THE GENESIS MOUSETRAP

WHAT IN THE WORLD IS GOING ON?

THE REASONS FOR CREATION

T. M. KYMALAINEN

© Copyright 2009 – T. M. KYMALAINEN

Published by:

Time to Return Ministries LLC
Willow Spring North Carolina

E-mail: timetoreturn@gmail.com

www.timetoreturnministries.com

Cover design by TTR, Publishing division: ttrinfo@gmail.com

ISBN: 978-0-9819871-0-1

All rights reserved. This book is protected under the copyright laws. This book may not be copied or reprinted for commercial gain or profit. The use of short quotations or occasional page copying for personal or group study is permitted and encouraged. Permission will be granted upon request.

Unless otherwise indicated, all Scripture quotations are from the King James Version (KJV) of the Bible, Public domain, no permission necessary for use of Scripture.

The following translations are also occasionally cited:

Scripture quotations marked "NKJV™" are taken from the New King James Version®. Copyright © 1982 by Thomas Nelson, Inc. Used by permission. All rights reserved.

Scripture quotations taken from Amplified® Bible, Copyright© 1954, 1958, 1962, 1965, 1987 by The Lockman Foundation Used by permission. (www.Lockman.org)

Scripture quotations marked NLT are taken from the Holy Bible, New Living Translation, copyright 1996, 2004. Used by permission of Tyndale House Publishers, Inc., Wheaton, Illinois 60189. All rights reserved.

American Standard Version (ASV), Public domain, no permission necessary for use of Scripture.

Noah Webster Version, Public domain, no permission necessary for use of Scripture.

Septuagint LXX Translation by Sir Lancelot C.L. Breton 1851, Public domain, no permission necessary for use of Scripture.

Judaica Press Complete Tanach, permission requested for use of scripture.

ACKNOWLEDGEMENTS

"Owe no man any thing, but to love one another: for he that loveth another hath fulfilled the law." Romans 13:8

The acknowledgements are said to be the place where everyone lists off who they are indebted to for inspiration, information, friendship and guidance. This attempt to do so will undoubtedly fall far short of expressing the proper appreciation for those who have held bright the lamp of truth in this day and for those who have faithfully labored in the fields of God throughout ages past. Yet, one must still try to say.... Thank you.

The Bible, Torah, the love of God that was given unto man in the revelation of the written Word has never ceased to bring forth those who love God and others more than they love themselves. These tireless servants of the Most High have in every generation given of themselves to help others find and stay on the way of life. It is to those who have sought out and brought forth wisdom from pure and humble hearts that thanks is given. May their rewards be great, may God honor their love.

Into every life God sends those who come as messengers or as witnesses to His will. Sometimes they come as a wind into a luffing sail; at other times as smoldering wicks which themselves need to be relit. In either case, they are always gifts unto us from a kind and patient God.

There are yet others, totally unaware of the testimonies they have in their everyday lives and of the impact which they have upon those around them. These are the living gems of the Almighty which He occasionally grants us the grace to see. Unto both Master and servants, I would like to say thank you.

The Bible tells us that the treasures of man need to be stored in heaven, but some of God's treasures walk among us upon this earth. May we have the wisdom to discern the footsteps of those who come our way bringing the message of truth.

Unto my people, those of Karelia, by the grace of God our day is not yet done. The generations of the past knew to respect the ways of old; they knew to honor the Holy One of Jacob. May we be granted the mercy to do the same in the remaining days we yet have. My prayer is that we are able to give God a reason to rejoice in the creation of our people before the tides of time wash over our now ragged shores.

And finally, it would not be prudent to leave out the One who makes all things possible: All thanks are given unto the Almighty, unto the LORD of Hosts and His Anointed One, the Mochiach Yeshua, the King of kings. It is only through the unending blessings of HaShem (The Name) that we are able to live in this day.

May we live our time well.

CONTENTS

The laws of life
One	A glimpse of creation's God	1
Two	The creation	19
Three	The anointing of life	41
Four	The rules of creation, the laws of life	49
Five	Where are they?	67
Six	The role of the Judge	81
Seven	Judgments: With Jude, Job, Jesus, and Joshua	93
Eight	A taste of God's wisdom	111

Finally, the beginning
Nine	Finally, the beginning	117
Ten	Rhyme and reason	141
Eleven	Adam's arrival	147
Twelve	The hidden agenda	161
Thirteen	Go with the flow	181
Fourteen	Back to the creative stream of thought	201
Fifteen	The Genesis Mousetrap	215
Sixteen	The result of Adam's appetite	241
Seventeen	Fruitful meanings	267

The return of Power
Eighteen	Back into the picture	279
Nineteen	This pair of Kings is always a winning hand	295
Twenty	Covert coverings	311
Twenty-one	It's getting dark out there	321
Twenty-two	The must attend event of the millennia(l) reign	339
Twenty-three	The end of the days	349
Twenty-four	Days, dreams, and visions	359
Twenty-five	A further explanation	367

PREFACE

Truth has always been the most precious and valuable commodity in existence; and from the time of the first angelic sin truth has also been the most obscured thing in creation as well. Wickedness has always attempted to hide, darken, and needlessly complicate truth for truth exposes the evil and weakness inherent to sin. That light of truth has been set forth to guide the errant children of Adam back unto the Lord God who created them; a fact which in itself leads to the weakening and removal of darkness and wickedness from upon the creation.

In the following pages, every effort has been made to shine the light of truth onto the reasons and effects of the creation. According to scripture the day will come when the limiting effects of time and space will no longer avail upon those who do love God. However, until that time arrives, everything is "known in part" as the Apostle Paul says. Nevertheless, it is our duty and privilege to increase, as best we can, the partial knowledge which we do have, so that the glass which we must look through would be less dim.

> "For now we see through a glass, darkly; but then face to face: now I know in part; but then shall I know even as also I am known." 1 Corinthians 13:12

There are a great many misconceptions among people as to what the Bible actually says about God, the beginning, satan, the redemption, and the world to come. My goal is to put some of these misconceptions to rest by presenting the Word of God to people without solely adhering to or depending upon any particular religious tradition or perspective. This allows the Word of God to be the foremost authority which we have in use. Due to that fact, the Bible ceases to be subservient to any specific "customary" perception of it which one or another select group or denomination may have. That lack of denominational bias, in turn, gives us the opportunity to answer the unknown from the Bible's perspective and thereby take the mystery out of things which man's traditions have often helped cause.

God never wanted His people unknowledgeable or uninformed about spiritual matters as they are vital to the proper function of all life. It was not His intent for people to be puzzled by His existence, unaware of the workings of the angelic host, or frightened of an unknown and mysterious devil. In the pages of this book, every attempt has been made to familiarize the reader with the spiritual matters of life and to take the unsubstantiated fear of the devil away from people by shining the light of truth upon that now darkened and shadowy cherub.

> *"The LORD by wisdom hath founded the earth; by understanding hath he established the heavens." Proverbs 3:19*

The creation of the universe has awed, perplexed, and puzzled mankind for many generations. It seems each person has within themselves an inborn longing to understand the reasons for the actions that take place behind the superficial structure of the world which has been fashioned around them. People are innately "programmed" to want to see beyond the veil of the obvious; and to search for a greater understanding of things, to find answers, as it were.

From our first cognizant thoughts we ask the question "Why?" We want to know, we want to understand. Why are we here? Where is here? Does life have a purpose? What is the universe? Who is God? Why does He do certain things? Who were Adam and Eve? Are angels really everywhere? What is satan? Will the world actually come to an end? Why does God seem so far removed from me? Is heaven eternal? The questions we have are as seemingly limitless as the universe in which we live. Hopefully, at least some of these questions will be adequately addressed and answered in the course of this book.

Every attempt has been made to keep the language used in the writing simple and straightforward; as the subjects in question can appear to be complex enough on their own and need no further complication.

The creation around us does, indeed, have a reason to exist; a unique and special job to carry out beyond just "being there". The creation is upheld by a multitude of ordering forces set by God, and chief among them is the law of free will which affects creation's beginning, course, and results. Yes, mankind and each individual child of Adam thereof does have an important part to play in the creative and redemptive journeys of the "olam"; a part so important that it required a special type of being to exist, one previously unseen until the creation of this being called man. This special type of being was to dwell in a most unique place and serve the Most High God by living as His image and likeness therein.

Some of the topics addressed in these pages are rather briefly touched upon, and any number of these "supporting" issues would well merit further independent study by the reader. Indeed, some topics would warrant much greater time and consideration as they are road marks, signposts, and guides found in the greatest map and guide of them all, the Bible. It is hoped, however, that enough information has been provided on each subject to keep the information necessary to the events studied flowing properly, as well as to whet the spiritual appetites of the readers and further increase their desires to learn more about the Almighty God of Israel.

A limited amount of Hebrew and Greek has been used on occasion to help convey depth of meaning and to clarify the understanding of the texts. However, the small amount of the two languages used and the way they are presented should pose no difficulty whatsoever to even the most uninitiated reader.

This book is designed to be read with a Bible close by, the Bible IS the topic after all. In many instances scripture will be cited or referred to with only the book name and chapter/verse numbers given in order to keep the book at a reasonable length. It is hoped that the readers will research the scriptures referred to, and perhaps even discover additional corroborative passages themselves while doing so.

All of the scriptural quotations used are from the King James Version of the Bible unless otherwise specifically mentioned directly before or after the quoted text.

The text of this book will break with the standard rules of English grammar and not have the word "satan" capitalized in any context, other than when directly quoting scriptural passages containing the word.

To sum it up; a brilliant man once said: "The Torah wants us to be amazed". It is my hope that these pages will add to, and increase, the reader's amazement and awe of God's Word and wisdom as we set out to explore the power and perfection of God as found evident in His Word.

The purpose in writing this book is to bring the reader to a place where s/he wil be able to say: "The Torah has me amazed."

May it be so.

Well, let's not dilly-dally any longer. Keep your Bibles handy; it's time to begin at the start of it all.

TK
Shavuot 5769

Chapter one

A glimpse of creation's God

THE PREQUEL

"In the beginning God created the heavens and the earth."
Genesis 1:1

Yes, the King James Version has this verse written as *"In the beginning God created the heaven and the earth."*, and as much as the King James is admired and respected in most aspects as an English translation, in the original language of the Bible, Hebrew, the word used for "heaven" is unmistakably the plural form of the word, which is "heavens".

These are then the very first words found in the Bible. This short and simple sentence is already quite amazing in what it tells us, and in the way it also immediately raises questions such as WHY, HOW, WHEN?

Well, in order to receive any perspective on the answers to these questions, we actually need to gain a better understanding of the questions themselves. In turn, for us to be able to do so, we need to first look at the One who made the heavens and the earth; the Creator, God Himself, from the perspective of the creation and of the creative process.

Who is He? What is He like? What does He do? Once these questions are addressed then we can better understand the questions and answers of why, how, and when He created the heavens and the earth that are in existence today.

He is One God; a single triune being: Soul, body, and spirit; Father, Son, and Holy Spirit, inseparable and perfect in all things.

THE FATHER

The Father is the portion of God we would commonly refer to as "God" in English. He is the "part" of God that we would call the soul. The soul is the mind, will, intellect, emotions, reason, personality, and judgment of a being; it's what makes an individual unique. For example, the soul is what makes you... well... you. It's the part of a person that makes the being an individual, with an identifiable unique personality, taste, and outlook; it gives the person character and attributes of will. Without a soul, a being would exist without persona and behave as a robotic, unfeeling individual.

THE SON

The Son is the body of God. The body is the portion of a being that enables the individual to partake of and affect the things around it. The body is also the part of the being which is manifestly revealed and only a body can credibly reveal a person to others in a tangible way. The body is the active "container" in which the spirit and soul reside. It is the physical essence and presence of a being; consisting of not only a body, but also consisting of the bodily manifestations of the will, such as the spoken word. The spoken word is also a physical attribute manifesting the will into the world around the individual in a very real and definite way.

THE HOLY SPIRIT

The Holy Spirit is the spirit of the One Indivisible God. The spirit is the life, ability, power, capability, and anointing of a being, the inherent rights of an individual to be and to do; the mobilizing force, the very breath and breathing of God. The spirit is the confirmation of an individual's life evidenced in the works done.

That is a brief and basic description of the structure of the eternal, inseparable, One God of creation.

Each characteristic or manifestation of the One inseparable God; whether of the soul, body, or spirit; whenever and wherever present, is of necessity always permeated, saturated, in filled, brought forth, and revealed by the other two. He is One after all, and not divisible one from the other.

The intellect (soul) cannot live without the breath (Spirit), and cannot affect anything without the body. The breath (Spirit) is powerless unless it carries the Word, and upholds and moves the body to do the will of the intellect (soul) which it empowers. The Word (body) cannot be brought forth or move without the breath (Spirit) to carry and empower it, and the intellect (soul) to give it the will and guidance to move.

Each form and part of the person of the One God comes with a different unique purpose in being and ability; different, but totally complimentary and necessary to the other parts of His personage. Each is also totally dependent on the others to function and bring about His purposes and goals. Such is the nature of the One God.

> *"For there are three that bear record in heaven, the Father, the Word, and the Holy Ghost: and these three are one."* 1 John 5:7

FURTHER DESCRIPTIONS

The Father: Where we read of God saying to Moses in Exodus 33:20, *"And he said, Thou canst not see my face: for there shall no man see me, and live."* We need to understand that this was the Father, or soul being spoken of, and we must realize the reason no man can see Him as the Father (the soul) is that we cannot see any soul with physical eyes. Not least of all the pure holy essence and manifestation of the Father, especially not in our present sinful physical state. Removal from the physical body would be the necessary requirement for a person to see a soul.

However, we CAN see God's body, the Word. For in Exodus 33:11, just a few verses prior to the previously mentioned verse it states, *"And the LORD spake unto Moses face to face, as a man speaketh unto his friend."*

This seemingly huge difference in these two closely sequenced verses is due precisely to the fact that Exodus 33:20 was speaking of the Father, the soul of God; and Exodus 33:11 was speaking of Moses conversing with the Son, the body of God, which like all bodies can be seen and is distinct in form.

Where we read of the Father seated on the throne or appearing in scripture in some way (see the following verses for examples) we are acutely aware of Him, but we see of Him that which can be seen manifested, which is His body; the Word, the Son.

> *"And above the firmament that [was] over their heads [was] the likeness of a throne, as the appearance of a sapphire stone: and upon the likeness of the throne [was] the likeness as the appearance of a man above upon it. And I saw as the colour of amber, as the appearance of fire round about within it, from the appearance of his loins even upward, and from the appearance of his loins even downward, I saw as it were the appearance of fire, and it had brightness round about. As the appearance of the bow that is in the cloud in the day of rain, so [was] the appearance of the brightness round about. This [was] the appearance of the likeness of the glory of the LORD. And when I saw [it], I fell upon my face, and I heard a voice of one that spake." Ezekiel 1:26-28*

> *"Again he said, Therefore hear the word of the LORD; I saw the LORD sitting upon his throne..." 2 Chronicle 18:18*

> *"And the LORD appeared unto him in the plains of Mamre: and he sat in the tent door in the heat of the day;" Genesis 18:1*

The name used in the original Hebrew for LORD in these verses, and actually, in all other verses throughout the King James Version where the title "LORD" appears fully capitalized is the sacred, personal name of God. It is the name which is used to signify His very totality, His full essence of being. That was a fact not lost on the English translators of the Bible as they chose to translate this name as "LORD" rather than making an attempt to mention it directly, and possibly risk defiling its sanctity in the process.

Within Judaism this unique name is considered to be the "unmentionable name" due to its holiness, and no attempt is ever made

A glimpse of creation's God

to utter it aloud. In English it is sometimes referred to as the "tetragrammaton" in reference to the four Hebrew letters of which this sacred name is comprised.

Now, out of respect for that name it will not be mentioned directly in this book. However, discussion of it brings us to our point. It was not the Father, the soul of the LORD God, who was visible in the previously mentioned verses, especially in Genesis chapter eighteen as He was physically visible while walking toward Abraham and visiting with him upon the plains of Mamre. Rather, it was the manifest presence of the LORD God visible in the only way He can be visible or known anywhere; particularly among mankind in this physical earth, and that is through His body, His Word, His Son. For as Solomon said in praying unto God in 1 Kings 8:27, *"...behold, the heaven and heaven of heavens cannot contain thee..."*

Needless to say, no physical or spiritual place, whether it is the plains of Mamre; the heights of Sinai; or the very throne found in the highest heaven, can even begin to contain the full essence of the One God called the LORD.

> *"No man hath seen God at any time; the only begotten Son, which is in the bosom of the Father, he hath declared [him]." John 1:18*

The Holy Spirit: The Spirit or breath of God carries the creative Word (the Son) which the Father speaks and the Spirit makes it (Him) manifest.

When the presence of God would fill the Temple, it was the Holy Spirit who was manifest in presence, but no one can deny the presence of the Father or of the Son in the Temple as brought forth by the Spirit to Isaiah in the vision mentioned in the sixth chapter of the Book of Isaiah.

To see the operational functioning of the Spirit as the enabling power of life let's look at the life and words of Jesus:

> *"And Jesus being full of the Holy Ghost returned from Jordan..." Luke 4:1*

> *"The Spirit of the Lord [is] upon me, because he hath anointed me to preach the gospel..." Luke 4:18*

> *"Howbeit when he, the Spirit of truth, is come, he will guide you into all truth: for he shall not speak of himself; but whatsoever he shall hear, [that] shall he speak: and he will shew you things to come. He shall glorify me: for he shall receive of mine, and shall shew [it] unto you. All things that the Father hath are mine: therefore said I, that he shall take of mine, and shall shew [it] unto you." John 16:13-15*

The Son: Without this portion of God which is the Word, the body of God, the Almighty could not affect or create anything, and we could have no understanding or concept of the Lord God. It is only through the Word and Son that we can have any way to relate to the being of God. The following verses make this fact perfectly clear:

> *"For in him dwelleth all the fulness of the Godhead bodily." Colossians 2:9*

> *"In the beginning was the Word, and the Word was with God, and the Word was God." John 1:1*

> *"I and [my] Father are one." John 10: 30*

> *"Philip saith unto him, Lord, shew us the Father, and it sufficeth us. Jesus saith unto him, Have I been so long time with you, and yet hast thou not known me, Philip? he that hath seen me hath seen the Father; and how sayest thou [then], Shew us the Father?" John 14:8-9*

The preceding verses are beautifully self explanatory, and bear ample witness to the fact that God is One. John 14:8-9 was especially telling on the matter. Please re-read the previous verses contemplatively.

Furthermore, it is the Word, body, Son of God speaking in the following verses; referring to Himself as "the *LORD thy God*", saying: "*the Lord GOD, and his Spirit, hath sent me*" and indeed, most of the words in the forty-eighth chapter of Isaiah are the words of the Son. Remember, the word "LORD" when capitalized in the King James Version refers to God's personal sacred name, and in these verses it is used by the Son in reference to Himself. This remarkable fact again bears witness to the fact that God is inseparably One:

> *"Come ye near unto me, hear ye this; I have not spoken in secret from the beginning; from the time that it was, there [am] I: and now the Lord GOD, and his Spirit, hath sent me. Thus saith the LORD, thy Redeemer, the Holy One of Israel; I [am] the LORD thy God which teacheth thee to profit, which leadeth thee by the way [that] thou shouldest go." Isaiah 48:16-17*

Speaking of Jesus, the Apostle Paul expressed His role as the body of God thusly in Colossians:

> *"Who is the image of the invisible God..."* Colossians 1:15

MADE IN THE IMAGE OF GOD

The existent and eternal nature of the One God is well represented and pictured in the being that was created to be in His image, and that, of course, is the being called man. (*Genesis 1: 26-27*)

Man is also a triune being consisting of a body, a soul, and a spirit which function in exactly the same way as the triune structure of the person of the One God Himself does; as unique dependent parts of one being.

A person is not made up of three separate people or entities that function together in symbiotic compatibility, and neither is God. However, a person does have a body, a soul, and a spirit which are integral and necessary parts of one whole just as God does, and lacking any of these three necessary parts of self would cause the individual to "not exist". That is the important difference between a being which is One, consisting of three inherent parts, as compared to a unity of three independent beings working together in cause. If one of these three individuals were to in some way cease to exist, the other two would still exist in the set cause; but if any of the three parts of the one individual were to somehow expire, be removed, or no longer exist, then the entire being ceases to be.

CALLING BOB

Let's use the following illustration of a telephone conversation between two people to give a simple example of the uniform integrity of these three parts of an individual in action:

If you were to call a person, let's say his name was Bob, and Bob then answers the call, who would you be talking to? Well, obviously you would be speaking with Bob. However, would you say, "Hello, I would like to speak with Bob's soul today." Or perhaps you would like to speak with Bob's body for a change. Could it be possible for you to say to Bob's soul that you want to keep a secret from his spirit? Of course not.

Maybe you could say that you really like Bob, but don't like his soul. That would be ridiculous! Bob is one, and all of Bob is always present and involved in anything he does. It is necessary for all of Bob to function and be present in order for him to carry out anything, including answering the telephone call. His body hears the call; his soul decides to answer; and his spirit enables both the body to answer; and the soul to decide what to say. The voice you then hear is the product of the body manifesting the will of the soul by the power of the spirit of the person you've telephoned whose name, as we have come to learn, is Bob. You did not speak with a part of Bob, or to one of three beings which made up the entity named Bob, you spoke with the entire being of Bob. Hopefully the two of you had something interesting to say after all this trouble!

GOD OR MAN?

The next issue which quite a few people seem to be a little confused about is that of the Son being simultaneously fully God and fully man. This is a matter of the division of offices which God holds, and an issue of what authority He uses in each particular office; of how, and where, and why He chooses to manifest Himself in order to interact with His creation.

A glimpse of creation's God

Let's try to bring some clarity to this very important subject. First of all, we need to state that the body, the Word, Messiah Jesus, always was, is now, and always shall be the Son of God; and although He was the Son, body, and Word of God He also became the sinless Son of man for the purposes of redemption.

"And the Word became flesh and dwelt among us..." John 1:14

It must be understood that during His time spent on earth in His natural body as the Son of man, Jesus could only operate in the authority and office that natural man had on this earth. That is to say, in the authority which Adam had before he sinned.

In issues which pertained to His life as a man on earth, Jesus did not operate in His role or authority as the body of God ever, because He could not do so and still have lived life as an ordinary man, which was a necessary requirement for the completion of the redemptive process. And remember, the redemption is the reason Jesus came in the flesh, after all.

Now, although He did not, and could not use his authority as God in issues that pertained to life in His physical body as a man and still atone for, and be classified a man, He was still constantly operating as the Son, Word, and body of God in all aspects of creation by spiritual and heavenly necessity. Jesus was, and is, always continually active in authorities pertaining to each respective office He holds as the Word and body of the omnipotent God.

These other offices were, and are, held by the Lord in concert with His office as Son of man and are a part of His eternal Godly duties. The Word of God never stopped tending to those other issues; however, they were not tended to through His office as the Son of man. The people living during the time that Messiah was in His physical bodily life here on earth would not have had any visible clue or idea whatsoever, that this Jesus who walked among them was also constantly spiritually present and functioning in the other myriad heavenly offices which He held. For these other Godly offices would not have affected or infringed upon His walk as a man in any way, as each office is held by the omnipotent God and Lord in total independence of one another.

The Genesis Mousetrap

A crude parallel to the Lord operating in multiple simultaneous offices can be seen in the following example:

A person can simultaneously hold and function in many different roles at the same time, without needing to separate or remove himself from the other roles which he also has. A person can simultaneously be a child, a parent, a sibling, a cousin, a friend, a customer, a citizen, an employer, or an employee; such as a lawyer, salesman, police officer, teacher, etc., and keep every role and relationship separate and independent of the others. Most people will never see the employee functioning as a parent; or the citizen functioning as a customer, so on and so forth. These are all different offices of authority that a person has and operates in without having one office interfere with the others.

So, let's try to state God's, and in this case specifically, Jesus' many roles in yet a different way. The Word of God, the Body of God, the Son of God, Jesus, is of necessity always omnipresent, and constantly working in and overseeing ALL aspects of creation at ALL times, and those other authorities which He has are not a part of or seen in the office that He holds as the Son of man.

In fact, Jesus could not have been, and cannot be, removed from His Godly duties and functions during His earthly tenure as the Son of man, for all of creation is eternally dependent on Him to function in His office as the Word of God for its existence. (*John 1:1-4*)

> *"Yet to us [there is but] one God, the Father, from whom [are] all things, and we in him; and one Lord Jesus Christ, by whom [are] all things, and we by him."* Noah Webster translation. *1 Corinthians 8:6*

> *"For by him were all things created, that are in heaven, and that are in earth, visible and invisible, whether [they be] thrones, or dominions, or principalities, or powers: all things were created by him, and for him: And he is before all things, and by him all things consist." Colossians 1:16-17*

> *"Who being the brightness of [his] glory, and the express image of his person, and upholding all things by the word of*

A glimpse of creation's God

his power, when he had by himself purged our sins, sat down on the right hand of the Majesty on high;" Hebrews 1:3

"And to make all [men] see what [is] the fellowship of the mystery, which from the beginning of the world hath been hid in God, who created all things by Jesus Christ:" Ephesians 3:9
"...I live by the faith of the Son of God..." Galatians 2:20

Not by faith IN the Son of God, but by the faith OF the Son of God all things and everyone exist. WOW!

So that which is being referred to when it is said that the Lord was fully "man" is that He was born as a man, lived as a man, and just like a man while in His earthly body; and He never functioned in or used His authority as God in this earth through His physical bodily revelation and offices. He was, however, constantly present, moving, working, and upholding all things in the heavens and their functionings as the Son of God, in the many different authorities and offices He held.

Different duties require different offices and authorities in order to allow any being the rights to legally act in God's creation. Redemption simply required God to take flesh upon Himself; and while the flesh contained God in fullness, it wasn't evident of nearly all of Him, nor did the flesh office He was in involve itself in the operation of any other office or aspect of creation held by God.

"...behold, the heaven and heaven of heavens cannot contain thee..." 1 Kings 8:27

What therefore needs to be understood about Jesus' physical presence here on earth is that He was, indeed, fully God. However, He was not operating AS God here in His bodily form. What was physically visible of Jesus, the Word of God, to mankind during His physical time on earth was not nearly all there was of Him to see. He is, and was seen functioning as, the Son of man unto who power was given.

THE ESTABLISHMENT OF THE AUTHORITY OF JESUS

Since we are briefly looking at Jesus' role on earth, we need to look at how and where the authority of Jesus to rule on this earth as a man was established. This event did not occur at His conception, or at His birth, or at His bar mitzvah preparations in the temple at age twelve. Yes, that's right, Jesus lived a Jewish life, and accordingly He was preparing for His bar mitzvah at the proper time. (*Luke 2:42-49*)

The authority of Jesus to rule came at thirty years of age, when He went down to the Jordan river to be baptized by John; at which time the Holy Spirit settled upon Him in the visible form of a dove to specifically anoint and empower Him with the blessings and authority of the last Adam, those of the sinless Son of man. At that time the audible voice of God the Father was heard saying the following in Matthew 3:17: *"This is my beloved Son, in whom I am well pleased."* (*Mark 1:11, Luke 3:22*)

At this event the Father gave the command to all beings and things to hear and submit to Jesus' Adamic authority on earth from that time forward. Why at that particular time? Simply because righteousness took time to prove. It would not have been legally possible for Jesus to operate in Adamic authority from the time of His physical birth, as only a person proven righteous and sinless before God could rightly do so, and as stated, righteousness took time to prove.

The righteousness which Jesus needed to establish here on earth in order to receive authority to rule from the Father was the righteousness originally lost by the man Adam, as Jesus was to receive the right to the full anointing of that first sinless man. This is the very reason Jesus is called the last Adam. (*1 Corinthians 15:45*)

Before His baptism and empowerment by the Spirit to hold the authority and office of Adam, Jesus had lived thirty sinless years on this earth to establish His credentials and qualifications; to prove in that time that He was, indeed, sinless as a man, and therefore eligible to operate in Adamic authority. That authority is the full original blessing and anointing which God gave Adam initially, and which Adam subsequently squandered away through sin. At the end of that thirty year timespan Jesus was judged to be sinless by the Father, and the right to inherit Adam's authority was attested to and bestowed upon Him by the Holy Spirit at the time of His baptism.

The Holy Spirit descending upon Jesus in the visible form of a dove wasn't to signify the first encounter Jesus had with His own Holy Spirit,

A glimpse of creation's God

far from it. Jesus, the Word and body of God, as we have seen, was the very bodily essence and manifestation of the Holy Spirit; for He was, and is, the pre-existent God. However, this visible descending of the Spirit upon Him marked the moment Jesus received the legal right to, and anointing of, the Adamic kingship; something no man had received and no being had held since the sin of Adam those many years ago in the garden of Eden. This Adamic anointing included the right of Jesus to be the promised Messiah of scripture, since the Messiah had to be judged perfect in all things.

"And hath given him authority to execute judgment also, because he is the Son of man." John 5:27

The age thirty is also significant in accordance with the Jewish practice of considering a man to be fully mature and able to teach at this age if he was versed in scripture. Hence after this time and event Jesus was also called rabbi or teacher. This anointing event is the occasion which signified the beginning of Jesus' ministry on earth.

FOR ADDED CLARITY

To help further clarify the issue of the Word of God, the Son, being revealed scripturally in different ways, that is, to clarify the matter of God being able to manifest Himself in different authorities and offices simultaneously, we can look at the Father (soul), and the Holy Spirit (spirit) of God, and how they were revealed to us in certain specific ways to bring about God's will. And how they were revealing His intentions in, during, or about a specific event, and how such revelations were by no means limiting the power or the presence of the omnipotent God as seen in the Father or the Spirit elsewhere in creation infinitely beyond what was revealed unto finite man in these specific instances; just as Jesus' presence in His physical body did not limit His presence and operating authority elsewhere in creation.

We can see a good example of the Holy Spirit coming down from heaven in the revealed form of a dove at the water baptism of Jesus in the River Jordan in Matthew 3:16, and also as tongues of fire during Pentecost in Acts 2:3-4.

Now, despite the presence of the Holy Spirit at these events we can clearly understand that the tangible revealed presence of the Holy Spirit at these times and in these events does not in any way limit the presence of the Spirit or His ongoing activity in any other area of creation. However, the Spirit of God came visibly in those unique ways to show, prophecy, or impart something specific to man during those and other similar instances.

The Father was present and revealed in Isaiah's vision of the Temple; again this revelation of the Father by no means lessens the Father's role, presence, or activity in any other area of His Kingdom during the time Isaiah saw His presence in the vision of the Temple. However, God chose to reveal Himself at that location in the vision for a specific non-limiting reason. (*Isaiah 6*)

Also, the Father was revealed to Moses on Mt. Sinai as He walked past where Moses was; there, Moses was able to catch a glimpse of God moving in the Father's office. We know this to be a revelation of the Father because the Bible states in Exodus 33:20 that Moses wasn't able to see His face and remain alive. However, in Exodus 33:11 it clearly states that Moses spoke with God face to face. In the instances where Moses did speak with God face to face he was conversing with God who was in the office of the Son, but in this specific instance of Exodus 33:20 it was God manifesting the Father's office and His presence in such as He walked by the hidden Moses.

The point to be stressed here is that although the Father appeared before Isaiah and Moses, being omnipotent, He was not limited to those specific times or places. One mere mountain or building certainly couldn't contain Him in His entirety if the heavens themselves could not.

EVERYTHING WE KNOW OF GOD IS REVELATION

Being omnipresent the Lord God holds many offices simultaneously and functions in any number of these offices concurrently. References to this fact are found throughout the Bible, and many people are confused by these actions and events thinking they signify a division of God or even a composite unity because man cannot fathom omnipotence or

A glimpse of creation's God

omnipresence. Indeed, everything man knows of God, everything man has ever seen or heard of God, is revelation of omnipotence to a finite being.

A great example of a situation where we can see the Lord in two offices at the same time is found in Revelation 5:6-7. Here we are given a simultaneous look at the Father seated on the throne and the Lamb that was slain receiving the sealed book from Him. This does not mean that either of the revelations of God was somehow less God than the other, but we are seeing the Lord move in two distinct and unique offices at the same time for the purpose of bringing about a specific goal. In this circumstance the goal was the opening of the sealed book which could only be accomplished by the sacrificed Lamb, the righteous sacrificial atonement prepared by God in the person of the Son of man, the slain Lamb Jesus. Without whose atoning work the book would have remained closed, as no one would have had the right to open it.

A further current of thought to bring understanding to this and other similar events is that this sealed book of God could naturally not have been opened by the soul, which is the Father, or by the Spirit of God without the presence and use of God's own body who is Jesus, the Lamb.

In the cases where the Lord is revealed through scripture unto man in separate distinct offices simultaneously it is always about issues that relate directly to man and redemption. Always. That is very important to realize, for in these simultaneous revelations of His being, the Lord God is trying to impart very important information about the redemptive process to man through the use of His Word. (*Psalm 110:1, Hebrews 1:8, Luke 22:69, Acts 7:56, Revelation 5:1-14*)

HE IS....

He is the Father, the Son, the Holy Spirit, the last Adam, the angel of the Lord, the Word of God, the King of Israel, the Lamb that was slain, the lion of the tribe of Judah, the bread of life, the Judge of all, the Ancient of days, the bright and morning star, and the list goes on.... He is the I AM.

In Revelation 19:11-13 we see the Lord Messiah returning triumphantly to earth wearing many crowns.... Let that sink in a moment.... Wearing many crowns.... These crowns are representative of all His different offices and authorities, as well as representative of all the crowns that He has taken away from the wicked angels upon His triumphant victory over hell and the grave, as He stripped the wicked ones of their rights to rule in the offices which they had held for so long.

We need to understand that the One God of Creation always has a specific purpose in choosing to reveal Himself in a certain way at a certain time. He always has a particular reason for operating in a given revelation, manifestation, or office to bring about a specific goal. The entire person of God: Father, Son, Holy Spirit (or soul, body, spirit) is, was, and always shall be, limitless in time and place. But how He reveals Himself, and how limitedly or limitlessly He does so, and why, is up to Him. Although He will never reveal Himself or do anything contrary to His previously established Word.

> "...for thou hast magnified thy word above all thy name."
> Psalm 138:2

Keep in mind that the Word of God is not merely a book, a document, an historical record, or a prophetic future account of events; it is Himself, in written form a revelation of Himself; a witness and testament to the will and power of God.

The Word of God is the beginning of His creation. *Revelation 3:14*. The Word is Jesus the Son of God Himself (*John 1:1*), given unto us by the will of the Father (*Galatians 1:4*), and revealed to us through His Holy Spirit (*1 Corinthians 2:10*).

> "And without controversy great is the mystery of godliness: God was manifest in the flesh, justified in the Spirit, seen of angels, preached unto the Gentiles, believed on in the world, received up into glory." 1 Timothy 3:16

The preceding verse in Timothy really said it well; God is One, regardless of what office He is revealed in.

> "...he is a rewarder of them that diligently seek him."
> Hebrews 11:6

Accordingly, it is our duty to humble ourselves before the Word He has given unto us so that we can grow into the best possible understanding of the Almighty God; an understanding which is necessary for those who wish to know Him in a true way. Those who incline themselves to do so are the "meek" which shall inherit the earth.

Just a few of the characteristics of the Almighty Lord of creation are mentioned next:

- All things are made by His Word.
- All things are made by Him.
- All His ways are peace.
- He has always existed.
- He exists outside of time.
- He is the King of all things.
- He desires perfect unity in His creation.
- He cannot lie.
- He cannot abide sin.
- He is faithful.
- He is longsuffering.
- He is a giver.
- He is love.
- He is life.
- He is perfection.
- He is totality.

The Genesis Mousetrap

Chapter two

The creation

THE ABSOLUTE THOROUGHNESS OF HIS WORD

We need to realize that when the One God does anything; whether He creates, gives, makes covenant, or speaks His Word; He will not and actually cannot alter, undo, or contradict what He has previously said or done. Since we know that His Word is God, permeated, filled, carried, anointed, empowered, and made alive by the will and Spirit of God, perfect in all aspects; we can get a slight inkling of why it cannot be changed.

In the following verses it is clearly evident that the Lord has said He will absolutely not go back on His Word:

> "...because I have spoken [it], I have purposed [it], and will not repent, neither will I turn back from it." *Jeremiah 4:28*

> "So shall my word be that goeth forth out of my mouth: it shall not return unto me void, but it shall accomplish that which I please, and it shall prosper [in the thing] whereto I sent it." *Isaiah 55:11*

> "For the gifts and calling of God [are] without repentance." *Romans 11:29*

Now, although this last particular verse in Romans was written within the context of God's covenant promises to Israel, it is nevertheless an unalterable principle of God which is inclusive of everything He says and does.

The Genesis Mousetrap

Each and every time God the Father speaks, He creates; there is literally no other possibility or outcome. His Word is God in pure unalterable power, and as a result, it not only creates, but it also limits and restricts what can be said and created when He subsequently speaks, so that the original Word is not infringed upon by following Words. That is an essential point to understand. The Words spoken by God not only create, but they also limit what can be spoken or created by Him later, so that the previous Words are not contradicted by the newly uttered ones. That is very important to realize!

The following Words can clarify, enhance, and strengthen the previously spoken, but cannot undo or contradict them, unless the previous has left specific room for a change or a refinement to take place as exemplified in the following verses: *Deuteronomy 11:13-17; 28:1-68, Hebrew 3:15.*

Since His Word is life itself, anything that would contradict His Word or even attempt to contradict it in any way is, or becomes, death; which is the antithesis of life. This is why He, and He alone, is eternally perfect in all things, as life Himself, He needs to be.

COUNTING TO.... TREE

For an example of the limiting power of God's Word upon creation let's use a simple, common, everyday tree in our following illustration. Where that tree exists another tree cannot grow in the same location, taking up the same space. The second tree can grow near the first tree, but it cannot exist in the same place at the same time. If such a thing were somehow to happen, though we know it cannot, it would result in chaos, confusion, anarchy, perversion, and in the ultimate death of both trees. A real mess would ensue, and we all know that God is not the author of confusion or messes. If He were, nothing could exist. The first tree therefore limits the location of the second. Just as the earlier Words of God limit the latter, but in the case of the Words of God they still only limit what He in His infinite wisdom has chosen beforehand to limit.

A biblical example of this would be found where the Lord said, *"...Let there be light..." Genesis 1:3-4.*

The creation

In saying and doing so, He also effectively limited darkness, as the two cannot be present in the same place at the same time. The ensuing outcome to that newly uttered and established Word was that God called the result of limiting the darkness "good".

In other words, He has said and done just what He intended to say and do, and it brought about a wonderful and darkness-limiting outcome: only a God that dwells outside of time, and yet in all times, is even capable of such amazing thoroughness of thought and speech necessary to establish and maintain this complex and infinite creation.

By speaking forth His creative Words, God has set boundaries and limits on not only the creation and the created within it, but shockingly, He has also limited that which He Himself can subsequently say and do, for He will never contradict Himself. Ponder that for a moment.

Now we need to understand that this holy and magnificent God preexisted, and also transcends all things in existence: The earth, as well as the heavens and all therein. Next we'll begin looking into the reason for the creation of the heavens from the beginning of it all. (*Hebrews 1:8-10, Revelation 1:8, I Kings 8:27, 2 Chronicles 2:6, 2 Chronicles 6:18*)

THE HEAVENS

"Thou art worthy, O Lord, to receive glory and honour and power: for thou hast created all things, and for thy pleasure they are and were created." Revelation 4:11

Nothing in scripture is mentioned or included by chance, not even the smallest word or phrase, or the way the phrase is written; such as Genesis 1:1, *"In the beginning God created the heaven(s) and the earth."*

Notice that in this passage of scripture in Genesis the heavens were mentioned first, and then the earth was spoken of. That is no accident. The point which needs to be emphasized here is that the spiritual heavens were mentioned first because they were made first; and then the earth was spoken of as it was made after the creation of the heavens due to the fact that it was brought forth from them. This is very similar to the manner in which Adam was first created, and Eve was later found in him, then separated from him and brought forth. (*Genesis 2:18-22*)

The spiritual heavens were a "place" where God's will could become evident, and His glory would be seen. They were a "place" where His creation was manifest and His works first made known. Then, and only then, were the physical heavens and earth made. (*Genesis 1:1-16, Job 38:1-7*)

The angels were already created and existing in the heavens watching the astounding creation of the physical universe unfold. The heavens are made and upheld, like all things, with the power of God's Word.

Yes, there is more than one heaven in God's creation, and each is important for His plans. Unfortunately, the Christian and Jewish views on this topic seemingly contrast with each other quite markedly. Therefore, a brief look at both is in order.

First, the common Christian view; centered mainly on the words of the Apostle Paul as found in 2 Corinthians 12:2.

> "*I knew a man in Christ above fourteen years ago, (whether in the body, I cannot tell; or whether out of the body, I cannot tell: God knoweth;) such an one caught up to the third heaven.*" *2 Corinthians 12:2*

From this single verse of scripture traditional Christianity has developed and maintained a belief in the existence of three unique and independent heavens.

The traditional Christian understanding of these three heavens and a brief description of them follows:

- The first heaven would be the atmosphere of the earth.
- The second heaven is space; the planets and stars therein, etc.
- The third heaven is considered the abode of God, angels, the righteous dead, new Jerusalem, etc.

The preceding understanding became an accepted and common Christian view on the heavens. It basically divides the livable sphere of the physical earth from the unlivable portions of the universe, and further divides them both from the spiritual world, from "heaven"; this, even though Paul nowhere gave an absolute definition, number, or designation to the heavens in his writings. He simply stated the existence of the third heaven and the fact that someone he knew (himself) had been there. How he saw the division of the heavens, and what precisely he meant by the "third", is something we do not definitively know; although, Paul did make a clear reference to paradise being located in the third heaven.

That being said, however, it is quite possible that he was making reference to the fact that paradise was in the third inhabited heaven of God's heavens, in the "upper heavens", as it were, and if such is the case this view would then coincide perfectly with the understanding which is found within certain traditions of Judaism. If that is, indeed, the issue, then the difference in viewpoints between Christianity and Judaism on this subject is really only a case of misunderstanding, not a chasm of total disagreement.

In the traditional Christian understanding, the earth itself is not really a part of any of these aforementioned three heavens, but it is a unique place of its own, created for the use of man, and central in the struggle between good and evil. This understanding, though, is simply not an entirely full or accurate depiction of the location and placement of the earth as found in the biblical narrative. For, as we shall soon learn, the earth is, indeed, an integral part of the heavens, which actually seem to appear ordered quite differently from the previously mentioned traditional concept, at least upon superficial inspection.

As stated, the three heavens of traditional Christianity contrast markedly with the description found within Judaism. This Jewish view actually speaks of seven heavens. This is, at least apparently, an unusually large difference of opinions between the two related beliefs, and what is considered to be an individual heaven is even quite differently defined by the two respective parties.

The general rabbinic consensus on the seven heavens found in the traditions of Judaism is as follows, starting with the heaven which is usually mentioned first:

- The first heaven, Vilon: Is said to retire in the morning and come out in the evening, renewing creation daily.

- The second, Rakia: The firmament. This is the physical creation which can be seen.

- The third, Shechakim: The atmosphere. Its original root meaning is clouds; alluding to the intangible.

- The fourth, Zevul: Site of heavenly Jerusalem.

- The fifth, Maon: The habitation of angels.

- The sixth, Machon: A storehouse of natural elements, weather, etc.

- The seventh, Aravot: The place of the Throne of God, the righteous dead etc. This is the place that would most commonly be referred to and viewed as "heaven" by the majority of people today.

As we can see, there is quite a contrast in viewpoints between the two theological camps. However, the Jewish view on the subject (although it may not be entirely accurate in its description of the design and function of these heavens) gives a basic understanding which is more thorough. Therefore, the fullest attempt shall be made to use elements of both views in order to give the most accurate descriptions of the heavens from not only the traditional Christian and Jewish accounts, but also from a viewpoint that favors neither tradition over the other; as both traditions contain elements of biblical truth, as well as human cultural inaccuracies which have seeped into truth over the course of time.

That being the case, the following is the explanation and structure of the heavens which will be used in this book; and the explanations found for the different heavens is by no means meant to be an exhaustive analysis, merely a brief summary to bring a little light to a complex, and seemingly endless subject.

Four of the seven heavens are to be considered as upper heavens, and three as lower heavens. A total of four of the seven are also apparently spiritually inhabitable; made in a sense prior to, and separate from, the physical heaven located within our universe and the substance it is made of which we call matter. Furthermore, in order to lose any wrong misconceptions we might have about the heavenlies, let's first understand that when we mention spiritual or heavenly things it doesn't mean that they are ghostly, wispy, marshmallowy, cloudlike realms where everything is more unreal than real. No, in fact you are actually living in a heaven right now. Surprise! That's right, a heaven! And let me be among the first to welcome you to heaven! Welcome! Moreover, you will find in our further readings that God did not intend mankind to function in only this one heaven as it now seems so natural for man to do.

If we can truly understand that this natural creation is actually a spiritual heaven in its own right then we can also better relate to the fact that in each heaven the spiritual substance it is made of is its own solid matter or reality, its own nature, and that they are all very tangible and concrete places. Each heaven has its own regulated structure and format, its own solidity which keeps a beautiful order in what many people would just assume to be a place of strange incomprehensible chaos. Although, obviously the substances present in the respective heavens aren't the same substances as what we're used to seeing and feeling here in this natural part of the universe, that difference is precisely what sets them apart one from another. It's exactly the structural and material variations which make the heavens unique and keep them separate from each other.

The following are the Hebrew/Jewish names for the heavens as well as their English meanings and a short explanation about their different functions. Keep in mind that a heaven is not a part of another realm, but it is a realm itself; autonomous from the other heavens around, above, or below it. That being said, however, the actions, and inactions in one heaven can have a great deal of influence on the activities which occur in the others. It was designed to be so by the Most High God from the beginning to keep balance and order in His creation and to bring His plans to fruition.

Some of the information that will be mentioned regarding these heavens is, or has been held by minority elements within both Christianity and Judaism throughout the ages. Furthermore, some of the information may be little known, and yet other parts of the following descriptions may be quite controversial to some in either religious camp. However, as the reader progresses through this book it is hoped that s/he will come to not only receive a better understanding of the workings of God's heavens, but also to find the following descriptions both informative and beneficial.

The first three heavens are all integral parts of our universe, and the following four heavens function as solely spiritual "heavenly" places.

"THE LOWER HEAVENS"

VILON

The first heaven is Vilon. Vilon means "curtain" in Hebrew. It is the spiritual ordering force; the separative workings of this universe, as well as the laws of physics which apply to all matter and keep a set orderly division to all matter. It is a complex three dimensional spiritual curtain, and literally functions as a curtain to separate the following two heavens from each other, and also from the others. Without this heaven acting as a separative curtain, it would be possible to freely reach into or move from one heaven into another at will. This is an uninhabited heaven which serves as a divider.

RAKIA

The second heaven is Rakia. This name means "expanse" or "firmament". It is the natural physical part of this creation which we would call matter, space, planets, galaxies, etc. It's the physical part of our universe which the heaven of Vilon separates from the other "spiritual" heavens. Rakia is that which can be seen with the natural eye and felt with the natural hand. Also, as an example, plants and animals are made to live and dwell in Rakia, the natural physical world.

SHECHAKIM

The third heaven is Shechakim. Shechakim means "dust" or "cloud". It's the spiritual "atmosphere" of the earth, and an integral native part of this universe. This is also an inhabited heaven, and it's in this level that man's spirit was created to function and dwell in; where the Spirit of God is and functions in this universe, and where angels function in their respective offices when in this universe. This is the heaven satan operates in when he is called: *"the god of this world"* in 2 Corinthians 4:4, *"the prince of this world"* in John 12:31, 14:30, and 16:11, and called *"the prince of the power of the air"* in Ephesians 2:2.

It's precisely in this heaven where those titles apply, and where all angelic authority in this universe is based. This heaven was also a foundational source of, and location for, the Garden of Eden on this earth. This Shechakim was also the place where Adam continuously functioned as guardian of Eden until he fell. And quite literally he did fall, into a lower, more physical existence, into the purely physical heaven of Rakia.

When Adam was expelled from the garden into this natural world which he was never created to be subject to, he had no way to re-enter the garden located by then in Shechakim, as the unity between Rakia (the physical), and Shechakim (the spiritual) was broken by the sin of Adam. The garden was then moved by God to another location in Shechakim away from the fallen Adam's presence. Since the time of the atonement work of Messiah Jesus the garden has been yet again moved by God. It is now in the highest heaven, in His presence.

Since the fall of man most people are unaware of the existence of Shechakim as a functioning place, or the way it affects the natural material creation of Rakia, or least of all, as a place in which man was meant to exist. Instead, mankind tends to now concentrate solely on the physical world around them (Rakia), which unbeknownst to most people is still ruled over and affected by spiritual activity that takes place in Shechakim, the place where man's spirit once held authority upon the earth.

The distorted state of this purely physical world around us in this day is the result of Adam losing his dominion and rights located in the spiritual heaven of Shechakim, thereby allowing evil to hold sway in this creation. However, a saved, born again, blood washed believer in the last Adam, the Messiah Jesus, as Lord of their life and, indeed, of all creation has his, or her, spirit reborn; and is able to function again through and under the authority of Jesus, the Last Adam, in this heaven of Shechakim, for Messiah came to restore all things to their rightful state.

Examples of the continued link man has with the Shechakim heaven can be seen in the following: If you are in prayer or in a church service, and the whole building seems saturated in holiness, or if you notice the ambiance of a restaurant; or the uncomfortable, perhaps evil atmosphere in a certain building, it's the spiritual activity in the heaven of Shechakim you are sensing in your spirit. Or if you are unsettled or bothered by a certain individual or activity for no apparent reason, again, it's due to the spiritual activity taking place in Shechakim. If you have ever seen into "the spirit"; or heard someone speak of such a thing; it was into the heaven of Shechakim that you or they were in all likelihood seeing. Shechakim is the "spirit world" which may be spoken of in charismatic and Pentecostal circles of Christians.

Again, Shechakim is the integral spiritual side of this universe, and being "spiritual" it's the part of the universe which in most cases carries a greater influence in matters affecting this triune universe than the physical Rakia heaven does.

These previous three heavens, the "lower heavens", make up our universe. They are in some way actually quite reminiscent of the spirit, soul, body, structure found in the makeup of mankind. Vilon functions similarly to the way the spirit does within man, as the ordering force of life; Rakia would be the counterpart to the body; both Rakia and the body are the physical parts of these two extraordinary triune entities, which are the universe and man. Shechakim would represent the soul, the determining factor, the place where decision is made.

God has organization and reason in everything he does, and these patterns and similarities which are found in creation and in scripture are not mere coincidence of chance. They are ordered.

"THE UPPER HEAVENS"

ZEVUL

The fourth heaven is Zevul; Zevul means "residence" or "habitation" in Hebrew. It is said to be the site of the heavenly new Jerusalem which will descend onto the new earth at the start of the eighth day in the world to come. (*Revelation 21:2*)

MAON

The fifth heaven is Maon. Its Hebrew meaning is "dwelling place"; this is most likely the place where the angels are based in their ministering roles throughout the other heavens. This is apparently the site of the seats of angelic authority; the location of the angelic thrones of office, and the center of heavenly conflict between the holy and wicked angels.

MACHON

The sixth heaven is Machon. Its meaning is a "fixed place", or "foundation". It is considered to be the location for the storehouses of blessings so often spoken of in the Bible. It does not appear to be inhabited per se, but seems to be the structural basis of the other three "upper heavens", not dissimilar to the way Vilon functions as an organizational structure for our triune universe. It is to be considered the foundational structure of the other three spiritual heavens. Hence, it is the storehouse of blessings.

ARAVOT

The seventh heaven is Aravot and it has as a meaning: "Plains" or "sterile place". This is the site of God's Throne; the river of life; the streets of gold; and the place where the garden of Eden and all the righteous dead are located since the time of their sanctification by the blood of Jesus. This is the place commonly referred to as "heaven" by most people.

IT'S ABOUT THE REASONS AND MOTIVES

It is the reasons and motives for the creation of our triune universe that we will try to focus on in our study, therefore the Christian and Jewish views will actually function quite symbiotically, and with little conflict throughout the course of our look into things. The question of the number of heavens will not be as important as the fact that there exists any division in them at all; or the subsequent understanding of what functioning capacities exist within the heavens as a whole.

Furthermore, although the physical and the spiritual realms are innately linked and conjoined (this fact will become more and more evident as we go on), however, in at least one sense the physical universe and the heavens that are linked to it were created for a different reason than the spiritual heavens were. It is that reason which shall be primarily discussed and discovered.

THE CREATED ANGELS

In order to more fully understand the reason for the creation of this physical universe from a biblical standpoint we need to have some understanding of not only the Creator, but of the created angelic beings also. For their story is integrally linked to that of creation as well; and we can shed a lot of light on the creation narrative with an understanding of God's relationship to the angels in view of His perfection and thoroughness.

The angels are beings which were created by God to dwell in His creation. They were brought forth to not only serve the Holy God in His heavens, but also to be children unto Him; to bring Him joy and to also enjoy Him and His work; to receive from Him great and myriad blessings which He so eagerly seeks to give. (*Psalm 148, Hebrews 1:13-14, Job 38:4-7*)

The following verses indicate that the angels had already been created and were present witnessing the foundation of the earth at the time the Lord God brought it forth:

> *"Where wast thou when I laid the foundations of the earth? declare, if thou hast understanding."......"When the morning stars sang together, and all the sons of God shouted for joy?" Job 38:4+7*

On the surface of things it may seem a little odd that the stars would "sing for joy", but stars are actually common biblical metaphors for heavenly, that is, for angelic beings. God, not only being alive, but life Himself, as we see in Genesis 1:11-12, creates life and life after its own kind to share His goodness with. Knowing God to be not only the Creator, but actually the Father of all spiritual life, including angelic, should cause us to not be surprised to find that angels are actually called the "sons of God" in scripture. (*Genesis 6:2; 6:4, Job 1:6; 2:1*)

The creation

These sons of God are not spiritual robots as many have assumed. Neither are they without their own free will to do as they choose. It simply isn't in God's creative DNA to have "offspring" that would not have His defining characteristics such as: free will, power, and authority. Such beings which are created to lack the right of free will could only be described as slaves, and God would then have to be described as an enslaver of His own children. That title clearly is not on His biblical resume. Isaiah 14:13-14 speaks of the free will of one angel in particular, and Jude 1:9 speaks about that of another.

Now it is very important to note when referring to angels, or to other beings, as the "sons of God", that they should not be confused with the Son of God: His Body and Word, Jesus the Anointed, who is totally unique in all things in that He is the pre-existent God Himself and should never be thought of as, or compared to, created spiritual beings, angelic or otherwise. (*Micah 5:2, John 1:1, 6:62, 17:24, 1 Peter 1:20, Revelation 13:8*)

IT'S NOT MYSTERIOUS

People keep trying to develop and imagine all kinds of silly things in regards to angelic beings. Many like to think of them as chubby little babies with halos and diapers. Some consider them to be the spirits of deceased people which have been granted birdlike wings. While yet others think of them as some type of aliens or mysterious phantoms which are a totally different form of life from anything we could possibly relate to or comprehend. Actually, quite the opposite is true in regards to such views.

We can see an example of one of the angels of God guiding John through the end time events in the Book of Revelation. In Revelation 19:10 John bows down to worship the angel who has accompanied him through this series of events and the angel forbids him; saying he is a fellow servant of John and of his brothers in the Lord.

> *"And I fell at his feet to worship him. And he said unto me, See [thou do it] not: I am thy fellowservant, and of thy brethren that have the testimony of Jesus: worship God: for the testimony of Jesus is the spirit of prophecy." Revelation 19:10*

The Genesis Mousetrap

In Daniel 9:21, Daniel refers to one of the great archangels as *"the man Gabriel"*, which shows us the close resemblance and likeness of appearance angels have to man.

In fact, so similar to people are these angels in all ways that some of these angels/sons of God even came to earth and had children with the daughters of men; although they did not have the legal authority from God to do so and were sentenced to hell as a result of their rebellious deeds. For further clarity on this issue, it must be noted that lustful desire wasn't the sole or dominant motivating factor in their forbidden actions. Rather, their goal was the defiling of the Adamic bloodline through the mixing of seed in an outlandish attempt to prevent the promised and pure Adamic heir, the seed of the woman, from being brought forth into creation. (*Genesis 6:4, Jude 1:6, 2 Peter 2:4*)

Furthermore, as Revelation 21:17 points out, the angels use a measurement called the "cubit". It is an ancient measurement which Semitic people commonly used in the Middle East. The cubit is based upon the length of the distance from a person's elbow to his outstretched middle finger. Since both types of beings use the same measure and as it is used interchangeably between the two in this verse it must be concluded that the size of the average angel is apparently quite similar to the size of the average person.

> *"Then he measured its wall: one hundred and forty-four cubits, according to the measure of a man, that is, of an angel." Revelation 21:17 NKJV*™

Also, when the children of Israel were wandering in the desert for forty years they were given the food of the angels, manna, to sustain them. From this we see that both men and angels have a need and an ability to sustain themselves with similar foods, in their respective heavens, of course.

> *"Though he had commanded the clouds from above, and opened the doors of heaven, And had rained down manna upon them to eat, and had given them of the corn of heaven. Man did eat angels' food: he sent them meat to the full." Psalm 78:23-25*

The creation

The similarity continues in the fact that the ungodly from among the children of men will be spending eternity with their ungodly angelic compatriots in the lake of fire. The same punishment fits both types of beings equally well. (*Matthew 25:41*)

The close similarity between man and angels should not be surprising when you realize that Adam, the first man, was called "the son of God", and angels are called "the sons of God". In that sense we are in the same genus, although perhaps not of the same species.

Actually, the largest tangible difference between angels and man is found in the authorities of their respective offices. Man was created to rule over a dominion as a king would: Guarding, protecting, and controlling vast and myriad things and issues simultaneously; while angels were created to assist and minister in specific functions and areas within God's heavens.

This leads us to the answer of why man has procreative authority while angels who are also sons of God do not. Angels as the unreproducing sons of God are so not due to lack of ability, but rather, due to the way they were blessed to function in their offices of authority. Angels are job specific, that is to say, they are authorized by God to move in exclusive areas, to be and to do, to move from point "A" to point "B" as it were. They were created to get specific tasks done, and not to delve into different issues, causes, or effects outside of their granted assignments.

In that way angels are isolationists, or sterile in existence, as their established authority is to carry out the cause or causes that were assigned to them; whereas man, a being with a dominion, is created to be multifaceted, involved with many countless issues on many levels simultaneously, a jack of all trades if you will. Man as a ruler, that is, one engaged in the domain of the endless and the infinite is created to have the possibility to produce endless and infinite answers, and to create solutions endlessly and infinitely in all ways, to allow for the meeting of the endless and infinite needs found within his dominion.

In other words, procreation is in the authority of a being that is designed and authorized to hold dominion in, and care for, all manner of things, such as man, but not for those brought forth to assist, meet,

33

answer, oversee and transform specific needs and issues, which is the case with angels. The need simply isn't there within the angelic authorities to require it.

Put yet another way, man was made to govern and control things in a "big picture" way, and needed to be a being which could come up with infinite solutions to infinite needs, and one of these infinite solutions was found in the ability to increase the numbers of man infinitely through procreation, whereas angels were made to manage the specific "nitty-gritty" details of things. No job given to them was too much for any of them to handle alone. (*Genesis 19:1-22, Ezekiel 1:9, Matthew 22:30, Mark 12:25, Luke 20:35-36*)

A LOOK AT BLESSINGS, ETC.

Without having an understanding of the blessings God grants unto His children it would be hard to grasp how the creations of God function. God's blessings are spiritual gifts that are actually bestowals of His Word, of His Spirit, of His grace and authority in certain specific areas of His Kingdom to empower the receiver with certain particular abilities, attributes, and/or benefits with which the recipient is able to function in a proficient and active way within God's creation. The beauty of the blessings of God is that they are not limited to, and do not exist to benefit the recipient exclusively, but convey or flow through the recipient for the advantage and benefit of others as well.

As a giver, God always wants to, and seeks opportunity to bless anyone and anything He can, in any way He can. He gets blessed Himself when doing it. It is a reciprocal cycle at work in creation, a law of reciprocity as it were, and in the same vein He has wanted to give that identical opportunity to His own; to have His children be able to receive the magnified blessings available to them when His blessings flow through the individual recipients unto others in creation as well. The amazing thing about all God given blessings is that they flow throughout creation very much like ripples in a pond, only with a magnifying, rather than a diminishing effect; eventually returning in an exponentially greater size and number to bless Him and the original recipients of His blessings as well. (*Luke 6:38*)

The creation

Some things which are important for us to understand and clarify in our minds are the types and functions of blessings that exist. The following is a brief outline to help bring some of the different varieties or classes of blessings to light.

- Anointing: The anointings of God are enablers. They are empowerments of the blessings and gifts He gives through the workings of His Spirit. All but one of the countless anointings are given without regret. That is to say, they permanently belong to the recipient upon issuance. The only anointing that does not belong to an individual is the anointing of life, which shall be discussed later in detail. The anointings make possible the successful operation of His gifts and blessings all.

- Ability: Ability is given without regret, it belongs permanently to the individual, and it is the power to do certain things, though not the right to do them. Certain abilities are perpetual, and some are temporal; bestowed unto the individual for a specific task or season of time.

- Authority: Authority is the right of an individual to use some or all of the ability given by God to the individual within a certain particular office, role, or task. Importantly, it is given without regret, and belongs to the individual.

- Office: The office is the place where the authority is used, and it does not belong to an individual. It belongs solely to God and His Kingdom. Therefore a being can be removed from his office (or job), regardless of his anointings, abilities, or authorities should he sin against God or His creation, and the office will remain to be filled by someone else.

THE ANGELS WERE EXCEEDINGLY BLESSED

Throughout the Bible we see the angelic host being exceedingly blessed by the Almighty and being anointed, authorized, and empowered to take care of God's handiwork each in his own specific way according to their God given authorities in a particular area of responsibility in a certain given office. (*Isaiah 45:12, Colossians 1:16*)

The Genesis Mousetrap

These areas of responsibility are quite autonomous in character and need to be, since angels are independent living beings, sons of the Most High, and not spiritual slaves without will; nor are they a fundamentally integral part of God essential for His will to exist and to be done. They are actually beings with their own will and choice, and are holding offices of great rank and honor within God's Kingdom, and as scripture reveals, many are even referred to as princes within God's Kingdom. *(Daniel 10:13; 10:20, Ephesians 3:10, Colossians 1:16)*

Looking at this issue from the viewpoint of the Lord being the Almighty Creator God; it is improper to assume that He in His magnificence wouldn't delegate tasks of responsibility to others. And looking at the issue from the perspective of Him being a constant source of blessing, and an absolute giver; it is His great joy to share all manner of blessings, rights, and authorities with others who have the capability to enjoy and accept Him and His gifts of their own free will and choice.

In the angelic organizational structure there is hierarchy and rank to be considered as well. These come as a result of the amount, size, and variety of blessings that have been bestowed upon individual angels in order for them to carry out their assignments within creation. Some angels may not have been given many abilities or authorities in comparison to others, and the offices they hold may appear to be quite humble in relation to those of others who may hold many great anointings and numerous powerful offices. However, even the least anointed and empowered of the angels has to be respected, and his office honored by all other beings in creation.

Even the most powerful angels dare not trespass against, or treat lightly the anointings of any other, no matter how limited in scope the anointings of the other may appear in comparison to their own. Nor would they have had any reason to do so, for that which the individual angel has, and represents, has come as a result of God's blessing of him; as such, that being, no matter how humble in appearance, is the most powerful force in his particular sphere of authority, and that fact cannot be overlooked by anyone. For if any angelic authority is wrongfully interfered with by another being, or rather, should any being attempt to wrongfully interfere with the rights of another, that being is then trespassing against the very Word of God, encroaching upon His will, and offending against God Himself in the process.

Furthermore, as a part of the issuance of the blessings of God, the Lord has also issued unto the respective angels abilities and authorities necessary for them to protect the given blessings against any and all form of possible trespass or threat to the blessings that could conceivably arise from any source. The protection of the bestowed blessings also then becomes the individual recipient's responsibility of free will, and an important part of his tribute of homage unto the Almighty God.

In the angelic visitation to the pre-judgment Sodom we can find an example of the way angelic beings are fully able to defend themselves and their assignments in the face of attempted trespass by corrupt and willfully offending individuals. It was precisely in the angels' defense of themselves, and subsequently in the defense of their missions, that these angels were showing reverence to God by protecting themselves against an evil onslaught which would have hindered or stopped them from doing that which God had sent them to do. (*Genesis 19:1-29*)

Hebrews 2:2 shows us that when angels are operating in their God given authorities, whatever those authorities happen to be, there is a severe consequence for those who would trespass against them and violate their offices.

> *"For if the word spoken through angels proved steadfast, and every transgression and disobedience received a just reward, ..." Hebrews 2:2 NKJV*™

Whether it is stewardship, praise, protection, or the ministry of that of a messenger/herald; different angels have different anointings or ministerial roles in God's domain, to oversee the things they've been given charge of as individuals; for the benefit of God's creation as well as for the benefit of others therein. These anointings of ability and authority are huge honors to receive from the Lord, and are often associated with crowns of glory that are given. Hence the biblical use of the terms principalities, powers, rulers, etc. when referring to those of the angelic host.

ABILITY ALWAYS EXCEEDS AUTHORITY!

Now, in order to keep things clear it is important to realize that in God's Kingdom ability always exceeds authority. Did you catch that? Let me say it again: In God's Kingdom ABILITY ALWAYS EXCEEDS AUTHORITY! This is a concept that is ABSOLUTELY necessary to grasp. If you don't focus in on anything else, focus in on this fact like a laser, absorb it and understand it, because it is a truth inherently present in all aspects of creation and vital to our coming look at the creation narrative. For what you CAN do is always MORE than you have a RIGHT to do, and that one fact is central to the very cause of our creation saga, and it is also the reason for creation's present state of being.

The following are some examples of how ability exceeds authority in the realm of man, and like most other things these examples from the realm of man convey perfectly into our look at the angelic hierarchy:

You can murder, but you don't have any right to. You can steal, but you don't have any right to. You can destroy, but you don't have any right to. You can blaspheme, but you don't have any right to. Your ability exceeds your authority in these and many other instances. It's the very same in the heavenly realms among angelic beings as it is among men in the physical creation. An angel anointed to do a certain job is not limited by strength, wisdom, or power to do only the job or jobs that he has been given; the angel is limited by the spiritual authority or anointing he was given by God to do that specific task.

Also, equally important to understand is that the individual angel is yet further limited by the spiritual authority or rights given to other angelic beings, or to man, or is naturally reserved by God for Himself. The angels cannot go running haphazardly around doing just any old thing they choose. Not at all. Their rights are only in the specific anointings and blessings that God has given or gives unto them.

If an individual angel doesn't remain in the area of his anointing or authority, but instead goes and arbitrarily interferes in some other role or assignment he infringes and trespasses against the rights and authority of another, bringing conflict and quite possibly sin into his own life. Nor can angelic beings freely act in any way they choose just because they remain in the field of their authority while doing so. No, every authority is contingent upon and subjected to the rights of others with overlapping rights of authority in any given situation, and the angelic being must move only to the extent of his given authority to the point that it does not interfere with the legal rights of other beings in each specific situation. To do otherwise would bring conflict, chaos, and disorder, and once again, these are attributes not in the Creator's character.

THE STAR OF THE GAME?

To use an earthly example of ability exceeding authority let's say you were a wonderful football player, one of the very best; that ability alone doesn't give you the right to just walk into a football stadium in the middle of a pro game, and run out onto the field to take the ball and score touchdowns whenever you wanted to, does it? Of course not.

There is procedure involved. First the coaching staff needs to see what you are capable of, then management has to sign you to a contract, then you need to put on a uniform, and familiarize yourself with the team's plays. Only then will the coach decide if and when to put you in the game and in what position, and what plays your team will make when you are on the field. You have then been authorized to use your ability in a certain position. That is not to say you aren't able to fill other roles, you just aren't authorized to.

If a quarterback suddenly decided to be a running back, or a tight end abruptly pushed the tackle aside and said, "I'll do this job", chaos would ensue. The other players and coaches would be quite upset as their game and rights would be interfered with by someone who had no authority to do so. No, actually they would be furious! They all would have had their rights infringed upon to some degree by someone on a massive ego trip. It would be time to get rid of that loose cannon, wouldn't it? You may have had the ability to do those jobs, and to do them well, perhaps even better then the people who were rightfully assigned to those other positions, but you don't have the authority to do those jobs of your own accord without the proper permission or authority given to you by those in command.

It's quite the same in regards to the angels and their respective anointings. They cannot overstep their bounds for as they do, they step into the authority of another. This in turn would cause conflict, chaos, and disorder; and once again, none of these are found in God's Spiritual DNA.

As long as there was perfect unity, love of God, and of other beings, things went on beautifully and in perfection; and God always desires perfect peace and unity. (*Matthew 22:37-39*)

Chapter three

The anointing of life

"THE BLESSING"

One of the most eloquent and accurate examples of life in the blessing of God is found in Psalm 23. It entails precisely what it means to operate in God's anointing of life. Please read Psalm 23.

The anointing of the Holy Spirit for life is the most precious anointing an angel or person could have, and this anointing is also the most important one, for the personal presence of the Holy Spirit of God Himself is this anointing. In this anointing the Spirit of God is present in the lives of God's servants to ensure that life in all its properties; prosperity, abundance, multiplication, and overflow would function in and through those beings which have been blessed by the Almighty into their anointings of office. He is the catalyst and enabler of the very dynamic forces of God that were to move and pervade creation through all of the blessings which God had given unto His created. Do notice that all the positive elements of existence are attributes of the pure will of God Himself.

The anointing of life is present to ensure that whatever the obedient recipient of the blessings of God does prospers. This particular blessing ensures that the gifts, blessings, abilities, and authorities can be successfully operational in an individual's office so that the will of God may be fully done in each and through each particular blessing and anointing.

This particular anointing is also very different from all others in that it belongs only to the Holy Spirit of God; it is His manifest presence and is only with an individual when He is. Therefore, this is the one anointing that can be taken away, for it leaves a being when He does, should a being choose to transgress against God. This is the only anointing of God that is not permanently transferred in issuance of blessing. For it is the personal presence of His own Spirit which brings this anointing and causes it to have effect, and is always with those who choose to stay in obedience to God and serve Him.

To further keep things in perspective; we need to understand that all other blessings and anointings a being receives from God become the individual recipients own to do with as he pleases; whether the being chooses to serve God with his received blessings or not then becomes the individual's own decision. It's all a part of having free will, and this is true among all God's offspring whether angel or man. However, for the personally received blessings to have any success or lasting benefit to any in creation this anointing of life must be present to enable them to function properly.

THE ANOINTING OF SAUL

To see a scriptural example of how the anointing of life relates to individuals, and how it functions, let's look at King Saul. Saul wasn't born to be a king of Israel, he was anointed by God to be the King of Israel as an adult; and because he wasn't born with the anointing to rule as a king of Israel, he couldn't function as such. That is, until God sent the prophet Samuel to anoint Saul to be King; to give Saul the specific authority and right to stand in that particular office from that time forward.

This anointing did not take away any of the privileges or rights that Saul may otherwise have had in his life prior to this bestowal of the kingly anointing, but being the greatest authorization and the highest office Saul received from God it was the one blessing he was most renown for having.

We read that when the Spirit came upon Saul, he changed; he was no longer the same man that he had been. Actually, he wasn't even of the same mindset as that of the other men of Israel any longer. For after the time of his blessing he had become encompassed with the necessary anointing which brought with it the kingly characteristics essential for Saul to function in his new office, and that changed him permanently.

The anointing of life

Now, this is not to say that Saul had been totally alien to the Spirit of God up to that time. If he were, God would never have chosen him to be King of Israel. However, what took place upon Saul receiving the kingly anointing was that the Spirit of God gave unto Saul, without regret, the anointing of the kingship of Israel to be his permanently, and in doing so the Spirit of God was also able to ensure the successful operation of the kingly anointing through His presence in Saul's life.

Actually, this fact of God granting Saul the kingship of Israel in and of itself would not have been legal for God to accomplish without Israel's overwhelming desire and national request to willingly subjugate itself before a king of its own. The people of the nation needed to voluntarily allow that king to share in their own national, tribal, familial, and personal blessings. The anointing of life, the personal presence of the Holy Spirit of God then came into Saul's life in a particularly strong way to enable him to function successfully in his new anointing as King of Israel due to the fact that Saul was humble and willing to serve the Lord through that office. Saul had at that point become not only full of the courage and the authority needed to be king, but he also carried with himself the anointing of life which brings about the successful operation of all other blessings, including the kingly one.

Please note that while Saul was blessed and authorized by the Lord God to be the King of Israel it is the separate blessing, the anointing of life, which is the presence of the Holy Spirit Himself upon Saul that caused him to be very successful as a king. (*1 Samuel 11*)

After a time, Saul, through direct disobedience defied the Lord in his office of king; he knowingly rebelled against the Word of God given through the prophet Samuel, and as a consequence the Holy Spirit with the anointing of life departed from Saul and Saul did not even realize it. This departure of the anointing of life happened even though Saul yet remained King due to the fact that the anointings of kingship which were given unto him by God were given without regret, and belonged to Saul all the days of his life. (*1 Samuel chapter 15; 15:35; 16:1; 16:13-14*)

That is the very reason why David, after he was anointed by the prophet Samuel to replace the disobedient Saul as King of Israel, when he accidentally came across the vulnerable and disobedient Saul during his arduous flight from the pursuant king, held back his sword when he had a chance to kill Saul in a cave near Engedi as recorded in 1 Samuel 24:6 saying, "...*The LORD forbid that I should do this thing unto my master, the LORD'S anointed, to stretch forth mine hand against him, seeing he [is] the anointed of the LORD.*"

Although God had seen fit to arrange for the removal of Saul from his kingly office, which could only be accomplished through Saul's death, and although the anointing of life (the personal presence of the Spirit of God Himself) had already left Saul by this point, David nevertheless understood that the kingly anointing was Saul's permanently. It was given by God without regret, and David dared not commit a sin against God by coming against the kingly anointing of God which was permanently upon the errant Saul. This kingly anointing was Saul's to the day he died, and because of it he would always be known as Saul, King of Israel.

Did you notice that the Spirit departed from Saul, yet the anointing of kingship remained? This fact is very important to realize as the same laws apply to all beings in creation, be it to man or to angels. The anointing of kingship, like all anointings, was given without repentance by the Lord, but the presence of His Spirit which was with Saul to establish life and success, to prosper Saul as a king, and to bring blessing to the entire nation of Israel through him, had to depart from Saul's life when he chose to rebel against God's Word. And in leaving, the personal presence of the Spirit, the anointing of life, didn't just leave Saul's anointing as king; he left Saul in all other aspects of his life as well. This caused Saul to be far more spiritually destitute than he was prior to his receiving the kingly anointing.

Why did the Spirit of God need to depart from Saul's life? First of all, the Lord God is extremely polite and will never insist upon His presence remaining where He isn't welcome. He needed to respect the desires of Saul to do things other than His will. Furthermore, God's Spirit cannot, and will not, remain to prosper or strengthen any who choose to move outside of His will. He cannot remain with such individuals to enable them to walk successfully in transgression or rebellion. That would result in God taking part in transgressions and rebellion against God, and that simply is not possible for Him to do. Though, as we can clearly see, the other gifts of anointing remain permanently for the life of the individual, whether man or angel.

DAVID KNEW

King David was well aware of this fact as attested to by the example found in 2 Samuel, chapters 11 and 12. In this case, David had sinned grievously against both God and man, but after the prophet Nathan, under the direction of God's Holy Spirit, made David conscious of his sin David quickly repented and cried out in remorse unto the Lord. His words of grief are found in Psalm 51.

> *"Cast me not away from thy presence; and take not thy holy spirit from me." Psalm 51:11*

David knew the hopelessly unsuccessful result of trying to function without the personal presence of the Holy Spirit in his life, as He is the anointing of life; the enabler of all God's blessings.

SAMSON'S ANOINTING

Samson is also a very telling illustration. He was born to be a lifelong Nazarite, set apart unto God from the day of his birth unto the day of his death, as he was declared to be a Nazarite by the angel of the Lord, and so he was. Although, when he stopped valuing the permanent gifts and abilities God had given unto him and let the visible expression of his anointing, which was his hair, be cut off or separated from him due to his apathetical indifference to God's will and command, the anointing of the Spirit for life left this lifelong Nazarite. The one who enabled Samson to function successfully in all of his blessings departed due to Samson's lack of respect for the Word of God and for the blessings he had received.

Now that is very important to realize. For the personal presence of the Holy Spirit that was with Samson did not depart due to any alleged dalliances or sins of the flesh, real or imagined, by the readers of his biblical account. The Spirit of God did depart, however, due to Samson's lack of respect for the blessings and Spirit of God, due to the sins of his heart. Once again, as with Saul, the Spirit left unbeknownst to Samson.

The Genesis Mousetrap

Samson had no idea that the anointing of life had departed from him until he first tasted defeat, and his unending success as a Nazarite came to a close.

Notice that it was only after Samson was greatly shamed by his enemies that he came to realize that the Spirit of God had departed from him. It was only the lack of the anointing of life and its successful enablement of Samson's permanently bestowed blessings which bore witness to the Holy Spirit's departure. Now, although the Spirit did depart from him, Samson still retained the lifelong office which he was blessed with. Although without the Spirit, the anointing of life upon him, the permanently bestowed blessings of Samson actually became a source of grief for him.

All the sorrow which the Bible mentions actually took place in Samson's life even though his walk in the anointing of a Nazarite continued unabated from his birth through unto his death in fulfillment of God's Word as spoken by the angel of the Lord unto Samson's mother. The hatred his enemies had for him, due to Samson being firstly: an heir of Abraham through Israel, and secondly: blessed with the office of a Nazarite, was able to manifest itself to his harm without the blessing of life, the personal presence of God's Spirit, present in his life to enable his successful walk in the office.

It is important to realize that without the personal presence of the Spirit of God in his life to enable his successful operation as a Nazarite, Samson also became unable to function effectively in his other blessings as well. With the Holy Spirit's departure, Sampson was no longer capable of properly operating in any of the blessings which were permanently given unto him, Nazarite or otherwise; and he was greatly grieved by the enemies of God as a consequence. *(Judges 13:1-16:31)*

How unobtrusive the Holy Spirit is in this anointing of His personal presence is amazing; for He is not present to forcibly change or alter the individual's life, but rather to enable, assist, and protect the recipient of God's blessings so that the recipient can properly function in the received blessings and carry out God's will. Consequently, when the personal presence of the Holy Spirit departs from an individual, due to some transgression or another, the transgressors do not readily realize the moment when God's Spirit lifts from their lives and his anointing leaves, for the other blessings which God bestowed upon them still remain.

The only evidence of His departure is that the ungodliness which was present in their lives, the lack of Godly attributes which caused the presence of God to depart in the first place, begins to bear the fruit of corruption. When the Spirit of the Lord God departs from the transgressors in this level of presence and this anointing consequently lifts, they don't even realize it.

The point to be made in all of this is that the angelic host in the heavens functions in exactly the same way as we do here on earth in regard to the Creator's given anointings, abilities, authorities, and offices. The abilities, authorities, and anointings of office are permanent, but the anointing of the Spirit of God for life is only present as a result of our/their willingness to be obedient to God.

The Genesis Mousetrap

Chapter four

The rules of creation, the laws of life

PRIDE CAME, HONOR LEFT

Having been given ability, authority, and autonomy of office, many of the created angels began to resent the service portion of their authority. Authority comes with responsibility; thusly, the functioning power of the blessings of God are strongest when they are flowing through the recipient to benefit others in the upholding and strengthening of God's blessings, will, and laws in their lives.

However, some of the angels had the notion that it would be more advantageous for them to keep all possible benefits of God's bestowed blessings for themselves, and to decline the use of their authorities and offices in the service of others. The operational impossibility in doing that, however, is that the blessings of God are "living" like everything about Him, and must therefore flow through a being in order to come to and benefit the being.

Much like water in a faucet: if the faucet is open, the water flows freely and comes forth to benefit those who need water. As long as that faucet remains open, all receive the benefits of the open faucet, including the individual who opened the faucet. But, if the faucet is closed and the water stops flowing, no one will benefit, as the water isn't "living", or flowing, anymore. It becomes "dead" or still, and doesn't benefit anyone at all while trapped up in pipes. This lack of receiving the benefits of the blessings therefore also includes the individual who greedily closed the faucet to keep his blessings away from other individuals.

The Genesis Mousetrap

This leads us to the foundational law of God's creation, and that law is love. Love is the greatest rule, and the most necessary attribute in His Kingdom; love, but not pride, which is exclusive love of self. Exclusively self-centered love was the first ungodly act committed by the angelic beings; it was the deed which brought forth all other wickedness.

The first, and also most anointed, of these angels to stray into transgressional behavior through self-love or pride was Lucifer, the angel anointed as the covering cherub of the Most High God; the first to receive the radiance of God's great glory. Lucifer, before pride was found in him, was attested by scripture to be perfect in all his ways.

> *"Thou [wast] perfect in thy ways from the day that thou wast created, till iniquity was found in thee." Ezekiel 28:15*

This Lucifer was also one of the most highly honored of the great angels. (*Ezekiel 28:13-14*)

Lucifer, in self pride and conceit, decided through his own free will that the lofty position which he was blessed with was insufficient for one such as he. This great cherub angel decided to attempt a further elevation of himself to the only office that was higher than the one he already held. Lucifer decided to elevate himself to the role of God. (*Isaiah 14:12-14*)

Having thoroughly convinced himself as to his own grandeur, pridefully overlooking the fact that he was operating in blessings given by God and faithfully upheld by His Word, this cherub chose to ignore the obvious truth; that he was basking in the glory of God's radiance, anointings, and abilities, and not in beauty of his own making. He then further convinced one third of all angels to covenant with him in his wicked conspiracy, with the prospect of attempting to elevate themselves into more glorious positions of office at the expense of the Creator and His creation being the prize for their selfish efforts.

In order to implement their plans these now wicked beings needed to end the service portions of their authorities which they felt did not sufficiently benefit their newfound need for prominence. Their thinking went thusly: If I am a blessing to you, helping you, and upholding you, then I can never get ahead of you, but if I stop benefiting you and use all of my resources and power to further myself and to hinder you then I can advance myself beyond you and fittingly "bless" myself with greater power and position than you have, eventually getting everything that I truly deserve.

> *"And his tail drew the third part of the stars of heaven..."*
> *Revelation 12:4*

These angels being acutely more aware of the ways and laws of God than man is today felt that through their God given abilities, authorities, anointings, offices, and newly formed joint covenant, they could stand a very good chance of elevating their own status and power.

This they hoped to accomplish using the unrepentant laws and permanently given gifts of God as hindrances and stumbling blocks against the kind and benevolent God Himself and against His remaining holy angels. In this way of legal maneuvering and twisting, these wicked angels felt that they could operate safely and legally within the established framework of God's Kingdom and effectively work toward His demise without the risk of openly breaking the unwavering law's of God; thereby entering into an unwinnable open rebellion against the Lord God of Hosts and consequently being sentenced to hell for their crimes, rebellion, and sin.

Thus ended the wicked angels love of God and of fellow angel, and the once brilliant angel, Lucifer, literally became death since He went counter the Word, Spirit, and will (soul) of God who is life (that's the entire being of God which we looked at in chapter one, by the way). The anointing of the Spirit for life left both this darkened cherub angel and his wicked compatriots, thus the title "satan' was given. The word "satan" simply means adversary in Hebrew, and this dark cherub angel literally became the adversary of all righteousness, the adversary of all who continued to walk in God's love; the adversary of all who sought to do God's will through the blessings they were given. This wicked angelic event of "exclusive self love" took place between Genesis 1:1 and Genesis 1:2.

> *"In the beginning God created the heavens and the earth"*
> *Genesis 1:1*

> *"And the earth was without form, and void; and darkness was upon the face of the deep. And the Spirit of God moved upon the face of the waters." Genesis 1:2*

WHAT'S IN A NAME? MORE THAN WE REALIZE.

Now, to further our knowledge, let's look at one additional fact of interest. When Lucifer transgressed, he was consequently given the descriptive title "satan", which as we have already learned holds the meaning of adversary. He wasn't given the title "rebellious", or "fallen being", or "convicted one", or "one who burns in hell", or "totally banished sinful being" simply because those titles were not fittingly descriptive of this errant angel or of his activities.

He was called "adversary" in order to describe the way in which he began to use his offices and blessings in his attempt to accomplish his goals of usurping God's throne by manipulation, through the blocking of blessings, and in efforts to abolish all things holy through every legal means at his disposal. The title satan was given to him precisely because it was fittingly descriptive for one who in his free will was wickedly, albeit legally, trying to engage in activities which were adversarial to God, His will, and His intent.

Furthermore, the term "satan" though specifically referring to the cherub angel once called Lucifer, can also refer to any of the angels in the wicked angelic covenant under satan's authority. This is exemplified in the way the legion of spirits in the demoniac of Gadarenes, spoken of in Mark 5:1-21, was often referred to as one spirit despite the multitude of spirits present. There had been one spirit there in the demoniac of a higher rank, that is to say, previously blessed of God before the angelic transgression took place with more authority than any of the others present there had, one to whom the others deferred and submitted to. So, they were all referred to in the singular since they were being led by one main spirit.

The same is true of the term "satan"; since it is not a being's personal name, it can refer to the former Lucifer, or it can refer to all beings in the satanic covenant, or it can refer to a single wicked being other than the former Lucifer, or it can refer to any portion of the cabal of beings that took part in the transgression and are operating against God's will, but beneficially to the former Lucifer's goals.

THE POWER OF COVENANT

This brings us to one of the most important Godly laws in operation; one that has already been touched upon, and that is the law of covenant. The power of the law of covenant has at its core two very basic and very strong laws of God's Kingdom.

UNITY

The first law is unity; in covenanting two or more individuals agree to unite or work together for certain specific reasons or stated goals, and in uniting the parties involved will always find it easier to achieve their goals as they are mutually strengthened by each others unique abilities and rights. The laws of unity actually make possible for the parties united in the set effort some things which would not have been possible for any of the individuals to achieve alone, as the united parties can build on and benefit from each others individual strengths and blessings, combining them for the mutual achievement of the set goal.

ASK MOM AND DAD

An example of the power of unity is seen in the way a man and a woman can unite in marriage to raise a family. Neither one could accomplish bringing a family into the world alone, but when they are united together in marriage the unique inherent blessings and abilities of each individual together, huband and wife, can bring about children and family.

Something which was impossible for a single being to accomplish alone became possible for two when the law of unity was acted upon and the two were joined together in the unity of marriage.

THE SECOND LAW

The second law of covenant is the law of giving, which is essential for any of the blessings of God to properly function in an individual's life; as the purpose of the blessings that are first given by God to the individual are for the edification and enrichment of His overall creation in general.

In a covenant these two laws are united by the voluntary consent of the parties involved, as they agree to unite for a set purpose by giving something of themselves specifically to each other in order to bring about an agreed upon goal.

The rules of covenant are quite simple, when you give, you are blessing, and when you are blessing, you get. It brings about, and causes, the law of multiplication to take effect for all parties involved in the pre-agreed to united effort of achieving their common goal. It is one of the basic foundational building blocks on which everything in all the heavens function. In essence, the ingredients of the law of covenant are two basic spiritual laws: those of unity and giving, themselves joined or covenanted together, in order to form and create a new law, the law of covenant.

The act of covenanting was absolutely necessary for the wicked angels in the satanic conspiracy to carry out if they were to have any chance of advancing their causes in God's Kingdom. For no created being was even remotely capable of achieving such an insolent and selfish outcome as these wicked ones had planned to achieve, alone. Remember, the wicked still needed to abide by the laws of God, and in order for them to keep any semblance of blessing flowing to themselves they had to give forth their blessings to others.

In the case of the satanic covenant the wicked were able to arrange a format in which they could legally pervert the intent of God's will by "blessing" only each other in order to keep some manner of blessings flowing to themselves. By doing this they were trying to keep their inherent blessings away from creation as a whole while still attempting to benefit from them to the utmost by sharing the blessings only amongst the wickedly covenanted ones. It is a perversion of purity which defines this evil at its core.

The rules of creation, the laws of life

To make covenant is one of the most powerful things a being can do in life. It enables one to establish order and draw on the resources, skills, or capabilities of another. And in the case of a large covenant like this satanic one, the rights and capabilities of an individual were soon multiplied by the number of partakers in it. In this particular case up to one third of the angels in heaven were sworn to one another, in effect making it one of the largest and seemingly most influential covenants in all of creation.

Since individual angels had only a limited ability, and/or a limited power in their own granted areas of authority in a pre-established number of offices, they would need the aid of other angels in other different offices to advance their cause. They would further enable each other through their own particular and unique authorities by lending access to their legal offices and rights where the abilities of another could be put to use.

Or more commonly, the covenanted would work to advance each other through direct mutual aid of one another. This is done through each angel working for the gain of the whole in their own offices. These are the standard ways the wicked use in advancing each other in their attempts of limiting righteousness for their mutual ends.

Now, for most people in this modern world today where it is incorrectly taught by society that making a promise or giving your word is a rather meaningless exercise, and that keeping your word is tantamount to simplicity (read foolishness), it's hard to understand the impact and strength of a true binding covenant. Being a Godly law, and an act carried out in accordance to Godly law, any break of a covenant by its members is a transgressionary offense, and a premeditated break of a covenant by its participants would result in a rebellious sin occurring against God Himself.

That sin against God and His laws would result in a judgment, leading to a removal from office, and a likely sentence to hell for the guilty angelic party. Therefore, any and all angels who took part in the satanic covenant are tied into it forever, they cannot attempt to undo or alter their agreements or deeds because a break in covenant is a sin against God.

A break against a covenant by a participant is also a break against one's own word which had been given to the other participants, and is therefore a break against the very essence of one's own being. Hence, the offense of breaking covenant is most serious as the offending party is actually sinning against the part of self that was given in covenant to the other partaker(s). These personal blessings and rights willingly offered to the other parties in the covenant are blessings which the individual participant had received from God Himself. Therefore, the breech also becomes a sin against God's Word in that way as well, because it is God's Word that established both the blessings and the law that provided the participant the opportunity to share the blessings and partake of the covenant. It is those facts which involve God in the enforcement and judgment of every covenant whether angelic, manmade, or Godly.

GOD WILL JEALOUSLY DEFEND HIS WORD

This fact of God so jealously defending His laws and statutes, even those applicable to covenants made among the wicked beings may seem quite amazing to us, and truthfully it should be, but we must understand that God will defend His Word and His laws at all cost, and it can make no difference to Him if that includes protecting the rights of the righteous, or the rights of the wicked malevolent beings in His Kingdom. Regardless of whether He spoke blessings, rights, and free will to the angels, to man, or even unto Himself, He will honor and defend the Word He has spoke and the rights He has given to the full extent of His immeasurable power.

Such is the case even when a being chooses to work against Him, and hate Him, and although the being thinks he can attempt to outsmart God by manipulating, perverting, and twisting his rights, using God's own Words, laws, and blessings against Him. Now, this is not to say that God likes, condones, or defends wicked behavior among His angels or any other being, but as a God of order, and a Dispenser of justice, He must always defend His Word and His laws, as well as uphold the blessings and anointings that He has bestowed upon individual beings for His own sake, and for the sake of His great and Holy name. (*Jer 11:5, Psalm 138:2, Isaiah 14:24*)

An example of wicked beings forming allegiances and acting in loyal covenant among themselves is found in Revelation 17:12-14.

> *"These have one mind, and shall give their power and strength unto the beast."* Revelation 17:13

To better understand this issue we can find examples of covenant, and the power of covenanting in the operational laws of democratic nations that can serve as good illustrations for us. The governments of democratic countries establish legal frameworks for their citizens to make business contracts, marriage covenants, etc. These covenants and the rights to make them are deemed to be beneficial to the entire nation as a whole. As such, the individually made covenants are then upheld and respected by the governments of the nations in which the covenants were made as long as these agreements were judged to be in accordance with the existing laws of the land, whether the head of government personally approves of the terms of the covenants, or not.

A breech of contract, or a break in covenant would have legal repercussions which would likely result in harm or possible financial loss to one or more of the parties in question; as well as in a loss of confidence in the laws and governments of the countries in which the agreements were made, should the parties who made the contracts in accordance to the laws of the particular country go unpunished in the case of a break in the covenant.

The democratic country will also defend its citizens rights to disagree with government policy, to work for legal removal of its elected officials, to behave in a way that would bring shame upon the country and its citizens, and to be as objectionable as the citizen wishes to be. As long as the citizen doesn't break the existing established laws of the country in doing so, he could be as malevolent as he pleases, and the government would defend his rights to behave that way. This is regardless of whether or not such behavior was detrimental to the government, its citizens, or the individual malcontent in question.

It is a telling parallel to the way God allows His angels the right of free choice within His Kingdom. Each individual being may choose how obedient and faithful to God they will, or will not be. For as long as they stay within the laws of God's Kingdom they have the free will to walk away from the will of God and from His life, and choose death for themselves by behaving in such ways that lead them into destruction.

THEY BELIEVE AND TREMBLE (James 2:19)

Our look at the angelic would not be complete without our receiving a better understanding of the results and consequences of their noncompliance with God's will. Remember, angels are not perfect; although they do have the ability to perfectly comply with God's will. However, only God is perfect in all things, therefore imperfection is subject to happen in anyone, anywhere free will is present.

The gift of free will like all God's gifts is, indeed, perfect, but the use of one's own will in any way other than in harmony and conjunction with the will of God is imperfect and may well lead to disobedience, transgressions, and/or rebellion. Actually, there are really only three kinds of purposed transgressions that exist in creation, and these are:

- Disobedience
- Wickedness
- Rebellion

Moreover, each is judged and punished in vastly different ways. The following is a brief look at the three different types of transgressions.

DISOBEDIENCE

Disobedience is when a being either purposefully or unknowingly chooses to do something other than God's established and unmistakable will, but does so without evil or malicious intent. Examples of this are found in the following:

- Adam eating the fruit of the tree of the knowledge of good and evil. (*Genesis 3:6*)

- Moses striking the rock twice. (*Numbers 20:11-12*)

- Peter choosing to look at and respect the power of the waves instead of obeying the Lord's command to walk on the water. (*Matthew 14:25-33*)

The rules of creation, the laws of life

WICKEDNESS

Wickedness is a purposeful twisting or perversion of God's will, and/or Word. The word "wick" actually comes from an old root word meaning to bend or twist. Something wicked is therefore inherently twisted, changed, or perverted from its original design. Examples of wickedness are found in:

- The serpent's twisting of God's Words to Eve. *(Genesis 3:1-6)*

- Balaam after having blessed Israel advising the Moabite king on how to bring the wrath of God upon the same Israel. *(Numbers 31:16)*

- Simon the sorcerer attempting to purchase the anointing and power of the Holy Spirit for his own personal use. *(Acts 8 18-24)*

REBELLION

Rebellion is a deliberate breaking of Godly law by the blatant overstepping of one's authority. Examples of this are found in:

- The Korah rebellion which took place in the Sinai desert when the participants refused the leadership of Moses. *(Numbers 16)*

- Absalom attempting to steal the kingship away from David. *(2 Samuel 15:1 through 2 Samuel 18:17)*

- The pharaoh of Egypt deliberately impeding, lying, and trying to stop the will of God from taking place through the hand of Moses as he kept the Israelites in Egyptian slavery despite receiving God's clear instruction to the contrary. *(Reference found in the entire Book of Exodus.)*

PUNISHMENTS

Now, punishment for angelic beings is really not that hard to understand, and we're going to look at the way, the amazing way, God has of punishing the transgressors of His Word, of dealing with transgressions and sins. Are you ready for it?

First of all, the punishment for disobedience, this punishment is chastisement. If an individual errs in action or duty by disobeying God's will, the Lord will scold the individual. Usually by lessening or removing His presence from the individual's life; or by lessening the authority the individual has by allowing others with similar or overlapping authorities a more active or greater role in their areas of office.

It must be noted that all of the chastisements which occur due to disobedience are for a limited period of time only, and are the result of God's love for the errant being. The chastisement comes with the goal of guiding and teaching the being in question in order that the individual can learn to better, more obediently, and more successfully walk in the laws and blessings of God. So that the individual in question, as well as others who are affected by the individual, can avoid repeating such errors which can cause the being or creation harm, and thereby cause a rift between God and His sons.

Chastisement is not to primarily punish for sins, rather it is a carrot and stick approach that most parents use with their children. If a child does well he is rewarded, but if a child chooses to be negligent and/or disobedient then a scolding follows. Nevertheless, the Lord always acts out of love and hope that the individual would learn to choose life. (*Deuteronomy 30:19, Job 34:31, Hebrews 12:5-10*)

Secondly: The punishment for wickedness, wicked or perverse behavior if left unchecked will harm not only the individual who has already chosen evil over righteousness, but it will also attempt to cause damage to the righteous functioning of creation as well. Therefore the punishment for the wicked is to exist in separation, under the curse of darkness. This behavior of wickedness results in a being's separation from the presence of God, and a loss of all intimate knowledge of God and of His ways. That, in turn, separates the individual from being able to partake of the enjoyment of the creation of God and of the blessings originally given to the individual. However, this punishment is not a removal from office or a sentence to chains or hell. (*1 Samuel 2:9, Proverbs 4:19*)

Thirdly: Rebellion. This sin carries a high and unbearable cost associated with it. Which is for the perpetrators to be ultimately removed from office, and most importantly, from God's presence; from His power; and from His radiance; for them not to be in contact with His

The rules of creation, the laws of life

Holiness, which is the very essence of the power of all creation; to have the Great King and Creator, Life Himself, turn from you and shun you in His anger, then cast you out of His Kingdom is the most terrible punishment any being can have. And the conspirators know it well; because once you're out, it's eternal, and there is no hope for the damned. The result is an everlasting living death incomparable to anything that we can naturally conceive of, and the location of that living death at this time is hell.

Hell is the place where all rebellious beings are sent after being judged by God to be guilty of such open and premeditated breaks against His Word. Once again, it needs to be stated that whether His Word is of Himself, seeing that He is the Word, or of another individual through their obedient and proper use and defense of His blessings which are bestowals of His Word given without regret to the individual, the severity of the breach against the Word is the same, and the severity of the "crime" is the same.

The only difference comes in the fact that a breech against the Word of God given to an individual being is the individual's responsibility to defend against by standing firm on the blessings that have been attacked, and by calling the interloper to the heavenly court for a trial of justice before God to have their authorities validated. While a break against God's Word held by God Himself results in finding oneself immediately tried and removed from office.

Those beings which blatantly and knowingly choose to exercise their abilities in ways that exceed their authorities, and in so doing break any part of the Word of God once they have been informed of the illegality of their actions, come into rebellion against God and are systematically removed from their offices for their crime. (*Joshua 1:18, Isaiah 1:20; 14:9-15, Jeremiah 28:16, Revelation 12:7-8*)

That having been said, the removal from office can also be a temporary punishment as can be seen in the following scriptures: *Revelation 9:14-15; 20:3*.

Though wicked and rebellious, these spirits in the preceding verses are brought back from their temporal bonds into their respective offices to function in their previously given abilities for a set time to complete specific works that are assigned to their authorities.

This releasing of the chained angels is also to allow them the opportunity to complete their break against the Word of God in the way that they were intending to do before they were chained for a lesser offence, but their rebellious acts of free will are then carried out in a time and place "convenient" to God's design. This keeps their sinful break against God's Word from causing too great a harm against God's creation during an inappropriate or wrong time period of history. It basically allows God to set the terms for the sinful actions of rebellion which an individual plans on taking. God in this manner sets the time and the place for the rebellious actions to occur; after the rebellious being has been freed and actually carries out his sin then the Lord can permanently remove the rebellious from his place of office and sentence him to hell for the committed crimes.

AN ETERNAL EXILE

More commonly addressed in scripture, however, is the permanent removal from office that results in an eternal banishment to hell, and later into the lake of fire as a consequence of overstepping authority in a clear breach of Godly law. For these, and all other beings, nothing can be worse than losing the right to be in God's presence and creation for all eternity, first having been cast into hell, and then later into the lake of fire.

Yes, the lake of fire is a totally different place than hell. Hell is actually a temporary "jail" for the wicked that have been found guilty of breaking against God's Word, but the lake of fire is the eternal "prison" of the wicked that is yet to be occupied. For the wicked to be sent to the lake of fire the great and final judgment needs to occur, and the Judge must bring the wicked out of the jail of hell to face trial and sentencing before they can be sent to the permanent "prison" of the lake. Why, even hell itself will be cast into the lake of fire after it has been emptied of its occupants who will have been transferred to the lake of fire. Truthfully, God doesn't want to keep a place like hell around anymore than anyone wants to go there. (*Revelation 20:14*)

AND HELL FOLLOWED...

Since we are on the subject of hell and the angelic, it is interesting to note that hell is not only a place, but it is an angel as well; a spiritual being that goes by the name of the place. This angel is the one in whose authority it is to administer the operation and order of the place called hell. This Hell is a wicked angel who will be cast into the lake of fire himself at the same time the place called hell is thrown in and destroyed.

> "And I looked, and behold a pale horse: and his name that sat on him was Death, and Hell followed with him..." Revelation 6:8

This preceding verse clearly indicates a being called Hell, not a place. As the place of hell obviously does not, and cannot, tramp around another place such as the physical earth any more than the planet Saturn can run around Sweden doing summersaults! This verse in Revelation is actually the only place in the King James Version where the names Death and Hell are capitalized.

The reason that Death and Hell are capitalized here in this verse is that the Bible is using these words as proper names, referring to the spirits in question and not to the generic events, actions, or places which are their synonyms. In many other translations such as NKJV, NIV, English Standard Version, New American Standard, Revised Standard Version, American Standard Version, Robert Young Literal Translation, among others, the name Hell is translated as Hades in this particular verse. The reason for doing so is because the word used in the original Greek for hell in this verse is "hades", and Hades is the Greek name for the "god" otherwise known as the Latin "Pluto", and Pluto/Hades was in Greek cultural mythology the individual being considered to be in charge of the underworld which carried his Greek name, hades. This fact transferred directly through into these many translations, and shows us that the place of hell was, indeed, known by the writers and later translators of the Bible to be administered by a being of the same name.

In the following verse we can see that hell has emotion and action, things which in this specific verse are again clearly indicative of a being, and not of an inanimate place or location:

> *"Hell from beneath is excited about you, To meet you at your coming; It stirs up the dead for you, All the chief ones of the earth; It has raised up from their thrones All the kings of the nations." Isaiah 14:9 NKJV™*

Although the wicked are in a state of covenanted transgression with evil intent, these evil one third of all angels still dare not break into open rebellion against the Creator and His created; so how they operate in order to ensure that they can remain in office and use the power of their authorities while still actively conspiring against the Lord Most High is the challenge they face. They must try to twist, warp, pervert, and bend around the Word and will of God in a way that does not constitute a break against His Word; seeking every legal way they can to expand their power while still holding office in His Kingdom is their goal of conduct. They seek to constantly twist and bend His will, and in doing so hope to confuse other office holders as to the true will and intentions of God. Only in this way can their influence on creation look as if it increases. As brash as they are in their twisted pursuits, they are still rightly afraid to clearly break against God's Word themselves lest they are sentenced to chains, and/or hell for such rebellion. *(James 2:19)*

KING'S RULES, GENTLEMEN

> *"...the kingdom of heaven suffereth violence, and the violent take it by force." Matthew 11:12*

This verse in Matthew is a very important scripture that references the way things are done in the Kingdom of the Heavens. The wicked angels are constantly seeking, testing, and probing to see where they can access the blessings, authority, or rights of another being; and it is the responsibility of those who love God, and who prize His gifts to protect the blessings, anointings, authorities, and rights that have been bestowed upon them, as these unrepentantly given gifts are the sole responsibility of the ones who have received them.

This is where the concept of spiritual warfare comes from in its purest sense. Each and every being must constantly guard the blessings and the anointings God has given, and resisting those seeking to improperly

The rules of creation, the laws of life

limit the authorities, or move in the offices that God has given to the individual is the way such "warfare" is carried out.

The wicked angels knew very well that there was no way in which they could harm or defeat God, but their tactic for gaining power was to see if they could find a way to move into the area of responsibility of another to block, steal, or twist the other beings' blessings of office. This is possible for the wicked to attempt due to the other beings neglect of duty, misunderstanding of rights, or even through the voluntary misguided invitation and permission of the infringed upon individual. These facts would all legally allow one being to move into the authorities and offices of another without need of further Godly grant required, and without the interloper breaking any existing law. The previously issued gift of free will unto both parties is sufficient for such actions to legally occur.

In the case of the wicked angels, they would move in where they are allowed to (allowed either knowingly or unknowingly) by another individual to stop, limit, or usurp the blessings of the one they infringed upon, in an attempt to pervert God's will in his life and office thereby expanding their own sphere's of influence by limiting righteousness. So, Heaven's Kingdom has, indeed, suffered *"violence, and the violent take it by force"*, but the sneaky and wicked attempt to take it through subtlety.

Yes, the *"violent"* specifically referred to in this verse is, of course, Jesus, the Son of man, who did take Heaven's Kingdom by force, or rather is in the process of completely doing so, and He will ultimately end the age long suffering of violence in the Kingdom which the wicked had initiated.

To get a better idea of the workings of this process in which one being has the opportunity to legally frequent, use, appropriate, or limit the authority of another without causing sinful rebellious infractions while doing so, let's look at the following example:

If you allow or invite someone into your house they are not considered to be trespassing; and since they are allowed in, and aren't trespassing, they are not breaking the law; and since they are not breaking the law,

The Genesis Mousetrap

they can't and won't be arrested for being there; nor will they be forced out of your home by the police.

Further still, if an individual were to illegally enter and occupy your home without your consent and you did nothing to resist or to expel the unwanted individual either by evicting him or notifying the appropriate law enforcement agencies of the government about the illegal actions of the individual, then that individual would have the ability and de facto right to stay in your home due to your inaction. This matter is exactly the same among the angelic beings as it is among men; all must take heed to protect what is theirs through the use of their rights and the laws of God as decreed in His Word.

Chapter five

Where are they?

STILL THERE

Many have assumed that the one third of angels belonging to the evil transgression of the satanic conspiracy have been cast out, cast down, thrown out, thrown down, or use some other such term to indicate the thought that the wicked conspirators have been evicted from, and are no longer in God's heavens, but instead have been sent to dwell in our triune universe as some form of punitive consequence for their sinful actions.

Could anyone really imagine the punishment of the wicked as being moved from one heaven to another? Is it really a punishment for satan to be sent to occupy the paradise of God that was planted east of Eden? Was paradise the place for punishment? Would not most wicked angels and people gladly accept the "terrible punishment" of being cast into the paradise of God? This situation, quite simply, is not the case. Thinking that God sent satan and his ilk from "heaven" into paradise as a form of punishment is down right funny!

Can anyone imagine God actually saying, "satan, I have had it with your insolence! So as punishment for you, I'll make you go torment Adam for a change." Of course not! Hell is the place for sinners and haters of God to be cast into, not paradise! The time will, indeed, come for the total removal and eternal punishment of the wicked ones but it has not yet happened.

Yes, there have been biblical instances where we can see rebellious angelic behavior punished by a removal from office, followed by a binding and/or a sentencing to hell in order to await judgment in the case of individual angels or lesser groups thereof, but not of the satanic conspirators, as there hadn't yet been a rebellious infraction on their part that would warrant damnation. *(Genesis 6:4 refers to two such rebellious groups and events. 2 Peter 2:4, Jude 1:6)*

FALLEN ANGELS

Some have called the satanic conspirators "fallen angels", meaning to imply that they have been cast out of heaven or removed from office. However, what should really be meant when using the term "fallen angels" is that they have fallen from right standing with God, from the holiness of His pure and blessed ways; from the path of His love; from unity with the Father, and not that they are somehow fallen from the heavens, their authorities, or their offices and are now sentenced to an odd earthly exile where their actions face no further consequences.

One of the most popular verses used to defend the viewpoint that satan and his ilk are already eternally removed or fallen from the heavens onto a permanent earthly abode is Luke 10:18, which quotes the words of Jesus, *"And he said unto them, I beheld satan as lightning fall from heaven."*

As previously stated this "falling" of satan and of the wicked angels is better described as an exclusion from Godliness and from His blessings rather than as an expulsion from office. However, this statement by Jesus is taken by those who claim a pre-existent historic expulsion of satan to be a verse which refers to a past event occurring somewhere in the murky beginnings of creation, as proof of the removal of the satanic conspirators from the Kingdom of God, even though our Lord Jesus Himself dwells outside of time. As He does, this statement could just as easily have been describing an event which took place in what we would understand to be the future, even though it is spoken of in the past tense. Just as the apostle John somewhat similarly described the activities which he witnessed in Revelation during his trip in the Spirit to the Lord's Day which was to be at least some two thousand years after John's time, which was for John clearly in the far distant future.

In Revelation 21: 5-6 the Jesus of the "future" speaks with the John of our past:

Where are they?

> *"And he that sat upon the throne said, Behold, I make all things new. And he said unto me, Write: for these words are true and faithful. And he said unto me, It is done. I am Alpha and Omega, the beginning and the end. I will give unto him that is athirst of the fountain of the water of life freely."*
> *Revelation 21:5-6*

The words *"It is done"* speaks of future events yet to come; events surrounding, and leading to, the Lord's coronation, and it refers to them in the past tense, as though the events were history, since the Lord has already lived through and experienced those events even though they were in the far distant chronological future for John and his readers. Our chronological timeframe is irrelevant and nonrestrictive to the omnipresent God, since for God all of the events that will occur have occurred already, and have all been witnessed by our Lord from before time itself began.

Furthermore, this verse in Luke needs to be read in conjunction with the preceding verse to give it depth and place of context. So let's read both verses together and see what the Lord was saying:

> *"And the seventy returned again with joy, saying, Lord, even the devils are subject unto us through thy name. And he said unto them, I beheld Satan as lightning fall from heaven."* Luke 10:17-18

This shows us a more accurate picture of why the Lord made the statement. He was calming the exuberance of his followers in the matter of exorcism, for they were quite impressed and surprised that *"even the devils are subject unto us through thy name"*. He was teaching them that casting out devils in His name was not to be a rare or surprising occurrence by referring to the fact that while it seemed new and exciting for these seventy followers of Messiah to have devils obey them and leave in Jesus' name, for Him it was more than common. Going so far to make His point as to describe the greatest exorcism in all creation; that which He had already been a witness to, the removal of, and casting out of satan which is the end of wickedness in the heavens of our God, of which the earth is also a part.

For additional corroboration to this statement we need look no further than the next two sequential verses in Luke where Messiah states:

> *"Notwithstanding in this rejoice not, that the spirits are subject unto you..."*

> *"Behold, I give unto you power to tread on serpents and scorpions, and over all the power of the enemy: and nothing shall by any means hurt you. Notwithstanding in this rejoice not, that the spirits are subject unto you; but rather rejoice, because your names are written in heaven..." Luke 10:19-20*

A few additional verses which indicate that time as we know it is not applicable to God and is therefore of no limiting consequence follow:

> *"Declaring the end from the beginning, and from ancient times [the things] that are not [yet] done, saying, My counsel shall stand..." Isaiah 46:10*

> *"And all that dwell upon the earth shall worship him, whose names are not written in the book of life of the Lamb slain from the foundation of the world." Revelation 13:8*

The preceding verse clearly indicates Messiah was slain before the world was made! The Lord who dwells outside of time gave Himself to experience crucifixion before the chronological sequence of events happened in this time sensitive creation to materially bring his crucifixion to pass! The Lord would have had, and indeed, did have a right to say that He died on our behalf before the actual event occurred in our time dependent creation. Therefore, in a sense, all events that occur in the present are already limited and restricted by the fact that the future is already ruled by the Messianic Kingdom inclusive of the millennial age.

So, it's no wonder that Messiah said He beheld *"Satan as lightning fall from the heaven(s)."* The omnipotent and omnipresent God is in, and has seen, every time and has already declared the end from the beginning. The Torah wants us to be amazed at that!

Where are they?

Moreover, these verses nowhere state that the *"fall from heaven"* spoken of by Jesus would even remotely indicate that satan's "fall" would be to earth, to the Rakia heaven. The only place the errant angel is going to "fall" into is the pit of hell.

OUTLAWS?

"Spiritual outlaws" is a term that has also been used by some in reference to the wicked beings. However, we need to realize that these evil ones are actually not spiritual outlaws but are in fact astute spiritual legalists, functioning within the laws and Kingdom of God for their own wicked ends in a far greater knowledge of God's will and laws than natural man is able to do, or even has understanding of.

This inability of man to fully comprehend God's ways is actually due in large part to the very perverting and covering efforts of these wicked legalists themselves. The wicked ones are acutely more aware of God's great power and might than man is, and they exist in a justifiably massive fear of God and His power which mankind cannot easily understand, although it would be judicious of us to attempt to do so, for the wicked know that their very lives depend upon God's Words and ways.

There are, in fact, no angelic spiritual outlaws of any kind in existence. Either one stays in the office one has, and functions through God given free will in holiness to bless and do God's will, or one functions in wickedness to pervert His will and prevent blessings. Or thirdly, one chooses to rebel and is removed from office and is sent to eternal punishment. There is no other alternative existence available to somehow allow a being to exist and run around freely empowered by self to do any and every action desired by one's own heart in mysterious areas of creation hidden somehow outside of God's laws and reach, foreign to God's Kingdom. For God and His law are the basis for, and structure of, everything in existence.

To be in His creation is to be in His heavens; to be in His heavens is to be in His Kingdom; to be in His Kingdom is to be subject to His laws, and nothing exists outside of the laws and rules of the creation known as the Kingdom of Almighty God.

The Genesis Mousetrap

As previously mentioned Romans 11:29 states: *"For the gifts and calling of God [are] without repentance."*, and that when God speaks, or does anything, it is unalterable since His Word is perfect. We have also seen how God loves to bless and give. It's His nature; blessings, anointings, abilities, authorities, autonomies, and providing that these beings wouldn't overstep their rights they were actually protected and sheltered by God's Word within their offices in perpetuity. The intents and actions of their free will were their own affair as long as they didn't intrude upon God's or another being's blessings in a way that overreached their own; as long as their actions didn't become illegal.

THE VOICE OF AHAB'S PROPHETS

"He cast upon them the fierceness of his anger, wrath, and indignation, and trouble, by sending evil angels [among them]." Psalm 78:49

A great example that we have in scripture of the evil angels still being present in the heavens is found in 1 Kings 22:19-23.

In this instance we can see that the Lord was on the throne, and ALL the host of heaven was there, present before the throne. It's interesting to see that the Lord actually would bother to ask the heavenly host *"Who shall persuade Ahab, that he may go up and fall at Ramoth-gilead?"* The Lord didn't command an individual angel to do this task, rather He was asking which of His sons was willing and able to go and get the job done. This is very important to realize. The Almighty as the basis of all free will allows and respects the viewpoints and opinions of His created; even the wicked ones found among them, and He apparently carries out practical discussions with them all, including conversations on ways to implement and carry out His judgments.

Some of the angels gave their different opinions on the matter, one saying this, one saying that, and since ALL the host of heaven included the wicked angels as we have clearly seen, a spirit came forth from among the others and said, *"I will persuade him."* The Lord then inquired of this spirit how he intends to do so; and the spirit replied, "I'll be a lying spirit in the mouths of his prophets". This was the evil spirit's proposal to God of how he could get the job done, all within the constraints of heavenly decree, all carried out by the wicked spirit working within the confines of Godly law. It's quite fascinating to see that God accepted his proposal and gave him the authority to do what he had suggested by blessing him saying, *"Thou shalt persuade him, and prevail also: go forth, and do so"*.

This express command/consent order from the Lord is what gave the wicked spirit the authority to do what the Lord Himself sought to have done. Amazingly, of all the different suggestions given from among the host, it was this spirit's proposal which God accepted as the best way to get things done!

We need to be aware that the spirit could not have legally done such a thing as intruding upon the king's prophets' anointings without the Lord's specific permission or granting of authority to the spirit to embark upon the venture even if it was in the spirit's previously held ability to do so, as it was. However, to intrude upon the lives of the king's prophets the spirit needed permission from God, a permission which was sought and granted in order to carry out the removal of the evil king.

Now, this was clearly not one of the holy angels, was it? Can anyone really envision Michael, or Gabriel, or one of the other faithful and holy angels of God going around and becoming a lying spirit in the mouths of the king's prophets for the purpose of bringing about the King of Israel's death? Of course not! It's offensive to even suggest that. So here we have a wicked being in among the host of heaven, standing before the throne of God, discussing things with the Most High and proposing answers to God's questions during the reign of King Ahab of Israel.

WHAT TO DO WHEN ONE THIRD OF YOUR ANGELS BECOME EVIL?

Alright, at this point the Creator has one third of all the angels in heaven in purposeful transgression against Him. You may be asking: "What to do? What now? Why doesn't He just send them straight to hell and clean house? He is the Almighty after all, and He can do any thing He wants, right? Why did He leave these evil beings around to cause trouble for Himself, as well as for all of us in His creation? Pride, jealousy, sickness, death, misery, bondage, affliction, war; the list is endless! All this started in the HEAVENS?! And the perpetrators are STILL THERE?! How can this be, I don't get it! What's to be done? OH! What's to be done?!"

Whoa! Take it easy, calm down, we'll get there, we just need patience.

> *"Better [is] the end of a thing than the beginning thereof..."*
> *Ecclesiastes 7:8*

Indeed, the end of satan IS better than the beginning. For all the rest of us that is.

ISAIAH 14

A close inspection of this chapter clearly indicates that the destruction of satan, the fall of Lucifer, the one indirectly referred to through the term "king of Babylon", is a future event, and not a past occurrence. It is a prophecy of things to come, and not a retelling of historical events. It tells of a time in the future when God again remembers the lost of Israel, and resettles them in His and their land. He will give them rest from the sorrow, fear, and the hard bondage which they have endured during the time the evil one roamed the heavens. A proverb will then be said of satan whose wicked works will have come to an end at the onset of the time of liberty which shall come to encompass the whole earth during the Messianic age.

> *Isaiah 14, verses 1-3: "For the LORD will have mercy on Jacob, and will yet choose Israel, and set them in their own land: and the strangers shall be joined with them, and they shall cleave to the house of Jacob. And the people shall take them, and bring them to their place: and the house of Israel shall possess them in the land of the LORD for servants and handmaids: and they shall take them captives, whose captives they were; and they shall rule over their oppressors. And it shall come to pass in the day that the LORD shall give thee rest from thy sorrow, and from thy fear, and from the hard bondage wherein thou wast made to serve,"*

Where are they?

> *Verse 4: "That thou shalt take up this proverb against the king of Babylon, and say, How hath the oppressor ceased! the golden city ceased!"*

Do the people of Israel, or anyone else, go around commonly remarking "How hath the oppressor ceased! The golden city ceased!" No, quite pointedly, they do not. And the reason they don't is precisely because to this day the oppressor (satan) has not ceased; one look around will confirm that evil is rampant upon the earth. The golden city? Babylon, its evil wickedness is abundant, and its influence is as corrupting as ever.

> *Verse 5: "The Lord hath broken the staff of the wicked, and the sceptre of the rulers."*

The staff is scripturally indicative of one's authority, and the sceptre is a picture of one's power. These are instruments of authority which the wicked hold and are not yet broken in any way. Contrarily, we see the Lord Himself granting the wicked spirits yet more authority and power in the end time events of the tribulation period to come, as mentioned in the Book of Revelation. (*Revelation 6:2-8; 9:3-5; 13:5-7*)

> *Verse 6: "He who smote the people with a continual stroke, he that ruled the nations in anger, is persecuted, and none hindereth."*

Ladies and gentlemen, the people are still being smitten continually by the evil one, aren't they? There are untold afflictions, bondages, sicknesses, and deaths in the world, aren't there? Therefore, the unhindered persecution of satan has not yet taken place. However, the unhindered persecution of satan by the righteous God is something to definitely look forward to!

> *Verse 7: "The whole earth is at rest, and is quiet: they break forth in singing."*

Is the whole earth at rest and quiet? No, on the contrary, it is still very tumultuous and chaotic due to the influence of evil which is still very much present and actively functioning in creation.

> *Verse 9: "Hell from beneath is moved for thee to meet [thee] at thy coming: it stirreth up the dead for thee, [even] all the chief ones of the earth; it hath raised up from their thrones all the kings of the nations."*

When a being, any being, is removed from heavenly office by God and is sentenced to punishment, that punishment is not a time of frivolity and wickedness upon the earth in the heavens of Shechakim and Rakia, or in the paradise of God where that wicked ones could freely run rampant outside of the confines of God's law causing untold misery to others while enjoying God's great blessings themselves. Such a punishment would sound more like a reward for a being! As this previous verse clearly indicates, hell is the location for the punishment of those rebellious individuals who choose to defy God, not another heaven or a part of one such as the earth, which is the abode of man. All creation longingly awaits the complete removal of the wicked ones from the heavens of our God, but for now they are still in office. (*Psalm 115:16*)

> *Verse 12: "How art thou fallen from heaven, O Lucifer, son of the morning! How art thou cut down to the ground, which didst weaken the nations!"*

As we have seen from the previous verses of this same chapter, satan is still in "heaven" weakening the nations, but this last verse really says it all. Lucifer (satan) couldn't have been weakening the nations unless he was still in his heavenly offices to do so at the time the nations existed upon the earth.

The pre-Adamic "fall" and *"cutting to the ground"* of satan would clearly preclude the presence of the evil one in the heavens at the time Adamic nations existed upon the earth. Therefore these verses in Isaiah are a clear prophesy of future events, not an explanation of bygone happenings. Once satan falls, or enters into illegal defiance, and commits the sin of rebellion then he loses the ability to weaken nations and torment people as he is "cut down" as a consequence of his rebellious actions. When satan is removed from his offices and cast down to hell, which we can see from this chapter is a result of his eventual rebellion, and the wicked conspiracy is finally ended, then this prophesy becomes fulfilled.

As Isaiah clearly states in the first verses of this fourteenth chapter, this proverb will be spoken by the regathered children of Israel in its applicable time as a celebratory reminder of a joyful past event; the utter destruction and removal of satan from his positions of office.

> *Verses 13-15: For thou hast said in thine heart, I will ascend into heaven, I will exalt my throne above the stars of God: I will sit also upon the mount of the congregation, in the sides of the north: I will ascend above the heights of the clouds; I will be like the most High. Yet thou shalt be brought down to hell, to the sides of the pit."*

Did you notice the tense changing in this series of verses? In verse thirteen satan *"hast said"* in his heart, he "hast" said at some point in the past, the past tense is therefore clearly used. Then these verses further expound that satan goes on to say *"I will"* quite a number of times, as he is referring to that which he plans to do in the future, but has not yet done. In verse fifteen we again encounter the future tense where scripture uses *"shalt be"* when referring to that which shall occur to satan as a result of his actions. The use of *"shalt be"* indicates the event in question had not yet happened, but will happen in a time to come. Lucifer (satan) *"shalt be brought down"* only when he attempts to enact the wicked rebellious things which he *"hast said"* he would do. The saying in his heart didn't cause satan to be cast down, the coming attempt to actually DO those things said is what convicts him.

All of creation is a witness to the fact that Lucifer *"hast said"*, and has decided to become wicked. His actions are readily visible in his perverted use of his God given authorities and offices which he grossly manipulates to this day. And all of creation, all of it, shall also be witness to the fact that the same being, satan, *"shalt be brought down"* and condemned to hell, the pit, and the lake of fire for all eternity, due to his soon to be committed rebellious actions at the time he attempts to actually DO the things he has said *"I will"* about. In the meantime, he is found in God's heavens, occupying the offices that he has been given, in and amongst all the other beings that are found in God's spiritual creation.

Now, some may say that satan's use of the term, *"I will ascend into heaven"* is proof that satan is no longer in (the) heaven(s) and in God's Kingdom as he needs to "ascend into heaven" to attempt his coup, and so, satan is able to just up and decide to ascend into heaven from his seemingly pleasant and happy exile here on the earth by use of his own strength to conquer the remaining portions of God's domain that are not already left to his control by God (That is SO silly it's difficult to even write down!).

If the Almighty God had cast satan down; how could satan possibly have the ability to get back up to "heaven" on his own accord whenever the mood struck him to do so? If a person were to say, "I will ascend into heaven" and then attempt to do so; you would laugh at him! For you know that he doesn't have the slightest ability to get there on his own. Neither would an exiled and previously cast down satan have that ability. No being enters any place God has forbidden them from entering. A cast down satan would have no way to hoist himself "up" into God's "abode" when the whim arose within him to do so. However, in order to quell such frivolous banter, let's reread verse thirteen and allow ourselves to indulge in this subject a little further.

> *Verses 13: For thou hast said in thine heart, I will ascend into heaven, I will exalt my throne above the stars of God: I will sit also upon the mount of the congregation, in the sides of the north."*

Let's start by looking at the phrase *"I will ascend into heaven"*. The word used in Hebrew for "heaven" is actually "shamayim" which means "the heavens", or more specifically, "the waters above". And the word *"into"* used in the King James translation is slightly misleading since going "into" something inherently means that one is outside of it. The more appropriate translation is, *"To the heavens will I ascend,"* as found in the Judaica Press Complete Tanach translation. The answer to the phrase, *"I will ascend"* is found in the context of this aforementioned fact, as one cannot go into something one is not out of.

The questions, rather, should be: Which of the heavens is satan planning on ascending to, and why? satan saying he will ascend to the heavens or to "the waters above" in order to exalt his throne above the stars of God refers to the fact that the heaven where the seats or thrones of angelic authority are located in by Godly decree is Maon the fifth heaven; and the heaven where the Lord's throne is located in is naturally the highest or seventh heaven. So, in satan's planned attempt to raise his angelic throne from the heaven of angelic authority to the heaven where God's authority is located he is not attempting to re-enter (the) heaven(s) after being permanently expelled; rather, he intends to rise up in a twisted attempt to elevate himself, an event that he has planned since wickedness first began. In the satanic plan to rise unto God's mount, satan was planning to exalt his throne *"above the stars of God"*; and stars, as we have previously read, are a common biblical metaphor for angels, above whose authority the throne of God towers, and above whom the lustful satan also wishes to see his own throne exalted. One must, indeed, rise up to the *"mount of the congregation"* if one wishes to set one's throne there, and one needn't be outside of the heavens for the need to exist to rise upward unto the place of God as He is the *"high and lofty One"* exalted in all ways. (*Isaiah 6:1*)

Furthermore, the term, *"I will ascend into heaven"*, need not mean that satan would enter into heaven for the first time since his supposed removal; not in the least. Have you ever ascended to the second story of a house? Have you ever ascended in an elevator to go to a higher story than where you were? Have you ever done so more than once? If you live or work in a multi-story house or building you have probably ascended to a higher floor countless times. As we have seen, the authorities of angelic beings extend into, or influence all heavens in some way; and that is the reason they are constantly coming and going, ascending and descending, into different heavens to carry out the responsibilities of their offices found throughout the heavens of God.

The Genesis Mousetrap

The illegality of the angel, satan's, ascent in this context, however, was the reason he had in his heart at the time. He was not planning on ascending to the heights of God to pay homage, or receive instruction, or to operate within his rightfully given offices; rather, in this verse, satan was planning and attempting to carry out an illegal coup, a wrongful seizure of power, and that sin is the basis of the issue encountered here.

The Book of Genesis tells us that the patriarch Jacob was shown a dream by God in which he saw ladders rising up to heaven, and angels both ASCENDING and descending upon it as they were moving from one heaven to another; and there was no illegality involved in the angels doing so, for they were all moving within their rightful authorities at that time.

> "And he dreamed, and behold a ladder set up on the earth, and the top of it reached to heaven: and behold the angels of God ascending and descending on it. And, behold, the LORD stood above it, and said, I [am] the LORD God of Abraham thy father, and the God of Isaac: the land whereon thou liest, to thee will I give it, and to thy seed;" Genesis 28:12-13

"And, behold, the Lord stood above it...". The Lord stands high and exalted above all, and only by His pre-established Word can the angels, or anyone else, function!

Speaking of the coming destruction of satan and evil, and of the liberation of His own; the Lord has said the following:

> "The Lord of Hosts hath sworn, saying, Surely as I have thought, so shall it come to pass; and as I have purposed, so shall it stand: That I will break the Assyrian in My land, and upon My mountains tread him under foot: then shall his yoke depart from off them, and his burden depart from off their shoulders. This is the purpose that is purposed upon the whole earth: and this is the hand that is stretched out upon all the nations. For the Lord of Hosts hath purposed, and who shall disannul it? And His hand is stretched out, and who shall turn it back?" Isaiah 14:24-27

Chapter six

The role of the Judge

THE WORD PROTECTED

"And ye are complete in him, which is the head of all principality and power:" Colossians 2:10

This brings us to one of the many roles that God had reserved for Himself: That of Judge of all creation. (*Genesis 15:14; 18:25, Judges 11:27, Psalm 9:8; 50:4, Daniel 7:22, Revelation 19:11*)

In the event clarity is needed on a particular issue, or a trespass such as the wrongful infringement upon the blessings and anointings of God had occurred somewhere, a judgment would be needed to ensure that peace and tranquility existed, and that the laws of God were kept so that the anointings of God wouldn't be disrespected by any. One of the most important reasons that God Himself has the role of Judge is to ensure that the proper respect is shown the Word which He has previously declared, and also that the blessings which He has given unto each individual being would not be illegally transgressed upon by others. We see the clear calls made by individuals for the judgment of God on particular issues occurring in the following scriptures: *Zechariah 3:1-2, Jude 1:9.*

It is most important to God, and indeed, necessary for the proper function of all creation, that the specific anointings and giftings, the very essence of His Spirit graced to one individual would not be disrespected, infringed upon, or blasphemed by another.

Now, we as people are told by the scriptures to judge ourselves so that we would not be judged, and to conversely not judge others, as we do not have the right of condemnation or the ability to know the intents of the hearts of others; nor do we possess the ability to understand the full legal complexities of the laws of God.

Another very important reason we are told to avoid judging others is that we as people are imperfect, and are also to some degree guilty of sin and trespass against others and against God. In denying us the right of judgment the Lord is trying to protect us from being held accountable to the high standards which we ourselves fall short of when we would condemn others as we stand to judge them of sin. This fact is born out of the law of reciprocity and is well explained in the following verse:

> *"Therefore thou art inexcusable, O man, whosoever thou art that judgest: for wherein thou judgest another, thou condemnest thyself; for thou that judgest doest the same things." Romans 2:1*

Yes, it is written that the day will come when man will, indeed, judge angels, but that comes at a certain time specified and ordered by the Almighty; in a time when man will walk and work in the full knowledge of God and in the understanding of His laws and of His justice. Until that day arrives, however, the office of judge is beyond the rights of man. *(James 5:9, 1 Chronicles 6:2-3)*

Why, even angelic beings do not have the right to judge others, rather they are to protect their own anointings from wrongful and illegal trespass by those who would seek to hinder the completion of their assigned tasks, and they are to guard their blessings from those who would defile them. For contested issues requiring a clarification in order to bring a conclusion to matters that come up, which don't yet have a pre-issued precedent existing, the angelic need to seek God's judgment. This judgment is required on anything which the overlapping angelic authorities and the intricate complexities of the laws of the infinite heavens would leave unclear.

As mentioned, areas of conflicting legal authority are issues which require the ever vigilant judgments of God to settle. Such conflicts are due to the satanic transgression in operation; for in true Godly love there is no desire to attempt to supersede, take from, or break against

The role of the Judge

the rights of another, or to encroach on the authorities of others. Rather, Godly love seeks to uphold and strengthen others, to help them in their authorities, so that their tasks can be completed for the glory and benefit of the Creator, and for the benefit of all that is found within His creation.

HOW TO DEAL WITH THE WICKED

Now, concerning the wicked beings, and how they need to be handled in light of the fact that they still walk in their privileges in the Kingdom of God, we need to understand that although we are not to judge and sentence anyone we are still commanded to *"prove all things"*, and to keep that which is good. (*1 Thessalonians 5:21*).

We need to weigh all things in light of God's Word; and all things which come our way that are found to be in conflict with the Word and Spirit of God, such as the will and actions of the wicked, must be resisted. This is to be done not only for our own sake, but for the sake of others in creation as well, and most of all, out of love and respect for the Lord God whose will and blessings upon us would be undermined, warped, and possibly usurped by the actions of the wicked.

The issues to watch for, however, is to not cast insult upon, or bring false accusation against, those who carry the anointings of God, no matter how deviantly they themselves choose to pervert their anointings. Care must be taken not to blaspheme the Word of God given as blessings to any individual, as that Word is upheld by the Holy Spirit and any disrespect shown the holder of the blessings is disrespect shown toward God. Such direct disrespect toward an individual is an indirect act of blasphemy against God, in point of fact.

We very well should, and are obligated to resist and rebuke those things which are not good and in accord with God's Word. Doing so would protect our own blessings and the Word of God that we've been given; and we should also endeavor to uphold and strengthen the blessings of others that walk in the light of the Lord who may be adversely affected by the actions of wickedness through the improper onslaught of the evil ones. However, we are not to insult or blaspheme those who in their perverted wills' and ways' still function within their own God given anointings, out of respect for the same Word of God which at one time was given unto them as well, no matter how wicked they may now be. For the absolute and unconditional Word of God still functions to uphold all.

Scripture also clearly states in 1 Peter 5:8-9, and James 4:7, in regards to dealing with the wicked beings that they are to be resisted. Resisted from what? From their attempts of wrongfully infringing upon, invading, or occupying any portion of the blessings which God has given unto us as individual beings, as these blessings are given without regret unto our care and are the responsibility of the recipients to protect.

The apostle Paul said it the following ways in regards to verifying the sanctity of beings and of the things they bring into our surroundings:

> *"Prove all things; hold fast that which is good."*
> *1 Thessalonians 5:21*

> *"But though we, or an angel from heaven, preach any other gospel unto you than that which we have preached unto you, let him be accursed."* Galatians 1:8

Anything that comes into conflict with the Word of God is cursed. Furthermore, it is a responsibility of our offices as recipients of God's blessings, and especially as believers in Messiah to curse, resist, and bind such things which come our way that are in conflict with God's Word. This is so that such things don't successfully continue perverting and undermining God's will in the areas of creation that are within our authorities, binding and deceiving us, hurting others around us, and blaspheming God in the process.

These things or beings which come to us and against us contrary to the Word and will of God are, indeed, accursed and doomed to failure, as they stand outside of God's will, and such need to be cursed and inhibited by those whose anointings the wicked come to assail. God's will needs to be affirmed and protected by resisting the intended assault of the wicked against the individual blessings of the obedient beings.

Those who carry His name and anointing of life must constantly guard against those who seek to bring destruction to God's creation. Due to the fact that those wicked beings are in conflict with God's Word and will no

The role of the Judge

individual should ever receive such spirits or the things they would represent, or submit to them in any way. For if we do, we either knowingly, or unknowingly, become enablers of the satanic transgressors by allowing them to use our authorities and offices to defile creation and further conceal God's will in the earth.

The word "accursed" which Paul uses in Galatians to describe such wicked beings is the Greek word "anathema", and it refers to something left to the Lord, marked for death, and unredeemable from death. In other words, it is utterly doomed to destruction and eradication; such is the lot of the wicked.

The point to be made in all of this is that we must not slur, shame, or blaspheme the anointings and blessings which are unrepentantly given by the Lord unto any, and are present with even the worst transgressor within His kingdom. However, we are to resist the wicked, reiterate the will and the laws of God, and call for the judgment of the Lord to destroy that which is evil according to His Word, so that the will of the Lord would be carried out in His creation. So that the permanent blessings of the Lord that are upon the righteous will not be hindered by the unchecked presence of wickedness attempting to grow its power at the expense of others.

JESUS GAVE THE EXAMPLE

An example that we are given as to how the wicked are to be resisted without blaspheming or insulting the anointings that are upon them when they move in their attempts of procuring power from the righteous, or when suppressing the anointings thereof, is given to us in the actions of Messiah Jesus Himself in Matthew 4:1-11, and in Luke 4:1-14.

Jesus wasn't the least bit surprised that satan would dare come near unto Him, not at all. Jesus knew that satan had every right to come and see if Jesus or any other being would be willing to sin against God; and since satan had the right to do so, he was not sinning himself in the process.

Notice that the Lord did not cast satan into hell for attempting to annoy Him. Nor did the Lord attempt to seize satan's authority; and nowhere did Jesus speak insultingly, or behave rudely toward satan. Certainly not out of fondness for the wicked satan, but out of respect for the offices and blessings that satan holds from God. So that God's blessings wouldn't be sullied by improper or blasphemous words which would result in an insult to God, the giver of the blessings.

Rather, Jesus always responded to satan's ploys and perversions with the truth of the Word of God, and He resisted any satanic attempt to weaken Him and lessen His abilities to walk in His own offices. When so countered, satan needed to leave Messiah having been unable to usurp, or lessen, any of His authority or find any cause to accuse Messiah of improper or illegal conduct before the Father God, the righteous Judge of all creation.

What did Messiah do to counter satan's remarks? He always referred to the Word of God, the legal groundwork and basis for all blessings issued in creation. Jesus spoke the Word of God as it was written in scripture. In this desert encounter recorded in Matthew's Gospel, Jesus quoted strictly from Deuteronomy; responding to every satanic twisting of truth by stating the pure and perfect will of the Almighty as written in the Torah, the source that protected His, and indeed, all anointings.

The Word of God alone upholds all things. The Word of God is the source of all rights and laws in creation, and it alone is that which rebuffs the wicked. (*Hebrews 4:12*)

MOSES, MOSES

Let's look at one specific event that is detailed in scripture which brings to light the way in which the angelic are affected by God's judgments: That of satan confronting Israel's angel prince, Michael, demanding from him the body of Moses. (*Deuteronomy 34:1-8, Jude 1:9*)

What actually happened to bring about this noteworthy confrontation? We read of God telling Moses that he would not be allowed to go into the Promised Land due to Moses' disobedience; instead, he was to climb to the top of Mt.Pisgah where he would be shown the good land and there on the mountaintop he would then pass away.

The role of the Judge

So, what was at the root of the angelic conflict here in this seemingly straightforward issue? First, this was a holy meeting, where God showed His servant the blessings He had in store for His people. No evil was, or could have been present in attendance. Second, Moses had many years prior to this event, during Israel's stay at Mt. Sinai, wanted to and prayerfully asked God if he could see His glory, to which the Lord replied: *"there shall no man see me, and live"* (*Exodus 33:18-20*).

Well, now at Mt.Pisgah, Moses received the answer to his prayer. Moses went up to the glory of God; he was given the privilege to see the Lord's full glory, and his physical body simply couldn't take it; it just expired. What a way to go!

However, satan was upset because he was the angel of death; the being assigned to the office which had the right to end physical life, and he felt cheated because he wasn't present to end Moses' bodily life. As a result, satan came to confront Michael about it, since Moses' body had been given over to the care of Israel's angel, Michael, for burial. satan came to Michael demanding what he claimed was his rightful authority to take part in, and to cause, the death of Moses' body. To this Michael wisely replied: *"The Lord rebuke thee"* (*Jude 1:9*).

It's important to realize that Michael wasn't afraid of satan, or powerless against him in this issue, as Michael held the authority and legal rights to care for Israel, and Moses was of Israel; but Michael did not want to speak injuriously against the anointings or rights of satan; who as the angel of death did have a strong form of a claim to the death of Moses, lest he would have blasphemed the authority given satan by God, and thus blaspheme God in the process.

What Michael did do when he said, *"The Lord rebuke thee"* was to call satan and his issue before the judgment of God for a trial and a reprimand. This is an extremely powerful thing that Michael did. He had called satan before the heavenly judgment seat of the Most High God, the great Judge of all.

Should satan have continued in his attempt to claim authority in this matter beyond what God had already decided was in accordance with His Word (the issue here being that God, indeed, did have the right to have a physical body expire due to the presence of His glory without the involvement of the angel of death) satan would most likely not have been present in the creation anymore. In all likelihood he would have become guilty of purposefully defying God's judgments; a rebellious act which would lead to being cast into hell.

The result of this call to heavenly trial was that satan never got to take part in the physical death of Moses since it was the power of the radiance of the glory of God that caused Moses to pass. This was a legal, although very unusual way for a person to pass without the "help" of the angel of death; who, indeed, did hold the right to end a person's physical life; however, clearly not the exclusive right. The angel, Michael, knew what he was doing.

In the following verse Jesus effectively spoke of the right of God to extinguish both the life of the physical body, as well as to destroy the very soul itself:

> *"And fear not them which kill the body, but are not able to kill the soul: but rather fear him which is able to destroy both soul and body in hell."* Matthew 10:28

So, Moses entered into God's presence and passed away from seeing the power of the glory of God, and his body was buried by Israel's angel prince, the archangel Michael, in accordance with the Word and will of God, in an unknown valley, in the land of Moab.

Another telling event of judgment can be found in the Book of Daniel in chapter four, verse seventeen. There, the scriptures clearly state that judgments were brought upon a man: In this particular case, upon Nebuchadnezzar, so that all may know that God rules in the affairs of men and gives authority to whoever He wills.

Notice that it was the holy angels, the watchers, who brought forth this decree which enabled the effects of the judgment to take place upon Nebuchadnezzar, even though the holy angels themselves were not responsible for carrying out the negative impacts of the judgment upon the person in question. However, their relaying of the Godly decree was necessary for the judgment to begin.

The role of the Judge

THE WORD IS THE LAW

We must further understand that the Almighty God Himself cannot, neither can His holy angels, break His eternal Words which He has given unto the angelic host, whether the angels themselves choose to be holy or wicked is inconsequential. Yes, that may seem shocking, but we must remember that the wicked weren't wicked when the blessings were first given unto them. Therefore, from the viewpoint of Godliness the bestowed Word of God is always sacred and perfect; regardless of whom it rests upon, and even if the empowered individual and his works may not be in God's will.

The Word cannot, and will not, be compromised or broken by God, not unless the wicked ones themselves first openly defy and break against God's Words or anointings in a way that leads Him to act in order to safeguard the sanctity of His Word which rests upon others in creation. As the wicked themselves defile or attempt to impugn the integrity of the Word bestowed unto others they run the risk of rebellion should their efforts which often border on and occasionally cross into illegality be called to a halt by the infringed upon being through the legal mechanisms provided for by the Word of God.

If such infringements by the wicked upon the blessings of others continue after the interloper has been duly forbidden, the sin of rebellion against God, the issuer of the blessings occurs; and the only way the Word is kept Holy is for the unyielding wicked being(s) to be removed from office and sentenced. This is to defend the sanctity of God's Word, especially after the perpetrator has been resisted by the one whose anointings the wicked had originally attempted to violate.

Should the wicked have still chosen to keep violating the will of God after having been resisted by one in legal authority (the pre-judged wicked still retain the free will to try, after all) then, and only then, can they be brought to sentencing and be judged by God to be guilty of rebellion. At that time they can be legally removed from office, but not before.

This was the case with the son's of God coming to earth and having children with the daughters of men. They were in clear violation of God's laws, and they simply didn't care. They felt compelled to sully the

The Genesis Mousetrap

Adamic bloodline in an attempt to stop the Holy and promised "seed of Eve" from arriving and ultimately destroying the wicked conspiracy. So, although the wicked conspirators had full knowledge that they were rebelling against God's Words, they chose to defy Him anyway, and the result for them was a judgment of being bound with chains in hell as mentioned in Jude 1:6.

Why, even a wicked angel doesn't dare to trespass against the authority of another wicked one, unless the other wicked one first somehow cedes the right of authority in his office unto the interloper. This caution is out of a fear of being rightly resisted, and of being found guilty of trespass against the original right and blessing that God had given to the infringed upon wicked being. In this type of situation, the infringed upon wicked angel has the same rights as any other being in God's Kingdom and can resist the infringer, going to the heavenly court of God for an immediate trial by the Judge. A just verdict would be given, punishment would then follow, and depending on the offense, the possibility of the terrible prison of hell would ensue for the rebellious who continues to break against God's stated Word, even if the defender in question was wicked.

That which remains necessary for the infringed upon beings (whether righteous or wicked) to do is to vigilantly protect their individual rights and blessings by acquainting and reacquainting themselves with their bestowed rights and blessings and with the stated laws of God. Then, by standing firm not to yield to outside pressure whilst ensuring that their own will and action's are in line with God's; all the while vigorously calling for the judgment of God upon the breach and breacher in question. Both righteous and wicked can, and often do, make constant claim to their rights, or what they perceive to be as their rights, before God. This is due to the fact that the laws and anointings of God are enforced by the Judge of all creation, God Himself, of whose loyalty to His Word the following is written in Psalm 138:2 *"...thou hast magnified thy word above all thy name."*

THE RULES OF WAR

The fact of the matter is that there has been a constant battling over rights and authority in the angelic offices since the moment the satanic transgression first began, and that battling is actually legal wrangling over what rights belong to what individuals in what circumstances. The evil ones are always looking to gain power in God's Kingdom by using and/or limiting the authorities and offices of others if and where they can in order to increase their own power, and the righteous contrastingly seek to preserve their blessings and fulfill God's will.

The use and stewardship of rights within creation can be generally explained in the following ways:

First, all individual rights are determined by God on the basis of the blessings He has given.

Second, they are then guarded by the angelic individuals.

Third, the rights are judged by God in cases of conflict.

Fourth, the judgments are adhered to by all creation, especially by the interlopers in question, as they come under a clarified and specific heavenly mandate that consequently restricts the interlopers' access to the newly clarified rights of the other; which in this hypothetical scenario were judged as being wrongly infringed upon.

Fifth, should the wrongful parties not yield unto the newly given judgment they are then found to be in rebellion against the Lord God Himself, and against the very Kingdom of God in which the basis of their own authorities lay.

Sixth, the rebellious interlopers are then subsequently removed from their existing offices and punished.

In events of conflictive claims of authority the Lord would rule against the wrongdoer, and the one with the rightful anointing of authority in accordance with his pre-existent blessings and newly clarified Word would prevail in the battle; which, as it has been stated, is a legal conflict in which blessings and anointings are protected and/or expanded in accordance to the Word of God, or ultimately rescinded in the case of transgressive activity.

The Genesis Mousetrap

Chapter seven

Judgments:
With Jude, Job, Jesus, and Joshua

JUDE

In the short Book of Jude we are given a fine example of the importance of respecting the blessings and offices of others, including those of the wicked beings, and also of how God views those people who in their insolence slander and blaspheme other beings, whether good or evil. He views it as a grievous sin. For the blessings the others had originally received and presently operate under come from God, and the rights they have stem from authorities that are based in God's Kingdom. To wrongfully or illegally insult any being, or infringe upon their blessings is akin to insulting God Himself.

> "Likewise also these [filthy] dreamers defile the flesh, despise dominion, and speak evil of dignities." Jude 1:8

This verse speaks of those people who in their prideful ignorance have the nerve and the audacity to insult the blessings that are upon others whether on man, or on angels; and after doing so believe that they are impervious to the consequences of their blasphemy against the blessings of Almighty God. The following verse, nine, affirms that the words "dominion" and "dignity" used in this eighth verse refer to angels, not just to man.

> *"Yet Michael the archangel, when contending with the devil he disputed about the body of Moses, durst not bring against him a railing accusation, but said, The Lord rebuke thee." Jude 1:9*

As previously discussed, this verse shows that not even the great archangel Michael would injuriously or blasphemously speak against satan; rather, Michael chose to respect the ways of God and called satan before the Lord for a certain judgment. Quite tellingly, the term *"railing accusation"* used in this verse could just as accurately be translated from the original Greek word into the English word "blasphemy".

The honorable actions of the archangel Michael are in sharp contrast to that of the *"filthy dreamers"* mentioned in verse eight which despise dominion and speak evil of dignities, including spiritual dominions and dignities as this ninth verse makes abundantly clear. There's no way around it, this verse clearly cautions against bringing railing accusations and blasphemous rants against even the wicked ones in creation.

> *"But these speak evil of those things which they know not: but what they know naturally, as brute beasts, in those things they corrupt themselves." Jude 1:10*

The same Greek word used in verse nine and translated there as *"railing accusation"* is used here as *"speak evil"*, and it is the Greek word "blasphemeo", which actually also translates into the English word "blasphemy" (no surprise there). So this verse can be read as, "But these who speak blasphemously of those things which they know not..."

As we have seen from the previously read text this verse is not just speaking of those who only blaspheme the Personage of God directly, but rather makes reference to the unrepentant naturally minded people, religious or otherwise, who think that just because they have the ability to speak evil of others, including wicked angels, and since they can verbally deride them, that it is acceptable and right for them to do so. Jude says these people corrupt themselves exceedingly in all manner of sin, living only for the natural, totally blinded to the power and effects of the spiritual truths and laws which they break. All must take heed not to defile themselves in mindless speech against any who carry the

Judgments: With Jude, Job, Jesus, and Joshua

anointings of God; for in doing so the defilers become themselves corrupted away from the truth as they have injured the Spirit of Truth Himself.

In the Book of Second Peter we can find a strong second witness to these facts spoken of in Jude. The words "governments" and "dignities" as we have seen also apply to the angelic forms thereof and to angels as individual beings as well; in these following verses of Second Peter it states not even angels bring *"railing accusation"* against such dignities. This term *"railing accusation"* used in Second Peter is the same Greek word "blasphemeo" which we have previously seen used in Jude.

> *"But chiefly them that walk after the flesh in the lust of uncleanness, and despise government. Presumptuous [are they], selfwilled, they are not afraid to speak evil of dignities. Whereas angels, which are greater in power and might, bring not railing accusation against them before the Lord. But these, as natural brute beasts, made to be taken and destroyed, speak evil of the things that they understand not; and shall utterly perish in their own corruption;"* 2 Peter 2:10-12

> *"Woe unto them! for they have gone in the way of Cain, and ran greedily after the error of Balaam for reward, and perished in the gainsaying of Core."* Jude 1:11

Cain was extremely jealous that Abel's offering was accepted by God, while his wasn't. Cain broke the laws of God and came against Abel's blessings out of jealousy and wounded pride, losing his own peace with God in the process.

Balaam was willing to curse the nation that God had blessed for mere capital gain. Balaam was willing to transgress against the will and anointings of God for profit and love of money, causing God to leave this once great prophet to a heathen's death.

Core, which is the Geek transliteration of the Hebrew name "Korah", is the same person which led the Korah rebellion against Moses in the sixteenth chapter of the Book of Numbers. This Core began to begrudge the authority of Moses, and he stirred up the petty among the people into rebellion. It wasn't Moses alone that Core and his compatriots despised, it was the will of God that they defied and wished to dishonor. In attacking God's anointings on Moses, Core and his compatriots thought that they could advance themselves in the hierarchy of Israel and gain prominence at the expense of God's will.

All three individuals cited here are examples of those who dared belittle and blaspheme the Word and anointings of God; destruction awaited them all.

> *"These are spots in your feasts of charity, when they feast with you, feeding themselves without fear: clouds [they are] without water, carried about of winds; trees whose fruit withereth, without fruit, twice dead, plucked up by the roots; Raging waves of the sea, foaming out their own shame; wandering stars, to whom is reserved the blackness of darkness for ever. And Enoch also, the seventh from Adam, prophesied of these, saying, Behold, the Lord cometh with ten thousands of his saints, To execute judgment upon all, and to convince all that are ungodly among them of all their ungodly deeds which they have ungodly committed, and of all their hard [speeches] which ungodly sinners have spoken against him." Jude 1:13-15*

Ladies and gentlemen, the point which must be reemphasized here is that nothing, absolutely nothing, exists which has as a source of creation someone or something other than God; and when we wrongly violate the sanctity of the blessings which are on others in creation whether through word or deed, we transgress and sin against the Lord who created and blessed them. This is so, regardless of whether these individual beings, which the foolish would so willingly besmirch, are aware of their own rights or not. The Lord will come to judge all the ungodly of their evil actions, and of the hard words which they have spoken against Him; both directly and indirectly through their behaviors toward his created, and woe unto those who have not repented of their actions and stopped their sins before they are made known and judged.

> *"These are murmurers, complainers, walking after their own lusts; and their mouth speaketh great swelling [words], having men's persons in admiration because of advantage."* Jude 1:16

These ignorant people grandly speak kind things to others only in the hope of gaining something from them; everything they do is based in selfishness and their kindness is superficial, covering an otherwise bitter, backbiting, and faultfinding nature. Everyone else is unacceptable in their eyes, only useful to them for what they can provide to these lovers of self. Their own will and wicked desire is paramount; they do despise government of all kind, after all.

The Book of Jude makes it extremely clear that all beings in creation must be very aware of the sin of blaspheming the anointings of God upon others; and equally we must be cautious not to harden ourselves into a self-centered, self absorbed life which the Most High God considers to be a filthy abomination and an insult to His grace.

JOB IN JUDGMENT

In the Book of Job we can see examples of both the wicked angels being present in the heavens, as well as of God's use of the office of Judge. An in-depth study of the Book of Job would be best, but for the sake of brevity we'll only be looking at a few passages of the book.

> *"Now there was a day when the sons of God came to present themselves before the LORD, and Satan came also among them."* Job 1:6

Once again, we find the sons of God presenting themselves before the Lord just as they did in Ahab's day which was touched upon previously. Does the Bible say the Lord went to present Himself before the sons of God while they were upon the earth? No. Did it say God left His heavenly throne to visit the angelic host while they were engaged in their assigned tasks? Absolutely not! The Bible is quite clear about the matter. The sons of God clearly came before Him in this instance and the Bible goes out of its way to say that satan was also among them, present before

God in the highest heaven. Why was satan among the sons of God in heaven? It is simply because he is unquestionably still one of them.

It is a mandate from God that all the sons of God come before Him to pay homage; to give an account of their activities; as well as to each receive permissions and further orders which they need so that they may carry out the fulfillment of His decrees. They are there before Him to also settle any legal disputes which may arise among the angelic host due to the presence of the greed and lust of the wicked conspirators.

> *"And the LORD said unto Satan, Whence comest thou? Then Satan answered the LORD, and said, From going to and fro in the earth, and from walking up and down in it." Job 1:7*

This is a great example of God requiring a report from the angelic host, satan included, on their activities. It must be stressed that God doesn't require reports from the angelic to keep Him informed of what happens in His creation. Due to His omnipresence such a thing would be most unnecessary. However, as He is the Most High God, King of all creation, it is appropriate that all beings in His kingdom come before Him to show respect, and to share with him firsthand the news of the events that occur in their offices.

Also, this sharing with God of the happenings in their lives is a great privilege, an opportunity for the angels to commune with their Creator; to be able to approach His throne, to hear and to tell of things with God is an astounding privilege. This is one honor which most likely made satan and His fellow conspirators a little uncomfortable though.

> *"And the LORD said unto Satan, Hast thou considered my servant Job, that [there is] none like him in the earth, a perfect and an upright man, one that feareth God, and escheweth evil?" Job 1:8*

Here we have the Lord engaged in a very straightforward and almost amicable conversation with satan. Amazing! The Lord wasn't saying: "What are you doing here in heaven, satan? I threw you out ages ago!" No, the Lord wasn't saying that because satan was actually obliged to be there to fulfill the duties of his offices. The Lord was speaking of normal things with satan, even things which apparently weren't official Heavenly business such as bringing to light the faithful obedience of His servant Job and casually discussing the fellow's life with satan.

> "Then Satan answered the LORD, and said, Doth Job fear God for nought? Hast not thou made an hedge about him, and about his house, and about all that he hath on every side? thou hast blessed the work of his hands, and his substance is increased in the land. But put forth thine hand now, and touch all that he hath, and he will curse thee to thy face." Job 1:9-11

satan answered the Lord, and he answered using quite a bit of contrarian thought and audacity in his reply. The angels having free will are more than within their rights to discuss all things with the Lord, and to give their opinions on any matter that is open for discussion. However, it is never wise or prudent to do so in an impudent manner as satan will soon demonstrate for us.

> "And the LORD said unto Satan, Behold, all that he hath [is] in thy power; only upon himself put not forth thine hand. So Satan went forth from the presence of the LORD." Job 1:12

If satan wasn't in heaven, and a part of God's kingdom, the Lord as a righteous Judge could not have left all that Job had into his power. It would have been a tremendously illegal breach of His own Word for Him to do so.

> "Again there was a day when the sons of God came to present themselves before the LORD, and Satan came also among them to present himself before the LORD. And the LORD said unto Satan, From whence comest thou? And Satan answered the LORD, and said, From going to and fro in the earth, and from walking up and down in it. And the LORD said unto Satan, Hast thou considered my servant Job, that [there is] none like him in the earth, a perfect and an upright man, one that feareth God, and escheweth evil? and still he holdeth fast his integrity, although thou movedst me against him, to

> *destroy him without cause. And Satan answered the LORD, and said, Skin for skin, yea, all that a man hath will he give for his life. But put forth thine hand now, and touch his bone and his flesh, and he will curse thee to thy face. And the LORD said unto Satan, Behold, he [is] in thine hand; but save his life."* Job 2:1-7

In this sequence of verses satan is once again found before the Most High in heaven among all the sons of God presenting himself before the Lord. At this time the Lord again chooses to make the case for Job's righteousness, which satan eagerly tries to dismiss, and satan again brings up the fact that due to God's protection of Job he wasn't being hurt enough to cause him to sin against God. Once again, the Lord allowed satan to increase his attacks upon Job.

It's important to notice that it was the Lord who was constantly bringing Job to satan's attention, and not the other way around. It wasn't satan who was always trying to bring Job up as a topic for discussion, begging for the opportunity to attack Job. Why was that the case? Why would the Lord do that? Hmmm....

This is a perfect example of God's wisdom, and of the way things operate in His Kingdom in regards to His Judgeship. The Lord made it quite clear in the forty first chapter of the Book of Job, that He was baiting leviathan (satan).

satan is always trying to increase his power at the expense of others, and in this case Job was brought to satan's attention as a man greatly blessed because of his upright ways. satan thought he could manipulate the Lord into giving him the authority to cause Job to curse God, and thereby drive a wedge between the Lord and His servant.

In that way satan thought he could have cleverly gotten God's blessings to cease operating through Job. satan was claiming it was God's blessings on Job which caused Job to fear and obey the Lord, and not Job's fear and obedience which brought on the blessings. However, it was God who was directing the course of the conversation and putting ideas into satan's mind. The Lord gave satan the permission he needed for his attempt to bring Job into sin and separation from Him. This He did knowing full well that satan would fail in his attempt, and that Job would remain faithful to Him, leaving satan guilty of attacking the blessings of an upright man without cause. This was God's way of bringing leviathan, satan, into a place of sin and transgression against the laws and Word of God, thereby enabling God to place a hook into satan's jaws, so that he would be more restricted, controllable, and further limited in his future actions.

The following verse contains this statement of fact made by the Almighty:

> "Who hath prevented me, that I should repay [him? whatsoever is] under the whole heaven is mine." Job 41:11

The New Living Translation or NLT has this same verse, Job 41:11, written as:

> "Who will confront me and remain safe? Everything under heaven is mine." Job 41:11

satan (leviathan), was a bit too bold in his presumptuous attitude toward the Lord and His servant Job, and he brought a judgment upon himself by trying to impose his overbearing will into the life of an upright man; in trying to take the blessings of another where no cause existed. That judgment will follow him to his end. No one pridefully confronts the Lord of Hosts about anything, even the smallest thing, and gets away with it. As is often the case with the servants of God, Job, the servant of God, did his duty without even realizing it.

> "[It is] a fearful thing to fall into the hands of the living God." Hebrews 10:31

THE EXAMPLE OF THE DEMONIAC AND THE LEGION

In scripture where a certain event is documented in more than one book it's good practice to read all accounts simultaneously so that we can get the clearest possible understanding of what took place in the stated event. In the case of the demoniac and the legion we need to look at all three accounts to get the fullest picture of the transpiring events. This incident is referred to in the following places: *Matthew 8:28-34, Mark 5:1-21, and Luke 8:26-39.*

In these passages we see a very good example of a situation in which the wicked spirits try to make use of God's laws for their own benefit. In these three accounts of this one event we see that the man with an unclean spirit came forth immediately to meet Jesus as the Lord came out of the boat and stepped onto shore. Although the scriptures clearly state that there were two possessed men and multiple evil spirits present in the possessed men it also speaks of the men and spirits in the singular, as being one man and one spirit.

Why is this the case? Among the angelic there is order and rank; the reason the scriptures occasionally reference a group of spirits as one individual spirit is that there was a certain spirit present of greater rank than the others, and that is the case here.

In one of the men there was a spirit present of greater rank and authority than the others, one to whom the others deferred. It was a primary demon among the others which were present also possessing the men, it was there leading the other evil ones in their foul behavior. This spirit saw a far greater power entering its area of abode; in fact, the greatest power had entered the area of its habitation, and the spirit had a pressing need to go pay his respects. Also, he felt a vital urgency to make the case for his right to remain there undisturbed by the One who had the ability to exile this motley group of far lesser spirits which were there possessing the men.

EVEN DEMONS RUN TO WORSHIP THE LORD! ....WHAT!?!

The Bible says the spirit saw Jesus from afar off and ran to worship Him. Think of it, we as people many times consider it a task to worship the Lord, while these spirits RAN from afar off to worship Him! Maybe we can learn something from them after all. Of course, they had selfish motives in doing so, but nevertheless, they understood who the Lord was, and what His power is. So should we all.

Judgments: With Jude, Job, Jesus, and Joshua

Now, that being said, it was not out of love that the spirit went to the Lord to plead, but out of respectful fear that he came saying: *"what have I to do with thee, Jesus, thou Son of the Most High God? I adjure thee by God, that thou torment me not."* This legion of spirits was pleading its case before the Judge of all creation, and tried to legally get Jesus to leave them alone by questioning His right of office.

This wicked legion spirit was adjuring or charging Jesus, imploring Him to let them be, presenting before the Holy and righteous God its legal claims to stay in the demoniac. When the spirit was told by Jesus to leave the man, the spirit protested saying in essence: "Because you're the Son of the Most High God you don't have the authority to punish us or to interfere with our right to possess this man or to dwell in this area before the time. So leave us alone."

What time were they referring to? The time of the Great judgment of God to come; that which is spoken of throughout the pages of scripture.

The wicked knew that upon the final judgment the Lord God had the right to try and sentence them, but they were desperately claiming He didn't have the right to interfere with them at that present time according to God's own law, and according to the unrepentant authority which they were all operating under. You know what? They were right.

In the context of their argument these demons were absolutely correct; however, the wicked ones are never to be trusted to bring forth all the facts. It's never in their interest to bring forth the whole story. Their "strength" lies in their misrepresentation and distortion of God's laws. That's why it is, and remains, a defining characteristic of satan and his ilk to speak half-truths and lies, *"...because there is no truth in him* (John 8:44)."

For as the Son of God, Jesus truly didn't have the right at that time to rule and enforce righteousness in a totalitarian way upon the earth, but as the sinless Son of man, the last Adam, He did, and it was in that specific authority and office in which He came to operate that He cast them out everywhere on the earth He went.

The spirits knew very well that Jesus was also the Son of man, and that He operated in that anointing, but this protest was the only legal avenue available for them to try in their panicked attempt to stay. They attempted to invoke Jesus authority as the Son of God whose time to judge them hadn't yet come. They attempted to charge Jesus with using unlawful authority in casting them out, and they conveniently overlooked the fact that He was the Son of man operating in the full sinless authority of Adam, the King of this creation.

Such twisted legal cunning is precisely why it is so important that every righteous individual knows and understands their own God given rights and authority and becomes familiar with God's laws personally. satan and his ilk cannot be expected to keep others accurately informed or to impartially explain things out of a sense of "honesty and fair play". After the Lord made it quite clear that He knew His authority and that the spirits had to go, the spirit got quite desperate, pleading with the Lord: "don't send us into the deep (hell), but let us go into the nearby herd of pigs instead".

This evident fear of being sent to hell which the demons had isn't mentioned in any of the other exorcisms which the Lord performed, but it stems from the fact that this legion spirit offered up resistance to the rightful authority in the matter, the Son of man, Jesus, after his legal rights had been clearly established. The legion spirit was close to crossing into sinful rebellion by openly defying, and almost denying, God's rightful anointing on Jesus. So, having lost their case, in desperation they begged not to be sentenced to hell for their transgression, which they themselves feared had crossed into rebellion since they did not leave immediately when told to do so by the one with authority, the Son of man, Jesus.

There is a terrible and immediate price for spirits to pay who willfully choose to rebel against the anointings and Word of God. That price is being sentenced to hell.

Did you notice that the wicked spirits had to seek mercy and permission from the same Jesus who they had just tried to resist and whose rights they had tried to deny? They needed and sought Jesus' permission to not only stay out of hell, but to remain in the area, and also to enter into the heard of pigs. All these issues were separate and under judgmental review by the Lord individually.

Judgments: With Jude, Job, Jesus, and Joshua

This event goes to show that while the evil ones are fearful and careful, they are also extremely tenacious and legally prudent in their operating procedures of moving within God's established legal framework to achieve their goals. While they were begging for their lives they were still simultaneously trying to negotiate for themselves the best possible outcome to their desperate situation.

HOGGING ALL THE QUESTIONS

Alright, why the demonic interest in the herd of two thousand pigs? And why were these spirits so interested in staying in that specific area? And why did the Lord let the demons go into the pigs which belonged to someone else? And why did the pigs run off of the cliff and die?

Well, God is a God of order and justice. He would not have let the spirits go into the animals to cause them suffering and death, and to cause their owners a serious financial loss unless there were justifiable legal claims on the animals by the wicked spirits.

What were these claims?

Well, pigs under the God given biblical law are considered unclean, inedible animals. Strike one! These unclean animals were being raised in the Promised Land. Strike two! Pigs were commonly raised in that area to be used as sacrifices to idols. Pigs were, in fact, the favorite sacrificial animal used in idol worship in much of the ancient world. Strike three! This area of the Promised Land at that time was actually a center for idol worship, this is a chief reason the spirits wanted to remain in the area; the people there had been very hospitable to them, and made it very conducive for them to want to stay. The local people were so hospitable to the demons, in fact, that once they heard of Jesus' arrival and of the works which He had done, they came to ask Him to leave their area so they could continue sinning in peace. Notice the spirits asked that they not be sent away, while the people came to send Messiah away. Now, why would these evil spirits want to leave the land of such pleasant and welcoming people? Strike four!

Very well, since we're on the subject of Jesus' authority, this is as good a place as any to bring up the fact that Jesus did exactly what the people wanted Him to do; He left the area. He didn't stay to preach, or to heal, or to cast out more devils. Why? Simply because He wasn't welcome, He needed to accept the will and authority of the local people in the area who wanted to stay far from God. Jesus couldn't legally overrule the free will of those people who were also of Adamic descent and who didn't want His help. They had a right to either accept or reject His Lordship and they chose to reject Him.

The Word and the judgments of God are very clear in these matters. During His time on earth Jesus could only do the things for people which they wanted Him to do; they had to be willing, accepting, and faithful. If there was any sign of resistance, unbelief, or willful sin, His Adamic authority to help was hindered in their lives by their own fallen Adamic authority to resist. (*Mark 6:5, Matthew 23:37, Acts 7:51*)

Well, why did the pigs run off of the cliff and drown?

First: We're looking at wicked spirits here, so as such, nothing they do prospers. They don't have the anointing of life with them; therefore they are always unsuccessful in anything they attempt to do. They tried to move into the pigs, and naturally they failed.

Second: Since many of the pigs that were raised in Israel at the time were destined to be sacrificed unto idols, and the rest eaten contrary to biblical Jewish dietary law, it was evident that the swine farmers were operating outside of God's will and blessings themselves. When you choose to walk outside of God's laws and blessings you shouldn't be surprised to encounter His judgment, which in this case was the loss of a great herd unto evil.

Third: The sheer number of evil spirits in question, and their wickedness, overwhelmed the two thousand pigs, leading the animals to sheer insanity and madness. Animals don't have anywhere near the capacity for withstanding demonic torment that people do; they simply weren't made to function in the same spiritual context; they didn't have the capability to "house" such spirits.

If the name "legion" was an accurate indication of the amount of spirits present, there may have been from four thousand to six thousand evil spirits present in the man/men, as this was the number of soldiers most historians say made up a legion in the Roman army during that time. It isn't that important for us to know the exact number, but it is noteworthy that their number was significantly high enough to cause the destruction of two thousand swine.

Forth: From the viewpoint of the pigs, when faced with the prospect of living out your days with a legion of evil spirits, drowning may seem to be a feasible and welcome alternative (Just a little bit of humor on the last one folks).

THE ACCUSER

Zechariah 3:1-10

Here in this sequence of verses we find satan accusing the High Priest Joshua who is found standing before the angel of the Lord. satan is trying to show and explain why the High Priest wasn't worthy to receive the intended blessings of God according to the previously established laws of God. satan was there before the angel of the Lord to claim that due to the High Priest's sins, exemplified by his filthy clothes, the High Priest wasn't fit to walk in the blessings of God which were meant for him, and through him consequently for all of Israel. This portion of scripture is an excellent example of the way in which legal proceedings are carried out in the heavens.

The "accuser of the brethren" is one of the many job descriptions of satan. He is called that precisely because as Zechariah shows, it is legal for him to stand before God accusing all others of their faults and sins; hoping in that manner to limit their blessings through his knowledge of God's laws and his twisted fervor to see those laws implemented judgmentally on others to their fullest degree. This accusatory type of action by satan is an attempt to increase the authority of the wicked, who benefit from the chastisement or removal of the once righteous non-conspiratorial beings while the wicked themselves try to remain "sinless" in their legal, but twisted efforts of perverting the laws.

> *"...for the accuser of our brethren is cast down, which accused them before our God day and night." Revelation 12:10*

Remember, the word "satan" means "adversary", and as such, he is always looking for transgressions, mistakes, and sins committed by others in any degree which he can bring before the Great Judge in hopes that He would judge against the accused. Such judgments would, in satan's estimation, limit or remove the anointing of life that is on the accused being. Whether this occurs in one area of authority, or in every area, whether temporarily, or permanently, whether partially, or fully; it's for the Judge to decide, but the accuser works for as much limitation as he can get.

As mentioned earlier, God's anointing of life cannot and will not abide with transgressors of God's Word. The evil angels are well aware of this and are always looking to benefit from this fact by finding sin in others, perverting even the reasons for the judgments of God where possible. They tirelessly attempt to use every law, statute, and fact in existence against others, while seeking to benefit from the turmoil of sin themselves.

Why is it only for the advantage of the wicked ones to have others fall, and not also beneficial to the righteous? The wicked don't walk in love. They also have no will to see the Creator's blessings go forth into His creation to continually empower the righteous with life and blessings. Actually, the wicked seek to capitalize on the weaknesses of others for the enlargement of their own power, whereas those beings who walk in love gain nothing from the shortcomings of others and are actually hurt when God's will isn't done in an individual's life. For God's will being done in a life brings forth the blessings that benefit all of creation through the individual in question. If, for some reason, the blessings cannot come forth all will go without in a certain sense. These blessings would stop functioning through the affected being since the anointing of life has to leave, and any time God's blessings stop flowing anywhere; everything, everywhere is affected.

Again, it's satan's vast legal understanding of God's rules which has him constantly accusing and pointing out to the Almighty where and how an individual, particularly a righteous individual, has sinned so that the individual would be separated from God in any or all of the blessings the individual has.

This is why satan is specifically called, *"the accuser of our brethren"* (brethren is a common term for the righteous in God). satan's interest doesn't really lie in accusing those who have already lost contact with

God through sin, only that they stay out of contact by remaining in sin. It is all the more important, however, for him to get the righteous to be found guilty, and for the anointing of life, the personal presence of the Holy Spirit to leave their anointings, abilities, authorities, and offices.

OTHER'S SINS ARE SATAN'S TOOLS

Actually, the sins committed by others are the most effective tools or weapons which the wicked conspirators have available. So, their desire is to entice, coax, mislead, prod, or scare others into sinning through disobeying, doubting, transgressing, or rebelling against the Creator, and then bringing the sins of others before the Creator for judgment in a way that would result in some or all of the evil angelic conspirators gaining access into the rights and offices of the accused sinner. In that way they could stop the will of God from taking place by the use of God's own law.

satan's operational procedure is to use God's righteousness as a hindrance to unity between God and all beings who could err in sin. Having accomplished that, he then works to separate God's Spirit from the sinner in a way that allows the wicked entrance into the accused's office. This is the evil ploy of the conspirators: weaken the righteous by causing them to err, and they may lose what was theirs.

All things done in heaven and on earth are constantly being watched for infractions made against the Lord's anointings and laws; even the smallest things are observed in a process of legally attacking, defending, and ultimately bringing to judgment the actions, authorities, and offices of all beings. Not only are they watched for by other angels, both holy and wicked, but by God as well, and they are recorded and marked for times of judgment as found in scripture. *(Daniel 4, Job 1:7, Revelation 2:2; 2:9)*

The Genesis Mousetrap

Chapter eight

A taste of God's wisdom

THE PLAN

The question then arises: How can the Holy God who hates evil and sin, but also cannot break any of His Words ever cleanse His Kingdom of these evil ones and bring about order, peace, and wholeness?

> "Our God is the God of salvation; And to GOD the Lord belong escapes from death." Psalm 68:20 NKJV™

The Almighty always has the wisdom to bring about salvation and perfection in every situation. In this case, the Creator does what He always does; He creates. He creates a new realm of heaven and of earth; a new structure for the heavens, one with a unique inhabited heaven that is set apart from the others by way of the material used in its creation. That substance is what we call matter or what the Bible refers to as dust.

This unique universe was to contain an autonomous kingdom linked to the other heavens, but separate from them. It was prepared to exist before the angelic transgression happened, to bring about the end of an evil which had not yet occurred. God knows what events will transpire before they do, and He arranged a way to rid His creation of the wicked transgression that was going to take place before it even began, and that way, in this case, was the creation of this universe.

> "Thus saith the LORD, which maketh a way in the sea, and a path in the mighty waters;" Isaiah 43:16

So, to understand what happened we need to realize that God prepared this creation to exist before the angelic transgression began, with an eye toward ending it and removing the yet nonexistent evil from His midst before the evil ever took place. WOW! That sounds like the Almighty to me.

ANGELS, ANGELS, EVERYWHERE

Let's look at how it was done. It goes back to the very nature of God as a giver, and as one who dwells outside of time. He was giving out anointings, abilities, and authorities of blessing to angels for use in this universe before the actual physical areas for the offices were created, before the physical came into being. He established angelic principalities, powers, rulers, and gave out responsibilities to oversee the natural working of the universe: Everything from gravity and seed growth, wind and fire, to the passing of time, the movement of the planets and stars, and the princedoms of yet to be created nations. All given as gifts and blessings to the angels before the things themselves physically existed. Perhaps these blessings were given by God before the angels themselves knew exactly what they were receiving. All this before the angelic sin occurred.

That's right. God did not move defensively by creating a new universe that was to be a safe zone free of the wickedness which was to occur in the heavens by His exclusion of the yet to be wicked angels from its area. No, rather, He moved to engage the yet to occur evil situation proactively, by giving, and by appointing the yet to be wicked angels into offices in this unique universe. Through the act of giving He linked the angelic host into this heaven, this creation, where amazing things were going to occur.

Everything in this physical creation is overseen by the angelic through the authorities they have received as sons of God and as members of His Kingdom. Remember, they are ministering spirits, as stated in Hebrews 1:14. Also, in the Book of Daniel angels are referred to as "watchers" since they oversee the functions of the creation and the actions which occur therein. (*Daniel 4:17*)

A few other scriptural references which show angels to be linked to the operation of this natural universe are the following: *Matthew 18:10, Revelation 9:15; 16:4-5.*

> *"For by him were all things created, that are in heaven, and that are in earth, visible and invisible, whether [they be] thrones, or dominions, or principalities, or powers: all things were created by him, and for him:"* Colossians 1:16

The preceding verse clearly tells us that all thrones, dominions, principalities, and powers were made by and for God. The word "all" is used in this verse because it is inclusive of ...all... including beings now wicked and their offices. This verse has the word "all" used twice, to emphasize the point clearly.

The following are a few verses which indicate the wide variety of roles which the angels have in this universe:

> *"For he shall give his angels charge over thee, to keep thee in all thy ways."* Psalm 91:11

> *"And I saw another angel fly in the midst of heaven, having the everlasting gospel to preach unto them that dwell on the earth..."* Revelation 14:6

> *"And another angel came out from the altar, which had power over fire..."* Revelation 14:8

Next, we'll look at the political angelic principalities to see an example of the foresight God used in giving out these angelic offices. Every nation has an angel prince to guide and guard it, placed there by the Lord. We find many references to this fact in the Bible. (*Ezekiel 38:2, Daniel 10:13; 10:20-21; 12:1*)

Speaking of angelic principalities of the political persuasion, the Septuagint translation also renders Deuteronomy 32:8 quite unusually, and it is well worth noting.

The Septuagint English translation, by Sir Lancelot C.L. Breton:

> *"When the Most High divided the nations, when He scattered the children of Adam, He established the bounds of the nations according to the number of the angels of God."* Deuteronomy 32:8

The Genesis Mousetrap

SUNSTRUCK...MOONSTRUCK...STARSTRUCK

The following verse wil shed some additional light onto the state of the world from a political angelic perspective.

> *"and lest thou lift up thine eyes unto heaven, and when thou seest the sun and the moon and the stars, even all the host of heaven, thou be drawn away and worship them, and serve them, which Jehovah thy God hath allotted unto all the peoples under the whole heaven."* American Standard Version, Deuteronomy 4:19

This is a very interesting verse and it does not merely signify that the heathen nations were into avid sun worshipping, astrology, or some other fanciful lunacy, although sadly most were, and many still are, active partakers in bizarre moonstruck behavior. More pointedly, however, the preceding verse speaks of the fact that the host of heaven and the stars (both synonyms for angels) were allotted unto the heathen nations to be their leading angels and guiding principalities, for the wicked natures of the heathen nations were to desire such.

So, in order to placate the heathen lust for idolatry and sin, God pre-assigned those conspiratorial angels into positions of office which could satisfy the heathen will. In these offices the wicked ones could effectively use their authorities to begin warping and wicking the very identities and cultures of the individual nations which live under their respective offices. Each encouraging its populace to adopt particular evils which most appealed to the principalities and powers in question as they attempted to propel the heathen nations which turned from the true God into an ever deeper darkness.

Upon examining the political angelic principalities which are found spoken of in the scriptures, and after viewing the appalling state of nations, both past and present, it has become clear that most angels which specifically operate in the political offices of authority are conspiratorial and wicked; most, but thankfully, not all.

However, it appears that of all these political principalities, powers, and rulers, which guide and guard the nations, Israel's prince, Michael,

A taste of God's wisdom

is the only one not in the satanic conspiracy. The fact that Israel's prince is the only non-conspiratorial political angel is no accident. When God was giving out these rights He knew Michael would remain faithful to Him, and that the others would be in the satanic conspiracy.

So, He greatly blessed faithful Michael by making him prince of His yet to be created nation of Israel. God placed Michael in that position for He knew Israel's prince needed to be obedient and faithful to Him; as Israel was to be the vehicle or tool with which God would destroy all evil.

> "The Portion of Jacob is not like them, For He is the Maker of all things; And Israel is the tribe of His inheritance. The LORD of hosts is His name. You are My battle-ax and weapons of war: For with you I will break the nation in pieces; With you I will destroy kingdoms;" NKJV™ Jeremiah 51:19-20

Whereas, according to scripture, the angel princes of Babylon, Persia, Javan (Greece), Rome, Egypt, and others, were and are, wicked and conspiratorial.

The apostle Paul writes the following:

> "For we wrestle not against flesh and blood, but against principalities, against powers, against the rulers of the darkness of this world, against spiritual wickedness in high [places]." Ephesians 6:12

Paul was quite clear in specifying that we don't wrestle against all principalities or powers, only the evil ones, the rulers of the darkness of this world, the ones who are in wickedness trying to prevent and pervert the will of God.

This fact points out two things: One, that not all of the angels ministering in this realm are evil. And two, that both the righteous angels and the God fearing people need to wrestle against, or resist, these evil ones in their perverse attempts to cause the anointings and Word of God to be of no effect in the authorities and offices of the just.

THE CONTINUITY OF OFFICES

Many of the different authorities which these angelic beings hold in the physical creation are representative of, and complimentary to, the offices which they hold in the other spiritual heavens. God is a God of order after all.

Let's take satan as an example of this. satan as we have previously read is an accuser in the highest heaven standing before the Lord, but he is also constantly moving about the earth going around blaming people for their sins and mistakes, constantly condemning others for their actions, bringing guilt and blame to mankind, while he himself entices man to sin. He is able to do this because his office which includes the role of accuser is applicable in both the highest heaven and here in our earth.

Also, satan was a leader of praise and worship; in other words, he was a chief musician in the upper heavens when he was still known as Lucifer, and he is very involved in the presentation of a great deal of the music found here on earth, exemplified by all of the foul lyrics and perverted mood setting elements found in song which are clearly representative of a twisted spirit. satan was also the highest ranking angel to take part in the wicked conspiracy, and the first to transgress in the heavens, therefore he is also operating on earth as the "god" of this world.

A look at Israel's angel prince, the archangel Michael, also reveals parallels in office. Michael as an archangel in the Kingdom of God in the heavens is well suited for his role as the prince of the greatest nation in the history of the earth, Israel.

Michael is also said to be an angel of war, a fitting title for a protector of Israel; as Israel has historically been under constant threat and attack, and that peace loving nation has needed to, and will have to, step into war against its enemies time and time again.

These angelic earthly offices neatly fit with the offices each angel holds in the upper heavens.

Chapter nine

Finally, the beginning

DARKNESS UPON THE DEEP

"...for the devil sinneth from the beginning..." 1 John 3:8

"He was a murderer from the beginning, and abode not in the truth..." John 8:44

"In the beginning God created the heaven and the earth." Genesis 1:1

"And the earth was without form, and void; and darkness was upon the face of the deep. And the Spirit of God moved upon the face of the waters." Genesis 1:2

Between Gen. 1:1 and Gen. 1:2 we have the angelic transgression occurring, and we see that the earth was *"without form, and void"*. The Hebrew reads: The earth was/ became/existed as chaos and waste; and *"darkness was upon the face of the deep"*.

The reason the earth was *"without form, and void"* was because of the darkness that was upon the face of the deep. This darkness was not ordinary night, neither was it the natural state of existence for anything in God's creation. It was a spiritual blackness brought about by the actions and plan of Lucifer both in the heavens and also upon the earth after he became satan.

How do we know this? Well, we need to remember that Lucifer was the highest ranking archangel in the heavens, and that he was the covering cherub of the most High God; these facts didn't change after his adversarial conversion. satan was still operating in those offices even though he chose to become wicked, as we have well seen. This now wicked cherub angel was still operating in his role as the covering cherub; only instead of serving as such to honor God, he was now covering creation in an evil darkness, shading from it the only light and life there is, the glory of the living God.

In fact, although every angel has the ability to pervert their authority due to their inherent free will, only the angel that was known as Lucifer held the specific offices and walked in the authorities necessary to attempt such a grandiose feat as darkening the deep. This act of perverting the use of his covering anointing was satan's strongest possible legal move. It was an action which he could take without exceeding his authority and without entering into open rebellion and thereby facing the judgment of God and a subsequent removal from his offices and God's Kingdom for the attempt.

In taking this specific action satan believed that he could bring about victory over the will of God through his twisting and wicking of the authorities and offices which he had been blessed with by the Lord. satan moved by perversely hiding the One who had originally given him the blessings he had. This wicked cherub was trying to separate God from His own creation, and in so doing, he was causing all creation to be cut off from the life of the Most High God.

Yes, even the holy angels had to hold firm in their faith and knowledge that God would not leave them in the shadow of the dark evil that was attempting to permanently envelope and choke everything in existence. They had to be firm in their trust of God's power, and of His promises to them that His blessings and the life which He gave were eternally with them as long as they were faithful and willing to protect all that they were given.

They had to stand fast to protect their blessings from the wicked seducing spirit which was now attempting to permanently conceal the source of those blessings. satan was now covering and completely hiding the majestic radiance of the glory of God so that no being would be able to partake of His light, or the beauty in the power of His love, since God was now perversely covered and cloaked by this wicked angel, leaving all creation in the hideous darkness of satan's shadow.

All creation was to become *"without form, and void"* under the satanically inspired darkness; the heavens and the earth were literally withering on the vine as creation was separated and choked off from the source of life itself. That is the reason the Bible describes the earth as *"without form, and void"*. It was dying a perverted death along with everything else in the heavens under the dark shadow of the being which chose to become the angel of death. Yes, this same satan who was once the highest ranking cherub in God's creation (and cherubs are the guardians of holiness and life), became the antithesis of holiness and life, twisting and perverting to become the angel of vile death itself.

In order to gain a better understanding of why satan chose to use this particular method to carry out his wicked plan we need to realize that God is the only omnipresent being in creation. He is the only one capable of being present in all places at all times, satan is not.

satan could not have begun to spread his evil upon even the smallest fraction of the heavens, let alone attempt to override the blessings of all other beings who were present in God's Kingdom. No, that would have been equivalent to an ant trying to hide an elephant by swallowing it whole. The very concept is laughable. Therefore, the most effective action satan could have taken in his wicked attempt of usurping God's authority was to use this one particular office of covering angel that he had been given, and its inherent proximity to God's throne, in his attempt to prove himself God's equal.

It wasn't that satan could affect everything in the heavens himself, but by blanketing God's throne satan effectively hid life itself from all things by using the location of his office to spread his darkness on the creation that would otherwise be receiving God's glory and life. It was the goal of satan to block the anointing of life, the personal presence of the Holy Spirit Himself, who upheld and kept all things in successful abundance, from upholding and blessing creation with the mantle of His presence.

In other words, satan capitalized on creation's dependence upon God's glory by separating creation from that glory. satan's formula went thusly: God is life; everything needs life, so separate, cover, and hide life from everything, and thereby nullify all God's works, in so doing, become an equal match to God. If one could legally bring death to all that God gives life to, if one could cause the destruction of all that the Lord creates, if one could thwart the works of the Lord, if one could negate His will and impede His actions, then one could claim to be His equal, and declare himself a god in the process.

AS A LAMPSHADE

To give a simplistic illustration of satan's plan of action let's use a lit table lamp as an example of our only source of light in a room. If a table lamp was lit in the middle of a room, the whole room would be illuminated, and it would be virtually impossible for you to try and cover everything in that room using just one blanket to shield the entire room from that light. It would be extremely difficult to do no matter how large the blanket may be.

You would need to cover the walls, floor, ceiling, furniture; everything in the room, with just one blanket. This would not be very easy; actually, it would be downright impossible. Add to these facts the presence of other people in the room who would undoubtedly object to your actions and begin removing the covers from off of themselves and you would probably never achieve your goals.

However, if you simply take your blanket and put it over the lamp, the light that it emits would be blocked from illuminating the room, and the entire room would then be in the shadow of the darkness which you have created by covering the source of the light.

This is how the covering angel, satan, legally carried out his actions in his attempt to exert his control over the heavens. Instead of being a complimentary and beautiful "lampshade" unto the glory of God, in the way he was meant to be, satan twisted his authority to become an obscuring blanket to hide the light of God that he was meant to compliment.

The term *"and darkness was upon the face of the deep"* refers to just that event, the covering of the heavens with the shadow of death. *"The deep"* refers to the condition of the heavens in a stagnant, deathish state due to the satanic covering of the source of all life and light, God.

Finally, the beginning

The original Hebrew word used in this verse from which the word "deep" is translated is "tehom", and it refers to the sea, the ocean, a place of great water in a bleakish way, the abyss, it could also refer to the grave.

This alludes to the fact that in the Hebrew language the word "mayim" which means waters, is also a base root for the word heavens, and the two words "tehom" and "mayim" are used in Genesis 1:2 to describe the same place, but from two very different perspectives: One from the perspective of death, and the other from that of life.

The actual word most often translated into heaven(s) from Hebrew is "shamayim", and it literally means "the waters above". This is really quite fitting since water is the essential substance necessary to sustain life. It is also the place where fish are found, and fish are biblically representative of the ones obedient to God. (*Jeremiah 16:16, Matthew 4:19, Mark 1:17*)

However, this darkness descended upon the face of the waters (the heavens) when satan twisted his authority and began his attempt to cover God's glory from creation, and the once life filled waters became the gravishly abysmal deep. Therefore, the "waters" (the heavens), a place of life and activity was referred to biblically as *"the deep"*: An abysmal place with no evidence of activity or life due to the choking darkness that was upon its surface.

SEDUCED INTO DEATH

It was at this point in the Genesis narrative that the one third of angels which decided to transgress joined with satan in his conspiracy and turned from God as they became wicked. They thought they saw a weakness in God, a God they once thought invincible and almighty. He was, and is, but they began to doubt His power and despise His ways due to the effects of the darkness upon creation. God's glory was blocked; hidden by one lone angel, and God seemed removed and weak.

The evil angels thought they saw how the Lord could be vulnerable to His own Word which He was obligated to keep. They understood that the Lord was bound to respect the anointings which he had given out to the angels in His blessing of them: God seemed imprisoned to His own

Word, and the power they appeared to possess in their manipulation of His laws and anointings was most seducing. So they decided to turn against the Lord their God in favor of the surprisingly successful satan, a mere angel.

In their free will these newly wicked angels had the choice to remain faithful to the Lord and trust in His power, or they could have done exactly what they did, which was to trust in what they perceived to be happening around them, and in their own abilities. They turned to hate, and began to despise the God who blessed them; the God who created them; the God who gave them His love, and they sought to do away with what they perceived to be His weak, simple, and ignorant ways of upholding others and constantly giving forth blessings, one to another, in order to build up creation and bring forth holiness.

In God's ways they saw foolishness; and in putting an end to His system of serving others, of giving in purity of heart, and of being a conduit for the love and blessings of God for the benefit of creation these wicked ones saw an opportunity to bring about the destruction of all God's works, and thereby cause the operational devastation of His Kingdom. They felt that God's love was His weakness, and that He in His kindness had foolishly given out far too much authority and power. Power which they hoped could now be used to stop Him from accomplishing anything, in essence, to stop Him from being God.

All the while, the newly wicked ones felt that the self-centered hoarding of power and the corrosive manipulation of others into their service would strengthen and increase the magnitude and scope of their own authorities, and further them in their ungodly quest for increased control of all things.

Can it be said of these angels who chose to become wicked that their love and faith in God, even in the best of events, was merely a shallow and superficial veneer since they were so ready to turn on Him when things seemingly got dark? Were these not just fair-weather friends who were happy to be with God when circumstances suited them and when the Lord appeared totally dominant in all things? This is precisely the reason God creates all beings with free will and choice, so that all may willfully choose whether to be with Him, or not.

Finally, the beginning

The love and blessings of God must be voluntarily reciprocated and shared by others in order for His created to bring Him joy. If He has to force His creation to love and respect Him, in other words, to be His robots or slaves, He wouldn't have any use or need of them. Remember, the great "I Am" doesn't need the help of servants to get things done; He is totality and sufficiency within Himself.

As the God of all truth and Father of all creation He wants to, and needs to, allow all beings to function freely in all truth, after the will of their own hearts. Anything less would, in fact, be God forcing creation to live out an existence of lies. In that case, God would be the father of those lies; that is a title reserved for satan, and not for God. *(John 8:44)*

God will never force any beings to live contrary to the will of their own hearts. Why, even in the final judgment spoken of in Romans 14:11 and Philippians 2:10-11, it is stated that every knee will bow and every tongue will confess that Messiah Jesus is Lord forever. Notice, however, that it does not state all beings will be forced to declare their love for Him; or that all will be forced to walk uprightly before Him, obey His ways, and to serve Him eternally with joy. No, the Lord will not force anyone to do so. Those who have chosen death will be given it, and those who have chosen God will be allowed into His presence to partake of His life. Freedom is paramount to His will.

REALITY VERSUS DECEPTION

Now, let's go back to the term *"and darkness was upon the face of the deep"*. The great contrast between God and satan, indeed, between God and any creation, is the difference between being totally saturated and permeated to the point of life and power radiating out of you and into all things to uphold and infill them, which is what God is and does, and merely covering or cloaking, placing a veneer on things to make something appear to be a certain way even though it may not be, which is what satan does. It's the difference between reality and deception.

It should be noted that the Bible says, *"darkness was upon the face* (on the surface) *of the deep."* satan did not change the basic makeup of creation from within, as that is beyond his capability. The darkness was

The Genesis Mousetrap

not in the deep, but upon it, encroaching upon its surface. That's the area where satan's effects were felt, on the surface of things.

satan's power and his ability to enact that power is strictly superficial without the blessing of life, the personal presence of the Holy Spirit which had departed from him when he chose wickedness. So, the surface was what satan was able to cover in darkness, and that's exactly where the Spirit of God moved as a result of satan's actions *"upon the face of the waters."*, upon the surface.

Notice that it was the anointing of life, the glory of the presence of the Holy Spirit that satan attempted to block and it was this very same Spirit of God that moved forth to undo satan's work. This is the first time the law of reciprocity is found in action in the Bible. That law can be simply stated in the following way: "What good you do to God's own will be repaid unto you, and what evil you attempt to do will be returned to you".

It was the attributes and function of the Holy Spirit which were particularly infringed upon in satan's attempt, and it was therefore the Holy Spirit that went forth to set things right. He moved in the same area where the problem was; *"upon the face"* of it. He moved *"upon the face"* to correct the problem. It was a superficial problem which only looked bad due to satan's actions, and not due to God's will. And since it was still God's creation and Kingdom; and because He had given His eternal irrevocable Word to the other still faithful beings in creation, the Lord had every right and more so, He had the obligation to begin rectifying the situation that came to infringe upon His will.

This is why, when the Bible refers to the situation from the perspective of darkness upon the heavens it uses the sullen term *"the deep"*, and when it refers to the very same heavens in the same situation, in the very same verse, but from the perspective of God's Spirit moving upon the heavens it refers to the heavens as *"the waters"*: A place of life and activity. The Lord moved to correct the situation, and when the presence of His Spirit merely moved upon the face of creation the result was that the sullen and abysmal *"deep"* was already being referred to as the *"waters"*, places of life. I hope you caught the significance of that! It's a "WOW" moment!

Finally, the beginning

God always moves in the area where the problem is to correct it, and to remove the results of evil from His creation. Astoundingly, just the presence of His Spirit upon the area was already sufficient to change the abysmal *"deep"* into life filled *"waters"* before the Lord did or said anything to bring about change. Once again, it's a "WOW" moment!

It brings to mind the title of the old song "Jesus your PRESENCE makes me whole." Just the presence of the Spirit of God, Life Himself, was already sufficient to begin restoring life to the heavens and begin negating satan's work.

There was never a question of satan catching the Lord off guard in his attempted wickedness, but satan did have the right to attempt his perversion within the legal boundaries of his offices. We have got to remember that God is all knowing, and knew about satan's attempts even before satan did. The Lord was well prepared for it, and the actions He began to take in healing and restoring His Kingdom were to be astounding.

MAYIM CHAIM-THE LIVING WATERS

This is where we need to bring some more Hebrew into the mix, because it really shows us some amazing things.

It was after satan darkened the deep that the Bible states: *"And the Spirit of God moved upon the face of the waters."*

The word "moved" used here is the Hebrew word "rachaph", and it means: He was affected by love for, and came to cherish with compassion.

The word for "waters" is "mayim". It is the base root of the Hebrew word for heavens, and "mayim" is also used as an occasional metaphor for heavens, since waters are places filled with life.

So, this portion of the second Genesis verse can well be read as: "...And the Spirit of God was affected by love for and came to cherish the heavens with compassion."

Let's look into the word "mayim" further; and see why it is biblically used as a metaphor for the word heavens in these early verses of Genesis. Well, as previously stated, the proper and most common

Hebrew word for heavens is "shamayim"; this word means: "The waters above". However, "shamayim" is a relative term; in order for there to be waters or heavens above, there had to be waters or heavens below; but, until the waters or heavens were separated and divided further on in the Genesis narrative and ordered into their present state, there was just one heaven, the heavens, and that's "mayim", or "the waters" as we find it in Genesis 1:2.

Interestingly, we can even see the two words, heavens "shamayim" and waters "mayim", used together in a biblical context to refer to the heavens in Psalm 148:4.

> "Praise him, ye heavens of heavens, and ye waters that [be] above the heavens." Psalm 148:4

Isn't that an interesting verse mentioning waters above the heavens? In order for the waters to be above the heavens in the strictest sense of the meaning, the waters would need to be outside of the heavens being referred to. And they are, for these waters are heavens themselves, they are some of the "mayim" of the "shamayim".

So we can see that once satan chose to pervert his authority in the offices he held as he initiated his attempt to do this wicked thing to the Creator and to His creation that the Spirit of God came to be so moved with love and had such great compassion upon the heavens He so cherishes that He began His work of removing the evil which sought to harm His creation from the heavens of God.

Isn't that just like the Lord? After He was greatly insulted and had His will assaulted by a hateful, greedy, satan and the other wicked angels, He didn't move out of hate or jealousy towards the wicked ones, He moved out of compassion and love for His creation and for His holy ones, and He began to give even more of Himself than He previously had to ensure that He, His light, and love would never again be totally hidden from His creation by anyone or anything. WOW!

satan thought God's undoing was found in the fact that He had given out too much of Himself. Whereas God saw that the best way to rid His Kingdom of this corrupting evil was to give even more of Himself. What

Finally, the beginning

a huge contrast in viewpoints and actions! Oh, that we would all learn from the wisdom of the Father and begin to walk as true children of God; to move in His ways and to live as vessels of blessings in this, His beloved creation.

PURE LOVE IS PURE POWER!

All of the Creator's actions and deeds are rooted in His great love, and all that is in existence is produced in that love, and is also defended by God in that same love. That's the reason he tells those of us who would be obedient as His children to walk in His love, and not merely in our love, but in His perfect love, nothing else is an acceptable form of respect for us to give His creation.

Godly love is the most powerful force there is, and it is by no means a submissive, passive, accepting spirit as the natural mind may assume. The love of God is the active source of the removal and destruction of all evil, and it is the basis of freedom for all things.

This must be said again, the love of God is a force; it is the most powerful force in existence, an incomparable power, the very pure will of God Himself, and shall always, always, bring about the peace and freedom of the righteous ones and the destruction of evil and bondage wherever His love is present and welcome. (*Zephaniah 3:17, Romans 5:5*)

It was the onset of precisely these wicked events initiated by satan that prompted the Lord God to begin the "tikkun olam" as it is called in Hebrew, which is the "repair and perfecting of creation". The Lord began to order a new format in the very waters (heavens) which satan tried to darken; a format which would serve Him in the removal of the wicked, and allow Him to bring about a day in which nothing would ever again be able to bring harm to the work of His Hands and separate His creation from His presence. (*Deuteronomy 10:14, Nehemiah 9:6*)

> *"Nay, in all these things we are more than conquerors through him that loved us. For I am persuaded, that neither death, nor life, nor angels, nor principalities, nor powers, nor things present, nor things to come, Nor height, nor depth, nor any*

> *other creature, shall be able to separate us from the love of God, which is in Christ Jesus our Lord." Romans 8:37-39*

THE NEXT STEPS

"And God said, Let there be light: and there was light."
Genesis 1:3

In the Hebrew, this third verse of Genesis reads, "and God said: Light be; and light was." The Lord spoke His light, the radiance of His Glory, His life itself back into the heavens. The light was found in His Words, indeed, the light was His Words, and it was brought forth out from under the cloak and covering of satan by the Holy Spirit.

It was at this point that the great office which satan held as covering angel was diminished in its obscuring effectiveness by God's ability to circumvent satan's covering through His spoken Word carried by His Spirit. He thereby limited the power of the place of the office that satan held.

The office of covering cherub wasn't dissolved, and the authority of satan to be in that office was still fully intact, as his activities were within his legal, albeit perversely used rights, but the location and effects of the office were circumvented by the very breath or Spirit of God which brought forth the light, God's Word, into the withering creation covered in darkness. As we know, Jesus, the Word of God, called Himself the light of this world. (*John 8:12*)

> *"Seek him that maketh the seven stars and Orion, and turneth the shadow of death into the morning..." Amos 5:8*

The shadow of death was literally turned into a very welcome morning for all of creation with the appearance of the light of God returning unto the heavens.

> *"For God, who commanded the light to shine out of darkness, hath shined in our hearts, to [give] the light of the knowledge of the glory of God in the face of Jesus Christ." 2 Corinthians 4:6*

Finally, the beginning

The above stated verse clearly shows one of God's first and continuing modes of response to the ongoing darkness upon the surface of His creation. He commanded the light (holiness, the essence of life), to shine out of the creation itself which the darkness was superficially covering. With the covering cherub still in office and still covering, the Lord God caused His light to shine forth from the faithful created ones in His heavens through an ever increased presence of His own Spirit given to reside upon, and indwell, the faithful in His life filled waters, the heavens.

This was a legal way for God to circumvent satan's shadow so that the shadow of the total darkness which was upon creation, caused by satan attempting to block out the personal glory of the Most High God as He was seated upon the throne, would no longer be total. God's light and life through the presence of His Spirit was now to shine forth from within the created themselves out into the heavens in a way which would ensure that all of obedient creation would be able to be blessed of God's life through the permanent presence of His Spirit and life in and through the lives of His faithful servants.

This is what was meant by scripture when it said, *"God, who commanded the light to shine out of darkness"*. The creation that was dying due to a lack of the presence of God's light was to now be infused with the hope of that glory which was brought to it by the personal indwelling presence of the Holy Spirit.

The Holy Spirit caused the essence of God's life to shine forth from creation itself through the life giving light of His presence despite the superficial shadow emanating from satan's dark cloaking attempt upon creation's surface. The Lord effectively and legally began to circumvent satan's perverted use of authority in this manner.

In the stunningly extraordinary events of the satanic transgression, and God's subsequent circumvention of satan's covering attempt, it must be understood that this initial restoration of His Spirit and His Word into creation was not yet a full restoration of God's complete presence into creation. Nor was it yet the completion of the repair and restoration of the heavens. Nor was the circumventing of satan's covering meant to be a permanent mode of operation for God or creation to function in.

The Genesis Mousetrap

The permanent restoration would take the removal of satan; and the removal of satan would take his open breach in the sin of rebellion committed against God; something satan was careful not to do.

Rather, the Godly actions of Genesis 1:3 were the first salvos fired in God's nonstop barrage of wisdom, holiness, and power; all within His pre-established legal framework against the actions of the wicked ones who attempt to carefully keep their offices from outright rebellious behavior.

The circumvention was, however, an amazing step in the Lord's plan for dealing with the actions of the evil conspirators, and a very legal action on God's part which started to negate the unwanted situation that satan brought upon God's heavens. The full presence of God, and unity with Him, was not to be known again by creation until the satanic conspirators were permanently removed; sin was totally dealt with; and the heavens finally cleansed. Pending that time, creation was given a hope, a promise, and an ability to wait for the day of fully uniting with and partaking of the glory of the unrestricted presence of the One God and His unhindered holy light.

> *"And God saw the light, that [it was] good: and God divided the light from the darkness." Genesis 1:4*

Here, in this fourth verse, God is separating the light from the darkness, causing the darkness (evil) to no longer ever partake in the glory and life it had just tried to cover and cloak. God is ensuring that the darkness, and those who would cause others to dwell therein, would never be able to enter into, and benefit from, the light which He brought forth into creation. This is one of the many reasons that satan was to remain in his office of covering angel; he was to now cover and cloak himself, as well as the other wicked one third of conspirators, in the same darkness that they themselves so eagerly had brought forth upon others.

Although the wicked angels were still a part of the creation of God, the blessing of life was far gone from them by this point, and they were decreed to exist in the same spiritual darkness and failure which they had tried to bring upon the rest of creation. We need to understand that

Finally, the beginning

this darkness which the evil ones were now subject to was of their own making, it was not of God's design. He simply sentenced them to exist in their own cold, black, evil, shadow of death which they attempted to foist upon others. In dividing the light from the darkness God had sentenced the wicked to continually exist in the darkness of their own doing even though they were still present within God's Kingdom.

The state of this darkness is well explained in the following verse:

> "And the light shineth in darkness; and the darkness comprehended it not." John 1:4-5

Here we have the light; Jesus, the Word of God, which came to shine in the darkness, and the darkness comprehended it not. The darkness was not able to comprehend the light because it was permanently separated and excluded from partaking of holiness and light at every level. This, even though it still dwelt in a creation that was formed and upheld by that same light.

Those of the darkness have no clue as to God's ways anymore. They cannot understand anything about His giving nature and will, or His goodness even when faced with it; they are absolutely omitted and prohibited from taking part in any aspect of God's holiness. Evil, and evil beings, are totally clouded and blackened by a self-absorbed, self-centered wickedness, and cannot any longer relate to the creation which exists around them; the creation of a God who is pure love and giving.

Now, this darkness in which the wicked beings presently exist is not the outer darkness of which Messiah Jesus spoke of. There is, indeed, an outer darkness as mentioned in Matthew 8:12 and Matthew 22:13. This outer darkness is the place of hell, where an individual is completely removed from his offices, the right of moving in the heavens, and consequently from the freedom of God's Kingdom, banished from all of the Lord's work, presence, and light. That outer darkness of hell is a separate darkness where an individual is cast as a result of a judgment; due to the breaking of God's laws which we have touched upon earlier.

However, the operational darkness in which the one third of angelic conspirators now find themselves is most akin to a person's sleep. Like the sleeping, the darkened evil ones cannot partake of the world around them in any perceptible manner. The one third of a person's life spent in sleep separated from the world and its activities by the darkness of an unconscious state in which the person is unaware of, and incapable of fully participating in the world around himself is an illustrative, corresponding, and telling matter. It is a living example of the state of existence in which the evil conspiracy finds itself and is an expression to man of its existence.

Amazingly, medical science after decades of study, to this day, cannot explain the need or the reasons mankind has for sleep. The fact that the average person spends a time in his life in the state of darkness called sleep, which is correspondent to the percentage of conspiratorial angels that are sentenced into darkness is no coincidence. The flesh, the one third of the triune man that is eternally in league with satan and his one third of wicked angels from the time of the Adamic fall onwards, as stated in Romans 7:14, 8:6-7, Galatians 5:17, and 1 Peter 2:11, is in effect condemned to eternal darkness and separation from God in its present condition. In this present state of existence the darkness applies itself to the entire person of man through the physical portion of the triune man in the form of sleep. And sleep, as stated, consumes the proportionate amount of time in a person's life which the flesh has influence over, one third of life.

The event described in Genesis 1:4 falls under the law of reciprocity that was mentioned previously. Again, that law simply states: "What good you do to God's own will be repaid unto you, and what evil you attempt to do to God's own will be returned upon you". It's a theme which is found throughout the scriptures, and it is very evident in this occasion as we witness the wicked ones being left to stumble about in the darkness of their own making.

One thing needs to be made as clear as possible, so that there are no misunderstandings, and that is: although satan and his wicked cohorts retain their offices and exist in the heavens, they are by no means partakers of God's holy glory. Nor are they running up and down the golden streets annoying and harassing the holy ones of God. Nor is satan visibly present as a vile smothering cover over the Holy throne. As a part of the reciprocative decree of judgment brought upon the evil ones, they have been left to exist in their own darkness in the heavens, and they cannot partake of that which is in the light.

This fact is exemplified and explained in both the design of the Ark of the Covenant, and in the construction of the Holy Temple. When the ark of the covenant was built according to God's instructions as given unto Moses there wasn't a third large covering cherub over the ark of the covenant which symbolized God's throne and resting place (it is commonly held that there were originally three archangels: Michael, Gabriel, and Lucifer). One of the reasons the third angelic cherub, Lucifer, wasn't pictured as being over the ark was that the ark was representative of the functional structure in heaven which now lacked the visible presence of satan. This was quite evident in the architectural design of the Holy Temple as well; the walls and veil of the Holy place and those of the Holiest of Holies were to suffice as a separative covering until the day righteousness could be established in creation. (*Exodus 25:18-22, Luke 15:38*)

It must be reiterated, this does not mean satan was removed from the office of covering angel, only that the office itself was, in essence, shrouded in what became a darkness that existed apart from God's light in such a way that satan would no longer be free to enjoy and consequently defile God's creation in the same manner that he had through his previous presence in that same light. When God said, *"let there be light"* (Genesis 1:3); that light suredly did not shine forth from satan.

THE WORDS OF PAUL

Perhaps the words of the apostle Paul could give us yet one more opportunity to delve into this subject, and to show that the wicked, while they are able to function in God's Kingdom in their authorities, are excluded from benefiting from the light and life thereof.

The Apostle Paul in writing the first epistle to the Corinthians states the following:

> *"And now abide faith, hope, love, these three; but the greatest of these is love."* NKJV™ *1 Corinthians 13:13*

Let's look into Paul's amazing statement and see what can be gleaned from it:

Can the wicked angels operate in faith? Yes, James 2:19 says: *"Thou believest that there is one God; thou doest well: the devils also believe, and tremble."* For the wicked angels to believe so requires faith; and the very fact that they are such adept spiritual legalists shows that they not only have faith, but that they have great faith in the very laws and Word of God which they themselves seek to pervert and misuse.

Can the wicked angels operate in hope? It can be assumed by their actions that they can, as no other reason can be given for the tireless efforts of the wicked conspiracy other than the hope they have of achieving greater power for themselves. So, the answer must once again be: Yes, the wicked can have hope, however misguided and perverted it may be.

Can the wicked angels operate in love? No! As we have seen, there is no love in them, only the desire *"to steal, and to kill, and to destroy"*, as stated in John 10:10. Love is something that is totally alien to them. It can be said, pardon the pun, that they're in the dark about it. They are separated from the light of love which, as Paul states, is the greatest of the three which abide. Without love the faith and hope that would abide are ineffective, and are incapable of bringing an issue to a complete and permanent realization.

This is because the personal presence of the Holy Spirit Himself is that love; He is the one who is lacking from them, and as a consequence they dwell in darkness even when they are surrounded by light. This one third of angels which chose wickedness are lacking the basic ability to partake of the essential one third of the elemental and eternal foundations of God's blessings and characteristics. Faith and hope are essential and important, *"...but the greatest of these is love."*

> *"And God called the light Day, and the darkness he called Night..."* Genesis 1:5

This is where God sets up a division between holiness and wickedness, creating a place of dwelling in the light (righteousness) called day, and of dwelling in darkness (separation from light) called night.

Finally, the beginning

"...*and the darkness He called night...*" The Hebrew word for night is "laila", and this word literally has a meaning of "protective shadow". We can see the subtle reference to the covering angel in the meaning of this word. As a part of God's Kingdom, albeit an undesired one, satan was still obliged to carry out the duties of his offices. satan was to be used of God to further His goals of ridding the heavens of the evil conspirators (which include satan himself) in a way that kept the now sullied and imperfect creation and the yet to be created repentant sinner (man), from being destroyed by God's holiness in the process.

This, even though satan was the most evil and ungodly being of all. satan and all wicked angels still have to fulfill the commissions of their offices where required; for if they don't, judgment with a removal from office would most assuredly await them. The wicked ones were subject to do the bidding of the Most High and serve Him where the Lord demanded in order to remain in God's Kingdom and avoid hell. Indeed, God was to use satan as a protective shadow often, in order to shield sinful man from His Holy glory, and thereby from His absolute judgments.

This seemingly unusual situation of evil serving the will of God is somewhat paralleled in Israel's sojourn in Egypt. That epic story is found in reading Genesis chapter 45 through Exodus chapter 14.

Although Egypt had kept Israel as an enslaved people, Israel was protected by Egypt from destruction by hostile and violent foreign nations, and from migrating into and assimilating with the cultures of welcoming alien lands. Both matters were accomplished through Egypt's great strength and authority. The shadow of Egypt protected Israel from hostile enemy attack, and it allowed Israel to live and to grow in number without assimilating into alien cultures. Egypt had unknowingly served God so well that enslaved Israel began to outnumber Egypt. That was God's plan as He explained it to Abraham in Genesis 15:13-16.

Evil having to serve good is also well documented in the Book of Esther where we find the example of wicked Haman unwittingly building gallows that were to be used to hang him and his own sons. (*Esther 5:14; 8:7; 9:12-14*)

> *"And God said, Let there be a firmament in the midst of the waters, and let it divide the waters from the waters." Genesis 1:6*

This is an amazing verse that tells us of God's plan for the division of the waters, the heavens. Remember, originally there was only one heaven, *"the waters"*, but here God in His wisdom began to speak of His plan to separate the heavens in order to implement His design to remove satan and all evil from His midst. He decided to make a firmament in the midst of the waters (heavens) to divide the waters from the waters. This firmament spoken of is the heaven of Rakia: the "to be" physical part of our triune universe which the Lord decided to bring forth at this point. Rakia was found by God in the heavens (the waters) and He decided to bring it forth, to separate it for special use. This unique individual heaven was created by the bringing forth of the firmament.

> *"Through faith we understand that the worlds were framed by the word of God, so that things which are seen were not made of things which do appear." Hebrews 11:3*

Hebrews 11:3 speaks of this event, and how it was the power of the Word of God that brought about this seen creation from the unseen where it previously existed. In other words, the seen physical universe pre-existed itself in the spiritual waters from which it was taken. The earth and the entire physical universe were at one time a part of the single waters, the heavens; which preceded the present day arrangement of separation.

> *"And God made the firmament, and divided the waters which [were] under the firmament from the waters which [were] above the firmament: and it was so." Genesis 1:7*

Here, the Lord is actually taking and dividing the Rakia heaven out from among the other heavens which surround it according to His decision in the previous verse. This "to be" physical place was originally of the same spiritual matter as the other heavens were; it was a part of, and surrounded by, *"the waters"*. God was literally doing an astonishing thing; establishing a new order in His Kingdom to bring about His plans.

Finally, the beginning

We have read something about this heaven in an earlier chapter under the subheading "the heavens".

> *"And God called the firmament Heaven..." Genesis 1:8*

God declares the newly created firmament, which is the Hebrew word Rakia (this physical creation), that He brought forth from *"the waters"* to be a Heaven; because, and even though, it was totally unique and different in structure from the other waters. This firmament was unlike anything seen before in creation due to the changes God made and was intending to make in it.

In the Hebrew, this verse literally reads "God called the Rakia shamayim." Isn't that interesting? God had declared the firmament (Rakia) which separates the waters "mayim", from the waters "mayim", to be upper waters "shamayim". This could be a really befuddling thing if we don't pay attention and realize that He was declaring this newly separated part of the heavens to be an individual, independent heaven of its own, equal to the other heavens, and part of the structure of heavens that He was establishing.

> *"And God said, Let the waters under the heaven be gathered together unto one place, and let the dry [land] appear: and it was so." Genesis 1:9*

The word for heaven used in this verse is once again the Hebrew word "shamayim"; and as previously stated, "shamayim" literally means "the waters above" or the "heavens". Here in this verse we can see that the Lord is gathering the waters or heavens which were to be below the upper heavens, together. These are the waters or heavens that belong to this universe: the heavens of Vilon, Rakia, and Shechakim. He was setting an order of compatibility to the waters beneath (the heavens; mayim) which are below the waters above (the heavens above; shamayim), to cause our unique universe to take shape and cause solid matter to be able to appear in its present composition.

It was at this point that God changed the nature of the material found in the lower heavens which include Rakia, and physical matter appeared in the midst of the heavens: dry land in the midst of the waters appeared. The physical creation as we would know it came into being, and was purposely unique and distinctive from the substances of the other heavens. Our familiar matter and the rules that govern it were brought into a form which we could relate to today.

The Psalmist makes the following statement in the sixth verse of the thirty-third Psalm:

> "By the word of the LORD were the heavens made; and all the host of them by the breath of his mouth." Psalm 33:6

> "And God called the dry [land] Earth; and the gathering together of the waters called he Seas: and God saw that [it was] good." Genesis 1:10

As we look back at Genesis 1:1, we can see that, *"In the beginning God created the Heavens and the earth."* The earth at that time was a spiritual place. Well, it still is; but at that time it was of the same spiritual material as found throughout the then unified heavens, the waters. It was only with the separation of the heavens and the following establishment of the unique design of the heaven of Rakia, which entailed the changing of its substance to its present state, that the earth shows up and is mentioned again in the creation narrative in Genesis 1:9 and 1:10 as dry land or a solid substance found in the midst of "the waters" (the mayim) of God.

From this point forward the creation narrative then concentrates itself upon the development of the earth and those things native to Rakia.

The changing of the Rakia heaven portion of the universe into the particular matter which the Bible calls dust was quite necessary, as this "dust matter heaven" has one peculiar attribute which doesn't seem to exist in the other heavens, that attribute is time. Time is able to affect it, limit it, and eventually bring it to an end.

Physicists will tell you that in order for time to exist, matter must first exist for time to "attach" itself to. Time cannot function or even exist without matter to affect, change, and measure. This was an important feature in the great plan of the Creator; the making of a unique place where the limiting law called time could operate in order to serve the vital purpose of bringing everything in this universe to a conclusion. That conclusion is His judgment day; the removal of the evil conspirators, and the sanctification of all creation, as time sets limits to all things. This creation, including all beings associated with it, is to face the judgment seat of God after the Adamic time, the week of days, has ended.

In other words, in this heaven of Rakia we have a secret agent of God at work to limit all things and to allow change to occur in the function and the duration of everything in existence. This is so that God can use the events and actions that happen in this universe for the benefit of all creation; to thereby restore all things throughout all the heavens to a state of peace and unity.

A RECAP

Everything which the Lord God had done to date in the creation narrative was done with an eye toward totally removing the satanic conspirators from the heavens. His will is to put an end to all darkness in His creation, and not have it existing with the light, apart from the light, or even as subservient to the light. The very existence of darkness is contrary to the intent and character of God. He will therefore remove the darkness (wickedness) totally. (*1 John 1:5, Revelation 21:23; 22:5*)

The elaborate dividing of the heavens into multiple unique places was a tool which the Lord God used, and is using, to bring about the downfall, judgment, and subsequent removal of the satanic conspirators. Once this removal of evil has been fully accomplished, He will then remove the divisions from the heavens, and reunite them to be as one again. The Bible states in the following passages that heaven and earth shall be together and the Lord God shall dwell in their midst. (*Revelation 3:12; 21:1-2, 2 Peter 3:13*)

The Genesis Mousetrap

Chapter ten

Rhyme and reason

SEVEN'S UP

The use by God of the number seven, and multiples thereof, in the establishing of a temporary format in which the interim division of a previously unified structure or entity is carried out for the benefit of all parts is well represented in scripture and a few examples of such are following:

THE NATIONS

This design format is clearly evident in the eleventh chapter of Genesis where we see the Lord God first confounding or dividing both the speech and unity of man. The division of nations and languages was designed to establish and safeguard a unique people, Israel (just as the heavens were divided to create Rakia as a unique heaven). This unique people was to be one who would be willing and able to accept and preserve the "to be" given Word of God, and to also allow for the entry of Messiah into the earth which the scattering of people, and the later establishment of the SEVENTY (a multiple of seven) root nations or peoples which are ethnically descended from the post-Noachian forefathers listed in this eleventh chapter of Genesis was created to facilitate.

This temporary dividing of mankind was done with a goal of preserving man's independence and free will. It also allowed for the subsequent reuniting of those of Adam who accept God's will through faith in Messiah, the last Adam, in whom the threat of satan's oppression toward creation and man's existence ends. This division was also brought about to preserve and guard the earth from the overwhelmingly deviant traits of a unified, but sinful mankind; traits which if left unchecked would have led to ultimate death and destruction for man, and through man, for all creation.

THE TONGUES

A further comment on the confounding of languages spoken of in Genesis chapter eleven: it was precisely that, a confounding or a confusing of the one existent language which the Lord gave unto man to speak with. The original Hebrew is very clear about that indicating a "confounding" rather than a "replacing" of language. The initial blessing of language was not taken away, nor was the original tongue replaced with a myriad of languages never before spoken by man. God had given the one language to man as an unrepentant blessing, and He never took that blessing away. He altered it, He confused it, He allowed it to become perverted from the original language due to man's sin; but He never removed from man the originally bestowed blessing.

This point again reaffirms the fact that the blessings and anointings of God are always given without regret. That is to say, He cannot, and will not take away something which He has blessed a being or beings with; including the language He gave. Rather, He confounded or mixed the language mankind originally spoke; changing their use of it, and altering man's authority to use the language He gave. The people then began using altered forms of the original language of man; further altering the changed versions of the original language as time went on.

Due to the fact that man lost the proper respect for this blessing, man also lost the proper use of it. The altered or distorted languages of our post-Babel world came into use as a result of mankind using this great blessing of speech in wickedness, without the blessing of life upon them in the matter. That fact resulted in their lack of success in using the blessing which God gave.

Each person using a corrupt form of the original language is mired in a poor relation to the original intent of God and has lost the ability to: Firstly, naturally understand the Godly mindset found hidden in the Hebrew/Jewish/biblical train of thought. And secondly, lost the ability to communicate effectively and fluently with all other people as the variety of languages and the nuances of speech and comprehension make perfect communication with anyone else a near impossibility for post-Babel man.

Rhyme and reason

LAND, HO!

The continents; the actual dry land itself, was at one time a unified single landmass as described in Genesis 1:9. This landmass was later divided, either during or most likely, after the flood of Noah during the days of one Peleg, spoken of in 1 Chronicles 1:19, into the SEVEN continents that we have today.

It's quite evident to most geography buffs that the continents are a relatively simple, but giant jigsaw puzzle. Perhaps the reason for the seven continents is to have them in some way represent the seven heavens that exist as unique areas of life. It's also interesting, but possibly only a coincidence, that one of these continents: Antarctica, has historically been, and is still considered to be, permanently uninhabited much like the heaven of Vilon is.

> *"For God speaketh once, yea twice, [yet man] perceiveth it not." Job 33:14*

THE NATION

The patriarch Abraham was the first Hebrew, and the one who received the promises of God, but the Hebrews numbered SEVENTY (a multiple of seven) as they first entered into Egypt on their long and difficult journey to bring forth the nation of Israel and the One promised seed of Abraham, the Messiah. The One in whom all men that believe can again be united as one through faith. (*Genesis 46:26-27, Galatians 3:6*)

THE LIGHT OF THE WORLD

The very design of the menorah which stood in the Holy place of the Holy Temple bears witness to this format of the number seven being used to establish a temporary division which again leads to a later unity.

The menorah starts with a single base that rises up to separate into a SEVEN pronged candle stick: and when lit, the seven candles bring about a greater unified light than a single candle on a single base could have. (*Exodus 25:31-40*)

SEVEN SEALS

In the Book of Revelation, chapter five and onwards, we read of a book with SEVEN seals. These seals; seven in number, were as seals are; placed upon the document, book, or scroll to temporarily keep it closed until it could be opened by the correct and authorized party. They were placed there to temporarily separate the outcome of unity from the divided format of creation, and every time a seal was opened the process for the removal of a certain divisional barrier began.

ETERNITY

Even eternity itself, as we have seen, was temporarily divided into the SEVEN days of creation, which are also indicative of the seven thousand years of man; when both of these structures of division have run their courses creation will then be led into a reunified and purified structure of eternity.

THE SEVEN FEASTS

This use of the number seven in temporal divisions is further attested to by the SEVEN great feasts of the LORD. As mentioned before, God does not waste words; everything written in the scriptures is there for an important reason, vital for the functioning of, or explanation of creation. In His Word, God gave specific instructions for His people to eternally keep certain yearly feasts, these were set appointments which He had established and declared holy. These feasts were to mark events that were extremely important in the redemption of His people, Israel; and indeed, vital for the redemption of all creation. The feasts were to be set aside as permanent memorials to His faithfulness and grace.

However, there was also another reason that the feasts were to be kept; they were living prophesies of the coming redemption through the personal works of Messiah, and Israel was to be a testimonial witness to God's Word and Messiah's coming deeds. There were seven of these great biblical feasts of God with four occurring in the spring and three occurring in the fall.

The four spring feasts were:

- "Pesach" (Passover)
- Unleavened bread
- First fruits
- "Shavuot", the feast of weeks called "Pentecost"

The three fall feasts were

- "Yom Teruah", the feast of trumpets. Known more commonly today as "Rosh Hashanah", the civil New Year's Day
- "Yom Kippur" known as "the Day of Atonement"
- "Sukkot", the Feast of Tabernacles

Amazingly, each of these seven feasts confirms and explains its corresponding day within the creative/redemptive week.

*

Day one has the creation of light and its separation from darkness.

Feast one: "Pesach" (Passover) is the feast of liberty from oppression; the freedom from the darkness of slavery. It is a witness of God's ability and will to free His own from tyranny.

*

Day two has the firmament in the midst of the waters, and the dividing of the waters beneath from the waters above.

Feast two: Unleavened Bread is the feast of freedom from sin. Those people of the waters beneath are those of sin, and are separated from those of the waters above; the sanctified, unleavened, and sinless. It's another separation of darkness from light.

*

Day three has the coming forth of the herb yielding seed and of the fruit bearing tree.

Feast three: This is none other than First fruits. Enough said about that!

*

Day four is the establishing of lights in the heavens, and the giving of rule over day and night to the lights; the sun, moon, and stars. The celestial bodies were given the authority to bring forth light, and to divide the light from darkness.

Feast four: "Shavuot" (Pentecost). This is the commemoration of the giving of God's Word through Moses on Mt. Sinai, and later of the giving of His Spirit on the Temple mount after the death and resurrection of Messiah. The Word and the Spirit were the lights in the heavenlies that shone upon the earth; they were the ones unto whom it was given to rule over and divide the light and darkness.

*

Day five finds the creation of sea creatures and birds (winged fowl) into their respective and separate habitats.

Feast five: "Yom Teruah" (Rosh Hashanah), finds the faithful, the "fish" as it were, being separated from the sinner, the "fowl", in great multitudes at the trumpet call, leaving all to go and worship the Lord during this feast. This is a further dividing of darkness from light.

*

Day six sees the creation of different cattle upon the earth, and then the creation of man to rule over creation.

Feast six: "Yom Kippur" (the Day of Atonement), has the separation of the sheep and goats (the different cattle) taking place upon the judgment which occurs at the arrival of the Son of man to rule and reign: Yet a further division of darkness from light.

*

Day seven is the day of rest, the Sabbath.

Feast seven: "Sukkot" (the feast of tabernacles): A seven day period of rejoicing and resting in the goodness of God.

So, the way the heavens were originally arranged was temporarily modified; and this temporary structure of division which is explained throughout scripture in the use of the number seven will have soon run its course in this creative/redemptive matter. The heavens will then be restored again to unity when this divisional state has served its purpose. It was God's original intent to have one unified heaven, *"the waters"*; and His original intent always comes about. It has to.

"For I [am] the LORD, I change not..." Malachi 3:6

Chapter eleven

Adam's arrival

THE BLESSING OF THE CREATED

In Genesis 1:11-25 we can see the physical creation of living things unfolding. The creation of life that is solely unique to this natural heaven of Rakia. Had the creation of plant and animal life taken place upon the earth before this time; before this heaven was separated from the other created heavens, the plant and animal life here would have been spiritual in nature as well as being physical. This would have caused legal difficulty in the separation of the heavens as the "to be" physical plants and animals as pre-existant living things would have had "roots" in the other heavens: spiritual rights that would have made separating this heaven from the others pointless and plainly impossible.

The spiritual side of plants and animals would have given them the ability and rights to compromise this distinct physical heaven which needed to be uniquely isolated from the others. Such multiheavenly flora and fauna would have left a legal pathway open for the wicked angels who are solely spiritual, and unable to partake of Rakia on their own, to possibly enter into and affect the physical creation through access to the yielded rights of such mixed spiritual/physical creations.

The creation of the individual plants and animals prior to the division of the heavens would have resulted in them being both spiritual and physical in nature. Through such a mixed spiritual heritage these plants and animals could have been able to open the door for wicked angels and the curse that is upon them to access the physical heaven of Rakia and contaminate it. Therefore, it was essential that all living things in this heaven of Rakia were unique to this heaven, made solely of and for this heaven.

However, that being said, everything in this physical heaven of Rakia has a spiritual component inherent to it, a link to the other of our heavens, that of Shechakim, but it is a spiritual component, not a root. All matter has that spiritual component which links it to the Shechakim side of this universe where angels as overseers in their offices of authority attend, care for, and influence the natural, and are meant to bring about the will of God on earth in its fullness through their particular authorities.

When referring to the function of our universe, it's important to remember that this universe consists of three heavens functioning together: Rakia, the physical; Shechakim, the spiritual; and Vilon, the separating laws, the curtain.

It is also notable that Adam himself was also created after the division of the heavens precisely to keep him separate from the upper heavens; to keep him innocent; and to prevent his kingdom and future sin from contaminating and interfering with God's Kingdom. There is always order and reason in everything the Lord does.

Now back to the creation of plants and animals; we read that God blessed them to bring forth after their own kind. One thing stands out in these blessings: it's clear that the Lord was careful to limit the right He gave the flora and the fauna to bring forth life ONLY after their own kinds. Otherwise the power of His spoken Word without the phrase, "after their own kind", would have allowed any and all life native to the physical creation to be brought forth by the plants and animals that He blessed with the ability and authority to produce life.

Here are some silly examples of this: the pear tree could have produced bears, and lions could have produced celery in the unlimited authority which they would have all been given through the all powerful Word of God, had it not been specifically stated that they were to bring forth life only after their own kind. Again, God needs to be very thorough and perfect when He does or says anything, as His Words are absolute, and His blessings are empowerments.

A MAN CALLED ADAM, AN ADAM CALLED MAN

"And God said, Let us make man in our image, after our likeness: and let them have dominion over the fish of the sea, and over the fowl of the air, and over the cattle, and over all the earth, and over every creeping thing that creepeth upon the earth." Genesis 1: 26

Having made this unique separate place we call the universe, the Creator created someone to keep order, rule over, and protect it from the evil ones which were within His creation, from those who were constantly trying to pervert God's will in all aspects of their authorities, and that someone was Adam.

Why couldn't God have kept the kingship over this creation for Himself? Well, this is another multipart answer: First; if God would have kept the kingship, the dominion, of this newly created universe for Himself, it would have defeated the purpose of Him separating it from the other heavens in the first place. And second; if God would have kept the kingship for Himself. He would not have been able to keep and guard the garden of Eden which God Himself was to plant upon the earth in such a high state of purity and holiness as Adam was able to. This is due to the presence of the wicked angelic transgression occurring in His Kingdom. Adam's kingship was free of the weight of wickedness, while God's was not.

Now, this does not mean the effects of the wicked conspiracy were absent in the area that Adam was given to rule; but it does mean that Adam's rule over the wicked was to be more complete and dominant in the issues relating to his domain than God's rule was in His own Kingdom. This is due to the fact that the wicked conspirators were operating in God's Kingdom, and out of authority which they derived from their offices within God's Kingdom. We need to remember that these wicked heavenly legalists were in God's Kingdom, and that He was actively constructing and preparing a mechanism for their removal and judgment.

Establishing a separate kingship was a legal pathway for God to move toward that goal. For in the creation of the separate Adamic kingship,

God was able to create an independent format which did not need to respect or uphold the free will of errant beings based in God's Kingdom to the degree that the issuer of the free will, God, did within His own Kingdom. Third, as a Creator and a giver it is in His nature to create and give; and to delegate as much authority as possible. What a tremendous joy it must have been for God to give such a magnificent honor, the dominion of this realm, to His son Adam.

ANGELS CANNOT BE KINGS

Why couldn't this protector have been an angel who God could authorize to fill the role? Why did it need to be a totally new type of being?

First of all, angels were made to be solely in the Kingdom of God, and as a part of God's Kingdom they can never be independent in operational authority; they can be autonomous, but not independent. They can be, and many are, princes, but they do not have the authority to be kings. There is only one King in the Kingdom of God: and that is God Himself.

Second, in order to have the governing say in this universe within God's pre-existing legal framework, a being had to be an integral part of this universe, made of the same material as this universe was made of, and that is dust, otherwise known as physical matter. There had to be that unifying thread to legalize authority and to allow a being to hold an office based solely in this triune universe.

Also, the need for spiritual separation was there; angels were created before the separation of the heavens occurred; that fact precluded their "use" by God in this circumstance as well. And as it was previously stated about the plants and animals: the spiritual roots of angels would have contaminated this isolated heaven of Rakia and defeated the purpose for creating it. This explains why angels, as the spirit beings they are, couldn't interject themselves dominantly into the physical world.

However, in Hebrew, even the name "Adam" (man) is similar to the word "adamah" (ground). Both words have a common and evident root in Hebrew. This was to be a reference to Adam's bodily origin, and the source of his authority in this creation over all things including over the purely spiritual angels who function in the upkeep of this universe. Man was of this creation; and since he was, his say in all matters of the earth was greater than any other spiritual being's was. When man would address matters relating to physical things he would be speaking about issues which were of himself, directly related to him and his habitation, his dwelling. No other spiritual beings had the ability to do that or claim that since they were not of this creation, this heaven of Rakia.

The angels were in their offices here in our triune universe as overseers of the laws God had put in place, as overseers and servants of God to carry out those laws within their respective mandates. Therefore, they didn't have the ability to rule or issue decrees on physical matters since they were not of this physical heaven even though they had access to, and were present in, this triune universe to manage the operation of it.

THE NEED TO BE NATIVE BORN

Even in the natural world we see an example of this situation occurring in the laws of the United States, in that, according to the law of the land, the Constitution, a person who would be the President of the United States needs to have been a native born citizen of the United States.

The founders believed that a native born person would have more reason to look after the best interests of the country than a foreign born person would who may have only recently moved into the country. The native born person having roots and blood ties in the U.S. would be less likely to purposefully mismanage the country when such strong bonds exist. The foreign born person could rise to the highest support position in the land to advise and assist the native born president, but like the angels in Rakia, the foreign born could not legally assume the governing role.

So, God created the body of man from the dust of the earth in order to establish that link of unity between man and the universe he was created to rule. This creation of Adam was also deliberately planned by God to occur after the separation of the heavens took place to ensure that the total spiritual separation of this universe from the upper heavens wouldn't be compromised by Adam having roots and rights in the upper heavens, and through such, allow Adam access to the upper heavens with his kingly authority. This fact also limited those of the upper heavens, such as the wicked angels, from using a witting or an unwitting Adam as a conduit of flow for their corrupt activities to enter into Rakia from any of the other heavens except Shechakim, the spiritual heaven of this triune universe where Adam held sway.

God in His perfect order had to limit the authority of man to this creation only, and by creating Adam after the division of the heavens took place no improper overlapping of authority came about. There can only be one King in power at a time per kingdom, and the Lord reserved what was in the other heavens exclusively for Himself.

Adam's authority as King in this creation was a necessity, in order to bring about the total redemption of all the heavens of God, as we shall discover in further reading. Still, man could not be considered the son of God if he was purely made of dust like animals or plants. This is why the Lord God breathed the breath of life into Adam's body after He fashioned it out of the Rakia dust of this physical creation. In doing so God put of His own Spirit into the dust body of man, and Adam became a living soul; he became God's son the moment God's Spirit entered into him. (*Genesis 2:7*)

This was the fact which established man as the son of God; man was born from the indwelling presence of God's own Spirit. Light came to shine out of darkness.... (*Genesis 1:3*)

It must have been quite an amazing thing for the angels to witness. God, the great King of all creation, took the seemingly worthless dust of the earth and formed a new being; one into which He put His own Spirit and then He further blessed that being to rule this creation. Giving the seemingly worthless dust of the earth greater authority and power over God's creation and these heavens than the angelic host had.

> "And base things of the world, and things which are despised, hath God chosen, [yea], and things which are not, to bring to nought things that are:" 1 Corinthians 1:28
>
> "For this purpose the Son of God was manifested, that he might destroy the works of the devil." 1 John 3:8

And finally, the facts that Adam was made after the angels, apart from the angels, and differently from the angels; established the further fact that Adam in his rule over this triune heaven was totally removed from the knowledge about what happens in the other heavens. Adam had no concern over what legal rights and authorities the angelic had or didn't have in the other heavens, or what actions they may or may not have taken prior to, or outside of his creation, and whether the actions were good or evil. It didn't concern him in the least. Adam was totally separated from, and oblivious to, the occurrences outside of his domain. He was innocent, and removed from all the events and the reasons for them occurring in the heavens of God's Kingdom.

IN THE COOL OF THE DAY

This is also why scripture states in Genesis 3:8 that "God came" to visit Adam in the cool of the day, and not the other way around.

Adam as a being created of this universe and as a part of this universe was limited to this universe, and didn't have the access or ability which the angels did to go bodily before the Lord in the upper heavens to present himself to God and pay homage, to give an account of things, and to be in God's direct presence. Therefore the Lord God Himself would come down to visit with His friend, His son Adam, in the *"cool of the day"*; or to use a slightly more accurate translation from Hebrew one could say: "God came to visit Adam in the Spirit". God would come and visit with man "in the Spirit" in the Shechakim portion of the universe that Adam's spirit dwelled in because Adam couldn't go to visit God. The Bible gives no indication of the Lord showing such a great honor as this to any being other than to man.

This is another veiled reference to the fact that while man cannot rise to the holy heights of God, the Lord can, will, and has come down to our level. That is so amazing. The Lord God of all creation would willingly trouble Himself to come and visit man in the domain God gave him to rule since man didn't have the ability to go up before God as His other sons did. It's time for another one of my "WOW's".... WOW!

THE KINGSHIP OF ADAM

Alright, before we continue along any further we need to establish the fact that there are only two beings in all creation that can be called "king" in accordance with God's will; that is to say legally, in accordance to God's Word. As we read earlier, angelic beings aren't entitled to hold this office, although we do see an angel called Abaddon, whose name means "destruction" in Hebrew, being referred to as a king in the Book of Revelation.

Abaddon is the angel of the bottomless pit and he is mentioned in Revelation 9:11. In the Greek language which was said to be the original language used to write the Book of Revelation, the word "basileus" was used in this verse in reference to Abaddon's kingship. This word was then translated into English as the word "king", but unlike the English word "king", the Greek word "basileus" does not always necessarily carry the definite and absolute meaning of the word "king" in its use. "Basileus" may also mean leader, commander, ruler, or prince, and should be read as such in this passage.

Also, this verse reads in reference to the demons in question *"they had a king over them"*. If someone were to insist on the title king being the most fitting translation from the Greek language in this situation, and therefore appropriately belonging to the angel Abaddon, it could well be pointed out that it was the demons who submitted to his rule and who chose him as their king of their own accord and decided to yield unto this particular angelic being the very high level of authority in their lives that would allow such a being to be thought of in that regal way. It should not be considered to be a God given office, or an accurate portrayal of such an office existing in the creation of God.

"A KING OVER ALL THE CHILDREN OF PRIDE"

The next point of contention on this issue may come from the forty first chapter of the Book of Job, where God speaks of a mighty creature called leviathan. The description of this creature; while it may be portraying an animal is also among other things to be considered a picture of satan. In this chapter the leviathan is called *"a king over all the children of pride."* In the Hebrew, the word used for king in this verse is clearly "melech", which does, indeed, unmistakably mean "king".

Should this be taken to mean that satan has been crowned a king by God? Or that God has somehow resigned Himself to the fact that satan is in an independent authority outside of the laws of God? Of course not. It simply means that satan is the instigator of the sin, the spirit behind the prideful; the one who all the uppity are emulating; the one who is seducing the foolish to follow in his wicked ways. Remember, pride was satan's first recorded sin, so he gets the prize for 'discovering" it.

In an earlier chapter we read of satan being referred to as the king of Babylon in Isaiah 14:4; he is also alluded to as the king of Tyrus in Ezekiel 28:12. There are also a few more passages referring to satan which use a physical man in a substitutional form of reference, in a veiling way; and we need to realize that in every case in which this happens, the form of satanic "kingship" which exists is always veiled behind a man precisely for the reason that satan himself cannot legally hold the title or the office.

God goes out of His way to ensure that the title of king is never directly bestowed upon satan, either by His prophets or through His own Words. These veiled references are due to the fact that satan has been ceded great authority in the dominion of Adam, and apparently also among the wicked angels, and consequently the evil works carried out through the power of those authorities are originating from satan, the instigator and controlling influence of evil. However, it does not mean in any way that God has granted the title of king to that dark angel.

Again, it is a question of individuals in their free will choosing to grant or cede authority over themselves to another being; choosing in their free will to have another being as a king over themselves, one which God did not authorize or anoint to that position, but nevertheless, has the ability to be a king over others if they choose to submit their lives to that individual's reign.

"BASILEIA" DIDN"T ORIGINALLY CARRY THE MEANING OF "INDEPENDENT KINGDOM"

Yet another issue which may be brought up, and the final one to be dealt with in this look at kingship, is the fact that Jesus Himself referred to a "kingdom" of satan as recorded in both the Books of Matthew and Luke.

> *"And if Satan cast out Satan, he is divided against himself; how shall then his kingdom stand?"* Matthew 12:26
> *"If Satan also be divided against himself, how shall his kingdom stand? because ye say that I cast out devils through Beelzebub."* Luke 11:18

The issue here circles around another form of the previously mentioned and dealt with Greek word of "basileus"; which in these cases is the word "basileia". This word "basileia" is commonly translated into English as "kingdom". However, "basileia" can also be translated as an area of "rule" or "reign"; this is something a prince can do in a principality, which is his area of "rule" or "reign". A prince can have an area of rule within a kingdom without being a king or ruling in an independent kingdom himself.

If it were to be incorrectly insisted that the word "basileia" retains only the meaning of the English word "kingdom" and that satan would be understood to be the absolute king of that absolute kingdom, then we must understand that the "kingdom" which satan, the adversary of righteousness, rules in his wickedness is the rightful kingdom of the fallen and exiled Adam. It is not a kingdom of his own, but rather, a kingdom ruled (overseen) by a "lesser" due to the rightful rulers absence. Such a situation could at best only be described as a rule caused by Adamic default, one which came about solely due to the rightful king's negligence and sin, not due to any regal rights inherent to the antagonistic angel.

Actually, verses 23-26 of the third chapter of the Gospel of Mark explain the situation in question quite well. These verses clearly state that when Jesus was referring to the kingdom of satan in the other gospels (see Matthew 12:22-29, and Luke 11:14-22), He was speaking of it in a parable.

> *"And he called them [unto him], and said unto them in parables, How can Satan cast out Satan? And if a kingdom be divided against itself, that kingdom cannot stand. And if a house be divided against itself, that house cannot stand. And if Satan rise up against himself, and be divided, he cannot stand, but hath an end." Mark 3:23-26*

ONLY TWO KINGS

Thus, the only two beings scripturally entitled, that means chosen and authorized by God, to hold the office of king are God and man. It should be safe to assume that God's kingship has been established well enough that no further comments on it are necessary to prove His right of crown, so we'll concentrate our focus on man's right to be called king.

Adam was given dominion over the physical creation, that's unquestionable (*Genesis 1:26-28*). Man was also given the right to establish kingdoms upon the earth. These kingdoms were accepted by God, with the kings of Israel in particular being chosen and anointed by God for their offices. If it were contrary to man's authority to operate in such offices God would not have sanctioned it in any form either individually, nationally, physically, or spiritually. (*1 Samuel 8:22; 11:15; 15:1, 1 Kings 19:15, Genesis 14:18, Hebrew 7:1*)

In God's plan it is necessary in order for the redemption of all creation to succeed that the Messiah be sovereign and independent of all outside influence. He must be a supreme power in the earth, in other words: He must be a king. This was God's intent from the beginning and also indicates His will which is to have a man hold the office of King Messiah, ruler of this creation. Therefore we can see it was, and is, God's will for man to have and hold the office of king. (*John 18:36-37*)

What we many times forget, or do not even realize in this day, is that the kingly rights and authority of Adam still rest on every person saved and unsaved, as all are of Adam's lineage. It's the way, and the why, God created man; it's an integral part of mankind inherent to the spiritual DNA of Adam. Although, due to the fall of Adam unsaved man cannot function successfully in this role as the anointing of life departed from mankind at man's departure from God's will, and our father Adam lost the kingdom he was meant to rule.

In essence, natural unsaved man became a king without a crown, an exile from the garden; a being with ability but not authority; a king without a country, but nevertheless, a king.

Often in scripture we read about the kings of the earth; such as in the following passages: *(Psalm 2:2; 138:4, Isaiah 14:9; 14:18; 24:21, Revelation 1:5; 17:18)*

The kings mentioned in these and other verses are not mere national leaders, although they are obviously also included in the rendering; but more specifically they refer to each and every person, all those who are of Adamic descent. The God of creation who blessed man originally still sees every person as a king no matter how far removed from Him that person may be. No matter what state an individual is in, no matter how low any person may have sunk, God still sees and calls mankind "the kings of the earth", as that is the office He Himself gave unto man. He never changed His original intentions, and He never does. We all still carry the anointing which He gave Adam even though we may have moved away from Him in sin and unbelief. Even so, He still sees man as, and calls man a king.

> *"God, who quickeneth the dead, and calleth those things which be not as though they were." Romans 4:17*

Through the redemptive work of the King Messiah we can see the Word of this preceding verse coming to pass; for in Jesus, man can once again step back into the will of God and receive the anointing of life, and actually walk in the authority of the office that is now held by Messiah to do the things God originally established the Adamic kingship to do. Furthermore, with the crown now firmly secure upon the head of the body, who is Jesus, the kingship of saved and redeemed mankind is eternally secure in Him and accessible only through obedience to Him. That is why Jesus said, *"...without me ye can do nothing (John 15:5)."*

One of the things which we will be held accountable for, and judged on by God, is how we as heirs of Adam operated in the office of king which

He gave unto each one of us; and more specifically, why we chose not to operate in that office which He made available to us. Instead, we as people have let the curse and wickedness run rampant through the creation which God has charged to our care.

The Genesis Mousetrap

Chapter twelve

The hidden agenda

THE TRAP BEING SET

In the preceding chapters we have read about the way God was preparing the heavens, this universe in particular, to serve in the removal of evil from the midst of His creation. In this chapter we'll be looking at what role man and his dominion had to do with it.

Once God had separated the three heavens that make up this universe from the others, modifying the substance of their structures to allow them to function for unique and independent purposes, and by allowing time to affect Rakia; He then created a unique being: man, to rule this creation and expand the garden God had planted here east of Eden. As we know, man was sinless and holy, having dominion in these heavens over all matter, animals, and beings on earth both in the physical part of the universe, Rakia, as well as over the spiritual matter and angelic beings in the heavenly part of this universe, Shechakim, in issues which pertained to the function of Adam's domain. All things were subject to him in matters concerning the operation of the garden of Eden, the seat and basis of Adam's kingdom.

However, we need to be clear that the angelic beings were only subject to Adam in the portions of their authorities and offices that were connected to the operation of this universe. They were not subject to Adam in the other heavens in any way; there they were under the sole authority and kingship of God. Nevertheless, it was, and is, the creating and establishing of Adamic authority in this creation that was one of the most important steps God had taken to rid the heavens of wickedness.

This situation of having two kingships in existence caused two very interesting things to occur: First, the angels had an obligation to oversee the functioning of all the heavens, so they had natural access to this universe. They had a right and obligation to function in accordance with their God given anointings and authorities in the offices they were assigned to in this universe. This meant they had unrestricted access and undeniable rights to this universe, but God didn't have His kingly access to the domain of Adam anymore.

Having given Adam the right to rule this unique realm, God gave up the privilege of having those same rights residing in His person, although one specific role that He did keep for Himself was the role of Judge. However, at the time God blessed Adam with dominion He took on a more advisory role in the operation of the domain of Adam in this universe in the context of man's ruling relationship to it, and in man's role in the tending of the garden.

This is one of the important reasons that Adam was the last of God's creations. Once man was made and blessed to rule, God limited His own authority to continue creating in this universe, leaving the continuing function and growth of spiritual and physical things in the care of the angelic, on autopilot, so to speak, while the purification and order of this universe He left in the care of Adam, the newly crowned king.

The continuous flow of creative events stopped at the blessing and crowning of Adam and Eve. This is why the Sabbath immediately followed the creation of man and the time of rest came on the seventh day; with man being created late on the sixth. All was completed beforehand because all needed to be; there was no adding to the creation by God any more. He had given the governing role to Adam, and excluded Himself from the direct control of the everyday operation of the garden from that point forward.

THE GARDEN

The scriptures state that the garden of Eden was planted by God Himself upon the earth. (*Genesis 2:8-9*)

This is a separate event from the creation narrative which is read about prior to and after God's planting of this garden in the Genesis narrative.

The hidden agenda

The garden was to be a "seed", a prototype, an example to Adam of what God wanted this universe to be. Again, this universe is a triune creation consisting of the heavens of Vilon, Rakia, and Shechakim.

The reason God had for planting a garden in this universe separate from the rest of the creation was that although this creation was separated from the other heavens, as we have read in earlier chapters; the angelic, specifically the angelic satanic conspirators, had too much authority in it and influence on it for it to be considered a place where God's perfect will could be done or brought to pass. The garden, however, was to be His separate and perfect showpiece of design for Adam to follow in his assignment of subduing the earth and filling it with God's will, His blessing of life.

The garden was to be the tangible foundation of Adam's Kingdom and the instrument of His power. Now, that is very important to realize, for, as we have seen, all of creation, all the heavens, were and are still God's according to scripture, but to establish an independent kingship God needed to establish an independent kingdom. The place and cornerstone of that kingdom was the ever expandable garden which He Himself "planted" upon the earth.

This kingdom was to rule over the universe, but not to own it, as all things created eternally belong to God. Hence the legal right for those in God's Kingdom such as God Himself and the angels to still operate in this universe to varying degrees. (*Psalm 50:10-11; 24:1, 1 Corinthians 10:26*)

Let's put the matter another way: Adam's kingship was to be over the creation, and not inclusive of it, as all things eternally belong to God. Creation belonging to God is what allowed the angelic beings the rights to function in this universe and serve in its upkeep without becoming integral parts of Adam's Kingdom. That is a very, very, important fact: for the angelic beings had to remain outside of Adam's kingship lest the wicked among them contaminate the Adamic Kingdom in their transgressions. In a slightly more practical mode, as we have previously read, the angels were in God's Kingdom, and as such, they couldn't legally be made to become a part of another kingdom such as Adam's.

Therefore we can say that this Adamic kingdom with its roots in the holy garden was on the earth, but was not of the earth.

This is also what Jesus, the last Adam, had to say about His own Kingdom; the Kingdom of the first Adam which He came to inherit, expand, and rule.

> *"Jesus answered, My kingdom is not of this world: if my kingdom were of this world, then would my servants fight, that I should not be delivered to the Jews: but now is my kingdom not from hence." John 18:36*

Adam was to grow his kingdom, multiply it, and fill the earth with it thereby changing the earth both physically and spiritually into the intended will of God. This garden, the manifest blessing of God's will on the earth, was to be expanded by man to be the dominant force in these heavens by restricting and controlling the angelic presence here.

In the formation of the garden we see another example of the fact that God never asks anyone to do anything which He hasn't previously in some way shown an example of. After first seeing God's will in regards to His design for the earth manifested in the garden, it was then possible for Adam to do the things he had seen His Father do; Adam was then able to go about caring for the garden and expanding it according to God's design. Again, this is also what Jesus the last Adam said of Himself.

> *"Then Jesus answered and said to them, "Most assuredly, I say to you, the Son can do nothing of Himself, but what He sees the Father do; for whatever He does, the Son also does in like manner." NKJV™ John 5:19*

> *"And He who sent Me is with Me. The Father has not left Me alone, for I always do those things that please Him." John 8:29*

> *"If I do not the works of my Father, believe me not." John 10:37*

The hidden agenda

The garden itself was divided from the rest of creation by the heavenly laws of Vilon. Evidence of this is seen in the fact that the Cherubim and the flaming sword were placed on the outside of the garden to guard it, separate it, and prevent the reentry of man into it after man's expulsion from it due to sin, and to bar the entry of anything else such as evil into it. (*Genesis 3:24*)

The reason for Vilon to operate as a dividing wall was to keep out of the perfect garden any things or operational conducts that were inherent to the physical Rakia, or the spiritual Shechakim, which were not considered by God originally, and Adam subsequently, to be in accord with God's will of love, unity, and mutual benefit to all life and blessing. Adam as the guardian of the garden had to maintain the integrity of its purity by functioning in accordance with the specific laws of all three of the heavens that make up our universe, and it was the laws of Vilon which allowed this garden to be moved and removed from place to place within the heavens as we will later see.

THE GARDEN; A HOLY PLACE

Now, a point which needs to be emphasized, one that is quite monumental in scope and not easy for many to digest immediately, is that the garden was created to be the most holy place in all the heavens as it was planted by God Himself in His Holiness exclusive of the activities happening in creation. As such, it wasn't marred by any corruption caused by the angelic transgression which existed outside of it. Hence the need to have a kingly guardian such as man there.

The garden as protected by the kingly Adam was actually the first place in any of the heavens where the will of God and the blessing of life could function in their fullest measures since the attempt by satan to bring the cover of darkness upon the heavens. Let those thoughts sink in for a moment....

In the garden the satanic transgression was unknown. Therefore the garden was unpolluted by what can only be described as internally based wickedness, that which existed in the rest of creation. The garden was, indeed, the holiest place in all the heavens. In fact, amazingly, the garden was on par with the throne of God itself in purity.

As stated, this is attested to by the fact that it was specifically the cherubs which were sent to guard the garden after man's banishment. In scripture cherubs are always and only present to guard and bear the holiness of God, they are found nowhere else. Therefore when the original protector of the garden, Adam, became unable to fulfill his role of protecting the garden due to his own disobedience and sin, cherubs were sent to guard this holy place of God.

Again, cherubs are only found protecting the throne of God, bearing and protecting His personal holiness, and protecting the garden which God originally planted east of Eden, nowhere else. These protective cherubs were sent to guard the garden precisely because the garden and that which it entailed was so holy to the Lord.

Notice that even these great cherubs stood outside of the garden while protecting it. They were not in it like Adam was, as they were not native to it, and also due to the fact that they as angels did not have the authority to rule the garden in Adam's stead; rather their duty was to protect it as it was. This is also similar to the conduct of cherubs when they are around the holiness of God in their other protective duties. The cherubs are pictured outside of the Ark of the Covenant; not inside. They are found carrying God's throne above them; they are not seated upon it, etc. So, here again we find the cherubs located outside of the holy place, guarding the garden.

Why was the garden just a small area and not originally planted by God to cover the whole earth, or to take up the whole Rakia heaven? First, one of the operating principles of the laws of the Creator is seed planting and growth. Everything He did, or does, or will do has a growth component built into it, an element of expansion, a life force. It is a "God factor", His fingerprint on all things. It's an unstoppable attribute which comes from the fact that everything is made with the living Word of God, and therefore that life must manifest itself in some form in all things created by God, and that form is growth, expansion, and increase.

So God planted the seeds of His will in the garden, and then authorized Adam to begin the expansion process, that of filling the earth with the garden. As it was filled with the life of God the garden needed room for

The hidden agenda

expansion and growth, hence like all things it started small and was to fill all the earth with its blessing.

Second, at that time God created only one Adam to tend the garden. This was clearly not enough manpower to mind a garden as large as the whole earth. It had to be an Adam sized garden so he could manage it, keep it clean of unwanted spiritual wickedness, and grow it at a pace man could handle. God would have been negligent to make the garden so large that Adam couldn't properly oversee its operation, function, and protection. It would have been wasteful, and God is never wasteful. Therefore the garden was designed to grow along with the population of mankind who were created to tend it.

All right, as the Bible makes clear, Eden was not the garden itself, merely its location. Eden was an area or land on this earth, the Bible says that the Lord planted a garden eastward in Eden. The garden was God's ideal for this earth, a place outside of the influence of the wicked angels, protected by His son Adam the king, a place where God's total will could feasibly be done.

In many ways the garden was the only place in all of the heavens where God's will could have been perfectly carried out as satan and the wicked angels had absolutely no say in the realm that was given unto Adam. It could be said that they didn't have citizenship in Adam's kingdom, and couldn't legally challenge him or insist on any say in any matters. In this way the perversions of the wicked angels were restricted by Adam's authority.

This was God's intent. The angels were absolutely subservient to the will of Adam in all things relating to his domain. The wicked angels had to obey Adam's authority and submit to his will in a fuller sense than they had to submit unto God's; for in God's Kingdom bestowed free will and God's unrepentant blessings had to leave the angelic room for autonomous action and even legalistic perversion if they chose it.

Contrastingly, Adam's God given authority on this earth was dictatorial and absolute. It was so by God's design. This place called the garden was more perfect than the upper heavens in all ways but one, the personified presence of God the Father was not there, His son Adam was. He was there serving his Father by keeping the garden holy.

The Genesis Mousetrap

> *"And the LORD God took the man, and put him into the garden of Eden to dress it and to keep it." Genesis 2:15*

Let's look at the words from the preceding verse *"to dress it and to keep it."* The word "dress" in Hebrew is the word "abad" and it means "to serve" or "serve in", and the word "keep" is the word "shamar" which also carries the meaning of "to guard". So we can see that the job of Adam was to serve in the garden and to guard it.

How was Adam to serve in it? By maintaining life and order; by bringing growth to the garden, expanding it to fill the whole earth as God instructed him to in Genesis 1:28 saying: *"replenish the earth, and subdue it"*.

Again, a look at the Hebrew will show us that the word for "replenish" is "maleh" and it actually means "to fill", and the word for "subdue" is "kabash" and it means "to force into bondage". Adam was to serve by expanding the garden, and by filling the earth with it and God's will right along with it, His blessing of life; by forcing all things including and especially, the wicked angelic beings into bondage to God's perfect will regardless of their own intents and will. This was God's design for the Adamic rule of the heavens of Rakia and Shechakim.

One of the specific things that Adam was to subjugate unto God's will was death in the natural creation which was found outside of the garden. Like all things, the plant and animal species here in the natural creation were under the oversight of the angelic authorities, and the wicked unclean angels were doing their best to nullify God's will in their areas of authority. They were busily perverting God's intentions for the natural creation by causing the destruction of life through the twisted use of their offices.

How? By bringing about the implementation of death through all means at their disposal: predatory feeding, natural disasters, starvation, disease, unnatural aging, genetic decay, etc. etc. Hey, such is life when you're stuck in the shadow of the angel of death and his ilk.

All the things that are contrary to life and godliness were found outside of the garden in a world still tinged with the satanic shadow of perversion. Adam's job was to put a stop to such evil behavior by expanding the garden, and by reintroducing God's will into the earth in such an absolute and dominant way that it could not be distorted by anyone, not even by the cleverest of legal perverts.

Now, as we've read earlier, God didn't have the right to act contrary to His own Word by sentencing the wicked conspirators to hell without just and legal cause, which the wicked conspirators in His free will kingdom were careful not to give. Adam the king naturally didn't have the right to punish without cause either.

Nevertheless, the wicked ones were to languish in bondage to Adam's will as long as they were to be in offices affected by Adam's Kingdom. This was God's design for His new creation, this triune universe; and the new Adamic Kingdom that He established here was His tool for implementing His will regardless of the will of the otherwise uncooperative wicked angels in creation.

The legalistic twisting of the satanic conspirators could not be accomplished in the areas of creation where the garden held ground, not with the garden under the protection of Adam. Adam in his separate kingdom simply was not under any legal obligation to put up with any perversions or transgressions. Actually, he was under Godly mandate to expand the garden and its holiness and bring into submission or bondage all things that were contrary to holiness. This was one of the obligatory duties that went with the Adamic kingship.

How was Adam to guard the garden? As a place where God's perfect and pure will was to be done it was a very holy place. Adam needed to keep out all unclean influence which existed outside of the garden under angelic control, and much of it under wicked angelic control at that. Now, this is not to say that the evil angels were absent from the garden. In fact, they were well represented there as their offices of operating authority overlapped with the garden while it was on this physical earth, on Rakia. This is attested to by satan's presence in the garden as a serpent, but the wicked were in total unquestionable submission to Adam's authority in all things pertaining to the operation of the garden.

These angels were actually bound to do Adam's will; and Adam's will was to do God's will. Actually, one can only be in bondage to the will of another if there is a difference in wills, and one is forced to acquiesce to the demands of the other which are made contrary to ones own intent. So, in that regard, the righteous angels wouldn't have been considered to be in any bondage at all, for they also wanted to do God's will wherever their offices of authority brought them. Contrastingly, the wicked angels were in a state of near total unwilling submission to Adam's will, unable to resist, lest they rebel. Can we say that satan was getting boxed in here?

ADAM..... BORN HERE, RAISED ELSEWHERE

Very well, scripture clearly states that when God created man, He did so outside of the garden itself, and then God brought man into the garden. (*Genesis 2:8*)

The reasons the Lord created man outside of the garden were:

First, the garden was a unique place. Being as much spiritual, of the Shechakim part of our universe, as it was physical, of Rakia, and Adam needed to be made unmistakably of dust, or earth, of this physical matter found in the natural Rakia part of our universe to establish his authority here as he was to expand the garden throughout the entire earth both physically, as well as spiritually.

Second, the Creator foreknew Adam's fall and made him in a way that would allow the Creator to exile Adam and his sin from the garden while still allowing Adam to survive on the outside in a non-transformed earth. This exile allowed God to keep the garden (Adam's Kingdom) holy and uncontaminated by Adam's sin. Since Adam was of Rakia he was able to be exiled from his kingdom, the garden, into Rakia without complication.

Had Adam been of the garden his sin would have also been of the garden and would have contaminated it. That would have compromised God's vehicle of removing the wicked angels from the heavens, negating all the work that God had done up to that point.

Third, had Adam been made in the garden, native to it, God could not have sent him out into the physical creation. Adam would have been indigenous to the garden, and the only place he could have been sent when he was removed from the garden was to hell; banishing a sinful

Adam to an eternity in hell was something God clearly did not want to do.

Fourth, Adam's creation outside of the garden and the reference of God bringing him into the garden is a picture or prophesy of God bringing a sinful mankind which was not born in holiness into a place where God's holiness abounds through His grace and works. It's a depiction of salvation.

Fifth, Adam the king being created outside of the garden, his kingdom, is a veiled reference to the last Adam, Jesus, arriving in like fashion. Jesus was clearly not of this world, but was brought into it by the will of God to be filled therein with the Spirit, the breath of God, and then anointed to rule the kingdom into which He was brought; this is all similar to Adam's experience. Similarly also, Jesus, like Adam, was brought into a specific place that He was not quite "native" to, in order to bring peace and to subjugate wickedness.

Where is the garden now? Well, the garden was originally planted into our physical heaven, and as it was planted it was not indigenous or native to this Rakia; although the garden was firmly planted into it and as such was fully a part of it. However, the garden was actually more spiritual in nature and operation than it was physical; and the job of man was to subdue the less holy Rakia, fill it with the garden, and transform the entire Rakia into a gardenlike place.

This may seem a foreign concept to us, but at the time there wasn't the seemingly total division between the physical and spiritual parts of our universe that we now have due to the disobedience of Adam. The Adamic disobedience caused the laws of the heaven of Vilon to take the previously unheard of and never before experienced effect of separating for Adam the physical Rakia from the spiritual Shechakim, and man was sent into Rakia while the garden, paradise, became solely a part of Shechakim. (*Genesis 3:23-24*)

THE GARDEN WAS SENT TO HELL!?!

The garden was then transplanted to an area of Shechakim called "sheol" in Hebrew which is located in the spiritual bowels of the earth. This word "sheol" is commonly translated into English as "hell", but it's a little more complicated than that. Sheol did, indeed, contain hell which is the place of punishment and eternal excommunication from the life and presence of God, but it also became the place for paradise, the garden, to function as the abode for the souls of the righteous dead of mankind who were able to reside safely in this "spiritual" paradise upon their separation from their physical bodies at death. So, the garden was transported to sheol where it was to remain as an abode for the righteous dead up unto the time of the coming of the atonement work of Messiah.

> "Thou hast ascended on high, thou hast led away captives; Thou hast received gifts among men, Yea, among the rebellious also, that Jehovah God might dwell with them." American Standard Version *Psalm 68:18*

The garden is also referred to as Abraham's bosom, and in the following scripture it's clearly evident that the garden, paradise, was in sheol, separated by a large canyon from the torments of hell. Paradise was the place where the faithful could peacefully await the coming redemption that was arranged for by God. (*Luke 16:22-31*)

Now, there may be some who still wonder about the garden and paradise being the same place; well, let's refer back to the Word. (*Luke 23:43, Revelation 2:7; 22:2+14, Psalm 16:10, Ezekiel 31, Jonah 2:2, 2 Corinthians 12:1-4*)

Do the wicked angels still have access and entry into the garden?

No, the wicked angels had no further entry into the garden after Adam was exiled from it, it was separated from Rakia, and the Cherubim along with the flaming sword were sent to guard it. The righteous dead were not spending their days engaged in conversations or activities with any evil spirits. The wicked ones only had access into the garden when it was planted into the natural creation and Adam was there in His kingly role to give out the instructions for their angelic behavior and activities within his domain. Since Adam lost the effective use of his authority and lost his own access to the garden, the angelic also lost the reason and right to enter into it, which was to be in the presence of the king in order to hear his will.

The hidden agenda

It was very necessary for the garden to remain in the Shechakim heaven potion of our triune universe as the righteous dead were to abide in paradise until the resurrection of the righteous occurred. It must be remembered that the righteous dead were still man, that is, of Adam. Thusly, they were totally of this triune universe whether they were physically dead or not. That being the case, they did not have the ability or the right to leave this creation, this triune universe which man was created to inhabit.

The righteous dead were not able to enter into the upper heavens therefore they could not appear before God in His Kingdom. That is the reason they needed a legally acceptable place to abide, and that place was the garden, paradise, located in the Shechakim heaven of man's domain.

Add to this the fact that without the atonement of the sacrificial blood of the last Adam, Jesus, to totally remove their sins, not just to cover them as the blood of animals had done during their mortal lives on earth, and we can see that man was absolutely unable to approach the direct presence of God. Consequently, the righteous dead needed to stay in mankind's "native" heaven of Shechakim so that man wouldn't be destroyed by the holiness of God's presence and direct glory. (*Matthew 26:28, Romans 3:25, Hebrews 10:4*)

It must be remembered that regardless of whether or not Adam fell into sin, man was made to dwell only in this triune creation, and did not have the ability to enter into God's upper heavens under any circumstances. This issue alone brought about the need for our God, who loves unity, to establish a way to bring man into His full presence.

In addition, since the fall of man occurred, man was still further separated from God and further limited in area of existence. Fallen man was only able to dwell in Rakia until physical death occurred, at which time the soul would be brought to sheol located in Shechakim which was still a part of the original Adamic universe where the dead would stay in either the place of fire and punishment for the wicked, or in the paradise of God, the garden, where the righteous were brought.

In this way, man could survive in his "native" habitat, hidden away from God's Holy presence until God established a way to reunite with the righteous, and bring them into His presence. This he accomplished through the atoning death and subsequent salvation found in the Messiah.

One of the things that Messiah, the last Adam, accomplished through His sacrificial death was to give mankind something previously unknown by creation, and that is the right, through faith, to become a new creation. Not only was fallen man to have the opportunity to be restored unto his original Adamic state, but in Messiah, man was given the privilege to become an altogether new being; one who isn't limited to only this universe, but now had access to God's presence in the highest heaven as well. (*2 Corinthians 5:17, Matthew 28:18, Hebrews 4:16; 6:19-20*)

The need for the separation of mankind from God ended as their sins were washed away and the willing righteous of mankind received lawful access to go before the throne of grace through Jesus. These righteous were allowed to be in full Adamic contact with the Father for the first time since Adam fell. Additionally, mankind was allowed to enter the upper heavens for the first time ever, to be in the full presence of God's great glory. So, due to the redemptive work of Jesus the middle wall of separation came down, not just between Jews and gentiles, but between God and man as well. (*Ephesians 2:14*)

Continuing along in the same vein, the veil which hung in the temple between the Holy place and the Holiest of Holies was in many ways representative of the partition which existed between God's full presence and the creation that was separated from Him. When the veil of the temple was torn in two, rent down the middle at the time of Messiah's death; the spiritual veil of separation that it represented was torn apart as well.

As a result, man, both living and dead, was once again able to enter into the Father's presence through the atonement of the Messiah, and actually able to enter into it in a way which man, even Adam himself, never had before. Since man was now able to enter the throne room of God through faith in the atoning works of Messiah Jesus and in the sanctification power of His blood. Man therefore was able to become an altogether new creature in Messiah. (*Matthew 27:5, Mark 15:38*)

Also, speaking of the location of sheol, the hell area of sheol as a place of punishment for, and containment of, the sinful angels needed to be as far from the holy throne of God as possible, so sheol was located in the farthest applicable heaven from Him, the heaven of Shechakim. Due to the fact that angels weren't made to permanently exist in Rakia, sheol couldn't be placed there even though Rakia is actually more isolated from God's throne due to its unique purpose of existence. Sheol therefore had to be in the spiritual Shechakim as the angels weren't of this physical matter, nor was man's soul which separates from man's material body at death and still needs to be in its "native" triune environment.

In other words, since sheol or hell was prepared originally as a place of punishment for rebellious angels who didn't have the authority of physically existing in Rakia, sheol needed to be in a "spiritual" place, a place where these spirits could legally exist far from God's throne. (*Isaiah 14:15, 2 Peter 2:4*)

HEAVEN IS HEAVENLY

Now, an interesting thing happened after the Messiah Jesus sanctified the righteous dead with His blood and atoned for their sin: Paradise didn't have a reason to be in sheol anymore. The righteous dead were able to enter God's direct presence in Messiah, and the Lord was then able to relocate paradise, the heart of Adamic office, once more. So the Lord moved paradise into His presence, into the highest heaven where He is seated at the right hand of Power. He didn't want to keep His precious garden in sheol any longer than necessary, and since He no longer had a reason to, which was to house the righteous dead there away from God's presence, He was able to bring paradise "home".

Another very important reason for moving paradise to the highest heaven simultaneously with the righteous dead was to keep man's necessary link with his "native" triune heavens intact. Paradise was that tangible link; the essence of the place that man was made for and needed to be part of until the resurrection of the righteous and their receiving of the glorified bodies.

So, when a person speaks about the righteous dead being in "heaven" and in God's presence they are correct, but the righteous dead are in the highest heaven because that is where paradise is located today, and not because man has rights to abide in the highest heaven. The righteous dead of mankind are in the highest heaven because they are still linked to paradise now located therein. However, unlike the situation in sheol where paradise was mercifully separated from the unseemly areas of hell, paradise is now apparently fully overlapping in area with the highest heaven; and as such, those of paradise have unhindered access throughout the highest heaven in a manner fitting ones who belong there.

In other words, the righteous dead are in the highest heaven at this time, but not yet of the highest heaven as they are there due to the rights that they were originally given to exist in paradise, the garden of God. Not due to any new rights which they were given to become native to Aravot.

This is very similar to the way scripture explains the situation of believers in the world today: The unbeliever is born from the first Adam. That is, from a sinful nature and world. While the believer is born from the last Adam; that is, from the Spirit of God. In the same way, the believers physically dwell in a place which they are not a natural part of. Those who are born of the Spirit are in this world, but not of this world. The believer moves and functions on this earth in much the same manner as the unbeliever does, but the rights, authority, and reason to function on this earth come from a different source. They come from the will of the Lord, and not from the world. (*John 15:19; 17:6; 18:36*)

This relocation of the garden established yet another interesting fact. When paradise was taken out of sheol, the area reserved for the punishment of the rebellious angels and subsequently of sinful men who do not accept God's mercy further expanded to fill in the void left by the removal of paradise. Isaiah 5:14 and Proverbs 27:20 speak of hell/sheol enlarging itself in a desirous sense in preparation of receiving new arrivals, and of never being full.

The hidden agenda

ANOTHER RECAP

Now, let's briefly review some of the main points that have been touched upon in this section:

1 The garden, paradise; was planted in this physical heaven of Rakia, and not a native part of it.

2 Adam's sin caused man to be removed from the Shechakim heaven portion of his authorities; afterwards, man "existed" only in the Rakia heaven from whence his body was formed.

3 Man's sin was the decisive factor in the relocating of paradise into the area of the Shechakim heaven portion of this universe called "sheol".

4 Man being of this creation, and needing to stay in this creation until the redemption was the reason both sheol and paradise needed to stay located in the Shechakim heaven portion of our universe.

5 Messiah's atonement work brought about the removal of paradise from sheol, and allowed it to be brought into God's presence in the highest heaven, along with all of the righteous dead located therein.

6 Paradise, the garden, being relocated to the highest heaven was the necessary link to man's triune universe which allowed the righteous of mankind to enter into the highest heaven due to Messiah's atonement work.

So, to put it briefly: the garden is located in the highest heaven today in the presence of Almighty God Himself where it shelters the righteous of the Lord who have past from the earth.

A TREE GROWS IN THE GARDEN

> "And the LORD God commanded the man, saying, Of every tree of the garden thou mayest freely eat: But of the tree of the knowledge of good and evil, thou shalt not eat of it: for in the day that thou eatest thereof thou shalt surely die." Genesis 2: 16-17

A look at the garden would not be complete without discussing the tree of the knowledge of good and evil as it was the one instrument that could

The Genesis Mousetrap

have brought sin and death into the dominion of man and thusly lead to his subsequent fall, as it did.

To start with, we need to look back a few pages and see that Adam was innocent. He had no knowledge of the satanic conspiracy, or that there ever had been one. He was totally oblivious to the events which took place, or that were taking place in the other heavens.

Furthermore, when it came to the things in his domain in this creation that weren't in line with God's will and Adam's mandate, Adam simply gave the orders for things to line up with God's will and they obeyed. He didn't need to delve into the legal mechanisms which caused things outside of the garden to occasionally go counter to God's will. Adam didn't need to ask "Why?" When he came across something behaving out of line, he made it operate according to God's will, pure and simple. For his authority of kingship allowed him the power and innocence of heart to do so.

If there would have been any resistance to Adam's God given authority by any angelic officeholder the angel in question would have had the same judgment passed upon him as if he would have resisted the Lord God Himself. The act of rebellion against a king would have resulted in a Godly judgment with an immediate removal from office and expulsion from the heavens into hell.

The tree of the knowledge of good and evil, however, was in the garden, planted there by God Himself to stand as a free will choice. The tree had to be there as a witness and a testimony of the evil which the wicked conspirators had brought about in God's creation; as well as to offer Adam the opportunity to know of the evil and partake of it if he so desired. Remember, Adam was created innocent, but not without free will, and God had to respect Adam's God given right to choose and to know of everything there was to know of, including evil and the transgression.

God isn't about hiding anything that may appear to be unpleasant or unseemly, such as the satanic evil that was brought upon creation by prideful and lustful, power hungry angels. He isn't about concealing evil, or denying its existence. That would be lying, and God doesn't lie. But, like a loving Father He does want to protect His children from evil.

The hidden agenda

However, children can only be protected from hurt if they are obedient to their parent's instructions to stay away from harm. God had warned Adam that death would result from partaking of the fruit of the tree, but since He created Adam with free will there was no way for the Lord to stop Adam from eating of it if he so chose.

The tree had to be in the garden to offer Adam a choice to partake of things which didn't concern him in the least. It was also to be a witness unto man of the existence of the evil conspiracy, and of the transgressions which had taken place in the heavens; of the wickedness which was still sullying creation. The tree was a solemn witness of the very thing which had brought about darkness to all of creation.

THE BEAUTY OF THE TREE WAS ONLY "SIN" DEEP

Notice that in Genesis 3:6 the Bible states this tree was very beautiful and pleasant; its deceptive and alluring appearance is a picture of what is at the very heart of the satanic conspiracy: A false premise of self fulfillment through self effort.

The entire format and operation which the wicked conspirators developed is so seductively misleading. The lure of power, greed, self love, and self advancement over others at any cost is so very tempting and inviting. The actions an individual takes to increase the use of God's issued blessings to solely bless "self" with is extremely appealing, but such ways all lead to death for man as well as for angels. This tree needed to look as beautiful and as inviting as the deception it represented really was.

A LIFETIME SUPPLY OF FRUIT

> *"And out of the ground made the LORD God to grow every tree that is pleasant to the sight, and good for food; the tree of life also in the midst of the garden,...." Genesis 2:9*

The tree of life: This unique tree stood directly in the middle of the garden on the most prime property in existence in all of creation. It was the centerpiece of all Holiness, the heart of the garden's existence, and the very objective and destination of the way which the cherubs and flaming sword were later sent to guard. Any who would partake of its fruit were to live from its abundance and strength.

This most important of all trees was not the usual apple, orange, fig, or pear, rather, it was life itself, offering its blessings to those who would chose it. This tree was Torah; the Word of God given unto man through which he could live. It was in that sense God Himself, the focal point of all things and source of all blessing centered in the midst of the garden. It was God, the Word, the Spirit in living uncorrupted representation. That is why the fruit of this tree, and only of this tree, produced life. That is also the reason for its phenomenal location, importance, and power to uphold those who partook of it.

What kind of fruit does this tree bear? The fruits of the Spirit referred to in scripture. *(John 5:24, Philemon 2:16, Matthew 4:4, Luke 4:4, 1 John 1:1, Revelation 2:7)*

> *"Hope deferred maketh the heart sick: but [when] the desire cometh, [it is] a tree of life. Whoso despiseth the word shall be destroyed: but he that feareth the commandment shall be rewarded. The law of the wise [is] a fountain of life, to depart from the snares of death." Proverbs 13:12-14*

The words used in these previous verses: "Hope", "tree of life", "the word", the "commandment", and the "law" are all biblical synonyms for the Messiah, the Word of God, and to a lesser intent for Godly attributes.

Interestingly, the word "law" used in these verses is the Hebrew word "Torah" which means the "instruction" and it is referring to the Word of God, Jesus Himself. The "desire" that "cometh", spoken of in this case, is Messiah. His coming is a *"tree of life"* to those who have awaited Him.

Chapter thirteen

Go with the flow

THE FOUR GREAT RIVERS

Since the Lord God of all creation saw fit to interrupt the Genesis narrative with an unusually flowing geography lesson placed smack in the middle of the second chapter of Genesis it must be important! So, in order to show the proper respect due this curious current of information we will also interrupt our look at the narrative and dutifully dive into the Godly stream of thought.

The theologically minded may call this a look at God's ingenious method of hermeneutical studies, but not being theologically minded we'll just call it God's ways for us to read and understand the Word.

In Genesis 2:10-14 we read about a great river which flows through Eden into the garden where it branched off to form four other rivers that watered the land. This brings about a few interesting questions.

The first of which is: Why are these rivers so important to God and man that the Lord felt it necessary to interrupt the creation narrative in order to tell us so much about them? The second question is: Whoever saw one river splitting up into four rivers? Usually in nature, multiple smaller rivers or tributaries flow into and become one large river; but a single large river as a tributary for four others? What gives?

Well, to find the answer we need to realize that these rivers are also an explanation of how God does things, and how He reveals Himself through His Word. Remember, His Word is God, and as such, is alive and multidimensional, multileveled. In other words, it is full of life.

These four rivers come from the great river of life that flows from God's throne and becomes the four levels; the four spiritual streams of interpretation of the scriptures. This is why these unusual biblical rivers seem to defy nature by flowing out of the one large river rather than feeding into it.

This is also why they feature so prominently in the creation narrative. God is explaining the amazing ways He has given to understand His Words of scripture using these four great rivers of truth, which never contradict each other, as living examples. These rivers of interpretation always add to and bless one another with a more in-depth understanding of each other. These levels come with a multifaceted understanding only available through the blessing which each uniquely brings to the recipients. They each flow in order to add unto and strengthen the power of God's Word and will as it flows through the other three rivers.

Each waters the land with its own unique revelations of God. They flow throughout the scriptures from beginning to end; each revealing God's truth in its own distinct way; each adding insight and understanding which is found only in its particular currents. Their presence is what makes the Bible the living Word of God.

The names and meanings of the four rivers of the second chapter of Genesis are as follows:

The first river is Pison; it compasseth the whole land of Havilah, where there is gold. The meaning of Pison is "increase" or "overflowing".

The second river is Gihon; this compasseth the entire land of Ethiopia. Gihon means "bursting forth".

The third river is Hiddekel; it goes toward the east of Assyria. The word Hiddekel means "rapid"; as in the rapid flow of water down a river.

The forth river is Euphrates; its meaning is "fruitfulness", "to break forth".

These are the names and meanings of the four great rivers which represent the four flows of interpretation found in scripture.

Go with the flow

As an additional brief tidbit of corroborative knowledge to the existence of the four interpretational levels; in the biblical Hebrew there are even four different words that translate into "man" in English versions of the Bible.

These in their own right represent the flow of the four rivers, and they are: "Adam", "aish", "enosh", and "gever". Each of these individual words conveys a specific meaning or understanding to the original script which was meant to bring an added depth of knowledge to the Word. God has chosen each word to represent concepts of the four streams of interpretive wealth, and He uses them to reveal how issues which are important to man and his legal standing before God are affected.

These four names of man are used to describe mankind and his standing in ways that are spiritually important to a deeper understanding of God's scriptures. They are a part of the four currents of truth which have become hidden by time and tide.

To continue along the flow of the four rivers a bit further; the very Bible itself is actually a document which affects four very different groups of beings, and each of them very differently. It needs to be understood in that context as well; let's see how it does so:

First: It affects God and His relationship to the creation.

Second: It affects angels and their role in creation.

Third: It affects man and mankind's place within creation.

Fourth: It also affects the wicked beings and their activities within the creation.

Each of these four groups is tied to, and limited by, the Word's of God as expressed through scripture; and each views scripture from their own perspectives.

- God views His Word as the supreme and Holy Law of righteousness and love.
- The angels see His Word as something to be obeyed and carried out without question.

- Man sees His Word as a path to salvation and to right standing with God.
- The wicked see God's Word as something to be greatly feared and manipulated where possible for personal benefit.

Each has their own current of understanding arising from their relationship to the Word, and each is affected differently by the same scriptures.

Why, even the four seasons of the year bear witness to God's patterns in creation and scripture. Each of the four unique seasons brings forth elements and developments which compliment life and enable the processes inherent to the other three seasons to produce God's intended results. Each of these four seasons brings a different "face" to nature, and only by experiencing all four seaons can the natural world complete the cycle of the year. The four seasons are another reminder of the four streams of scriptural revelation.

A NEW TESTAMENT OCCURRENCE

Furthermore, to make sure that Christians don't segregate this issue to being merely an "Old Testament" occurrence, the Lord made sure to start the New Covenant with the four Gospels of Matthew, Mark, Luke, and John. These four books were meant to be a clear example and an open clue to the four rivers of God which flow straight through the scriptures into the "New Testament" as well.

These four books of the gospel were written on generally the same events from four different perspectives. Nowhere do they contradict each other, but when studied together they add to one another. Each shows a different level of interest in certain occurrences depending on what river they are representing; each bringing to light its respective stream of God.

The Lord wanted to make sure that the New Testament readers would be aware of His concepts, and the fact that His ways never change. However, mankind has managed to become what many would incorrectly describe as blissfully (and all too often blisterfully) ignorant of His concepts.

EVERY GARDEN NEEDS WATER

"[There is] a river, the streams whereof shall make glad the city of God, the holy [place] of the tabernacles of the most High." Psalms 46:5

Once again, the great river of God and its multiple streams are referenced in scripture. Only when they are revealed by God and become realized by man, and are seen for their beauty and life can they indeed bring gladness to the city of God and its inhabitants. His Spirit is the river of life, and its life; that which flows in it, is the pure current of God Himself.

The Jewish way of explaining the beautiful flow of the four rivers of God's Word is called "pardes". This is an acronym for the names and ways Jewish rabbis have historically had for describing and defining each of the four different streams or levels which the word pardes refers to.

Pardes, in Hebrew, means "garden", and it is a not so subtle reference to the garden of Eden through which the rivers flow. The term pardes is also the source of the English word "paradise", which is a synonym for the garden of Eden itself. Indeed, the word pardes is actually the basis for all paradisiacal words found to exist in every known language. These four rivers of truth were found to be flowing out of the garden, the paradise of God, and in a scriptural and spiritual context they are still flowing to bring us the life of God through the revelation of His Word by His Spirit.

To understand where the Hebrew word pardes comes from, we'll need to look at each of the four levels in question individually, and discover the meanings of their Hebrew names.

The first level is named "Pashat". It means "simple" or "literal", and it is the straightforward historical view of the written fact.

An example of this is: Did God really bring the children of Israel out of the slavery of Egypt and then lead them into the Promised Land? Of course He did. The Bible is quite clear on the matter, and the children of Israel aren't found in Egyptian slavery anymore. Are they?

The second level is named "Remez". Remez means "hint", "indicative", or "alluding to". It is the finding of parallels to what is written.

Such an example would be found in realizing that the slavery which the children of Israel experienced in Egypt was also an allusion to and a picture of the bondage of sin unto which all mankind was subject.

Another example would be found in Matthew 22:39 where it states: *"Love thy neighbour as thyself."* The question is: Does neighbor refer only to the person living directly next to you? Of course not, it means everyone we come into contact with, but we have to realize that ourselves. We must understand that the Bible in many places indicates that everyone is our neighbor and worthy of our love. This verse can well be read in that context as well.

The third level is named "D'rash". D'rash means "search"; it is the story or "parable" level. In D'rash one searches the scriptures or other complimentary sources for a fuller understanding of the verses or passages in question to enhance what is studied, read, or explained. D'rash is the word used unto this day to describe many rabbinic sermons or teachings which use stories and parables of other events from which a similar point can be taken or conclusion can be drawn in order to better strengthen or explain the original point.

Jesus Himself often used D'rash in His sermons. The fourth chapter of Mark is an example of this. So are most of Jesus' parables such as the story of the woman and the unjust judge in Luke 18:1-8.

The fourth level is named "Sod". Its meaning is "hidden" or "secret". It looks at the Bible as a book filled with prophesy, picture reference, types, and clandestine images. Basically one could say everything written in the Bible is, or carries, a hidden story in its words; a meaning behind the meaning.

Indeed, a great deal of the Book of Revelation is written with an eye toward this format being very much in evidence of use, as the Book of Revelation has the hidden "hard to understand" secret things foremost in its delivery.

Go with the flow

From the names of these four levels of interpretation: Pa(shat), R(emez), D(rash), and S(od), we get the term pardes. Together they are the rivers of Paradise.

Both Old and New Testaments are replete with references to four different functions, reactions, causes, or occurrences that represent these four rivers at work in some sense; such as Jesus' teaching in Mark chapter four about the sower who sowed the Word.

The seed of the Word fell into four distinct places: The wayside, stony ground, among thorns, and upon good ground. The location of the sowed seed brought about four vastly different results even though it was the same seed sown. Messiah then went on to further comment privately about this parable to His disciples saying that the simple explanation given to the general crowds was not nearly all there was to understand about His Words. Rather, the four results of the sown Word had yet further "hidden" meanings that were flowing through the parable, which He then explained to His disciples. These were the pardes rivers of interpretation at work. Please read the entire account found in the fourth chapter of the Book of Mark.

"THE MANY SOUNDS OF MANY WATERS"

> "And, behold, the glory of the God of Israel came from the way of the east: and his voice [was] like a noise of many waters: and the earth shined with his glory." Ezekiel 43:2

> "And his feet like unto fine brass, as if they burned in a furnace; and his voice as the sound of many waters." Revelation 1:15

The reason His voice is as the sound of many waters, outside of the obvious fact that it is beyond scale in magnitude and power echoing in unbounded might; is precisely because when He speaks, He speaks of many subjects simultaneously on many different levels of revelation and understanding; these are the many waters or streams of the voice of God found throughout the scriptures, the living waters of the Most High God.

The Genesis Mousetrap

The real heart of the issue, the true reason of why God went to the trouble of mentioning the four rivers in the middle of the creation narrative of Genesis is that He desires for everyone to know Him as well and as thoroughly as possible; by means of His Word and His Spirit which He has made accessible unto all those who will seek Him. Therefore He has made that information as richly available as He can in an effort to speak unto man as fully as possible and to bless mankind with God's own life, His Word. It would be a pity to read the Bible on only one level or in only one format and lose out on the truth which has been made readily available to all who would humbly seek Him.

A SECOND LOOK

Can we see an example of pardes at work in the Genesis narrative that we have been looking at? Of course we can.

However, just as the Most High interrupted the second chapter of Genesis with His explanation of the four great pardes rivers, so too must we also interrupt our look at the causes and effects of the darkening of the deep, and its ultimate end, to briefly look at the other Genesis currents of truth. These other flows of God's knowledge which shall be mentioned in no way contradict the creative stream that we have been and will again be looking at. Rather, each current adds to the richness of God's narrative and leads us into a deeper understanding of the Word as revealed in the Genesis account.

PASHAT

The first level is that of Pashat, the simple reading of the text. This stream of scriptural understanding is the most commonly used and well known of all. Many Sunday school students (and hopefully all Christians), will be familiar with the Pashat reading of the creation account.

Pashat acknowledges and moves in the infallibility of the literal meaning of scripture. It accepts the face value message of the Bible. For Example: God created the world in six days and rested on the seventh.

In Pashat, the creational activities which the Bible states took place unquestionably happened upon those seven individual creative twenty-four hour days just as they are written. Pashat seeks no interpretation to the written Word. Water was water; the earth was the earth; light was light; fish were fish; a day was a day; and Adam was Adam. It is so and amen.

Without the vital Pashat river of truth flowing forth from God's throne our understanding of scripture would be sorely limited, and all but void of understanding.

REMEZ

The second level is Remez, the allegorical reading of the text. Remez is the understanding of the indicative, the interpretational examination of metaphor and allegory as found in scripture.

In this particular stream of revelation which we shall be looking into, each creative day is representative of a one thousand year period of time as it is explained in Second Peter 3:8, and there it states, *"...that one day [is] with the Lord as a thousand years, and a thousand years as one day."*

This current, found flowing in the first chapter of Genesis, winds its way throughout the scriptures and can be called the Adamic week. From this perspective the Bible is giving us the details of the most important events that have occurred, or will occur, upon each day of the seven days spoken of in the creative/redemptive saga.

Each Genesis day was a chronologically ordered millennium of time representing mankind's Adamic duration upon the physical earth. It has the first Adam created on day one, and the Last Adam first appearing on day four and arriving to rule on day six when the creation of the first Adam is spoken of in the Pashat reading of the text.

Perhaps surprisingly, in this Remez reading of the text, the creation will not even be complete until the Millennial reign of Messiah begins at the start of the seventh day, the Sabbath; an event which has not yet begun! So, the Remez reading of the Genesis creation verses tells us that we are living in a day when the creation process is actually still "underway", and creation will remain "under development" until Adam is created on day six and blessed to rule creation. This indicates that Messiah (the last Adam) must arrive during the sixth day in order to usher in the perfection of His millennial kindom which shall rule the Sabbath day of rest and complete creation.

LIGHT FROM DARKNESS

The following is an example of reading in Remez:

On day one the Lord created light and He then divided it from the darkness, thereby creating day and night.

In the first one thousand year timespan of man's existence upon the earth what great event transpired? Mankind was created! Adam was made by God to be in His image. Adam was the Godly light of the world separated from the darkness which had until that point in time been the prevalent state of existence upon the earth.

On this day God also divided the two opposing elements of light (Adam), and of darkness (the shadow of satan), giving light the authority to displace darkness wherever the light was present. Adam (the light) had that displacing and overruling power because he was made in God's image, after all.

This first one thousand year timespan also saw another huge event take place in the realm of man; the further division of light from darkness. Adam's progeny (mankind) was essentially split into two groups: Those of darkness, the children of Cain with their likeminded Sethian counterparts in one group, and those of light in the other: these were the remnant of the faithful children of Seth, the ones who were the lights of righteousness upon the earth. It's a division of light from darkness.

WATER, WATER.... EVERYWHERE?

On day two God created a firmament in the midst of the waters, and separated the waters from the waters.

During the second millennia of man's existence, the flood of Noah, without question the biggest event of that particular "day" of the week occurred; it immersed the earth in the great waters, and equally importantly, the "firmament", the dry land was able to once again come forth and appear as the waters receded.

God caused the firmament to divide the waters that were under it from the waters that were over it. This was done to reapply His original will and format unto the structure of the earth, as the Noahcial flood saw the *"fountains of the deep"* opened and temporarily merged into one with the water from the opened *"windows of heaven"*. So, a separation needed to take place to reinstate the division of the waters. (*Genesis 7:11*)

This need to reapply the separation of the waters during the second day may also stem from the fact that the angels who inappropriately came to earth during the time prior to Noah's flood were those who had "mixed the waters" (the heavens) together by entering the abode of man, and they needed to be removed and separated from man before they could harm God's creation further than they had. Order needed to be restored; the "firmament" divider was set and reset between the two groups; angels and man. The angels were in this manner those of the waters from *"the windows of heaven"*, the upper waters which mingled and mixed with the waters from the *"fountains of the deep"*, the daughters of men. God ended such sin and contamination of creation during this second day event and brought the cleansed firmament forth unto Noah and his children.

ONE...TWO...TREE?

On day three, the waters were gathered together unto one place in what appears to be a seeming contradiction to the command decree of the previous day. It also saw the establishment of vegetation, the trees and shrubs, upon the earth.

On the third Adamic day of creation what great events do we witness? We see the waters coming together unto one place. Water is often biblically portrayed as a cleanser and as a blessing. All blessing (water) coming together into one place is explained in the fact that in this third millennia God found the man Abraham, the father of faith; the man He was able to call His friend. (*James 2:23*)

This Abraham was the sole person blessed of God to inherit the promises and the blessings of Adam, including the Messianic promise. All the water (blessing) that was issued unto man came together into one place (unto Abraham) in this way. That is why all those who are of faith are called the children of Abraham unto this day; the waters (the blessings) are still found in that one location, upon Abraham and his seed. (*Galatians 3:6-9*)

The trees and the shrubs which were created on this third day are biblically representative of the nations and also, but less applicably, of individuals from those nations. The green olive tree is Israel; the cedar is Lebanon; the tribe of Ephraim is likened to a fir tree; and the king of Babylon was called a great tree, etc.

Not coincidentally, it was precisely during the third millennia of man's existence upon the earth that the nations of the world began to form, grow, and mature into unique entities and cultures throughout the earth!

Most historians will recognize the fact that the early kingdoms, the first great nations of man, flowered in the centuries prior to, and specifically after, 2000 B.C. These "trees" came to the fore of human existence in the third Adamic day! Amazing!

The great old nations of the past: Israel, Egypt, Babylon, Persia, Assyria, the Indus valley civilization, the Chinese civilization, Greece, etc., all "formed" in strength and grew to a mature state during the time of this third day, as the seventy nations of the post-Babel dispersion formed, strengthened, split, reformed and finally developed into peoples, nations, kingdoms, and states.

In this third day blessing of the flora, God strengthened and allowed the "seventy nations" of man to legally exist upon the earth as separate entities for as long as man was to dwell upon the earth. Hence the term used in this "third day" verse, *"whose seed was in itself"*. Each nation was to be self perpetuating in population, culture, and ethnicity, each was to be unique among the others upon the earth.

LIGHTS AND NIGHTS

On day four God created the lights in the heavens to divide the day from the night; to be signs, to give light upon the earth. On this day He made the greater light to rule the day, and the lesser light to rule the night. And as scripture says, *"He made the stars also."*

The latter end of the fourth Adamic day saw the birth of Jesus the Messiah, *"the light of the world" (John 9:5)*.

Messiah came to divide those of the day (holiness), from those of the night (sin). Messiah and His followers were the spoken of signs given unto man. Messiah is the great light which rules the day; He was that which came forth during the latter moments of the fourth millennial day, and the corporate body of repentant believers in Him is the lesser light, that which rules the night. *(Matthew 5:14)*

Remember, night occurs only in the absence of day (in the absence of the sun), and the moon (the body of believers), which is decreed to rule the night has no light of its own. It only illuminates the earth when it receives and reflects the light of the sun (Messiah); how much light the moon shines onto the earth is dependent on how much sun can shine upon the moon. If the moon (the body of believers) allows the earth (the things of this world such as sin, etc.) to come between it and the sun (Messiah) then the moon cannot properly illuminate the earth as it was meant to, as the things of the earth were able to block out righteousness.

Almost as an afterthought the Bible states in this sixteenth verse that: Oh yeah, *"He made the stars also."* The existence of the angelic host, the stars, is not really central to the context focused on here, for the angelic are not the main agents of grace or of the gospel of Messiah unto man. This age of grace has the Holy Spirit witnessing of Messiah to man by man. It is the Adamic week after all.

DAY FIVE, THOSE OF THE WATER AND SKY COME ALIVE

On day five the Lord had the waters bring forth abundantly, "the moving creatures which have life". Also, on this day the fowl were decreed to fly above the earth in the heaven.

The fifth millennia of man saw the abundant spread of the truth of God in the gospel of Messiah Jesus preached throughout the world. This, in turn, caused the waters, the blessings of God which were previously all brought together into one place (upon Abraham and His seed the Messiah King of Israel), to bring forth an abundance of "fish". Fish being those obedient to God; they are the ones *"that hath life"*, as these verses say. That life is the redemptive resurrection life of God in Messiah.

The Genesis Mousetrap

These verses in Genesis state that the fish, and indeed, all aquatic life, were in myriad size and form from the smallest minnow to the greatest whale, and actually there is so much variety in the marine world that one species is almost unrecognizable to another. Nevertheless, the waters (God's blessings unto man as found in the Son of man, Jesus) brought forth these fish abundantly.

There is a telling significance to the wide variety and vast array of marine life found in the waters of God specifically spoken of in these verses. In their many apparent differences may lie a possible inability of the aquatic creatures (the believers) to distinguish one another as "fish", that is, as native inhabitants of God's blessings in Messiah.

These minnows, whales, salmon, et al. well represent the vast variety of different people who are believers and sanctified in the Lordship of Messiah: Unfortunately, one person who is a believer may not recognize another person who is also a believer due to their differences in dress, custom, manner, cultural tenets of religion, denominational doctrine, beliefs, and general understanding of Torah, which all serve to separate the multitude of believers one from another to the point that the great whale may not even see the little minnow swimming by its side. Similarly, the minnow may not realize that the "wall" it swims next to is actually a living creature, a whale, living in the waters of God just as the minnow itself is. Nor could the bass in a small pond envision a great school of cod swimming vast distances in the depths of the mighty ocean to be fish just as it is itself.

Yet, regardless of the believers' inabilities to recognize or conceive of each other as "fish", it is nonetheless the waters of God which *"bring forth abundantly"* and maintain those *"that hath life"*, and not the other way around.

Now for the fowl: Compared to the fish, these birds are a very different sort of animal. The Bible in Genesis 1:20-22 appears to treat the creation of fowl as an additional, supplementary, or even consequential fact to the commentary on the creation of fish spoken of first in each of these fifth day verses. Noticeably, however, it seems to purposely mix the mentioning of the two throughout the fifth day commentary.

However, the emphasis and importance of this day lies clearly on the creation of marine life, as the fish come first in every verse. The fowl almost seem to be considered as an antithetical afterthought to the creation of the fish, almost as if they were a leftover result, and in this level of Torah learning that is exactly what they are.

The fish are the saved and holy, but the fowl, those who reject the grace of God in Messiah, in this fifth day and beyond, come about as a result of their personal rejection of, and opposition to, the last Adam.

The spreading of the gospel, the creation of the fish (saving of souls), comes with a polarizing effect in that fowl are of necessity created on the very same day in which the same gospel message is heard and received by the fish. There are always those who accept grace and those who reject it; the fish and the fowl. Both were blessed of God (authorized) to bring forth abundantly after their kind (to exist and grow in number), and they still do.

The wrestling for souls to be in one camp or the other has never been more intense: May the fish bring forth in great abundance unto the Lord, amen. God declared that this separation and stark division among the children of man in this age of grace was "good". No soft middle; no compromising masses; no lukewarmity wanted.

Strikingly, Genesis 1:20 notes that the fowl (opposers) were created to fly above the earth in the open firmament; not to be of the earth. The fowl are to be in the "landscape", but not of it; this, even though it is the earth which brings forth these likeminded compatriots to the wicked angelic conspirators.

That is an important fact to note, as the earth and that which is of it were to be for the last Adam, Jesus, and for Him alone. No opposition can lay legal claim to it; or to anything belonging to the last Adam, the King Messiah. God therefore decreed the fowl (opposers of Messiah) to be created for the earth "realm", but not for the earth.

ADAM & CO.

On day six God first created the beasts of the earth, and then lastly, man. Man was made in His image, given dominion and blessed of God.

The sixth Adamic day saw the creation of the beasts of the field, and of that life which is of the earth. The beasts, etc. are representations of the third group of people which exist; the fish being the saved, the fowl the unsaved resisting element; and the beasts? They are the wishy-washy indecisive middle; neither open and accepting of the gospel, nor immediately rejecting and resisting of it. Their focus is on the things of this natural world, they are neither committed to God nor are they purposely evil.

It is over these massive herds of indecisive cattle that the battle rages: It is for the souls of these unsaved that both the fish of the sea and the fowl of the air contend. The population explosion of this sixth millennia has been, and is, unprecedented in scope. It is in this time, more than in any other, that the believer has the duty and incredible honor to be able to lead the vast assortment of these beasts of the field, the great herds of unsaved humanity, unto the waters of God so that they may drink of living waters and be saved from death in this now dry and dusty land.

The beasts need to be led to the Wellspring lest they fall by the way and become consumed by the ever ravenous fowl of the air.

It is also on this last creative work day that the earth was finally able to see and receive the one who was meant to rule over it: Man; Adam. The son of God was created and blessed to have dominion over creation on the sixth day. (*Luke 3:38*)

The end of the sixth millennia; in whose evening hours we now find ourselves, is the time in which the last Adam, Messiah, will come to rule and reign as the King of creation. At that time, *"every eye shall see Him";* just as creation witnessed the arrival of the first Adam at the beginning of man's journey along the redemptive plan of God. (*Revelation 1:7*)

This Lord of Glory who was first known as *"the light of the world"* on the fourth Adamic day when the sun was set to shine upon the earth will permanently arrive as the King of creation, as the Lord of Lords, in the closing moments of the sixth day to rule and reign over the Kingdom prepared for Him by His Father.

Go with the flow

This coming of the last Adam, the Messiah of Israel, is the last creative work of God prophesied, explained, and broadcast through the Genesis creation account of the first Adam. It is upon His arrival that His bride (the saved and faithful of all generations) shall also be brought forth and blessed to rule with Him; just as Eve was brought forth from Adam and blessed.

There is yet another reason why the beasts appear upon the sixth day, the same day that the last Adam comes to rule. It is precisely upon the coming of Messiah that He will judge between the different beasts, the sheep and goat nations; between those He accepts into His reign and those He does not. This sixth day has and will have witnessed the creation of myriad varieties of earthly man in all possible ways: ethnically, culturally, socially, mentally, and spiritually; but in the end Messiah will divide mankind into only one of two groups. Making a clear distinction between those who have been kind to His people here upon the earth (those are the sheep nations), and those who have not been kind to His own (the goats). (*Matthew 25:32-46*)

SHABBAT SHALOM

On day seven, God ended His work and then blessed and sanctified the day in which He rested.

The seventh millennia; the seventh Adamic day, will be the time of the millennial reign of the King Messiah, the last Adam. It will be a one thousand year time of rest, as creation will have been complete and sanctified through the rule of its King.

Thanks to a Remez reading of the creation narrative text we are able to gain a deeper understanding of the events taking place within the scriptures as we uncover the Adamic week. Each day of creation has alluded to the important events occurring in its corresponding counterpart within the seven thousand year grant of man.

D'RASH

The third level is D'rash. D'rash is defined as the "story" or "parable" format of interpretation. As an example of a Genesis creation D'rash: Dr. Gerald L. Schroeder has written and lectured extensively on the first chapter of Genesis using a scientific viewpoint to add a unique insight into the biblical narrative.

Dr. Schroeder expounds upon the physical beginnings of the creation using the knowledge available to man through scientific study. He does so in a fascinating manner totally compatible with, and complimentary to, the words of scripture. Dr. Shroeder uses the understanding available through both an accrued scientific knowledge of nature as well as the study of the spiritual physics of the universe to explain biblical creation beneficially to not only the student of the scriptural narrative, but to all who are interested in the accurately presented beginnings of our creation. He uses and unlocks the story of the physical creation itself to compliment and explain the information found in the Genesis narrative.

Incidentally, this is a great opportunity to illustrate the interaction of the four rivers. Dr. Schroeder's work draws heavily from the Sod level of interpretation to give us further insight into the straightforward P'shat reading of the creation text. A Schroeder D'rash is worth listening to.

SOD

Oh, and the fourth level? Sod, the "secret" or "hidden" level of scripture: An example of Sod can be seen in what has been previously touched upon in our look at creation in the preceding chapters, and what shall again be returned to in the next chapters: The darkening of the deep, the division of the heavens, the hidden reasons for the creation of man; the first Adam, the last Adam, Eve, the coming eighth day, leviathan, and so forth.

Now, although our look at creation is largely in the Sod level all interpretational rivers are present to some degree in order to advance the flow of information in an orderly manner. The rivers are all complimentary to each other, after all.

In this short while, we have attempted to quickly glimpse at the beauty of the four Torah rivers of Pardes as they make their way through the creation account and increase our understanding of God's amazing Word and creation.

Each river of God which comes to water the garden branches off from the main river, the Holy Spirit, containing the Torah Word itself. They

Go with the flow

complimentarily flow forth benefiting all creation with the wisdom, knowledge, and power unique to each individual river, never contradicting or crossing over each other in any way. Rivers never do cross each other; do they?

The Genesis Mousetrap

Chapter fourteen

Back to the creative stream of thought

SOMETHING FISHY HERE

Genesis 2:18-20 seems to be re-describing or even rehashing the events surrounding the creation of the animals corresponding to the narrative of Genesis 1:20-25, and it is; but a closer look at these two accounts will reveal some interesting things which are not readily apparent at first glance.

First of all, the simple reading of the second chapter of Genesis, verses 2:18-20 in particular, seems to imply that man was created before the animals; contrary to what the account in the first chapter of Genesis clearly states. Also, the second chapter doesn't mention the creation of marine life such as fish at all.

What is going on here? There seems to be a glaring inconsistency in the creation narrative which should never have occurred, especially right in the very next chapter.

Obviously there are no contradictions or inconsistencies; rather, the Bible is using these different orders and formats found in the first and second chapters to emphasize and point out important spiritual details in its amazingly resourceful manner.

First, it needs to be remembered that God dwells outside of time and as such, He set about creating this universe with Adam's creation foremost in mind, and in so doing, He recognized the need His yet to be created Adam had for company upon the earth and prepared the natural animals to be his companions even before Adam himself was made.

The Genesis Mousetrap

This explains the phraseology found in Genesis 2:18. The Lord God already had the yet to be created Adam in mind when He first created the animals which He intended to present unto Adam. It seems only logical that the house (creation) would be prepared with the occupant (Adam) in mind, and that it would be fully completed and furnished before he arrives. That completion and furnishing included the creation of the animals which Adam was to name.

Second, we need to see what else the creation of animals by God, and the later naming of them by Adam may refer to in a prophetic or spiritual sense; which in this instance alludes to the creation and formal establishing of the offices and authorities of the angelic host and the preparation of the place of those authorities.

As well, it refers to the placement of the angelic host into their offices in this triune universe as creation was finally prepared into a state where the offices previously blessed and bestowed unto the angelic could actually be implemented. As the Word of God in this creation became tangible the angelic were able to inherit the promises of God made unto them from before the creation of the physical earth.

For those who may wonder about the scriptural use of animals to picture or represent the angels (or men for that matter): the Bible is full of instances where the angelic, as well as people (and even the Lord Himself), are pictured as certain specific animal types that best characterize the being or the authority which the being represents. Such is the case here in this reading of Genesis 2.

Examples of this type of pictoral imagery are found in the following:

- Jesus being called the Lamb of God. (*John 1:29*)
- Jesus being called the Lion of Judah. (*Revelation 5:5*)
- satan referred to as the serpent, *"more subtil than any beast of the field"*. (*Genesis 3:1*)
- The Pharaoh of Egypt is called *"the great dragon"*. (*Ezekiel 29:3*)
- Herod was referred to as a fox by Jesus. (Luke 13:31-32)
- The verse of Isaiah 30:6 speaks of the burden of the "beasts" of the south.
- Daniel chapters 7 and 8 speak a great deal of the nations and of their angel princes as being an assorted variety of beasts.

THE THREE PICTURES OF OBEDIENCE

Furthermore, as we can quickly notice after reading through the first chapter of Genesis, as well as through other passages of scripture; the Bible divides the animal world into three distinct groups:

- The fowl of the air
- The beasts of the field
- The fish of the sea

These three groups in essence represent the three levels of legal obedience and adherence to the will of God as found among the sons of God in a spiritual context.

So, the instance in Genesis 2:19 where the beasts and the fowl were brought before Adam to see if any among them could prove to be a proper "help meet" for him, and also for them all to be named by him, is not merely referring to Adam coming to realize after intensive scrutiny and many long drawn-out interviews with the critters, that the beasts and fowl wouldn't make great employees or co-regents. Therefore Adam in his resulting frustration with them started calling them all manner of strange names. No.... rather, the beasts and the fowl were in this descriptive sense the angelic beings which had offices of authority in this universe, in this physical creation; and as such, they were the most likely candidates in creation to assist Adam in his kingly role.

These angels were all brought before Adam by the issuer of their anointings; the One in whose authority they served, and that, of course, is none other than God. In being presented to Adam they were also being introduced and brought into the service of Adam by God. As Adam was now the king to whom they would all need to be obedient in the matters that related to this universe which were given over to Adam's care.

It is precisely in the naming of the beasts and the fowl that Adam first began assigning tasks and limitations to the different beings which were brought under his authority; naming or assigning tasks to them which best suited each being individually. For in the Jewish/Hebrew/biblical way of thinking, the name is all important as it describes, denotes, and characterizes the individual or thing named.

Notice, that God brought unto Adam the beings to be named; He did not name them Himself. Undoubtedly, God already had fine names to call everything He created, but as a king, Adam had all rights in his domain to do as he saw fit. That included naming those brought before him and/or modifying or specifying their behavior, and assigning guidelines for their tasks. This was to be equally true of Adam's authority over the angelic beings in his domain as it was of the natural animals therein.

Now about the marine life, the fish, and their peculiar absence from the narrative given in the second chapter: First of all, we need to remember that the underlying theme in the second chapter is slightly different from the underlying theme in the first.

The first chapter speaks of creation, its establishment, and the reason for it, which was to remove the angelic conspiracy; while the undercurrent of the second chapter, as previously mentioned, draws our attention more toward Adam's role in the creation around him. It also alludes to the entry of the angelic into their respective offices in this universe and speaks of their subsequent submission to the Adamic kingship, their "naming". This also brings us to Adam's realization of the unsuitability of these beings to be a help meet for him.

So, the first chapter speaks of God's creative works; while the second familiarizes man and angel to Adam's unique role in his surroundings within that creation.

However, the unusually absent fish were not mentioned in the second chapter for the following reasons:

First, we need to realize that the fish biblically symbolize the obedient of God; those who are righteous before Him, and as such, these fish were not seeking to be "in" the garden on earth with Adam. Rather, they were dutifully functioning in the areas of their own offices. In essence, such righteous angels were already helping Adam by functioning in willing obedience to God in the places of authority they had received from the Almighty.

Back to the creative stream of thought

Second, Angels were not created to be solely of our triune universe or to have kingly authority here. So, the ones that were willing to be considered by Adam for the function of help meet, the ones that would willingly or eagerly partake of the Adamic anointing of kingship were already those who were living outside of the perfect will that God had for them. These were the beasts and the fowl. Such angels were willing to push the bounds of legality and authority in the pursuit of self interest.

This explains the need for Adam to "name" them, to define and/or restrict their roles in his domain. While the fish (obedient angels) weren't "named" by Adam in this instance because they were already functioning in the perfect will of God in voluntary willing obedience, with no need of further role definition, or naming, required.

Put simply, the fish weren't out to get Adam's job, those beings who were couldn't have been described as fish. Genesis 3:1 bears this fact out saying, *"Now the serpent was more subtil than any beast of the field which the LORD God had made."* Notice the use of the term *"more subtil"*, "more" is a purposefully comparative word. The serpent was more subtil than the other beasts who were less subtil than he, but accordingly, still subtil, a characteristic that is not of Godly origin in this context.

Also, notice that the serpent was not said to be more subtil than the fish, as the fish were not considered to be subtil at all in this matter since they were not seeking improper authorities or ways to access such authorities for themselves. Therefore the serpent was specifically called *"more subtil than any beast of the field"*.

THERE'S SOMETHING FISHY ABOUT ADAM

Moreover, it could be said that Adam himself was the fish not directly mentioned in the second chapter, as he was the only obedient one, the only "fish" that was found to be present on the earth. Adam was the only being which was able to fulfill his specific role on the "land" (in Rakia) while remaining in God's will. So, Adam was himself a fish in this perspective. Adam was the only being authorized to operate in his unique anointings and to have a physical presence in Rakia.

Any beings other than Adam which were willing to be considered for the role of help meet and to be named could not have been "fish". For fish (the obedient), first of all, didn't need naming (further role definition), and secondly, as we know, do not live on "land" (in Rakia) in the first place.

Actually, Adam's unique rights to this physical creation, the heaven of Rakia and the garden, which were his "lands" rather than the upper waters or heavens where angelic authority was based, is precisely what made him a fish in this unusual context. So, in a sense, the fish were mentioned, albeit clandestinely, in the second chapter of Genesis when it speaks of Adam himself.

JACOB'S UNUSUAL BLESSING

A further illustration of this point can be found in Genesis 48:16 where Jacob is blessing the two sons of Joseph who he had taken for his own.

The Judaica Press Complete Tanach translation is used here as it brings forth the intent found in the original Hebrew particularly well.

> *"may the angel who redeemed me from all harm bless the youths, and may they be called by my name and the name of my fathers, Abraham and Isaac, and may they multiply abundantly like fish, in the midst of the land."* Judaica Press Complete Tanach translation, *Breishit (GENESIS) 48:16*

Jacob prayed that the angel would bless the lads to multiply, *"like fish, in the midst of the land."* What an unusual blessing! To be a fish in the midst of the land would seem so out of place on the surface of things (pardon the pun).

But, it is in the very words of this blessing given by Jacob that clarity is found. Jacob stated that he was redeemed from all harm, which means he himself was brought out of the place of troubles by the angel; caught out of it like a "fish", as it were. Redeemed from troubles, and saved from experiencing them due to his lineage and faith.

In claiming the two lads as his own Jacob was bestowing unto them the same blessings that were given unto him and his fathers by God, the blessing of that first unique fish, Adam.

Back to the creative stream of thought

The sons of Jacob were to be removed from the place of troubles brought upon creation by the fall of man and they were to be placed on the "land" where only those blessed by God to dwell could function naturally.

Did not God also bless Adam originally to be fruitful, and to multiply? Well, here we have Jacob blessing the lads to *"multiply abundantly like fish, in the midst of the land"*. God was restoring the Adamic blessing unto the heirs of Israel.

It is commonly known that natural fish do not multiply very well on land; in fact, they do not even survive long on land. So, it is in the context of willful obedience, redemption, and in the subsequently restored blessing of Adam upon the children of Jacob that being a fish on land is considered to be not only logical, but desirable. It is a restoration of mankind to its natural place of abode.

Sadly, many translators couldn't understand the reasons for Jacob's use of the words, *"like fish, in the midst of the land."* in this seemingly unusual blessing, so they moderated and changed his words in their translations to make them appear more logical. Perhaps they were worried that if anyone read Jacob's true words they might think him a bit odd, or perhaps they felt that there was something a little "fishy" going on here!

ON A SIDE NOTE

On a side note, the returning of people unto God, and the subsequent reauthorization of the blessings of God in the lives of those individuals is precisely what is referred to in scripture as the catching of fish. In Matthew 4:19 Jesus Himself said the following unto Peter and Andrew: *"Follow me, and I will make you fishers of men."*

What takes place when fish are caught? They are brought to land! It is only when errant individuals are caught up from the great "sea" of wayward humanity and are subsequently brought out onto the "land of promise" which God initially intended for them to reside on, that these unusual fish called people, which were originally created to be native to the "land" are returned to their natural habitat in the will of God through salvation.

Alright, back to our subject. In order to be a help meet unto Adam a being had to be a fish. That meant one had to be in one's natural element in regards to Adamic authorities and offices of blessing, which in turn severely limited the legal options available in the choice of candidates to that of Adam alone.

THE EVE OF EVE

The unsuitability of any of the other beings to be a practical help meet, that is, to be a full partaker of his blessings of life became evident to Adam himself as he finished naming them, but questions remain to be asked about why God chose this particular course of action to begin the journey of mankind, so they will now be asked....

Why did God create only one Adam in the first place? The Lord could have created both Adam and Eve together originally; or he could have created untold billions of people simultaneously. So, why did the Lord choose to create only one man originally?

It must be understood that Adam was created to be a king in an independent kingdom; and there can be only one absolute king ruling in authority in one kingdom at a time. Adam's creation and grant of authority having occurred before the formation of Eve ensured that while the authority of man was shared by both equally the rights of kingship were kept securely upon Adam. For Eve had a special job to do which, as we shall see, required her to be without independently bestowed kingly authority.

Furthermore, the simultaneous creation of untold billions of people with independent total authority could not have accomplished anything more than unnecessary anarchy. There needed to be order. And order starts with the crowning of one king.

Looking at the fact that man was made in the image of the One God, it is also fitting that mankind was created as one to comply with that image perfectly.

Add to the previously mentioned reasons the fact that it was absolutely necessary for Adam, as a God appointed king, to come to the conclusion on his own that he needed a being to share authority with. He had to realize on his own that he needed someone to whom he could bestow authority, someone who would legally be able to act as king in all things in Adam's stead. Adam as king had to decide he needed a help meet on his own. God could not insist upon it and delegate Adamic authority once it had been issued without the consent of Adam, or even fully with his consent had Adam chosen a being incapable of doing the job. That is to say, if Adam had chosen a being lacking the given ability to reign, something which a then righteous Adam would never do.

EVE HAD TO BE OF ADAM

The only one fit for the job that Adam was to find in his search through all of creation was the one being which was essentially.... himself. Or rather, a being that was even more Adam than Adam himself was; for Adam was made from the dust of the earth, but Eve was made from Adam.

Hence Adam used the term: *"bone of my bones, and flesh of my flesh"* to describe her. Eve was the very core, the full essence of everything Adam was created to be. She was the very bone of bone, the flesh of flesh itself, and as such, there was no question as to her status or right of authority to stand in Adamic office. Only such a being that was so integrally Adam could be legally accepted by Adam to share his authority; as only a being created to be a king can fittingly rule as a king.

Please notice God's work in creation was otherwise completed at this time. His instructions were given, and Adam's necessary ground work in "naming" the animals was finished. All was finally prepared for the arrival of the one called Eve.

Why was it necessary for Adam to have named the animals before the arrival of Eve? Beyond the previously stated reasons, it was to leave the authority of establishing and/or defining the roles of the animals and specifically of the angelic host which they illustratively represent in the personal charge of Adam.

Eve was to have rule over the creation and the authority to enforce existing law; but not the right to further alter it. That responsibility was to rest solely upon Adam personally, as the specific rights of this particular first Adam were those that Messiah, and Messiah alone, was to inherit.

The Genesis Mousetrap

With the entry of Eve into the creation narrative, the plan God had initiated for the removal of the satanic conspirators really starts to come together. It's clear from scripture that Eve's creation took place late on the same day that Adam's did, that being the sixth day of creation, and that she was present to receive God's blessings. (*Genesis 1:27-28*)

ABILITY AND AUTHORITY

In these blessings we see a very good example of a being's ability and authority. We read that God created Adam and Eve; male and female; but this fact alone did not give them the authority to create life after their own kind, or to multiply. It gave them the ability to physically multiply, but not the authority. The angels, for example, have the same ability, but they don't have the authority; the authority to use their ability was specifically given to Adam and Eve by God in His blessing of them, and it's in that specific blessing where their authorization to *"Be fruitful, and multiply"* comes from.

Also, this blessing of Adam and Eve is often thought to be limited strictly to the reproductive sense, but that is far from accurate. It also meant that they were to cause everything in their care, in their dominion, to become full of abundance and blessings, and they were to ensure that everything blessed would then further spread those blessings into creation to benefit creation as a whole.

Let's take a look at one specific thing God intended in the blessings He gave unto Adam and Eve which many people are confused by in the reading of the King James, and that is the term *"replenish the earth"* as found in Genesis 1:28.

This command of blessing does not mean that the physical earth was at one time inhabited, then became desolate, and was to be filled again with people and/or other living things, nor does the Hebrew word used even carry the meaning "replenish". In Hebrew, the word used for "replenish" is "maleh" which means "to fill", or to a lesser extent "to satisfy". So, Adam and Eve were not to replenish anything, but rather they were to "satisfy" the earth by "filling" it with God's will and blessings.

Back to the creative stream of thought

That is to say, they were to bring light into an otherwise dark place and satisfy creation's need for God's holiness and blessings by enforcing His will and restricting wickedness. Since the darkening of the deep first occurred the creation had longed for, craved, and needed God's presence, righteousness, and life. Adam and Eve were to begin the process of restoring holiness back unto the creation robbed of purity by the evil ones. They were to be God's active partners in the "tikkun olam", in the repair and restoration of creation.

The point which needs to be emphasized here is that the blessings which God gave and gives unto any are not to be taken only one dimensionally, as in the procreative sense in this blessing. It also needs to be further understood that Adam and Eve were to be the guardians of, and conduits for, all the blessings found in the will of God for that portion of His creation given to their charge. They were to ensure that all things in their dominion were to be able to receive their intended blessings and function properly in them. In so doing, they were to bring about the successful institution and expansion of God's will in all things entrusted to their care.

As God's representatives, it was Adam's and Eve's duty to oversee the abundant and blessed operation of this creation at every level, and to ensure that every good thing in their charge would multiply and fill the earth. It was their assignment to expand the garden of Eden in all of its attributes to fill the whole earth, to make the kingdom which God had given unto man, with all its blessings, fill the entire earth. They were made in His image; in His own likeness; and they were the only visible look at God this natural world would seemingly ever behold.

It's very much the same with the situation of believers in the world today: in that the only glimpse most other people will see of God on this earth is in the believer; in the life and actions of those who love God. It's a walk of awesome responsibility which few take seriously.

BROUGHT FORTH

It could be said that Eve was the last to be created. In a way that is true; but we have to remember that Eve wasn't really a separate creation at all, as she was originally created in Adam as a part of him. She was then found by God in Adam, taken out of Adam, and then formed.

Eve really didn't have an independent creative event, but rather a time of being brought forth. This is evidenced by the fact that God did not breathe His Spirit into her nostrils as He did to Adam because she already had received His Spirit through her being in Adam when God breathed into him.

This bringing forth of Eve is very similar to the way God found this earth, this universe, in the heavenly waters. This triune universe was also originally a part of a greater unified body; the unified heavens. God then took the triune heavens out, dividing them from the other heavens; and He then made this separate universe to be an instrument of blessing to all the heavens and the creation within them through its unique ability to ensnare satan. In that same way, Eve was also brought forth from Adam to be a unique blessing unto all creation (by the way satan was to be ensnared through her).

The similarity also exists in the fact that as this universe was originally a part of the other heavens; divided for a time, and then will be rejoined and reunited with the other heavens; Eve was also originally part of Adam, separated for a time from him, and was then brought back to Adam to be joined with him in the unity of marriage.

> "And the rib, which the Lord God had taken from man, made He a woman, and brought her unto the man." Genesis 2:22

We can see from this scripture that it was God Himself who brought Eve back unto Adam, so that God's original intent would be done as He never changes. His will happened when He created them originally as one Adam, and He is actually obligated to Himself to ensure that His original intent is always carried out so that His Word is fulfilled.

So, although God separated them and it looked like His original plan was changed, and as such, found to be imperfect; hence needing modification at the time He brought Eve out from Adam, being true to His Word God brought them back together in a way that would bring a far greater blessing to His creation than what was first seen as possible

Back to the creative stream of thought

in Adam alone. Not just in the sense of expanding the number of guardians of the garden through procreation, but through Eve, the process for the entrapment, judgment, removal, and destruction of the evil ones was made possible, as we shall soon discover.

As we have seen, the Lord made Adam and Eve to be one flesh; and although they were separated for a short time, God brought them back together to be one flesh, and like this temporarily divided universe, Eve was going to play a very important role in the trapping of satan and in his coming to final judgment. An event the heavens have long awaited.

There is a very interesting prophetic picture found in Eve as well. She was the only living being to be created or brought forth inside of the perfect garden. All plants, animals, and even Adam himself were created outside of the garden or before the garden was planted upon the earth.

Everything else was created as a light brought forth to shine in darkness. However, Eve, the bride of Adam, who was called the son of God, was the only one specifically created or brought forth into the paradise of God. She was as a light brought forth into light, never having known the evil existing outside of the garden.

How was Eve brought forth into the garden?

> *"And the Lord God caused a deep sleep to fall upon Adam, and he slept: and He took one of his ribs, and closed up the flesh instead thereof"* Genesis 2: 21

This preceding verse is an illustrative picture which alludes to an event other than to itself. It is to show that the Son of God, the last Adam, Messiah Jesus, who like Adam, in sinless perfection ruled His kingdom, also fell into a "deep sleep"; that of death. He also similarly had His side opened like Adam as he was pierced upon the cross. Jesus had His side opened for the sake of His bride to come, much as Adam's side was opened for his, and from His piercing came forth blood and water; a birthing occurrence.

In this way, Jesus brought forth into God's perfect kingdom through His deep sleep, His death, a bride that never was affected by the wicked corruption of the creation found outside of the holy garden, a bride without spot or blemish.

Eve thusly, is the picture of the bride of Messiah born into holiness through God's redemptive work; who from her "birth" will never have known the evils of the wickedness found outside of the place God has prepared for her. (*Ephesians 5:27; 1:4, 2 Corinthians 11:2, Revelation 21:2; 21:9-10*)

> *"Thus the heavens and the earth were finished, and all the host of them." Genesis 2:1*

Chapter fifteen

The Genesis Mousetrap

THE TRAP GOING OFF

Now we have all the elements in place for the Lord God to begin setting His first hooks into the jaws of leviathan (satan). (*Job 41:1-2*)

The Lord had created a separate universe consisting of three heavens. He made this universe to be affected by and limited by time. He planted a most perfect garden in the earth, and chose to remove Himself from the everyday rule and protection of this creation. He then gave the dominion and responsibility of all this creation to man; a triune being with all procreative authority in the Rakia heaven; a being made in His image. He would conveniently only visit Adam in "the cool of the evening"; leaving Adam to be otherwise "unsupervised" by God. He also made sure that the angelic host, including the wicked angels, had free and easy access to Adam through their offices of authority in the triune heavens.

This was the most perfect set of circumstances that satan could have imagined. satan must have been elated with the prospect of being one of the highest ranking angels in all the heavens, and now he seemingly had so much opportunity to attempt the removal of God's anointed king from these heavens. This was an ideal situation for satan to silence the voice of God in this creation as spoken by man.

The shadowy cherub was also interested in the possibility of gaining a new or increased right to establish and increase the effects of the transgression in the Rakia and Shechakim heavens. Why, if he could accomplish this, he really would move closer to his goal of being like God in all ways; but how could he do it?

The Genesis Mousetrap

This was such a prize; such a great trophy, that the wicked, lustful satan simply could not leave it alone. He had to attempt to get man to either enter into his wicked conspiracy and bring his great anointings with him into the satanic transgression, or he needed to otherwise cause man to sin against God and loose his office and right to "meddle" in angelic affairs; but how could satan accomplish this? How could he do it? How?

The Lord God arranged for that as well. He had left in Adam's domain the tree of the knowledge of good and evil; a tool which satan could use in his attempt to silence the voice of God as spoken through man. It was just too good and convenient for satan to pass up using the fruit of the tree as bait, but little did he know that when Eve and Adam were to swallow the fruit, it was satan who was to receive the hooks in his jaws.

A DAY IN THE GARDEN

> *"Now the serpent was more subtil than any beast of the field which the Lord God had made. And he said unto the woman, Yea, hath God said, Ye shall not eat of every tree in the garden?" Genesis 3:1*

The serpent in question is clearly not an ordinary snake who happened to be an unusually inquisitive fellow with a penchant for theological conversation. No, this serpent was satan; milling about his business in the offices he held in this creation, making sure that everything was going "as it should" in the areas of his authority. He was working hard to make sure God's will was being done AS POORLY AS POSSIBLE, AND AS TWISTEDLY AS ONLY HE COULD DO IT!

As an angelic officeholder who had not yet committed a crime worthy of chains or hell, satan had every right to be in the garden.... and actually, he had an obligation to be there. Eve would have thought nothing of it. In fact, the serpent would have had a presence in the garden which predated Eve's own individual existence. Since the angels who held authorities of offices in this creation were a regular feature in the garden, nothing was out of place or unusual about their presence there.

Why, they even had a need to come and get direction from the one who had rights of dominion over all the physical creation, Adam; and one fine day (they were all fine days back then), the serpent was milling about....

What? You still have trouble believing that the serpent was satan himself? Let's take a fresh look at what the scriptures say about the subject. (*Matthew 23:33, Isaiah 27:1, Revelation 12:3-4; 12:7; 12:9; 12:13-17; 13:2-4; 20:2*)

The fact is that once the wicked and perverse angels decided to turn to their great deception their spiritual forms warped to represent the nature of their true hearts. They literally changed from being beautiful and majestic sons of God, into being totally twisted creatures fully consumed in their own lusts and desires, wicking into all manner of strange and unseemly beings.

Each individual twisted into the type of perverted being which best represented its own personal quest for power and desires; the nature of their hearts was revealed in the form of their beings.

The serpent or dragon, therefore, is a common biblical description for the angel once called Lucifer. He gained this appearance after his satanic conversion as it most suited his cunning, deceptive, and aloof nature. The permanent anointings, abilities, and authorities which these wicked angels hold, having been perverted by the angels themselves, evidenced the selfish change which their hearts experienced in the transformation of their spirits. The lusts of their hearts manifest themselves in their spiritual bodies in ways that are as grotesquely deviated from God's original will as they themselves now are, causing them to become unrecognizable from their original selves in both actions and appearances.

Actually, the perversional manifestation of the evil ones' desires appears to be in an antithetical lockstep with their original anointings which have been fiendishly warped by these wicked beings themselves. In other words, the individual wicked angels each pervert the use and purpose of their own personal blessings to be totally opposite to that of God's original intent for them.

The cherub angel of life, holiness, and light once known as Lucifer, became the angel of death and darkness. The angel assigned to strengthen others became one who now attempts to weaken others; the angel which was to be of faith became one which promotes fear; the angel sent forth to ensure plenteous supply became the spirit of lack, etc.

Furthermore, these deviant spirits are, as previously mentioned, always unsuccessful in everything they do; this is best exemplified in the loss of their original God given beauty.

For example: The spirit of cancer, while it may appear successful in finding a place, a body, to reside in and in bringing bondage to the person attacked; actually ends up killing the body which it finds to inhabit. The unsuccessful spirit actually makes itself homeless again by becoming successful in its purpose. As it seeks to strengthen its grip on the body in question it destroys its own habitation.

The spirit of famine, should it find a location to reside in, ends up impoverishing and destroying the place where it seeks to stay and thrive. It is therefore unsuccessful in its attempt to rule an area, for the spirit itself causes destruction to the places it resides.

The spirit of lust cannot ever be satiated as it always wants; and the more it consumes, the more it desires for things it cannot possess; it just cannot be satisfied. That is the epitomy of unsuccessful existence. The evil ones are caught in a hell of their own making even before they are sentenced to the place itself. The wicked can't win for trying.

HARD AT WORK

So, one fine day the serpent was milling about the garden doing his chores, while always seeking an opportunity to bring others into sin against God which causes them to lose their blessing of life, the unique presence of the Holy Spirit which we have read about in previous chapters. Or better yet, if he could get them to enter into outright rebellion they would be eternally removed from office and unable to resist the conspiracy.

This then leaves the wicked angels an opportunity to enlarge their areas of authority by attempting to fill the vacuum of power left in an office by a being that had broken communion with God.

The Genesis Mousetrap

The "industrious" serpent saw an opportunity to pose a seemingly innocent question to Eve; a little question that he hoped would lead to a loss of blessings by Eve. Everything the wicked one does is cloaked in a seeming innocence; the covering angel is very skilled at covering the wickedness in everything he does. No one would entertain the slightest thought of listening to him if he was open about his destructive plans for them and for all of creation.

The serpent came and asked Eve, *"hath God said"?* This is the one phrase each and every person is asked by the wicked ones in regard to God's Words: "Has God really said that? Could God really have meant that? How could God have said such a thing? Does He even exist? If He doesn't exist then how could He have said anything?" etc. etc.

The wicked angels come in their deceptive innocence to sow seeds of doubt into the lives of others, and also to gauge what kind of a response is given to see if there is any weakness in the answer which they can work with in order to cause that weakness in the authority of another to grow into some type of sin. The Word of God is the basis of all creation as well as the basis for all authority, blessing, and life; so the evil ones constantly need to attack the source of the power of others by causing them to begin doubting, then denying, and then defying the source and authority of their power: the Word of God.

Eve dutifully answered the inquisitive serpent by saying the following:

> *"We may eat of the fruit of the trees of the garden, but of the fruit of the tree which is in the midst of the garden, God hath said, Ye shall not eat of it, neither shall ye touch it, lest ye die."* Genesis 3:2-3

Now this answer was really something that the serpent was looking for. Eve responded by misquoting the Word of God with vagueness in her reply. First of all, she was leaving confusion or misunderstanding in her answer which incorrectly located the tree of the knowledge of good and evil in the "midst" of the garden, and by stating that man was not to eat of the tree which was located in the "midst" of it.

However, the Bible clearly says that the tree of life was the one in the midst of the garden, and not the tree of the knowledge of good and evil.

The Genesis Mousetrap

Actually, the Bible never mentions the location of the tree of the knowledge of good and evil, other than to say that it was located somewhere in the garden. Eve nonetheless places the tree of knowledge in the midst or middle of the garden using the same term for the location of this troublesome tree as the scriptures use for the tree of life; and as we know, two trees cannot occupy the same space at the same time.

Eve then further misquoted the Lord by saying, *"Ye shall not eat of it, NEITHER SHALL YE TOUCH IT, LEST YE DIE."* (emphasis mine). The Bible makes no reference anywhere to the fact that God said, *"neither shall ye touch it."*

Where did Eve come up with the fact that touching the tree was prohibited by God? Well, it appears that Eve wasn't yet formed when God told Adam not to eat of the tree. So either Adam changed the Word of God by misquoting His instructions to Eve (perhaps Adam was overly zealous, or too cautious about the matter; and out of well intentioned caution added His own comments to the warning given by God), or Eve added the change of her own accord. In either case, there was never a biblical prohibition denying man the right to touch the tree, although it was, indeed, prohibited to partake of or eat of its fruit.

Another thing that Eve changed in her answer was she said, *"lest ye die."* God had clearly said, *"thou shalt surely die."* Eve's answer left just a slight hint of uncertainty and ambiguity to the fact that death was, indeed, a guaranteed result of eating the fruit. Eve meant no harm to God, or to His Word in these little changes; but the consequences of these misquotes were to have staggering implications for all of creation.

So, Eve unfortunately morphed God's Word from saying, *"thou shalt surely die."* Into, *"neither shall ye touch it, lest ye die."* These facts in her answer left the serpent wiggle room to continue the corruption of God's Word that Eve, and/or Adam, had innocently begun without intending to compromise the truth. This is a serious lesson for all of us not to change, alter, soften, or purposely misquote the Word of God in any way; for any reason at all. The results of doing so, as we can all now see, can be most severe and the impacts can still be felt to this day. (*Deuteronomy 12:32, Revelation 22:19*)

The Genesis Mousetrap

"And the serpent said unto the woman, Ye shall not surely die:" Genesis 3:4

The seemingly innocent serpent with his, "let me get this straight just so I can understand the rules and will of God a little better" question of, "did God really say that?" had an answer all ready himself. What a surprise! How convenient! satan will always willingly provide the answers to the seemingly innocent questions he asks. Well, if he knows the answer why did he bother to ask the question? Precisely so that he can give a misleading answer himself; one which perverts the truth and leads the intended target into fear and doubt. satan responded with his prepared comment, *"Ye shall not surely die."*

Or to paraphrase him, "Eve, my dear friend, sister, trust me, you won't die if you eat the fruit. I happen to know better than you and God; I'm a snake after all. I slither through the trees all day and get a real close look at all the trees and their fruits. I should know what trees are the best for you to eat of." Here's a charming fellow who is so eager to make the lives of others better that he provides both the question and the answer, just to make things easy for you. That's satan, always thinking of others (and what he can get from them).

Did you notice that while Eve misquoted God for whatever reason when she used the term *"lest ye die"* the serpent actually quoted Him correctly in this matter? Since satan was already in existence when God commanded Adam about the tree, and he was obviously paying astute attention to any new legal decrees which were issued by God, the serpent was able to accurately state God's Word correctly while he was lying about it. Quite amazing isn't it?

"And the serpent said unto the woman, Ye shall not surely die", he used God's phrase of *"surely die"* which he heard spoken unto Adam in order to make his lie sound all the more credible and believable. Being the spiritual legalist that he is, satan knows scripture inside and out. Like all good lawyers he needs to know the laws that he is working with. Only he always endeavors to change or twist the terminology or intent of the Word in an attempt to disarm the very Word he uses, as there is no truth in him. (*John 8:44)*

The Genesis Mousetrap

It's also important to realize that the serpent was in full control of this conversation from the beginning. It's very typical of the evil one to try and dominate everything he can; his mode of operation is always one of attempting to seize control of whatever he can, wherever he is. Put simply, the manipulator seeks to manipulate everything.

In his conversation with Eve, satan started out questioning the intent of God's Word by asking, "did God say?" Then he went on to tell her, "Oh, God's Word can't be trusted to be accurate." Then he goes further and essentially says in Genesis 3:5, "Well, yea, God said it, but He had a jealous motive for saying it, and for keeping you from the fruit, so you shouldn't obey His Word even if He did say it because there's no benefit for you in obedience."

> *"For God doth know that in the day ye eat thereof, then your eyes shall be opened, and ye shall be as gods, knowing good, and evil." Genesis 3:5*

The actual Hebrew word used in this previous verse for "gods" is the word "Elohim", and while it may be used as an indicative word for gods in general; it is also a name of the One true God in particular. Therefore this verse can, and should, be read as, "and ye shall be as God, knowing good, and evil." The right to be like God is what satan had always been after for himself. It's the enticement that he used to bring the wicked conspirators into the transgression, and it is that same incentive which satan used in his controversial conversation with Eve.

This, actually, is an unusual verse of scripture in that the entire verse consists exclusively of a direct quote of the serpent himself (The Bible is quoting satan?!).

Being the perpetual opportunist that he is, and as the father of lies, satan knows more than anyone else how important it is to have an element of truth in all deceit in order to make it all the more believable. Therefore when he said, "ye shall be as God, knowing good, and evil." he was absolutely correct in that portion of his statement.

Man was created pure and innocent without any knowledge of the great evils which the satanic conspirators had been up to. Whereas God

The Genesis Mousetrap

knew of their evil very well; He saw the destruction that the wicked satanic conspiracy was continually trying to perpetuate upon His creation. He knew the evil that the holy angels had to war against continually to defend their anointings, offices, and His will. Whereas Adam was removed and oblivious to all of that unseemly activity in an oasis of God called the garden, having a complete say as to its operation and function.

Man didn't know if things were good because he didn't have evil to compare things to. For in Adam's domain, even the wicked angels had to obey his every will and couldn't freely manifest the twisting of their authorities which they had been able to do outside of the garden and in the other heavens. The wicked were in bondage to man's authority as God had intended, and God didn't want His son Adam to taste the same evil that He Himself had known in His Kingdom.

So, in that regard, satan was right; God didn't want Adam and Eve to know and experience the hardship of evil which He and the righteous in His kingdom were dealing with. The truth is that due to the effects of the satanic transgression in and upon God's Kingdom, knowledge of what was good unfortunately came with an unwanted knowledge of evil.

SATAN DIDN'T DARE EAT THE FRUIT HIMSELF

As we have seen, satan is an effective misrepresenter of the truth. He constantly works through schemes of manipulation; being the serpent that he is, twisting is the only thing he can do in his attempts to propel himself forward. He twists the Word to cause others to sin while he avoids commiting rebellious sin himself.

If the fruit was so amazing why didn't the serpent go to eat the fruit? No, no! He had already known both good and evil, and it sure didn't make him as God. No, he was goading Eve into doing it, he needed her to sin, he needed her to break fellowship with God.

satan himself wouldn't dare do anything to blatantly sin against God in such an openly rebellious manner with no hope of success coming from it. As a knowledgeable legalist satan knows better. He knows that by openly breaking God's laws, all any being gets is a sure way to an unpleasant judgment and sentence into hell. He'll always attempt to

The Genesis Mousetrap

manipulate others into sin while he himself will go before the Judge of all Creation and accuse them of breaking God's laws, which they may well do; but at satanic instigation and prodding.

The following is a hypothetical example of satan the accuser explaining the events surrounding Eve and the fruit to the Almighty:

"LOOK, GOD! LOOK! Did you see Eve, Sir? She ate the fruit! Punish her! Punish her! What? Me? Oh, no, Sir! I haven't done anything wrong, Sir. No... It was Eve. She ate it! I was an eyewitness, Sir. I just happened to be in the garden devotedly tending to my duties when I saw it all happen Sir; and I've dutifully come to report the terrible crime. I just knew you'd want to know about it, Sir. Could I suggest you burn her in hell forever, Sir? It seems a fitting punishment; and I really think she deserves it. And may I add that I think she may have even gone back to the tree for seconds." (Just a little humor there, folks.)

Seriously though, Adam's and Eve's eyes were, indeed, opened to evil, and they came to know what good was as well. The only problem was that since they became partakers of evil and death, they lost access to the goodness and life that they had in their kingdom.

BEHIND THE SCENES

Eve, in her biblically recorded conversation with the serpent, came to a very surprising conclusion. She actually came to believe that the serpent was correct about things. She bought into the idea that God wanted to keep her ignorant; that He wasn't looking out for her best interests, and that He was trying to hide good things from her. She came to "realize" that she had to begin looking after her own welfare. As such a God could not be trusted to take care of her since He was greedily trying to keep information and power for Himself and away from mankind.

Eve believed this seemingly petty God was not fit to have the final say in matters that would affect her and her life. That although He created and blessed her, and made mankind in His own image; the one essential thing which she really thought she needed was the one thing God had lovingly kept from her. Eve believed that the only thing missing from her life was for her to have the knowledge of good and evil; then she would truly be of God's likeness and be able to exist on a more Godlike level.

It was at this point that Eve, believing satan's lies, rebelled against the Lord God who created, and blessed her, and anointed her with glory and honor. Eve chose to become a stranger to the presence of God's love, and as she ate of the fruit, she died to the blessing of life. She chose to no longer be the conduit, or vessel, through which God's blessings and Spirit could flow into this creation. Instead, she attempted to partake of things which were not in her authority.

THE FIRST REBELLION

In this sequence of events Eve found her way into and actually joined the satanic conspiracy and chose to become an enemy of God. She really thought that He was being a greedy old scrooge; and she would outsmart Him and bring herself up to a more "appropriate" position of power.

She began to think as the wicked angels thought. She began to behave and operate as they did, and do the same works that they did; trying to elevate herself into a higher state of power at the expense of God's Word and love.

Notably, it was Eve, and not a wicked angel, who actually became the first being in the biblical narrative to enter into an open rebellion against the Lord God. There may have been, and most likely were, a number of wicked angels that rebelled openly against the Lord prior to her. Remember, rebellion is an action done in a way that would lead to total death and subsequent removal from God's creation, and an endless sojourn in the infernal regions. So, there may have been offending angels guilty of such deeds in times prior to Eve's actions; but there is no mention of these in the scriptural record. Therefore, our dear foremother Eve gets the regretful distinction of being the first to enter into open rebellion against the Lord.

Keep in mind that the wicked conspirators, being the adept legalists they were, kept a tight reign on their own actions not wanting to lose the rights to their own offices of authority by causing an open breach of rebellion in their own walk; knowing that God's sure judgment would await any who do so.

> *"And when the woman saw that the tree was good for food, and that it was pleasant to the eyes, and a tree to be desired to make one wise, she took of the fruit thereof, and did eat, and gave also unto her husband with her; and he did eat." Genesis 3:6*

Eve's actions were caused by the beliefs of her heart, of her spirit, and as the words of doubt and animosity which the serpent was able to plant in her heart began to grow and replace God's Word therein, Eve began to desire the undesirable. And because she allowed such thoughts to grow into fruition they were able to produce the fruit of rebellion against God. Eve believed the beguiling words which the serpent had spoken to her, and the result was her death; the separation of Eve from all things pertaining to the blessing of life and of things belonging to the Holy Spirit of God. Her spiritual separation, her death away from God, took place in the very same instant she chose to sin.

> *"But of the tree of the knowledge of good and evil, thou shalt not eat of it: for in the day that thou eatest thereof thou shalt surely die." Genesis 2:17*

Yes, Adam ate of the fruit; and yes, Adam died as well. But, with all that being said, there was nevertheless a huge and marked difference between what Eve did in eating the fruit, and in what Adam did when he ate of it.

Eve believed satan. She accepted the serpent's words as being more truthful than God's. She allowed herself to be deceived into believing God's Words and action's were evil; and thus, she entered into the satanic transgression in her attempts of self promotion through illicit consumption of arboreal produce. Whereas Adam had another reason entirely......

> *"But I fear, lest by any means, as the serpent beguiled Eve through his subtilty, so your minds should be corrupted from the simplicity that is in Christ." 2 Corinthians 11:3*

The Genesis Mousetrap

Notice that scripture makes no mention of the fact that Adam was "beguiled" into sin as Eve was. This detail is extremely important for us to realize as it was essential to the redemptive plan of God, and the repercussions of this one fact were meant to carry into all the heavens. For it was a vital difference between the actions of the two people; one necessary for the ensnaring of satan. Since the kingship rested with Adam, and not with Eve, and due to the fact that Adam and Eve were one body under the law of covenant; Eve's full entry into the transgression against God was not final without Adam's consent; a consent which he never gave. This is why it was so important that Eve was the one who chose to transgress, and not Adam, or both of them.

Indeed, had Adam been the one to yield to the serpent's words and enter into the transgression, the fall of man would have been final and without room for repentance. However, it was not so in Eve's situation. This was all in the design of God, for the kingly authority rested solely upon Adam, and only through Adam did Eve partake of that authority; so if it had been Adam who ate of the fruit and partook of the wicked transgression, mankind would have certainly been lost. Conversely, in Eve's case, her transgression as one who had the right to access Adamic authority while not being the head of creation was exactly the perfect mechanism for ensnaring satan in a way that did not eternally doom man.

However, it did hook satan firmly into the affairs of man, and brought this leviathan into a situation which caused him to unknowingly enter the place of the "great sea" before the "sea" was even created; so that Isaiah 27:1 could eventually be fulfilled according to God's design.

> "...and he shall slay the dragon that [is] in the sea." Isaiah 27:1

What, exactly, is the "sea" being referred to? Sea, in this context; refers to the nations or people of the earth, and it is precisely in among the seas, that is to say, in the area of the progeny of nations or peoples that have descended from Adam and Eve that leviathan will finally be caught by God.

For other examples of seas being used to refer to nations or peoples, see the following: *Luke 17:25, Revelation 17:15; 13:1; 12:12; 17:5.*

The Genesis Mousetrap

This is one of the most important reasons that man was divided into two unique beings. Through the Adamic division the redemptive possibility of man lived on in Adam who wore the "crown" and didn't enter into the transgression; while Eve, whose authority was contingent upon Adam's, and therefore couldn't be lost by her actions, was God's perfect decoy to lure satan into entering into the realm of man through her falling victim to satan's deception without being able to turn over or lose the control of the kingdom, or of herself.

Furthermore, as made clear in Genesis 2:17-18, the prohibition of eating of the fruit of the tree of good and evil was specifically given unto Adam prior to the creation of Eve. This fact is the basis for death being able to separate Eve from the Lord, while allowing Adam the right to "reclaim" her from death as long as he, the king, the one to whom both the authority of office and the prohibition were given, had not died in the sin of rebellion himself.

> "And Adam was not deceived, but the woman being deceived was in the transgression." Timothy 2:14

WITH AUTHORITY COMES RESPONSIBILITY

Why then did Adam partake of the fruit since he didn't believe the lies of the serpent and didn't suspect God of petty jealousy or some other greedy behavior? Well, as previously stated, Adam was the head of all creation. He was responsible for everything that took place in his domain. No matter what happened, it was his job to set everything into alignment with the Word of God. Regardless of what took place, he had to make things righteous in his kingdom; it was a part of his mandate of dominion. That also included the placing of all things into submission to Adam's will and the bringing into bondage of all things outside of God's will. This also meant any sin or improper action taken by any beings in this creation, including those of Eve and the serpent.

With authority comes responsibility; and the office of king came with a great responsibility. Add to these previously mentioned issues the fact that Adam and Eve were *"one flesh"*, as stated in Genesis 2:23-24. This is more than just a cute phrase created by Torah marketing professionals hired by Moses to increase sales of scripture; it meant they were, indeed, legally one, according to the original intent and will of God Himself. Eve had died away from God, and being one with her, Adam had no choice but to die as well.

ADAM HAD TO DIE!

Adam had to die! That's right. Adam HAD to die. Half of "one" does not make a whole. A half cannot survive on its own. With half of Adam already dead, the other half legally and practically could not live. He wasn't whole, and God's law, His nature, His very will itself, is for everything to operate as a whole, for all to function in "shalom". Not divided in pieces, shattered, or torn apart. The Hebrew word for "whole" is "shalom". It means: nothing lacking; a wholeness; peace.

So, first of all, the oneness of God and Eve was broken through her sins. This fact required Adam's actions as the living part of Eve to repair the breach. Second, the oneness of Adam and Eve was broken as Eve entered into spiritual death, which is separation from God, through her transgression. This left Adam considerably less than whole; and wholeness was a state he needed to be in for him to continue to comply with God's fundamental laws and intent. Again, Adam could not survive with half of him alive and the other half dead.

The previously mentioned law of covenant was strongly at work here. For as the being totally covenanted with Eve into oneness, Adam was fully responsible to make amends unto God for her breach of their covenant against Him. A price had to be paid for Eve's transgression against the Adamic covenant with God, restitution had to be made; Adam had to pay, for he was the only one who could.

Adam needed to make restitution unto God for Eve's transgression which he was, indeed, able to do as a righteous king and a husband. He was responsible for Eve according to the laws of God, in more ways than one, and only the shedding of the sinless blood of the righteous in a substitutional sacrificial death could accomplish the redemptive return of the wicked whose own lifeblood flowed tainted by sin.

In other words: Eve needed to have a blood transfusion; righteous sacrifice, when coupled with the personal repentance of the wicked, can and will lead to the washing away of sin. This fact is not only Godly law;

it is an obligatory way for covenanted members to maintain one another in good standing when a breach has been made by one against others.

Therefore, Adam had to die. That's right, Adam had to die to carry out and fulfill his kingly and covenantal mandate to pay for Eve's sin. She was his responsibility; a part of Adam, as well as a part of his kingdom; and Adam had to pay the price of returning Eve to good standing. If she was ever to receive God's mercy, she had to have a way of being brought back into wholeness and peace with God. She needed atonement.

Adam had to die; but he chose to act in disobedience. Adam ignored the established procedures of God and incorrectly sacrificed himself with the consumption of the same fruit Eve ate of. He chose to die in the same manner and context that she did, and that is spiritually; separating himself from the life of God and the innocence of the kingdom God gave him.

Adam should have chosen to die physically to bring about the redemption of Eve and of the physical world that Eve in her sin cursed by allowing the works of the wicked angelic transgression to enter into the physical realm unchecked through the subjugation of her authority to the deceptions of the serpent. Instead, Adam chose to disobey God's will and subjected himself to a spiritual death so that he could join with Eve in the darkness she was in. He did so rather than obediently shedding his blood and sacrificing physically to bring her out of the darkness to rejoin both himself and God in the unity of His light.

So, they both died away from the life of God, albeit for different reasons. And subsequently, they entered into the distorted world of the curse of evil where they became all too familiar with the satanic way of existing; which is the perverted manipulation of everything in one's life and sphere of influence in the futile hope of self advancement.

They received the knowledge of evil, however, by becoming partakers of it, they had no way to control it or subdue it anymore. In fact, the evil they came to know was attempting to constantly control them.

Adam's disobedience cost man and this creation the only apparent hope for restoration there was: his righteous sacrifice. What's more, through his disobedience, Adam left Eve's covenantal debt unpaid. Tellingly, Adam chose a spiritual death, such as Eve had partaken of, against the better knowledge he was privy to because the disobedient act was easier for him to carry out, but not because he wished to join the satanic transgression. Adam should have chosen the correct, but seemingly more unpleasant course of action, which was to die physically to atone for Eve's sin.

Eve thought the worst of God; and she joined into evil with the wicked conspiracy becoming the first recorded being to actually enter into outright rebellion against the Almighty in a needless and futile attempt to advance herself. Whereas Adam disobeyed the rules of governance and sought an easier way to comply with his mandate because he did not respect God or His Word the way he should have. But, Adam never sought to enter into outright rebellion.

This was the great difference between the actions of Adam and Eve in the case of the co-consumed fruit.

> "And almost all things are by the law purged with blood; and without shedding of blood is no remission." Hebrews 9:22

Eve's repentance; and Adam's physical death and blood sacrifice would have restored Eve into communion with God and allowed her to once again dwell in His presence. Also, since Adam would have been sinless at the time of his physical sacrifice, death would have had no legal power over him to keep him in its grip. Adam's body could not have stayed dead under any circumstances. Adam's blood atonement would have been more like a blood transfusion for Eve; and Eve's spiritual sin of rebellion manifested in the physical partaking of the fruit would have been physically atoned for by the substitutional shedding of righteous blood.

Only through that manner of sacrifice could Adam have reclaimed man's total dominance in the garden and in the physical creation, and ended the satanic corruption of his kingdom and of the earth which Eve allowed to enter through her newfound knowledge of evil. Instead, now there were two spiritually corrupt and sinful people rather than none, and no one was left to carry out God's will in this creation. This was the act and result of Adam's disobedience toward the instruction of God.

"For as by one man's disobedience many were made sinners, so by the obedience of one shall many be made righteous."
Romans 5:19

THE DIFFERENCE BETWEEN THE TWO

As we have seen, disobedience is very different from rebellion. Adam did not think evil of the Lord and attempt to subvert His will. Instead, Adam did what he had to do according to his responsibility of office and authority, however, he did it incorrectly.

Adam did not give the Word of God the proper respect it deserves; nor did he value the contact and unity he had with God. Adam had stepped out of love; he didn't hold fast to the will of God on this issue. Rather, he took the apparently easy way of incorrect compliance with the Word which totally changed the outcome of events from one that could have brought about reconciliation, to one that instead brought about the seeming loss of mankind and the heavens he was put in control of.

The Lord Himself spoke of the outcome of such tepid behavior when He was warning the church of Laodicea in Revelation 3:16:

"So then because thou art lukewarm, and neither cold nor hot, I will spue thee out of my mouth." Revelation 3:16

Unfortunately, Adam chose to be lukewarm about God and His Word, and lost his kingdom and his life as a consequence. The very cold satan was seemingly able to step into this lukewarm man's rights and spoil his blessings; and Adam was spued out of the holiness of God. The only thing which remained hot about Adam was the proverbial water he found himself in! (Pardon the pun.) (*Leviticus 19:2, Numbers 15:40*)

Now, let's be fully clear on the issue. It wasn't Eve's greater and much more serious sin of entering into the satanic transgression that brought about the fall of man, it was Adam's seemingly lesser offense; the sin of disobedience. Despite the fact that Eve committed her sin first and that it was a much more grievous offense; it was Adam's sin which brought about the fall as the responsibility of the kingdom ultimately rested upon him.

The Genesis Mousetrap

Although it appeared to be terrible, and indeed it was; and its effects still are, but Eve's entry into the transgression wasn't an unchangeable or an absolute result as long as she had a redeemer in Adam; but Adam neglected his duty.

As incredible as it may seem; this fall of man brought on by the separate, specific, and shockingly necessary acts of both people in the garden was God's plan from the beginning; for if the Adamic kingdom was ever to bring about the defeat of satan, it had to be done in a way that would bring about the total destruction of the wicked conspiracy by entrapping it into sin and rebellion through its involvement with mankind and through man's seeming submission to it.

The redemption process needed mankind to act both transgresively (Eve), and disobediently (Adam), in order to ensnare leviathan, and not just to give satan a slap on the twisted angelic wrist which Adam's obedience would have accomplished through his correct sacrifice for Eve.

Such Adamic compliance would have at best brought about the return of creation back into its original Adamic structure. No, a beast like leviathan was to require Adamic hooks set so firmly into its jaws that it couldn't possibly twist its way loose through legal maneuvering, and the placing of those hooks had to be done with such skill and wisdom that leviathan wouldn't even realize he was hooked until it was too late.

This serpent's cunning was to require God's detachment, Eve's susceptibility, Adam's disobedience, and a whole lot of patience by God and His servants in the family of man to complete its capture, judgment, and removal from the heavens. Unbeknownst to Adam or Eve, their apparent failings were needed to bring about the ultimate fall of the satanic conspirators.

Adam's incorrect sacrifice committed in disobedience was necessary to bring satan yet deeper into man's domain through the events initiated by Eve. These brought leviathan to a place where God would be able to outsmart the subtil beast, and outmaneuver the careful serpent, so that the last Adam would then be able to deliver the deathblow to God's enemies.

The Genesis Mousetrap

BACKTRACKING

Now, before moving on, let's briefly backtrack to the second chapter of Genesis which speaks of the creation of Eve. Doing so will give us the opportunity to glean more information from the biblical account on the state of things.

Concerning the arrival of Eve, the Bible makes the following two statements:

> "And Adam said, This [is] now bone of my bones, and flesh of my flesh: she shall be called Woman, because she was taken out of Man." Genesis 2:23

> "Therefore shall a man leave his father and his mother, and shall cleave unto his wife: and they shall be one flesh." Genesis 2:24

This last preceding verse seems quite poetic and even logical upon a quick superficial reading of the Bible. Many even find it to be among the most beautiful phrases found in the scriptures, but the clandestine strangeness of the location of this statement lies in the fact that Adam had no earthly father or mother to leave. He was the first man and he was alone on the planet. The reader of the biblical narrative may even wonder if this unique Adam knew what a father and mother was!

At best, this twenty fourth verse seems out of place. At worst, it seems to actually contradict the rest of the creation story with its hasty mention of man (Adam) needing to leave his parents. So, what is going on? Patience dear reader, patience....

The Bible also makes the following statements concerning the Godly design of life:

> "But I would have you know, that the head of every man is Christ; and the head of the woman [is] the man; and the head of Christ [is] God." 1 Corinthians 11:3

The Genesis Mousetrap

> *"For a man indeed ought not to cover [his] head, forasmuch as he is the image and glory of God: but the woman is the glory of the man. For the man is not of the woman; but the woman of the man. Neither was the man created for the woman; but the woman for the man." 1 Corinthians 11:7-9*

Man was made first. He was to be the head of woman; and woman was made for man, to be his help meet and friend. Yet Genesis 2:24 has man improbably cleaving unto woman. It does not have woman cleaving unto man for whom she was made; even though that would be the logical thing to expect. The fact that man (Adam) is the one who needs to be clinging, holding, bonding to, and staying with woman (Eve) seems quite bewildering when viewed in light of the other previously mentioned verses in the scriptural narrative which state that woman was made for man. A man she wasn't told to cling to! This odd fact is evidenced in another look at *Genesis 2:24*.

> *"Therefore shall a man leave his father and his mother, and shall cleave unto his wife: and they shall be one flesh." Genesis 2:24*

So, what is the Bible saying here? God was the parent of Adam. God was the Father which Adam had to leave in order to be with a wayward Eve. The Bible, in stating that Adam had to leave his parent (God) and cleave unto his wife (Eve) set the course of events, and laid the path for the servant of God (Adam) to follow.

If necessary, Adam was to emulate Eve and follow her at all costs through her dim journey into the depths of deception which started with the consumption of the forbidden fruit. Adam was to follow her into the darkness of a sin tainted existence in order to launch the events which would eventually draw satan into a place where the cloaking cherub would be forced to enter into outright rebellion in response to the actions that God was able to initiate through Adam's and Eve's wayward proximity to the serpentine angel.

This first man was to cleave unto his wife, even though she had willingly left God and entered into transgression. It was his duty to not let her go it alone. Adam was, in this way, under Godly instruction to follow his Eve wherever necessary; regardless of what she would do and how she would do it.

If there was ever to come a time when Eve and God went their separate ways, Adam was to follow Eve and cling to her even if this meant leaving His Father (God) in order to do it. The two were created one after all, and when God says one, He means one.

In these verses, God was preparing His creation and instructing His servant to bring the serpentine beast to trial; even if it meant ostensibly leaving Him to follow after the one who sinned in order to do it.

Actually, one of the Hebrew meanings for the word "cleave" found in Genesis 2:24 is: "to pursue closely"; so we can see that Adam was destined to pursue Eve closely regardless of where that journey would lead. However, this verse also ends with a promise: *"and they shall be one flesh."* God had a plan and a purpose to fulfill. Adam would be successful in his pursuit of Eve and together through their differing actions they would help in the humbling of the proud ones.

On a side note: This is also a wonderful prophesy of the way the last Adam would come to pursue His bride which had far travelled down the path of darkness into the valley of the shadow. The Son left the glory of His Father's might and came as a man to redeem the loved one He so clings to. The last Adam wouldn't let His bride go into the darkness of a sin tainted existence alone! Praise God!

EVE WAS NO ANGEL, THANKFULLY!

Alright, in all fairness; the following question may be asked: Why would Eve have had the opportunity to regain mercy after breaking the laws of God and entering into the satanic transgression, while the wicked angels were given no such opportunity for repentance?

First of all, Eve wasn't an actual partaker of the satanic covenant in the same manner as the wicked angels were. She was an independent transgressor, and she was beguiled into her sin of rebellion by the wicked without her full awareness of the issues involved. While contrastingly the wicked angels were voluntary participants in the satanic covenant with full prior knowledge of the conspiracy, and of the results of their own foul behaviors as partakers in it.

In other words, they bought into the transgression with a full understanding of things. Whereas the angelically exploited, cherubically beguiled Eve was not aware of all the facts and consequences involved in her actions; she had no prior knowledge of the evil she was entering into; hence the need to partake of the fruit.

Also, she was still fully covenanted by God to Adam, Genesis 2:22-24, who was not participatory in any conspiratorial efforts or acquiescent to Eve's partaking of them. Therefore, she was not bound to keep any such unrepentant covenantal agreements that she did not knowledgeably make, and indeed, could not make with others. Furthermore; since the information which lead to her actions came from a skewed and perverted source, Eve, though unable to claim any degree of innocence, was able to plead a measure of ignorance. That was something the wicked angels could not do. (*Genesis 3:13*)

Second, there are still some fundamental differences in both the spiritual structure of man (in this case Eve), and in that of the angels; as well as of the structure and location of their operational authorities.

Let's look at the locational and operational differences found between man and angels: The angels had unencumbered access to the presence of God where they stood in the direct knowledge of His will, majesty, and law. God was not hidden from them in any way. For such beings the use of faith in the issues of obedience is very limited. They can see, hear, and know the will and awesome power of the Most High constantly; so for them to deviate from His will, or for them to choose wickedness and perversion over holiness is totally purposed and without excuse.

Also, as they were based in heavenly offices which were under the direct control of God's Kingdom, angels did not have the liberty, authority, and independence of kingship that man had. So, for angelic beings to purposefully alter or ignore God's direct orders is blatant, willful sin.

Standing in the direct presence of God, the angels had absolute knowledge of what was Holy and what was sin, and in their absolute knowledge the wicked chose sin; being in an absolute state, once a choice is made, the choice itself is, and becomes absolute. The wicked don't want reconciliation with God even if they could get it.

Whereas man (in this case Eve in particular), was separated from God since the beginning by the fact that man was of this creation, purposefully removed from the upper heavens. Man was never in the throne room of the Most High and never stood in the awesome, heavenly physical presence of God. Man, from the first, had to operate in faith to a much higher degree than angels did, and needed to trust in the Word of God as expressed through His Spirit.

The following verse shows that the angels do, indeed, have direct access to God, and have the ability to walk in the full revelation of His will, whereas man did not have that opportunity.

> *"Take heed that ye despise not one of these little ones; for I say unto you, That in heaven their angels do always behold the face of my Father which is in heaven." Matthew 18:10*

So, the heavenly barrier to the absolute knowledge of God was one reason that Eve was offered the opportunity to regain grace which the angels did not have, or want to have. She knew His will and mandate, but was separated from the absolute knowledge of God, and that also included being separated from, and not knowing, good or evil.

Another perhaps more important reason specific to Eve was that although she did grievously sin in rebellion, and was therefore actually worthy of eternal separation from God; she was still one flesh with Adam: who, although disobedient, never rebelled against God.

Through that fact; and the fact that both Adam and Eve together were given the unique and exclusive joint blessing, the authority to procreate, and once the Word of God is given it cannot be rescinded; her blessings of authority were needed and vital to bring forth man's kinsman redeemer the Messiah to complete the will of the Lord in the redemption and cleansing of all creation.

For these reasons Eve was shown mercy, and specifically due to the fact that she held the necessary joint authority of procreation in the heaven of Rakia, an authority which could not be transferred away from her and given to another being.

> "...but the woman being deceived was in the transgression. Notwithstanding she shall be saved in childbearing, if they continue in faith and charity and holiness with sobriety." 1 Timothy 2:14-15

> "Neither was the man created for the woman; but the woman for the man. For this cause ought the woman to have power on [her] head because of the angels. Nevertheless neither is the man without the woman, neither the woman without the man, in the Lord." 1 Corinthians 11:9-11

God will never show undue favoritism to any of His children or use unfair weights and measures in dealing with them as He is never unjust. (*Proverbs 20:10*)

So as the preceding verses in 1 Timothy and 1 Corinthians explain Eve's right of return was due to her covenant and oneness with Adam, and the fact that she was functioning under authority established through his crown. This was a fair and legal pathway which God had pre-arranged for Eve to uniquely have. It gave her a way to come back unto God which the angels did not have.

Therefore it is stated, *"For this cause ought the woman to have power on [her] head because of the angels."* It was through Adam the wearer of the crown, and through the covenant Eve had with him, the holder of power, that she was kept from the devourer and allowed the possibility of return. As a tribute of respect for the plan of God, woman was to keep her head covered by power as a sign of her resumed submission unto the crown of mankind (as held by Adam the redeemer) for the sake of the angels who had no redeemer to allow them back into God's grace. Thankfully, Eve was no angel!

Lastly, but most significantly; Eve, Adam, and all of mankind, were uniquely created to be the servants of God in the great endeavor of ridding His creation of the evil conspirators by ostensibly falling prey to the serpent and spending most of man's mortal existence in an uncomfortably close proximity to the wicked ones, leading, and then causing, the errant angels to sin and finally rebel. Thus allowing God the legal right to then sentence the wicked ones and cast them into hell without having broken His eternally established Word while doing so.

This servant's work was, and will be rewarded by God unto those who remain faithful to Him in this undertaking. By attempting to swallow the bait of man the serpent was going to find itself with such a severe case of indigestion that it was to eventually go belly up!

Chapter sixteen

The result of Adam's appetite

THE DEVIL IN THE DETAILS

satan thought that he was now in an extremely desirable position due to the actions of Adam and Eve. Not only was he able to coax God's anointed rulers of this realm into a state of sin which caused them to lose the control they had of their kingdom due to the loss of their blessing's of life, but he also expected to gain access through them into their spiritual and physical authorities in and over creation where he would then be able to more fully bring about his will of covering everything in darkness and separation from God. This he would accomplish by using mankinds newly twisted wills and mandates to hinder God's will, and there was no one anointed or legally authorized to stop him anymore.

Adam and Eve had died away from their God; and while angels had authority in the operation of the spiritual and physical heavens that make up this universe, they didn't have authority over the heavens. Nor could God just create another new man to rule in Adam's place for He had rested from all His creative labors on the completion of creation upon the anointing of Adam as king; giving Adam the rights in this kingdom, including procreative rights. Therefore, God could not legally step into this situation and supersede or replace Adamic authority by creating a new king to rectify creation. There was no one existing or creatable who could enter into this situation in these heavens with the kingly authority necessary to subjugate the wicked angels as Adam and Eve had done earlier.

satan had understood this fact before he began his efforts to beguile Eve in his quest to secure those Adamic rights for himself; and what he couldn't secure use of, he hoped to hinder man from accessing by way of accusation of man's disobedience and sin. If it wouldn't have been for the apparently foolproof possibility; the seemingly safe opportunity in doing so, satan would never have attempted to dethrone God's anointed ones. Being the astute legalist that he is, the serpent would never have taken the bait of man if it didn't look edible and safe to do so, but it did. God made sure of that.

Things for satan finally had the appearance of looking up for the first time since God said "light be" in Genesis 1:3. The wicked spirits of the evil conspiracy thought if they could just behave carefully enough they would now have a "permanent kingdom" in Adam's domain; and due to Adam's actions satan as "leader" of the wicked transgression became the "god" of this world, as stated in 2 Corinthians 4:4.

What is meant by the term "world" in this context is the behavior of things, beings, and spirits that are of this creation which are now under the spiritual influence and subjugation of evil and satan, much in the same manner as they would have been under the protection and mandate of Adam. The term world in this context does not mean the physical earth itself.

> "...The earth [is] the LORD'S, and the fulness thereof; the world, and they that dwell therein." Psalm 24:1

However, all things which the Lord commended to Adam's domain became corrupted into death in what was now a perversion of God's will in an evil existence called satan's world. For Adam the anointed ruler had become a subordinate of the conspirators, he became a stranger to God, just as Eve was.

To put it yet another way, satan's newfound governance was a perverted corruption of the Adamic authority received by satan from an acquiescent Adam; and this authority was then twisted as far as an angelic being could possibly twist anything without breaking it. Though, all of the capability that satan had to affect things in mankind's authority was still to be dependent on man's continual cooperation and yielding of power through man's constant obedience to sin.

Now back to our continued look at the Genesis verses:

> *"And the eyes of both of them were opened, and they knew that they were naked; and they sewed fig leaves together, and made themselves aprons." Genesis 3:7*

This is not a question of mere physical nakedness alone, as is often assumed; but rather a cognizant realization by Adam and Eve that they were void of the glory which had encompassed them. They became aware that the presence of the Spirit of God had departed from them, and they no longer had the capability to do His will; that is, to function in their God given offices successfully.

The glory of the Lord had departed, and they were destitute. So they went to one of the trees which had sustained them in their blessings earlier; a tree that itself had been a provider of blessings to them, and they tried to use its leaves, its sign's of life, as a covering of life for themselves. They were hoping that the living (righteous) covering of the legal fruit tree would help cover them in their sins, in their death, and in so doing, return their lost lives.

An additional point: Trees need leaves to absorb energy from the light of the sun. A tree with fresh leaves is therefore known to be alive as its leaves are its contact point to the life bringing light. Adam and Eve had entered into the world of self effort in their attempt to benefit themselves by taking and using the tree's ability to live in order to cover and bring a semblance of life to themselves.

The creation, and the tree in it, weren't yet judged by God to be in the same curse of darkness that man had voluntarily entered into. During that short post-death/pre-judgment time, creation was still in the light of God that Adam's rule had made possible; Adam was hoping to reenter that light, that presence of God, by covering himself with these living and "light" absorbing leaves. In that way, Adam ended up putting the proverbial cart before the horse in this situation; for he was the one who was created to be the light and covering for creation, but due to sin he was now looking for creation to cover him.

The Genesis Mousetrap

> *"And they heard the voice of the LORD God walking in the garden in the cool of the day: and Adam and his wife hid themselves from the presence of the LORD God amongst the trees of the garden." Genesis 3:8*

Adam and Eve immediately realized that the leaves of the tree which they placed upon themselves were not enough of a covering to undue or hide the damage caused. Then when they heard the voice of the Lord they immediately ran for cover and hid themselves from the presence of the One they could no longer unite with, just as darkness needs to flee before the coming light. So, the two hid in among the other legal trees which had bountifully sustained them in the garden, but this too was a vain attempt for man to find righteousness and life to support and uphold him before the Lord God Most High, the Judge of all creation.

> *"And the LORD God called unto Adam, and said unto him, Where [art] thou? And he said, I heard thy voice in the garden, and I was afraid, because I [was] naked; and I hid myself." Genesis 3:9-10*

Adam responds to the Lord calling unto him by saying that he was afraid because he was naked; and so he hid himself. Was Adam naked? We just read that he and Eve had made aprons of fig leaves to cover themselves, so physical nakedness wasn't what he was solely referring to. Instead, he was also speaking of the lack of the blessing of life, of the fact that the anointing of the Holy Spirit had departed from him, leaving him exposed to all contrary spiritual elements, powerless to enforce God's will, or his own.

"ARAM"

Indeed, the very Hebrew word used to describe man's nakedness is essentially the same word used to describe the serpent being "subtil" in Genesis 3:1. They are both close variations of the word "aram", and this word can also mean "shrewd", "crafty", and "sly".

Thus, when Adam said that he was afraid of being naked before God, he was also referring to the fact that he had been subtil, or crafty, even brash in his actions, thinking he had an easier way to handle Eve's transgression than the procedure established and given by God. So in his brash, naked, shrewdness he disobeyed the Almighty and that brought about sin; his reason to be ashamed of his actions and afraid of the consequences that were to follow.

Yes, due to the fact that the words in Hebrew for "subtil" and "naked" are essentially the same in both spelling and pronunciation, coming from the same root as they do; that also means we can now see that the serpent as spoken of in Genesis 3:1 was more "naked" than any beast of the field which the Lord God had made. He was more forward with his intent, and bolder in the actuation of his own will than any other beast of the field was, or dared to be. The serpent was quite open and brash in his intent and actions, having the perverse gall of daring to deceive Eve by his twisting of the Word of God in order to seek personal power. Apparently, no other "beast" dared to go that far.

This type of action is very much in keeping with the brazen character of the former Lucifer as it was previously exemplified in his darkening of the deep, which was discussed in an earlier chapter. The covering cherub was both subtil in his carefully made plans, and audacious enough to nakedly implement them in the very face of God and His angels. The overly self-confident and thouroughly evil satan simply had no shame.

The fact that Adam and Eve used a fig tree's leaves for their coverings is no accident; it was quite prophetic and telling. The fig tree is always a biblical reference to the things of Israel; and in the prophetic sense, the fig tree's leaves used for covering man was the law that God gave Israel to live by. The law was the sign and way of life.

The explanation here is man had tried to better himself through self exertion, and through the self implementation of the holy laws, the ways of Godly purity. Doing so was man's attempt to attain holiness, righteousness, and life. This self effort of man was, as self effort always is, incorrectly motivated and simply insufficient to attain righteousness. It was a mere superficial shadow of the righteousness which comes through the substantial blessings of God brought about through His works, will, and actions.

The Genesis Mousetrap

Sinful man's attempts to cover himself with the holy and good laws of God were vain. Man realized that the leaves, the coverings of the fig tree, as legal, functional, and as beautiful as they were while on the tree, died themselves when they were broken off of the tree in man's attempted efforts to benefit from their substance.

The leaves simply did not have the ability to retain or restore life after man's effort to use them separated them from the life of the tree itself. The leaves couldn't function as an adequate cover for man's sin and weakness in the manner Adam had hoped. For the anointing of life, the personal presence of God's spirit had departed from man, and nothing man could do beyond that point, nothing in creation, could help Adam attain the wholeness that he needed, which was the presence of God in his life.

Even though the fruits of the same legal fig tree were well able to sustain man when he was whole and righteous, its leaves couldn't cover the lack of righteousness that Adam now had. They were never meant to. The leaves were to be the glory of the tree, and its own signs of life, not a sanctifying covering for man's sin and death.

The fig leaves which Adam used (the life sustaining and holy laws of God) did not have the ability (through man's self effort) to atone for man's sin, the source of man's shame. They merely covered it for a time, and how well the leaves temporarily would cover man was up to man's own limited effort to use them as effectively as he could.

The other trees, among which Adam hid; were they not pictures of the nations where the children of Israel migrated to in the long flight of exile from their home and love which was the fig tree, seeking refuge and safety in among the nations and their ways, which were the other trees? However, they found none, just as Adam didn't find a means to sustain himself among the other trees as there is no righteousness or rest outside of the holiness which is already provided for by God, a holiness that Adam had shunned.

This is also the reason that Jesus cursed the leafy but fruitless fig tree which he traveled by in Matthew 21:19 and Mark 11:13-14. Fig trees with leaves can also be expected to have fruit. It is an unusual attribute of that particular tree species, and when Messiah said, *"Let no fruit grow on thee henceforward for ever."* He was also saying that man's temporary system of works of self effort to attain right standing was eternally over with, as He had come to establish a permanent righteousness for man based on His grace, His fulfillment of the Godly laws, and His atoning sacrifice. Leave those leaves on the trees where they belong!

> *"Behold, the days come, saith the LORD, that I will make a new covenant with the house of Israel, and with the house of Judah:" Jeremiah 31:31*

THE FIRST JUDGMENT DAY ON EARTH

In Genesis 3:11-24 we enter into a period where the role of God as Judge comes into the fore. In these verses God begins to seek answers to the events that caused the apparent fall of Adam, his kingdom, and the loss of the dominion of the physical creation to wickedness. God asks Adam:

> *"...Hast thou eaten of the tree, whereof I commanded thee that thou shouldest not eat?" Genesis 3:11*

In Genesis 3:12 Adam's response to God's question was that he ate the fruit because the woman God had given him, gave it unto him. Adam explains he died because of the woman God gave him, saying, *"she gave me of the tree, and I did eat."*

In Genesis 3:13 the woman explains to God that the serpent had beguiled her, that he had utterly deceived and misled her into thinking that having thorough knowledge of good and evil, was beneficial to her and something she couldn't pass up having.

Both of the statements made by both of these two people were the absolute truth. No one will ever lie before God Almighty as no one CAN lie before God in a judgment situation. His power and majesty are so great that only the truth can be spoken by those in His overwhelming presence; in that sense, all are bare before Him. *(Hebrews 4:12-13)*

It is interesting to notice, however, that God did not ask the serpent for his explanation of events even though the serpent's actions were the original cause of this situation; and even though the serpent was there to face judgment as well, God nevertheless chose not to question him. Once again, there are multiple reasons for this.

The first reason is that man was given dominion of this creation; and therefore man was the one responsible to God for all explanations of the activities which took place here.

The second reason is that the occurrences had a detrimental effect on both Adam and Eve, but not on the serpent. They were the ones engaged in breaking God's commandments and choosing to die away from God, not the serpent. Thus, they were the ones responsible to explain what they did and why they did so.

The third reason is the serpent was the instigator of Adam's and Eve's sins. God did not need to hear the serpent's explanation of events as he was the cause of the trouble. All the serpent would have done was blame Adam and Eve for sinning and ruining the otherwise fine day he was having milling about in the garden doing his chores. On top of it all; in all likelihood God had already heard all of this from the accuser in the heavens and He didn't need to hear it again.

THE VERDICTS OF THE GREAT JUDGE

Next, the Lord God, the Great Judge of all things, begins to pass out His verdicts and judgments, to clarify the new order of things. This new order was not one that the Lord designed; but instead, it was an arrangement which came about because of satan's efforts and man's sin.

As the Great Judge of all creation, God had to make sure that all beings who had an active role in this universe understood the rules of operation in this new order. Once more, God totally and fully accepted Adam's and Eve's testimonies about the events which led to their sin because He knew they were the absolute truth. He therefore begins by responding in His judgments upon the now silent serpent first.

> *"And the Lord God said unto the serpent, Because thou hast done this, thou art cursed above all cattle, and above every beast of the field; upon thy belly shalt thou go, and dust shalt thou eat all the days of thy life." Genesis 3:14*

Now, in this judgment there are a number of interesting things to see: first of all, God said, *"Because thou hast done this"*. What exactly did the serpent do? Well, unlike satan's twisted and evil, but nevertheless legal actions taken in the darkening of the deep, in the garden he used quite a different tactic.

The serpent went beyond legal individual free will, choice, and self effort, and beyond prodding and instigation, into deception. He deceived Eve. He beguiled, or misled her; and it was the serpent's overt deception that caused Eve to sin. However, the serpent didn't openly lie to her because he could not clearly lie and accomplish his goals. If he would have clearly lied to Eve, he would not have been able to convince her of God not being perfect.

The serpent needed to use subtlety, and he needed to finesse Eve into coming up with his preconceived conclusions for her on her own. The serpent had to move smoothly and carefully in this situation lest he run the risk of exposing his intent, or worse yet, of moving into rebellion, an act no angelic being takes lightly. So he did the only thing which he felt capable of legally doing in that situation, and that was twisting the Word of God and the truth for his own benefit, and for the detriment of others.

In this case, the prize of having access to the physical creation that was under Adam's authority was simply too good to resist, so the serpent went just a little too far in his twisting of the Word, and in his convincing of Eve; he beguiled her. The serpent led her into the transgression without Eve having a complete knowledge of the consequences of her actions. Nor was she aware of the heavenly events which the angelic conspirators had initiated. She didn't fully know what she was getting into, and that is what brought God's judgment upon the serpent.

We have to keep in mind that the Lord God is not speaking to this twisted serpent in a strictly physical context. Contrary to our natural thinking, everything which exists is spiritual in nature and the spiritual context of all things is the greater operational truth. The Lord God was arranging in this new order of things the necessary format in which the hooks placed in leviathan's jaws at Eve's and Adam's swallowing of the fruit could be beneficially used for the purposes of dragging the serpent in for his final judgment and removal.

The sequence of events which led up to and followed Adam's fall, were enablers which allowed God to define the consequences of breaking against His will. These actions permitted Him to legally establish a new set of laws which further modified the ones that had been previously established in a way that caught satan off guard and set the wicked one on a path toward the inevitable.

The Lord was now implementing a way for the wicked conspirators to be removed from the heavens permanently without wrongly interfering in the previously given rights and blessings of the created; and satan never saw it coming.

A further breakdown of Genesis 3:14 reveals yet more things of interest.

> "...thou art cursed above all cattle, and above every beast of the field..."

As touched upon earlier, in the Bible we find many examples of illustrative terminology used to describe spiritual beings and their different authorities. Types of cattle and beasts are used in the Book of Daniel to refer to nations and their angel princes. (Daniel *chapter 7; Daniel 7:17; 8:4; 8:20-21, Ezekiel 29:3, Isaiah 30:6*)

Elsewhere in scripture, the pharaoh of Egypt is referred to as a dragon; the Messiah Himself is referred to as the Lion of the tribe of Judah, as well as the Lamb that was slain.

So the old serpent, the great dragon, satan himself, the angel once called Lucifer, while he hadn't yet committed any acts egregious enough to give God cause to condemn him to hell, became the most cursed, the most unsuccessful spiritual being in the heavens, for daring to take such brazen liberties with the Word of God in his beguiling of Adam's God decreed and anointed co-ruler of the garden; the woman called Eve.

The result of Adam's appetite

THE MOST ACCURSED BEAST

"...upon thy belly shalt thou go..."

The most accursed of all the beasts was to be the serpent; and one of the specific curses that the Lord God sentenced him to exist under was for him to be in a state of constant hunger and desire, lusting after things he could not have; ceaselessly trying to obtain that which is not his; incessantly longing for that which he will never possess; chasing after that which he cannot attain. satan's attempt to achieve a victory was in effect, turning into a very short lived joy as God's judgment upon him was that nothing he would do was ever to satisfy his endless lusts and hunger for power. *(Job 1:7)*

Contrast this to Psalm 23; the Psalm of life in the blessings of God, where it is written, *"The Lord is my shepherd I shall not want."* satan only wants, wants, wants; and it drives him constantly to no end. The belly, desire, and lust of this serpent move him to constantly seek the ever present more with no peace or rest possible. As it is written in 1 Peter 5:8, satan is like a roaring lion seeking who he may devour. Constantly seeking, seeking, seeking. There really is no rest for the wicked.

"...and dust shalt thou eat all the days of thy life."

This is a very important part of God's judging and of his clarification of the new order which satan and man developed through their activities.

When have you ever seen a serpent eating dust? Never! Snakes simply do not eat dust. Some will say this simply means that snakes basically look as if they eat dust, being so low to the ground and all, but that is not what God said. He said, "EAT", not look as if you will eat. God simply isn't capable of saying things that aren't truthful and accurate. So, what was He referring to? If God said it; it must be so, but what did He mean? This was the point in the first judgment which brought bare the first set hooks that had been firmly placed into the jaw of the unwitting leviathan.

The Genesis Mousetrap

Thank God for His mercy and kindness! Thank God for His grace! Although we stumble he shows us compassion and protection for His Word's sake. The Lord God Most High, His name shall be praised forever, limited the serpent's new authority over fallen man to only physical things; thing's of the flesh; thing's of the dust body of man. Yes, this was an enablement of satan over man, but it was only to be over part of man. The ability of the serpent was to only extend to the Rakia part of Adam, and his authority therein, the material dust part of man and no further.

This unexpected limitation of rights was legally possible for God to do because of the triune makeup of man and the physical nature of Eve's and Adam's sins which was the eating of the fruit. It was dust that man's body and the physical part of the universe was made of, and it was only dust that the serpent was to be allowed to eat. That is one reason the serpent incessantly hungers. He just didn't get much to eat; not nearly as much as he expected to get. God limited satan's authority and the operation of the curse to the natural physical body of man, and excluded the serpent from any rights over the soul and spirit of man due to satan's overreaching beguilement of Eve.

THE CURSE IS FLESHLY

The operation of the curse and of all sin which fallen mankind is subject to is fleshly, of the dust of the earth, of the Rakia heaven. Even the right of the angel of death, satan, to separate man from life was limited to existence in the dust body of man ONLY. This satanically enacted physical death is what is scripturally referred to as the first death. (*Revelation 2:11; 20:6; 21:8*)

satan was excluded from any power over man in the other two aspects of man's existence: the soul and the spirit. This is why Jesus said the following in Matthew 10:28:

> "*And fear not them which kill the body, but are not able to kill the soul: but rather fear him which is able to destroy both soul and body in hell." Matthew 10:28*

Had this exclusion of satan's power not been made by God at this judgment, man would have been totally under satan's rule, eternally

The result of Adam's appetite

removed from any possibility of redemption and cursed to a permanent separation from God; doomed to an existence of satanic servitude in hopeless damnation. This exclusion was made possible by the fact that man spiritually died immediately upon eating of the fruit, but more on that later.

This decree was absolutely not what the serpent wanted to hear. He thought that he had everything neatly and legally arranged for mankind's destruction and fall from authority, and for permanent satanic control of Adam's Kingdom. Instead, the serpent was dealt such a serious blow that not even a well versed legalist such as he could quite fathom its far reaching implications at the time this particular decree was issued by God.

This judgment of giving the serpent certain rights over a portion of fallen man's being, the dust body; and over things pertaining to the natural world that could affect man through physical sin and death also brought the wicked one under the laws of God which pertained to the physical part of this universe. This judgment was facilitated by the serpent's entanglement with man and man's authority as the entry of Eve into transgression also reciprocally brought the entry of leviathan into the seas of man. As a consequence, for the first time ever, the angelic beings were also to be affected by the laws of the Rakia heaven personally. That is why God said, *"and dust shalt thou eat ALL THE DAYS OF THY LIFE"* (emphasis mine).

To top it all off, the serpent now had a clock to deal with! His life, once eternal, was now to be numbered in days. God was able to place him under the limits and constraints of time which only exist in the natural physical world; and in phrasing His statement: *"all the days of thy life."* God was indicating that the angelic being called satan who believed himself to be everlasting in God's heavens because of his care, thoroughness, and legal maneuvering in the planning of his transgressions, would now have a limit to the days of his life.

Things weren't going well for the wicked ones after all. satan must have been quite dazed upon hearing the judgments of God upon him. On one hand, it was an apparent victory for the satanic transgressors with the advancement of the will of the wicked conspirators taking place, and the removal of man from his place of honor and authority in the Adamic Kingdom having been achieved, but access to most of the Adamic authority was barred from satan. Simultaneously, satan and the other wicked angels through him were brought into a very serious curse, as well as under the impending limit of time now placed upon their authorities, and indeed, a decree was issued by God Himself limiting, and thereby placing an end to the very life of satan.

Perhaps that's still one more reason why the serpent goes on his belly; he must be so staggered by these unexpected, but nevertheless legal decrees that he still hasn't recovered enough to stand! (Just a little more humor, folks.)

> *"and I will put enmity between thee and the woman, and between thy seed and her seed; it shall bruise thy head, and thou shalt bruise his heel." Genesis 3:15*

The declaration of the Lord was that although the woman was deceived, and had entered into the satanic conspiracy there would be enmity, hatred, and hostility between her and the serpent continually. She was not to be a pushover or a peaceful ally to satan, but a very powerful enemy. And because she was beguiled and fooled into entering into rebellion against God she would have the right and the privilege to bring about the ultimate judgment and punishment of God upon the serpent. This was to be accomplished through her seed, the promised Messiah, who was to bruise the serpent's head by subjugating and then destroying satan's power totally.

Once again, we are given a chance to see the law of reciprocity at work. Eve, the one who was wronged by the serpent and the one who allowed this creation to be defiled is the one who has the privilege of bringing forth the ultimate judgment of God upon the serpent. Furthermore, she was also given the right to return the creation which she lost back unto God, by way of her seed.

The previously mentioned verse was also the second direct prophecy made by God to an individual found in the Bible. That is to say, God is clearly telling an individual (in this case satan) what the results of his actions were, or shall be. This was in clear reference to the fact that the

The result of Adam's appetite

serpent's newly found dominance over the dust body of man was to be only temporary, and it was to come to a bruising end, along with the serpent's days.

satan was now going to have his very head crushed by one of Eve's children! satan's pride, his glory, the apparent victories he had accomplished, they were all to be absolutely destroyed by the Son of man, and there was nothing he could do to alter his destiny. Things are going from bad to worse for the evil one who thought himself able to match wits with the Most High God. By the way, the first direct prophesy God gave to an individual was given to Adam in Genesis 2:17 stating that the day he eats of the fruit he shall surely die.

> "Unto the woman He said, I will greatly multiply thy sorrow, and thy conception..." Genesis 3:16

NEXT UP, EVE.

Next, the Lord God addresses the woman in Genesis 3:16, declaring unto her that her sorrow and pain in childbirth would be greatly increased, and that the time of her conception would be lengthened. Notice the Lord had just declared to the serpent that the seed of the woman was to bruise the serpent's head, but now He declared to the woman that her difficulty and pain in bringing forth her seed, and the length of time it takes to bring the seed forth, would be greatly increased due to her partaking of the satanic transgression, and her attempted efforts of selfish advancement.

This decree does not refer to the increased natural birth pangs of a woman alone, as is often assumed; more specifically it also meant that the time and pain it would take to bring forth the Messiah (the woman's seed) into the earth and into a place of dominance became increasingly long and difficult due to the fact that she opened the door for satanic interference in the affairs of man through her partaking of the transgressions.

The Lord also continues to state in Genesis 3:16, *"...in sorrow thou shalt bring forth children..."*

The Genesis Mousetrap

> *"...but the woman being deceived was in the transgression. Notwithstanding she shall be saved in childbearing..."* 1 Timothy 2:14-15

Since Eve allowed herself to be beguiled by the serpent, and actively took part in the wicked rebellion against God, she would not have had an opportunity for repentance without the fact that she and Adam were deemed one flesh and co-recipients of the unrepentant blessings of God. Specifically, recipients of the rights of procreation, and as such, she was indispensable and necessary to bring forth the promised Messiah, the seed that would bruise the head of the serpent. Adam could not have done this alone, and God could not have created another woman since He had blessed and given the authority explicitly to Adam and Eve together. Only they could have passed along that authority, and indeed, all Adamic authority to others. That is to say, to their children, particularly unto their child, the Messiah. God couldn't go against His own Word and blessings; therefore Eve was shown immeasurable grace.

So, in a sense, Eve was reborn out of an impossible situation due to God's pre-established mercy and wisdom in issuing such conjoined and codependent blessings unto man.

Although, an event which should bring about great joy such as the birth of new life became one which correspondingly brought her great sorrow and pain as a reminder to her of the sorrows and pain the newly born child would experience in his or her existence as a result of inheriting her sin tainted life.

Now as we can see, the sorrows of the woman are mentioned twice and almost back to back in the same verse. This is to focus us on a different aspect of the sorrow which came about due to her actions. The woman, or feminine being as a wife or bride in some form is often biblically associated with and representative of the righteous, those who belong to God, including the corporate body of born again covenanted believers on earth.

Perhaps in Eve, the first woman; we can find a veiled picture of the first salvation from death and satan's conspiracy. As she was, in a way, the first to escape the darkness of rebellion, and was also the first to experience a merciful redemption from the wages of sin due to her pre-established covenants and authorities which were necessary for the afore stated will of God to be carried out.

However, as stated, this verse also alludes to the repentant believers; those who seek to do and bring about God's will. A great sorrow and longing has always been present among these faithful ones to accompany the bringing forth of the fruits of God in their time. Chief among these fruits is the growth in the number of new believers, new children of God. These children are brought forth in sorrows, prayers of anguish, and burdens for the lost until today. Examples of this are found in the following verses: John 16:21, Hebrews 5:7, Luke 7:38, Romans 8:26.

"They that sow in tears shall reap in joy." Psalm 126:5

"That I have great heaviness and continual sorrow in my heart." Romans 9:2

"For godly sorrow worketh repentance to salvation not to be repented of..." 2 Corinthians 7:10

THE BURDENS OF THE PROPHETS

Even the prophets, Isaiah foremost among them, often spoke of the burdens which they had for whoever their prophecies were concerning, actually calling many of their words or prophesies burdens. These supernatural burdens come with great sorrow and heaviness unknown and indescribable to natural man. It is a grieving in the spirit and through the Spirit for the things of God, for His will to be done and brought forth.

The great seven year tribulation period, itself a time of untold sorrow and anguish upon the earth, precedes the second coming of Messiah as a time of birth pangs with sorrows incomparable to anything known on earth previously, as the woman, Israel, brings forth the manchild (Messiah). (*Revelation 12:1-6*)

Every move of God, every salvation, miracle, deliverance, and healing has come through the prayer and travail of an obedient believer or group of believers somewhere seeking the Lord for His children to be brought forth into the life and freedom of Messiah. These obedient people are the ones who bring the life of God into this earth through their burdens, birth pangs, and sufferings on behalf of others; as well as on behalf of the Word of God. These intercessors weep the tears of God and bring forth His fruit and life into the creation.

The conclusion of Genesis 3:16:

> "...and thy desire shall be to thy husband, and he shall rule over thee."

The woman was given a way back to God's grace, and that way was through her descendent which was to come through her husband, as well as through his rule over her as Adam wasn't guilty of rebellion against God as she was. Therefore the path back to right standing with God for Eve was found in Adam, and she was allowed the ability to wait for and partake of the redemption to come due to her commitment to her covenant with Adam, hence "...*thy desire shall be to thy husband...*".

The Lord reiterated unto Eve His original decree signifying that His intent for her was still fully applicable, and that He considered her covenant with Adam to be fully in force regardless of the actions and events that took place. God helped Eve back by increasing her desire to be with her husband Adam, the source of her redemption; so that her one time desire to rebel and join the transgressional beings would be overridden by this original Godly intent.

This fact also refers to the believing body on earth, whether Israel or the church, longing for the Lord, who in His rulership of the woman (the body of believers) can sanctify her and empower her no matter what she has done as long as she remains with Him and submits to His rule over her.

> "And Adam was not deceived, but the woman being deceived was in the transgression." 1 Timothy 2:14

> " And unto Adam He said, Because thou hast hearkened unto the voice of thy wife, and hast eaten of the tree, of which I

commanded thee, saying, Thou shalt not eat of it; cursed is the ground for thy sake; in sorrow shalt thou eat of it all the days of thy life;" Genesis 3:17

ADAM'S TURN TO LEARN

Adam knew his responsibilities. He knew the will of God on the subject in question. He knew that he had to atone for Eve's sin, but in disobedience he chose to die away from God in the way Eve had, instead of dying God's way for Eve. Despite having ample knowledge Adam did not value the things and ways of God and chose to turn from them.

The serpent was cursed to long for that which he cannot have. The woman's sorrow and physical pain was increased in childbearing; but Adam was not directly cursed for His actions. God cursed the ground instead. God cursed the ground ("Adamah" in Hebrew) for man's (Adam's) sake. The earth received the punishment for Adam's disobedience; and the only way the curse was to affect Adam was through his involvement with the things of the ground, the physical, Rakia.

How was this transfer of punishment legally possible for the righteous and holy God to carry out without His committing a miscarriage of justice and breaking His own laws? Well, this decree coincides with what the Lord had previously said to the serpent, giving the serpent the right to eat dust, which is the part of Adam that is of the ground, the body, physical matter. Accordingly, due to the fact that Adam's body was made of dust, God was able to transfer the inevitable curse caused by Adam's actions and inactions to the ground, the dust of the earth.

Adam's physical body was of the dust of the earth after all, and that being the case, God was able to use that link to transfer the punishment which should have been on Adam onto the ground and that which was of it, thereby protecting His son Adam from the unavoidable judgments which He had to decree. God could not have legally done such a thing as using the ground as a substitute without the fact that Adam was of the ground; so God in His perfect foreknowledge saw this escape for Adam before He first created man.

The Lord did say, however, that Adam was to eat of the ground in sorrow all the days of his life; but the sorrow was only to apply to Adam through his partaking of the things of the physical earth. Or put yet another way: Adam was to partake of the things of the physical earth in sorrow all the days of his life as the physical was cursed so that the triune Adam himself wouldn't be.

So, the serpent was cursed. The woman's sorrow and time of physical pain was increased in childbearing; and Adam's curse was placed on the ground with Adam partaking of the things of the ground (physical things) in sorrow as long as he was to bodily live. This is also referring to the fact that everything which comes from the earth, the physical, the flesh, was no longer a blessing to Adam but became a hindrance. It became a vehicle for the curse to operate in, and a possible way for evil to bring about death since it was in the physical where the serpent obtained his power in Adam's domain under the rules of the newly established Adamic/serpentine order. Notice the phraseology used in this verse to limit man's physical life is the same as used in Genesis 3:14 making reference to a limit on the serpent's life. The countdown was underway to the great judgement day; tick, tock, tick, tock....

> *"Thorns also and thistles shall it bring forth to thee; and thou shalt eat the herb of the field; In the sweat of thy face shalt thou eat bread, till thou return unto the ground; for out of it wast thou taken: for dust thou [art], and unto dust shalt thou return." Genesis 3:18-19*

Up to this point in time Adam was able to live in the blessing of life, in the personal presence of the Holy Spirit of God; and all creation readily saw to his welfare according to the will of God. Man was never in need of exerting effort for his own behalf; his needs were more than provided for by the Almighty and His highly blessed creation.

Adam's job was to look after the will of God, and to look after the best interest of the portion of God's creation that was given unto his care. How? By blessing creation, enabling it to exist in the will of God; doing so allowed it to partake of, and correspondingly share the myriad blessings which God had issued it.

In the Godly way of doing things it simply isn't necessary, beneficial, or even advantageous to pursue one's own interest, but rather to be a conduit of blessings for the welfare and benefit of others. Conversely, the blessings of God, some received directly from the Lord, and some flowing through the lives and anointings of others, would as a consequence abundantly provide for you.

However, now that Adam had walked away from God's plans he had to squeeze out a livelihood from the earth which did not want to readily supply it for him. Through great personal effort and a subsequent manipulation of the natural laws that were now themselves under the effects of the curse, Adam was to eke out an existence from the earth that once served him as gladly as he served God. Adam, because he had died away from the blessings of God, now had to work in order to sustain himself.

THE LIE OF THE BIG "I"

Under the format of the curse established by the actions of Adam and the serpent in this now perverted world everything becomes self centered, self absorbed, and selfish. Nothing is as important as the great "I", and the needs "I" have in caring for "MYSELF" become the paramount concern for "individuals". In the backward deluded thinking of the natural mind ("natural" in this case really stands for "perverted") everything around "ME" must be made to serve "ME" as "I" am the most important thing in "MY" life.

The selfish tendencies that seem so logical to the natural mind are actually greatly contributing to the essence of the curse in operation in the lives of man, and that is a complete mirror image to the ways in which the blessings of God function and are brought about.

When God said, *"till thou return to the ground; for out of it wast thou taken: for dust thou art, and unto dust shalt thou return"*, He was referring to Adam's bodily death, and the fact that the curse, and satan's power over him through the flesh, actually ends upon Adam's physical death, upon man's separation from his dust body.

After the first death no elements of self effort, the curse, or any transgression, satanic or otherwise, would have any effect on man at all.

Ergo the use by God of the term, *"...till thou return to the ground..."* upon the issuance of this decree. The power of the curse was absolutely limited by God to stop at the first death; the death of the dust body. Yes, God had informed the serpent of this limiting fact earlier in Genesis 3:14, but as it affected both parties, both were made aware of the results and impacts of their actions from the standpoints of their individual positions.

THE TIME FOR THE NAME FINALLY CAME

"And Adam called his wife's name Eve; because she was the mother of all living." Genesis 3:20

This is actually the first time in the biblical narrative that the woman is referred to as Eve. Even more interestingly, the placement of this verse in the narrative is really quite odd on a superficial reading of events. It is located immediately after God's decrees of judgment; an all around strange time to be naming a wife and commenting about what seems to be an otherwise obvious fact.

Therefore, it is time for another question. Was Eve really *"the mother of all living"*? The answer is: not in the physical sense. She and Adam were both living at the time this statement was made; and Eve wasn't either of their mothers. However, *"all living"* is the operative phrase in this statement of Adam's. Adam was referring to the promise of God who had decreed that Eve's seed, her child the Messiah, was to bruise the serpent's head, thereby destroying satan's power over man. Adam understood the decrees and design of God in the matter and saw that the hope of redemption remained and was actually strengthened through these judgments of God.

The now dead unto God mankind was to once again live through the promised seed of Eve. Messiah was to restore life in wholeness back to mankind and Eve was in that restorative manner of redemption, *"the mother of all living"*. She was the one from whom all the redeemed descend through Messiah. Adam wasn't merely referring to the fact that Eve would be the mother of all who would physically exist upon the earth.

FRIEND AND FAMILY

In fact, a look at the original Hebrew shows us that "Eve" wasn't even the name which Adam called our dear foremother. Eve is merely the anglicized version of the name. The original name used by Adam was "Chava", and it has as a foundation of meaning and very close relative the word "chai" which means "life".

In faith, understanding, and obedience to God's decrees, Adam named the once transgressive, fallen, and appearently dead unto God woman, "Chava". The Eve who first entered into rebellion and who initially brought death into the realm of man was now being called the "being of life" by Adam in his faithful agreement and compliance to the spoken Words and prophecies of God. Adam had realized the promise of God that the woman's seed was coming to redeem fallen man, and that God was wonderfully restoring them both.

The name Chava is also closely related to the word "chaver" which means "friend" in Hebrew. Adam was calling Eve HIS friend. His ally in this earth, his friend FOR life; Adam was calling Chava his chaver for chai. Adam had never signed off on Eve's rebellious actions, and now with God's decrees of judgment set in place, Adam was able to reaffirm that Eve was, indeed, his friend and ally in the journey of redemption and not satan's collaborator in sin. In this verse we can see that Adam and his "friend" were coming into compliance with God's intent as Eve, the being who appeared dead, was now, "the being of life"; Adam's friend and ally in the Godly plan of redemption in which Eve was, *"the mother of all living."*

COATS OF SKINS

> *"Unto Adam also and to his wife did the Lord God make coats of skins, and clothed them." Genesis 3:21*

God made Adam and Eve coats of skins and clothed them. Once again, this was not to hide their physical state of nakedness, for they were previously clothed with fig leaves and hidden among the trees. However, it was necessary for them to have proper attire, proper cover for them to stand before God.

The Genesis Mousetrap

Why wouldn't cotton, linen, or some other plant substance have been sufficient? God could have woven a wonderful fabric, you know. The fact is that this was a blood sacrifice; the first blood sacrifice that is ever recorded in the Bible. God Himself came down to earth and sacrificed His own innocent animals on behalf of his wayward children. He shed innocent blood so that Adam and Eve would not have to immediately physically die for their own sins. He then clothed them with the skins of the sacrifice. This wasn't merely to cover their nakedness, but the death of the sacrificial animals covered Adam and Eve's lack of righteousness, their sins, and allowed them to stand covered by innocence before God and not be destroyed.

Notice, that of the entire sacrifice made, the skins of the sacrificial animals were the parts used as coverings for man. This is a very telling fact, and for a further explanation we must once more look at the Hebrew to see what is happening. The innocent sacrifice had its skin used to allow man to stand before the holy God, and markedly, the word for "skin" in Hebrew is spelled with the letters "ayin", "vav", "resh", and it is pronounced "or". This word "or" is interestingly a homonym of the Hebrew word for "light" which is spelled: "aleph", "vav", "resh", and it is also pronounced "or". That is no coincidence. This verse speaks of an amazing event and the use of the Hebrew word "or" to represent both words "skin" and "light" touches on the legal process of redemption.

Remember, it was light which satan first attempted to cover in the darkening of the deep; and the darkness was found to be upon the surface of creation, on its skin, as it were. As a result, it was light that God commanded to come forth from within creation itself in order to begin negating satan's actions. Thereby allowing creation to survive its unfortunate but thankfully temporary time in an otherwise choking darkness, and when Adam and Eve lost their light by falling into the darkness of sin the Lord God took of the yet innocent life found in Rakia, which still had, to some extent, the light of God, and He used that light, that skin, to cover, or recover man. This He did so that the dark cloak of sin could be dealt with and itself be covered by God's use of the light of creation.

It was a measure for measure action, another function of the law of reciprocity at work. In some sense, man could be "relit" by the use of a substitutional sacrificial light allowing man to return from the darkness back into the light of God; at least to some degree.

Yes, it could be said that this covering event is similar to the action taken by Adam and Eve when they tried to clothe themselves with the fig leaves, but there are striking differences at work.

First, the use of the fig leaves was full of self effort; Adam and Eve decided to put forth their own exertion in order to cover themselves with the leaves in an attempt to hide the truth of their actions from God. Contrarily, the sacrifice which God made for them required no effort on their part, only an admittance of fault, a humbling before Him, and their acceptance of His gifts.

Second, the fig leaves were only a part of the living thing in question; they were not a life sacrifice: Whereas the animal skins required the death and sacrifice of the entire animal in question.

Third, the leaves were used by Adam and Eve in greed and deceit. The leaves were very useful and beautifying for the tree so the opportunistic Adam and Eve couldn't help using them for themselves. An interesting thing about leaves is that they appear to be healthy and alive for a time after they have been cut off from the tree. So a deceptive individual (or in this case a pair of them) could try to use the freshly cut leaves in an attempt to return unto themselves the false appearance of life. Fallen man was into deceptive behavior from the start.

The living appearance of the leaves was in sharp contrast to the unmistakably dead skins of the animals which were to drape the sinful and fallen mankind in a clear and obvious display unto all that a life was forfeit due to sin. The skins displayed the fact that the individuals who were wearing them had sinned but had also received a substitute to cover their sin.

Fourth, the leaves of the tree didn't have blood; the animal bodies did. A blood sacrifice was absolutely necessary to cover (although it could not cleanse or remove) the blood debt which was made when Adam and Eve broke and left the covenantal debt unpaid to God.

Also, this event of the Holy God coming down to sacrifice and shed blood on behalf of man is a prophetic picture of the atoning death of

Messiah as He came down to shed His innocent blood on behalf of sinful man. Through this sacrifice sinful man now has the ability to be covered by the death of the innocent Messiah; the one whose physical sacrifice now covers our lack of righteousness so that God will see the body of the righteous Messiah, His skin (covering) and light, rather than our nakedness or lack of righteousness.

God will now see the light of Messiah clothing the acceptant, repentant, believer and not the person's own lack of such. This verse is a direct indication of the sacrificial work of Messiah and man's atonement that is found in Him.

Also, this event clearly indicates that Adam and Eve did not commit an unpardonable sin, for if they had, God certainly wouldn't have troubled Himself to establish a covering for them; a way that allowed them to stand before Him through His own efforts to sacrifice on their behalf.

Chapter seventeen

Fruitful meanings

TWO HIDDEN TWICE

The activities surrounding mankind's consumption of forbidden fruit had two issues which seem to cling to the narrative. The first one is betrayal; and the second is its close relative, the cover-up.

satan had betrayed God in the beginning during his attempt to cover up God's light from creation. The serpent then betrayed Eve by beguiling; that is, by deceiving her into transgression against God in a way which he felt adequately covered up his involvement in the matter.

Eve followed right along and betrayed God and Adam by breaking covenant with them. Then she tried to cover up her actions by blaming the serpent and clothing herself with fig leaves.

Adam betrayed God's trust in him by disobediently emulating Eve; and he then attempted to cover up his sin by blaming God for giving him Eve, and also by using the leaves of the fig tree to no avail.

satan was betrayed by his pride and greed into the hands of the Holy God who bared the wicked satan's lack of understanding by separating creation into the seven heavens and then by establishing the Adamic kingship; using it to coax satan into eventual outright rebellion, which shall prove to be his downfall. The same God also covered up His servants in the matter, Adam and Eve, with skins from His sacrifice. So betrayal and cover-up walk hand-in-glove through the events of the narrative.

CLOTHED IN A COVERUP

This brings us to the next point: In the Hebrew language the word for the covering of man, which is clothing, and the word for betray are inherently linked. In Hebrew, the word for clothing is "beged" it has as a root and relative the word "boged" which means betray.

Should that seem odd on the surface of things? Is there a strange cover-up going on? Could the link between these seemingly unrelated words betray buried knowledge? Is truth actually clothed in mystery? What's the answer?

Well, once betrayal entered creation it was necessary to cover, that is, to clothe the offense with something that appears less offensive or inoffensive. Eve and Adam's betraying actions committed through their physical bodies created the need for a physical covering. Clothing "beged" was the answer to, and result of, betrayal "boged". However, as we have seen, mankind could not adequately "beged" (clothe) itself to cover its "boged" (betrayal) of righteousness. God had to cover them Himself.

There is yet another interesting link between the two words: "beged" (clothes) are commonly used by the wearers thereof to present false images about themselves, so that they may deceive or "boged" (betray) those around them.

Many wear high-dollar suits and dresses to appear very successful or powerful in order to gain influence or trust among people. The wearer does this simply in order to gain the unearned and occasionally misplaced trust and respect of others.

Some will wear sports apparel to appear fitness minded, even though the wearers are most often found sitting on the couch.

A few will purposefully attire themselves in humble garb to hide the fact that they have great personal wealth.

There are also those who will put on very modest dress and require others in their society to do so in an attempt to hide the fact that the desires of their hearts and their crude hidden actions are actually extremely immodest.

Yet others array themselves immodestly in an attempt to use the way they cover their "shame" for their own benefit; seeking to exploit the selective use of cover in order to reveal the inappropriate, in an attempt to manipulate and betray, for personal gain, the weaknesses found in the base elements of society.

Religious leaders the world over tend to use prim, unique, and/or unusual dress to separate themselves from the common folk which they would seek to lead or hold sway over. These religiously arrayed individuals use their dress to deceive or "boged" (betray) people into thinking that the uniquely "beged" (clothed) leaders of religion have a special link to some supernatural truths which the normal people can only access by dutifully submitting to the specially appareled ones.

Mankind's use of "beged" (clothes) to "cover up" itself has from the beginning been inherently linked to "boged" (betrayal), from the very first sin even unto this day. Thankfully, this fact is no longer clothed in betrayal by the many layers of our Babel based languages. Nor is it covered up and lost under the thick garments of translation any longer, for the amazing Hebrew language which never betrays those who search for knowledge constantly uncovers the intent of God's Words and then clothes them with the light of truth.

NO MORE FRUIT

> *"And the Lord God said, Behold, the man is become as one of us, to know good and evil: and now, lest he put forth his hand, and take also of the tree of life, and eat, and live forever: Therefore the Lord God sent him forth from the garden of Eden, to till the ground from whence he was taken." Genesis 3:22-23*

The Lord God wasn't punishing Adam for eating the fruit of the tree of the knowledge of good and evil by denying him access to the tree of life.

Quite the contrary, a close inspection of these events will reveal that the decrees of judgment upon Adam and the others was already over with after God substitutionally cursed the ground for Adam's sake.

The Genesis Mousetrap

Markedly, in this previous verse, the Lord isn't decreeing judgments unto any of the three beings in question. Instead, God was actually protecting man from a terrible fate when He decided to send man out from the garden.

Had Adam and Eve eaten of the tree of life in their fallen sinful state they could not have died physically. Now remember, they had already died spiritually the moment they ate of the fruit of the tree of the knowledge of good and evil in accordance with God's Word.

So had they eaten the fruit from the tree of life in their fallen state of existence they and all their heirs (i.e. mankind) would have existed eternally under the subjugation of satan; the prince of the power of the air. The same being who received the de facto control of the remnants of Adam's Kingdom and the right to eat dust through Adam's willful disobedience and his subordination to satan's "invention", the evil conspiracy.

Should Adam have eaten of the tree of life, mankind in essence would have become a race of physical demons existing in eternal separation from the Lord and His holiness due to sin. Man would have had no possibility for redemption as death is needed to release one from life, and especially needed to release one from a sinful life.

Man would have lived in an eternal spiritual limbo with his spirit dead and his body alive, subjected to a perpetual rule of evil with no way to end satan's wicked reign over himself. For the first death, the physical death, which the angel of death was empowered to enforce would have become ineffective upon those who partook of the fruit of the tree of life.

A BEAUTIFUL PLAN

When God allowed the curse of sin and death to affect man's being, God also limited satan's power over man and man's kingdom strictly to the physical portion of man, the dust body. This brought about the fact that satan also loses all of his authority over man at man's physical death.

So, in an absolutely beautiful plan, one that could only have been designed by the wisdom of God, satan actually loses all authority over a person when satan functions in his most "powerful" anointing; that of the angel of death, to bring about the first death, the physical death of man.

Once again we see that due to the lack of the blessing, the anointing of life, on the wicked ones they are always unsuccessful in all that they do, including when they try to enforce their legal authority and will upon others.

That which satan considered his power move; the bringing on of death through the destruction of the physical body of man, is the one event which actually releases man from the curse and satan's control. Isn't that amazing!

But wait! There's more! Since it was only the physical death of the body that could release man from bondage to the evil one, Messiah Jesus came to die on behalf of all mankind as a sinless substitution.

This redemption would not have been possible if Adam would have eaten the fruit from the tree of life, as mankind, including the Messiah, who is the Son of man, could not have been able to die physically after that time. For that reason Messiah could not have come to redeem mankind from sin through His sacrificial death. This substitutional death became the salvation arranged and provided for by God from before the creation of the world, and was only possible because God forbade Adam from partaking of the tree of life by sending him out of the garden after his sin.

> "But with the precious blood of Christ, as of a lamb without blemish and without spot: Who verily was foreordained before the foundation of the world, but was manifest in these last times for you," 1 Peter 1:19-20

> "...the Lamb slain from the foundation of the world." Revelation 13:8

This banishment of Adam allowed for the process of redemption to proceed for all who now choose to take part in the death of the righteous Messiah Jesus, the last Adam. By laying down their lives in Him and taking part in His death they become free from the law of sin and death (the curse, and separation from God) as they no longer "live" of themselves, but it is Messiah who lives in them. And Messiah is free from sin and the power of satan!

It is a covenantal exchange of lives which occurs. Once we partake in the death of Messiah through faith; we become free of the power of sin and satan before we physically die ourselves. satan's powers of sin and manipulation stop upon our death through faith in the sacrificial works of the righteous Messiah. Remember, satan has no power over a dead man.

Those who humble themselves unto God and accept the sacrificial death and Lordship of Messiah upon themselves are thereby free from the power of sin and satan. So, once again we can see the wisdom of God in action for He actually saved mankind from a fate literally much worse than death when he sent Adam out from the garden before he could eat of the tree of life and live forever in bondage to sin and satan.

The beauty of God's wisdom is also evident in His bestowing of the power of death unto satan, for when God gave satan the authority (and obligation) to administer the first death, He actually gave satan the tool with which satan was to unknowingly relinquish his authority over man and release those who he held in bondage. What's more, with satan's use of this tool, he was to eventually destroy himself in his greed.

Genesis 3:23 is where God sends Adam out of the garden into the land from whence he was taken. Adam as a being who now existed solely physically was sent out from the garden to the solely physical heaven of Rakia from which Adam's physical body was made before Adam could permanently destroy himself through further disobedience or cause desecration to the holy garden.

With Adam removed from the garden, Adam's new "boss", satan, had no way to affect the garden or anything in it. As satan still needed Adam's cooperation, and/or consent in exercising Adam's now exiled authority and anointings to rule, change, or alter anything that was given to man's care.

> "So he drove out the man; and He placed at the east of the garden of Eden Cherubims, and a flaming sword which turned every way, to keep the way of the tree of life." Genesis 3:24

This was the exile.... the separation of the king from his crown, and consequently the removal of the king from his kingdom. A kingdom that was to remain without a king until the arrival of the Holy and Promised One; the Son of man, the last Adam, Messiah Jesus, whose inheritance of the intact Adamic Kingdom was necessary to affect the removal of the wicked conspirators and their effects from all creation.

Adam was God's chosen vessel for the removal of the wicked conspirators, and God's original intent must always come to pass, so the last Adam, the Word of God Himself was the one who would come to fulfill God's intent.

THE WAY OF THE TREE

Indeed, a close look at this verse indicates that the Cherubim mentioned therein were sent specifically *"to keep the way of the tree of life."* These angelic protectors of holiness were specifically sent to guard and protect the holiness of *"the way"* which leads to the tree of life.

What is *"the way of the tree of life"* referred to here, and why was it so holy? It was not only the garden or a blessing thereof. Actually, the answer is found in the Word....

> *"Jesus saith unto him, I am the way, the truth, and the life: no man cometh unto the Father, but by me." John 14:6*

Messiah Jesus, Himself, is the way! He is the way of the tree of life. He is the path to God. He is the road to salvation. He is the sanctifying passage. In Him, and only in Him, can one come to the tree of life, which is the revealed, applied, and sanctified Word of God, made alive by the presence of the Holy Spirit to those who come to it, the very Torah will of God Himself. To partake of Him is to live. The Son revealed as the Word of God is the tree of life.

As demonstrated in the following verse the Word of God is life by which man is to live:

> *"But he answered and said, It is written, Man shall not live by bread alone, but by every word that proceedeth out of the mouth of God." Luke 4:4*

The Genesis Mousetrap

It was therefore of the utmost importance to the Lord that the garden, the foundational basis for the dominion of Adam remained holy as it, and everything in it, was to be inherited by Messiah.

It was also equally important to God as a loving Father that His children would not be eternally separated from Him through their partaking of the fruit of the tree of life while they were sinful, an event that would have kept them in a state of permanent darkness subjugated to eternal wickedness as they further would defile His will.

It was at this point in the narrative that the garden which was "planted" by God into this heaven of Rakia was removed from upon it for its protection, uprooted as it were, and moved into sheol to be a resting place for the souls of the righteous dead who were to await the coming Messiah.

The overly self-confident astute legalist, satan, had been brilliantly lured by God through the modification of the heavens, the planting of the garden upon the earth, the establishment of the Adamic kingship, and specifically through the creation of Eve and the presence of the tree of knowledge of good and evil in the garden to attempt his beguiling endeavor.

satan's goal was to entice man into evil and into partaking of transgression, and through that route satan hoped to have Adam submit his kingly authorities unto satan's use. That is what he hoped to accomplish and this thought was the temptation satan succumbed to.

God in His great wisdom and foreknowledge had planned and designed a format for these seemingly terrible events to serve in the task of ensnaring satan in a way which would lead to the benefit of all creation, and not to its detriment and demise.

ADAM, DEAD BEFORE THE JUDGMENT

What satan received was not at all what he had hoped for; through the spiritual death of man which the Lord wisely arranged to happen *BEFORE* God's judgment of man's transgressive actions began, man lost access to the source of his great authority and dominion, which was inherent to his spirit. God in His wisdom protected Adam by allowing him to spiritually die upon eating the fruit *BEFORE* the necessary judgment took place, so that God didn't need to judge Adam on a spiritual level.

This fact is attested to in Adam's realization of his nakedness or lack of holiness, and his lack of capability to function in peace, which is why Adam used the word "afraid" when he explained the reason he hid. He was never afraid beforehand; he had nothing to be afraid of. He was shalom.

In the prejudgment spiritual death of Adam, satan lost the right to interfere with and infringe upon man's spiritual authority. This left every authority that was in the spiritual portion of Adam's existence holy and protected from evil by being separated and protected from the fallen Adam himself.

This in turn meant that only the rights that were inherent to the lone portion of Adam which yet lived at the time of the Adamic/serpentine judgment, which were those of man's physical body, remained to be judged. Only the remaining innate physical rights were decreed to be under the influence, and/or subjugation of evil and even those only for the time man was to physically live upon the earth. Ponder that a moment.... Keep pondering.... Alright, you can stop pondering now.

Did you realize the effects this had? satan really just got an empty shell to attempt to manipulate, didn't he?

satan was after man's dominion, and almost all of man's power and authority are based in man's spirit which had previously died. The only part of man that was judged by God to be within the reach of evil is the flesh. The only part of man that has ever been within the reach of evil is the flesh, the Rakia portion of man, and even that for only the time man exists upon the earth.

It must also be realized that when Adam and Eve ate the fruit of the tree it wasn't satan that brought about their spiritual death, this is due to the fact that satan couldn't kill them spiritually. He never could and never will kill any person spiritually. satan never had one bit of authority over any person's spirit; and by the grace of Almighty God he never will!

It was God who decreed man's spiritual death as a consequence to sin before Adam and Eve ever sinned. God protected Adam and Eve by letting them die away from their source of authority before He needed to judge them and their actions. He designed and foreknew the events that were to transpire, and knew that He needed to allow man to be subject to satan's transgression for a time for reasons of redeeming all creation and ultimately for ridding the heavens of the wicked ones entirely. God was preparing His servants for a most holy work.

Man, and man's authority, was the bait needed to hook leviathan. And since man was to serve in the important task of ensnaring the beast, God prearranged for all the necessary legalities to be in place to ensure that Adam would not be needlessly lost, and to ensure that the old dragon wouldn't get anything he expected.

The Lord therefore hid Adam's authority away from His own inevitable judgments through Adam's spiritual death; for these judgments which are decreed according to God's pre-established laws, would have obligatorily placed Adam's full authorities into satan's grasp. God ensured the authorities were hidden before the judgments took place; before He would have had to allow satan access to the spiritual authority of man due to man's sin.

This still undefiled spiritual authority is the same God given authority that would once again be taken up and utilized by the woman's seed; the sinless last Adam, Messiah Jesus, of whom the Father said in Mark 9:7, *"This is my beloved Son: hear Him."*

It is this same Jesus who liberates from satan's evil all those who accept His kingship. It is this same Jesus that will rid the heavens of the evil conspiracy in its totality. It is this same Jesus who is *LORD*.

A few verses which speak of the separation and enmity that exists between the flesh and the spirit of man follow:

> *"For the flesh lusteth against the Spirit, and the Spirit against the flesh: and these are contrary the one to the other: so that ye cannot do the things that ye would." Galatians 5:17*

> *"For I know that in me (that is, in my flesh,) dwelleth no good thing: for to will is present with me; but [how] to perform that*

which is good I find not. For the good that I would I do not: but the evil which I would not, that I do." Romans 7:18-19

"O wretched man that I am! who shall deliver me from the body of this death?" Romans 7:24

THE RECAP

As an answer to satan's wicked perversion of attempting to cover creation in darkness, the Lord set about to change the format of creation in such a complex and brilliant way, while of course still respecting His own laws, that satan couldn't fully follow the complexities and intricacies of what the Lord was doing.

So, still thinking himself as clever, or more clever than the Lord God, satan greedily entangled himself in the affairs of man; and it was precisely because satan did so that God was able to instigate the process of satan's soon to be affected demise.

In subjecting fallen man's physical rights to the serpent, God linked satan into this physical creation in a deeper way than satan as an angel could have ever been without his involvement with and infringement upon man's authority.

This series of events tied satan into the time limited physical heaven of Rakia; in effect making satan an adopted part of it, and that allowed God to include the satanic conspirators into His great coming Adamic judgment at the end of the prophetic week of creation.

All of the creative events which occurred following the satanic covering of creation were organized, planned, and foreseen by the Lord God Most High as a way of ridding His Kingdom of the wicked conspirators and their evil shadow.

The Lord perfectly designed every detail of the creation, including the Adamic kingship and its seeming fall, to draw satan into a place where he and the other evil ones could be enticed to fall prey to their own greed and lust; and in so doing, cause them to eventually sin in open rebellion. That in turn, will allow God to judge them, find them guilty, and remove them from their offices eternally by casting them out of the heavens and into hell, and later into the lake of fire.

The Genesis Mousetrap

The bait of Adam was swallowed, and the hooks in the jaws of leviathan were firmly set. God was now able to begin tightening the line, and adding yet more hooks into the great beast in His awesome plan of pulling satan toward his final judgment.

Chapter eighteen

Back into the picture

WHO'S DOING WHAT?

Alright, Adam and Eve were expelled from the holy garden and exiled into the physical creation from whence their bodies originated to toil in an unnatural existence until their bodies succumbed to death; but how was it that they were able to survive one single minute in a sinful state before the Holy God without being utterly consumed by the glory of His holiness?

First, we saw that there was a division established between this universe and God's other heavens which acted to separate God's direct presence from this creation before man even fell.

Second, we saw God offering a substitutional blood sacrifice on behalf of Adam and Eve to enable them to stand before Him.

Third, satan was still the covering cherub of God; and also, due to Adam's sin, the new "god" of this world; and as those who sadly came to know sin and evil all too well, Adam and Eve were further removed from God's presence than ever. Neatly tucked away from God under satan's dark shadow, as unwilling de facto members of his conspiratorial transgression.

These facts are what enabled sinful man to survive bodily for a time in the physical creation before expiring.

So, as strange as it seems, satan's perverted works as the covering angel became indispensable for fallen man's physical survival; for as satan was attempting to cloak God from creation, he inadvertently ended up shielding sinful man and the wickedly influenced creation from God's awesome holy presence.

In fact, God has used, is using, and will continue to use the dark covering of the wicked angel satan to protect sinful and imperfect man from the glory of His radiance until the day righteousness is established and satan is removed from office.

The satanic shadow cover under which mankind found itself was one that would constantly and tirelessly attempt to make and remake mankind into the image or copy of the evil ones under whose influence man's flesh was so firmly entrenched.

That is not merely an empty filler phrase; the wicked beings were, and are, committed to seeing fallen mankind behave as duplicates of themselves; for a mankind which is made or remade in the image of the evil ones is the greatest "tool" available for them to use in this triune universe in their attempts to steal, kill, and destroy that which is not theirs.

Having been separated from God and exiled from their garden home, Adam and Eve entered their existence in the wickedly affected creation. In it, mankind was to dwell in *"...the valley of the shadow of death..."* made mention of in Psalm 23:4 for the duration of its remaining physical existence, which was to last the week of days.

That is where mankind found itself, and that is also where mankind finds itself to this day: In *"the valley of the shadow of death"*, covered and separated from God by the "god" of this world; half swallowed by the hungry leviathan and his wicked conspiracy, but not yet left for dead.

This servant of God known as mankind was the bait covering the hooks of the Holy One now embedded deep in the serpent's gullet. It's dirty work, but someone had to do it; and that someone was man.

Although it may be a dark and arduous sojourn in the dim dell of the angel soon to be sent to hell, as man exists in *"the valley of the shadow"*; the Lord had still arranged for man to find light in the shadowed land.

He made *"paths of righteousness"* for man to follow. He prepared *"tables"* in the very presence of the wicked ones for the unwilling and repentant rebels in the family of man to partake of. He arranged for feasts which the wicked could not touch. The Lord had His rod and His staff (signs of His authority and power) extending into the valley, visible to all who would see.

Yes, even while man's life as experienced through his physical body was *"in the valley of the shadow"*, this same Psalm 23 speaks of the reward for the just. It also speaks of the fact that hope was not meant to be taken from the servants of God in this great endeavor of cleansing creation of satan's dark stain.

> *"Surely goodness and mercy shall follow me all the days of my life: and I will dwell in the house of the LORD for ever." Psalm 23:6*

For a more detailed explanation on what it means to dwell in the shadow of a being we need to look at Genesis 1:26. Particularly one word found therein.

> *"And God said, Let us make man in our image, after our likeness..." Genesis 1:26*

Now, any time the Bible repeats two similar statements about a single issue as it does here, it does so for a reason; it is not merely waxing eloquent. The word that will be looked at in this verse to help us understand the effects of the satanic shadow which was hovering over man is found in the first of these two phrases of this verse, and that is the word *"image"*.

The word used for "image" here is the Hebrew word "tselem" and it means "a picture of" or "copy", and is a form of the word "tsel" which means "shadow". *"Let us make man in our image,"* could be understood in more detail if it were also seen translated as "Let us make man in our shadow".

Man was made in God's shadow, under His protection, His influence, and also to be His representation; following God's will and actions much in the same manner as a shadow represents and follows a person as an image of the person.

The following verses speak of man, the image and "tselem" of God, being shielded under the shadow of God, under His "tsel":

> *"How excellent [is] thy lovingkindness, O God! therefore the children of men put their trust under the shadow of thy wings." Psalm 36:7*

> *"He that dwelleth in the secret place of the most High shall abide under the shadow of the Almighty." Psalm 91:1*

It is in the shadow of God that man was created to dwell, influenced and protected by His will. As such, Adam was constantly being formed and transformed into the picture or image of the Living One who was covering, protecting, and overshadowing him in glory and in Spirit when man dwelt in righteousness.

Adam dwelling in the protective shadow; the "tsel" of God, was created to also emulate His heavenly Father just as a young child born in its natural father's image would instinctively want to emulate him by "shadowing" his father, by imitating him. A child naturally wants to be his father's image, his "tselem"; dressing the same, speaking the same, acting the same, and constantly growing into his father's likeness. For the father is the young child's role model and ideal.

This constant formation and transformation of man is well illustrated in the following verse.

> *"But we all, with unveiled face, beholding as in a mirror the glory of the Lord, are being transformed into the same image from glory to glory, just as by the Spirit of the Lord." 2 Corinthians 3:18*

Now, back to the words "tselem", image; and "tsel", shadow, and their implications for the being of man; as we have already seen, man was made in the image, the "tselem" of God to dwell in the shadow, the "tsel" of the Lord. Let's take this thought a little further; man as the image, or "tselem" was to not only exist in the shadow, the "tsel" protection of God; but man was to function exactly as a shadow, a "tsel" does.

Man was to be the shadow or image of God in this universe which consists of the lower heavens, moving here in the same manner and ways of power and holiness as the Father moves in throughout all creation, particularly within the upper heavens.

Man was to be upon the earth as a silhouette of God, shadowing or imitating the Father in all actions, words, and deeds. Man was to not only be in a part of the shadow of God protected by Him, but man was made to also *BE* the shadow of God emulating Him, and visibly bringing forth the will of the Almighty into this creation; just as man was empowered to do by the breath of life which was breathed into him by God. In that way, man would be His image.

Let us refer once again to the words of Jesus, the Son of man, who came to emulate (shadow) His Father upon the earth:

> *"Then Jesus answered and said to them, "Most assuredly, I say to you, the Son can do nothing of Himself, but what He sees the Father do; for whatever He does, the Son also does in like manner." NKJV™ John 5:19*

When we realize this we can better understand more of what it meant for fallen man to languish under satan's shadow during the many years of the Adamic exile. In fact, from the very beginning satan has attempted to imitate the ways and procedures of God in all things, for the formats God uses are most harmonious to His laws and statutes which must be complied with. So, the very shadowing process that satan used in the "darkening of the deep", mentioned previously, was by no means satan's own original thought; rather it was a perverted replica, a weak and twisted imitation of what he had seen God doing as God was shadowing and protecting His creation in the period before the wicked satan began his darkening attempt.

WHOSE KINGDOM IS IT?

For God to be able to fulfill His Word, which He must do once He has uttered it; and for His original intent to be done in all ways; and for Him to be able to restore creation unto righteousness; He had to arrange for man to exist somehow, despite the fact that man died away from Him.

It is quite clear that the way man was to exist was in a state of living physically; that is, bodily; under the shadow of the angel of death until the arrival of Eve's promised seed, the last Adam, who would come and return all things to their original state of wholeness.

This process of Messianic restoration centered around one legal process more than any other; and that is the willful ceding of rights to God by men who would not turn around and subsequently withdraw the authorities which they had yielded to Him.

In yielding their rights and themselves to God, these men were able to legally authorize God to begin establishing an eternal and inheritable series of covenants which allowed the Lord God to circumvent satanic authority, and begin the restorative process of the restitution of the Adamic Kingdom. In yielding to God, these men opened a way for God to gain access to themselves and activate the dormant blessings inherent to their lives through their acceptance of, and yielding to, the presence of God's Holy Spirit in their lives.

Was yielding to God possible for fallen man to do? Yes, for although man had died spiritually, and was in submission to the satanic conspiracy physically; man was not a demonic robot having to blindly follow every whim of the wicked in total obedience. Quite the contrary, every blessing, anointing, ability, and authority which the Lord gives to an individual being belongs to that individual alone. No matter who or what they are, and no matter who or what would attempt to claim authority over that individual.

So, although man had come under satan's shadow, and the enactment of the curse upon man was the result of man's submission to satan's authority; man still had the one basic spiritual element, the one right which inherently belongs to all beings called the sons of God, and that is free will.

Even though the wicked beings were now in a strengthened legal position to enact their goals of negating holiness in their newly acquired authorities due to Adam's fall, they were still totally dependent on the cooperation of the children of man upon the earth to enact their perversions through man's permanent abilities and authorities that were inherent to the body of man, the dust of Rakia.

Back into the picture

Man still had to yield permission for these wicked spirits to bring evil through himself into the physical creation, and as Genesis 3:15 so aptly informs us: God Himself has *"put enmity"* or hatred between mankind and satan, ensuring that mankind as a whole would never fully yield itself to satan's perversions or wish to completely do so. Contrarily, mankind was to have an ingrained resistance to evil dominance. So, after the exile, fallen man was still free to choose whether he would submit to the apparently dominant oppressor, satan, or whether he would seek the grace and presence of the "hidden" God.

It is an interesting thing to note that when man was in the garden, a place of holiness and perfection; God came calling for man, as described in Genesis 3:8, but now when man is in the physical Rakia, in a place which isn't holy and perfect, man has had to call out to God. Since the fall of Adam, it became man's obligation to seek the Lord, as it was man who chose to separate himself from God originally.

Now it had become man's duty to call out, "Lord God, Lord God, where are you?", as the Lord needed to become ever more hidden from man, for man's sake, due to man's sin. Those in the family of man who chose to humble themselves and seek God, and quiet their flesh before Him, found that as they sought the Lord and yielded these remaining inherent rights to God they would become strengthened against the ongoing attempts of satan to manipulate them into evil and destruction as they ceded themselves and their authorities to God for protection.

In essence, they were returning of themselves what they could unto God. They were returning from satan's shadow unto God's shadow; and as mentioned earlier, this alludes to man returning unto the likeness or image of God as well. They were starting the process of man's return back to that which God had originally made, and thereby unto His original unchanging will for man. Doing so brought multiple benefits for these willingly obedient, not least of which was that it gave God Himself a legal pathway to begin restoring man to his proper place in God's will.

This yielding gave God the rights to begin dealing with man on the issues of Adamic restoration and salvation, and it also brought about the beginning of the re-establishment of God's blessings upon those people who would humble themselves before Him.

What manner of blessings could these have possibly been that the Lord God saw fit to bless these humble ones with? Why, they were the exact same blessings that the Lord God had blessed Adam and Eve with originally!

Through the spiritual death of Adam, man had lost access to the anointings that were inherent to his spirit, and thereby lost much control of the blessings that were upon his earthly body, and consequently, man lost control of the events surrounding himself as well: Hence the presence of the curse in creation.

Man lost access to the anointings that were upon his spirit, but the anointings were still present; hidden in each man's dead spirit so that satan couldn't access these rights through Adam's disobedient submission to him through the partaking of sin.

So, when God was able to find individuals to bless and to later covenant with; when He found individuals who hungered after God's righteousness and allowed His anointing of life to rest upon themselves, the Holy Spirit of God who subsequently came upon them was then able to access and enable the dormant hidden blessings inherent to the dead spirits of these people. The Holy Spirit was then able to bring these blessings forth into the lives of men. By being allowed to include His Spirit of life into the lives of men, God was able to allow the blessings inherent to man's spirit to be accessed through His Spirit, and only through His Spirit.

In that manner God was able to keep the blessings of Adam protected from satan and the evil ones, while still being able to bring forth the benefits of the blessings and anointings into the lives of these humble individuals; blessings which had been spiritually dead and inaccessible to mankind since the time man first sinned.

In this way, the blessings that God brought forth and anointed the humble with stayed hidden away from the wicked satan who had inherited influence over the physical bodily life of the disobedient Adam, but not over his spirit. That is why the Bible quite clearly states that it is in Him and in His presence that we have liberty and strength as it is only through His Spirit that mankind can function the way man was meant to. (*John 15:5, Philippians 2:13*)

THE UNCHANGING WORD

God's Word never changes. His will never changes. His goals never change. The Lord God was looking to enact the very blessings that were already upon man from the original blessing of Adam. The vast majority and most important of those residing in the "dead" spirit of man, and the presence of God's own Spirit upon the humble and righteous who called upon Him was the way in which He could bring this about. This was the legal way for God to begin the restoration of the Adamic kingdom upon the earth.

Slowly but surely; generation after generation; people would come along and say something to the effect of: "Existing in satan's shadow isn't good enough. Separation from the God of Creation is horrible, and being subjected to sins that I don't want any part of isn't life. I weary of this bondage! God of Creation, help me!"

Through this sort of seeking, yielding, and humbling; the Lord was able to begin answering those prayers through the presence of His empowering Holy Spirit given into people's lives. The Lord was then able to begin covenanting with these humble ones and restoring through them the legal framework necessary for the arrival of the great King, the last Adam, who would finally complete God's will.

In the duration of time that was to be the exile of man from his Adamic kingdom, the garden; the Lord God was implementing the next step in His course of action of cleansing the heavens from evil; that being the Adamic process of redemption. A process which He had prepared from before the beginning of time; this redemptive procedure was designed by the Lord to take place in much the same manner as the fall of man happened, only now the roles of the beings involved were changed.

satan was now the one who was having to protect his newly acquired rights in the realm of man from the promise of God to send one man that would reinstitute Adamic dominance. satan was now the one who had to attempt to guard what he had (or thought he had). He also had to be mindful of losing his life in the same manner in which Adam had lost his since God had already prophesied the end of satan's days.

The serpent may have been the most subtil beast in the garden, but the Lord God was proving Himself to be, by far, the wisest being in existence.

The Genesis Mousetrap

The following verses may shed a bit of light on the afore mentioned topic. Please notice it is the intent of God that through the church (the believing repentant ones of the corporate body of Messiah) that all men would be made aware of the mystery of the fellowship which exists between God and His created; to the intent that the principalities and powers would also be made aware of the manifold (great and myriad) wisdom of God. The body of Messiah (the believers), was the instrument which God decided to use to prove His great wisdom unto the angels, specifically unto the conspiratorial ones, satan foremost among them:

> "And to make all [men] see what [is] the fellowship of the mystery, which from the beginning of the world hath been hid in God, who created all things by Jesus Christ: To the intent that now unto the principalities and powers in heavenly [places] might be known by the church the manifold wisdom of God," Ephesians 3:9-10

A MULTI-LAYERED SAGA

The process of ridding the heavens of the satanic conspirators was showing itself to be a multi-layered saga in which the Lord was establishing the legal framework necessary for the promised "seed of the woman" to arrive and crush the serpent's head. Adam and Eve became the initial partners of God in the redemptive process when they accepted the Lord's substitutive animal blood sacrifice and God's Word concerning Eve's seed to come. They had shown humility and regret in accepting His mercy and coverings upon themselves. Some of Adam's original wisdom seems to have remained with him through it all!

With the birth of other humble people such as: Enoch, Noah, Abraham, Isaac, Jacob, and their wives, Joseph, Moses, Joshua, Ruth, Samuel, David, the prophets, and Mary, among many others; God was able to construct and increasingly establish a way for the Kingdom of Adam to begin reentering the abode of man on earth, and that way was the nation of Israel. Through the covenants He made to bring about this nation, and then later with this nation, God was also able to reestablish a format for His authority and His will in the affairs of man to again be done through Eve's promised seed; the righteous heir to the Kingdom of Adam.

Back into the picture

Little by little, the Creator with the faithful acquiescence of these obedient servants was opening the legal pathway for the last Adam to come and inherit His Kingdom; the kingdom that was established to be the vehicle for redemption and restoration known as Israel. This last Adam has the same kingdom and therefore the same mandate of dominion as the first Adam did, which was to bring all things that were outside of the will of God into bondage to God's will and fill the earth with God's blessings, leaving no room for contradictory elements to exist in the realm of His authority.

THE REALM OF HIS AUTHORITY

From the beginning it was clear that in the design of this unique being called man; blood ties of kinship were to be extremely important. First, Adam was blessed to be God's son. Second, the blessings of God reissued unto man were always passed down throughout the progressive generations of mankind; never ceasing to exist even though the original recipient may have slept away. Rather, the blessings increased in clarity and strength building upon each successive generation toward the day the promised heir would arrive to reclaim the rights and kingship of man.

> "For unto us a child is born, unto us a son is given: and the government shall be upon his shoulder: and his name shall be called Wonderful, Counsellor, The mighty God, The everlasting Father, The Prince of Peace. Of the increase of [his] government and peace [there shall be] no end, upon the throne of David, and upon his kingdom, to order it, and to establish it with judgment and with justice from henceforth even for ever. The zeal of the LORD of hosts will perform this."
> Isaiah 9:6-7

A momentous event occurred in the restoration process with the establishing of the Abrahamic covenant. This covenant marked the implementation of an arrangement that saw one humble man ceding his expected, but yet to be born lineage entirely to the care of the Lord God.

In return for being yielded the adoption rights to Abraham's children, the Lord God promised this particular man, Abraham, that He would make his lineage a nation great upon the earth; heirs to the land of Canaan, His land, and establish them forever as trustees of the things of God. (*Genesis Chapter 15, Genesis 17:5; 17:7-9; 18:18-19; 26:3, Isaiah 41:8, Micah 7:20*)

This covenanting with, and blessing of, Abraham was to allow God to form a people who could receive the blessings that God had intended mankind to have in Adam. This people needed to be an independent nation, free from any ties with this world and its wicked god; it needed to be a nation that dwells alone.

> "Israel then shall dwell in safety alone: the fountain of Jacob [shall be] upon a land of corn and wine..." Deuteronomy 33:28

> "...it is a nation that will dwell alone, and will not be reckoned among the nations." Judaica Press Complete Tanach Translation, *Bamidbar* (Numbers) 23:9

Therefore, this Abrahamic covenant was vitally important to the reconstruction of Adam's Kingdom. For in it, this nation that was to be born of Abraham lost some of the rights of its free will.

Now, this is not to say that the people of Israel were all to be blindly obedient slaves, not at all. Every person born has the same amount of individual free will as any other person has; and individuals from the nation of Israel have the right to choose for themselves whether to follow God and remain faithful to Him, or they can choose to become as one of those who dwell in darkness.

However, in the case of Israel, the nation and lineage of Abraham through Jacob as an entity was destined to become the vehicle used in redemption; and as such, it was to be instrumental in the ending of the satanic involvement in creation, whether individual members of the nation chose to participate in the process, or not. (*Deuteronomy 2:25; 14:2, Micah 4:11-13*)

A further ratification of a yet more detailed covenant by a new generation of Abraham's seed occurred at the giving of the law at Mount Sinai by God through Moses. In this event, the nation of Israel as a whole covenanted with God in what can only be described as a wedding ceremony.

Israel gave itself to God, and God gave His Word unto Israel. Remember, God's Word is also called His Son, and His Son is Jesus the Messiah. This event further strengthened the relationship between God and the nation of Israel, having established yet a new bond between them, and consequentially this further limited the free will rights of Israel as a nation.

Through Israel's acceptance of the Word of God, the responsibility upon the nation to fulfill everything which the Lord had given them to do in the Word reduced their rights to stray after their own will; although it did not reduce their ability to stray. The nation of Israel was bound to God by this Word which was the "way" to freedom from death and from the bondage to sin that had come upon man at the fall of Adam.

This covenant provided a way for God to allow Israel to corporately re-enter and become conduits for the blessings inherent to the lost Kingdom of Adam through adherence to the Word and obedience to the covenants.

In so doing, God was also able to bring into the natural creation His will and Word for the creation; as well as for man which was to rule over it, making tangible His Word in the earth through the Abrahamically adopted children of God, the nation of Israel. Through its attachment to Israel, this Word of God was able to be made an integral part of the natural physical earth, the Rakia heaven, for the first time since Adam left the garden. Israel was being prepared to be the kingdom that the arriving Messiah could inherit and rule over. *(Exodus Chapters 19-31, Jeremiah 31:32, Deuteronomy 18:15)*

Through yet another covenant; this time with an individual of the Abrahamic line, King David of Israel; the Lord was able to secure rights for the Messiah to come as David's heir and rule the Kingdom of Israel upon the Davidic throne as an eternal king of an eternal kingdom which itself was the heir of the promise's of God through covenants. In exchange for yielding such rights to God David secured the throne of Israel and through it eventual eternal rule of the entire creation for His lineage. Note: A covenant with God is always mutually beneficial. (*2 Chronicles 21:7, Psalm 89:3-4; 89:34-36, Isaiah 55:3*)

All this, and infinitely more, was part of the framework necessary for the establishment of the independent kingship of the Last Adam in whom all of God's blessings resided bodily, as He had, and has, the Spirit of God without measure.

What was there that Messiah and His Kingdom had to be independent of? Absolutely everything which the fallen state of man and the subsequent satanically enabled curse could affect. All things "natural" to the state of fallen man were contaminated by evil and Messiah's Kingdom needed to be separated from that world where satan was "god".

Messiah was coming to restore holiness into an unholy place and to shine the light of God into the world of the fallen Adam, to redeem of Adam's seed all who would humble themselves unto Him. He came to salvage and sanctify the blessings of God that were given to man. To strive against the remnant of the old fallen Adam which preferred to dwell in the darkness of satan's shadow, and to establish His kingship in the Kingdom of Israel which would not only be separate of, but ultimately bind and destroy all power that dwelled in satan's world. That is why His kingdom needed to be independent.

So, there are two events unfolding simultaneously in this restorative process:

First, the founding of an independent kingdom free of all dependencies upon, and ties with, the world and its god, satan. This kingdom was one in which the King Messiah could rule; a realm where His will could be dominant, and eventually universal in scale.

Second, the establishment of a legal structure in which the blessings of God that were upon Adam could once again be accessed by all the remnant of man through the restored kingship of the last Adam, the King of the Kingdom of Israel.

Both of these: The King and the Kingdom were necessary for the restoration of man.

How should it be put? The last Adam inherited what belonged to the first; and similarly His Kingdom, the Kingdom of Israel, inherited the rights of the Kingdom of the first Adam and became the vehicle and structure of Messianic/Adamic will upon the earth.

The Genesis Mousetrap

Chapter nineteen

This pair of Kings is always a winning hand

THE RETURN OF POWER

With the reintroduction of the Adamic kingship upon the anointing of Messiah Jesus, after He underwent John's baptism in the Jordan River, there were once again two empowered and blessed Kings in creation, and their Kingdoms differed quite dramatically in reason of existence and structure of rule, as we well know.

The first Kingdom: the Kingdom of the Most High God, Creator of all things, is by His very essence enabling. He is a giving, merciful, freedom loving God who has bequeathed all beings in His Kingdom absolute blessings and free will. As long as these beings were careful in the exercising of their rights, so that they didn't illegally interfere with the rights of others, they were safe in the Kingdom of God. This was regardless of whether or not they became wicked, as God never rescinds His Word or blessings.

The second Kingdom: the Kingdom of God's son, Adam, was established by God to be an absolute force, a tyranny of love, an enforcer of blessings, a dictatorship of God's will upon the earth. This was to be a realm of rule with an iron rod; created to subjugate any and all of the wicked spiritual beings who in their God given free will chose to pervert their authorities and dishonor God's Word in the areas that were affected by Adam's Kingdom in this universe. And it was so, until the sin of Adam, his spiritual death, and his subsequent exile from the garden.

The Genesis Mousetrap

Only with the arrival of the sinless Messiah, the last Adam, who came to regain the lost authority of this Kingdom, was a man again able to begin operating in the anointing of the Adamic kingship.

This last Adam did in obedience what the first Adam in disobedience failed to do. After He had been anointed to begin functioning in His kingly Adamic power at the age of thirty, He began His demonstration of God's will as it was exemplified in the Torah. At the end of His demonstration of the proper meaning and application of God's will and Word, His authority to function in Adamic office having been fully established, Messiah sacrificed Himself physically for His wayward bride; something Adam never did. This sinless King of creation voluntarily laid down His life on behalf of a sinful creation.

Well, how were the evil ones to respond when the opportunity to kill Him who could not be killed, arose? What did satan and his fellow conspirators think when they saw an opportunity to rid this physical creation of the one being who had reestablished the most terrifying and powerful rule of love they had ever had to submit to? We know.

They were all too eager to bring about His death and subsequent removal from the physical creation. These evil spirits using their influence over their like minded and spiritually blind accomplices in the family of man eagerly seized the first possible opportunity to exert their powers over the last Adam, Jesus. They couldn't wait to destroy any part of Him they could and His physical death, His removal from the earth, seemed most rewarding for them.

> *"Many bulls have compassed me: strong [bulls] of Bashan have beset me round. They gaped upon me [with] their mouths, [as] a ravening and a roaring lion." Psalm 22:12-13*

> *"For dogs have compassed me: the assembly of the wicked have inclosed me: they pierced my hands and my feet." Psalm 22:16*

However, the wicked conspirators once again succumbed to their own greed and lust in their haste to remove the anointed King from the earth. Now remember, a being's ability always exceeds its authority, always;

and due to the fact that the righteous Messiah's death was a substitutional sacrifice, the satanic conspirator's ability to engulf the righteous last Adam with sin and death far exceeded their authority to do so. Their enthusiastic implementation of the penalty of sin upon the sinless one, the manifestation of the curse which they brought upon the holy King Messiah, became a literal death sentence which the wicked angels brought upon themselves and their own wicked conspiracy. For without realizing it, they had violently broken against the Word of God and His anointings which resided permanently and without measure upon the King Messiah.

The evil ones had thought that just because they could kill Messiah it was their right to do so. This time, however, the evil ones were openly offending against the rights of a sinless Adam, the last Adam, and therefore, they were subject to losing the rights which they received in this natural creation due to the first Adam's sin.

satan's overenthusiasm in the implementation of his will and abilities upon an upright man was to cost him dearly. For in the substitutionary death of the sinless Messiah, all of the promises of God, all of the covenants that He had made with man, all of the blessings of God which were removed from mankind in the sinful death of the first Adam, were fully reinstituted by God unto the last Adam when He reinherited His life after His wrongfully implemented death.

Didn't Messiah already have those same rights before His death occurred? Messiah had those rights personally due to His sinless nature and life; and yes, Messiah did use His rights to benefit others who had faith in God. This He did through physical healings, forgiving of sins, casting out devils, and the teaching of righteousness. All of this was a part of His kingly authority.

However, at His death, He not only arranged for the forgiveness of all sin, but He was also able to destroy the root source of its power, as well as its byproducts. In so doing, He was able to sanctify all those who were still under the confines of the fall of the first Adam, allowing those who so chose to be remade in His image, enabling them to walk in the righteousness of His kingdom just as free from sin as He is through their personal acceptance of His Lordship, sacrifice, and grace. Therefore it is through Him and His atonement work alone that all who believe are saved.

Notice that all men weren't made heirs to the Adamic Kingdom, the only heir of the Adamic Kingdom was to be Messiah, for it was He who was wronged by satan, the one who held power over physical man due to Adam's sin. satan became obligated to repatriate all the rights which he had received in the first judgment to, and specifically to, the wronged sinless Son of man.

Also, in Messiah's inheriting of the sole rights of all the promises and covenants of God, He inherited the responsibilities for upholding the same covenants and blessings. This Son of man therefore became the only one who could break covenant with and tarnish the blessings of God. And since this Son of man is also God Himself, and God is not able to break His Word without breaking Himself, the covenants and promises have become eternally safe, made by God with God for the blessing of His own and for the restoration of His creation.

In other words, all of the anointings that were ever bestowed upon man became the sole property and responsibility of this last Adam who is God. Due to that fact man cannot lose the blessings of God to satan, death, or eternal death, or even break covenant with God anymore. No one can. God's Word belongs to God and became God's to protect once again due to the humble obedience of the Messiah.

This is what is meant by having a better promise in Messiah; man cannot break the covenant, or defile it in any way. The only thing individual man is able to do is to choose to accept God's mercy and to walk in the righteousness offered in Messiah or refuse to do so and correspondingly choose to walk in the de facto curse of sin and death subservient to the perversional actions of the wicked angels.

> *"But now hath he obtained a more excellent ministry, by how much also he is the mediator of a better covenant, which was established upon better promises." Hebrews 8:6*

> *"If ye abide in me, and my words abide in you, ye shall ask what ye will, and it shall be done unto you." John 15:7*

But that's not the half of it! What the wicked angels did in their application of the curse and implementation of death upon the last Adam was something which they eternally regret ever doing. In fact, had they been aware of the results of their actions, likely, they would have done whatever they could have to ensure the permanent safety and well being of the Lord upon the earth. satan may have even considered becoming the Lord's personal body guard! (Okay, that's pushing it; just another attempt at a bit of humor!)

> "... for had they known [it], they would not have crucified the Lord of glory." 1 Corinthians 2:8

Back to the matter at hand; satan and his ilk in physically killing the sinless last Adam were not only guilty of a terrible sin, but in doing so they also inadvertently released Messiah from His natural body and from the laws which apply to it as found in the natural creation. This means the body of the slain and resurrected Messiah was no longer under the constraints of the heaven of Rakia or under the laws of the heaven of Vilon which serve to divide the heavens and enforce limitations and restrictions upon dust matter. It was free from such restrictions as the laws of physics which apply to the physical creation and as a result apply to the natural physical body of man.

For these reasons and more, Jesus upon His resurrection didn't merely reacquire His physical body in its normal state; He acquired His body in a glorified state instead. This was a body which was free of these previously mentioned restrictive elements, and that brings about two very important results:

First, all the actions which left the rights and authorities inherent to the body of man under the influence of sin and satan due to Adam's sin, and the decrees resulting from God's judgments of that Adamic sin, were not applicable to the glorified body. This new glorified body was now totally separated from the source of satanic influence and subjugation. It was a body which was no longer subject to the wicked satanic twisting that was saturating Rakia. Such legal twisting is exemplified in what Jesus Himself experienced in His encounter with satan during His forty day fast in the desert. (*Matthew 4:1-11, Luke 4:1-14*)

The Genesis Mousetrap

The establishment of the right to receive a resurrection body was essential to Adamic redemption, for in this same way, all who were to sleep away in the sinless Messiah were to rise in like manner at the resurrection of the righteous, along with those who yet remain alive in their physical bodies at the catching away of the saints. These will all be raised into a sinless glorified body that is not affected by either the weight of the curse and the influence of satan which is upon the physical dust body of man, or by the natural and unperverted Godly laws of the heavens that limit man to this triune universe.

> *"Now this I say, brethren, that flesh and blood cannot inherit the kingdom of God; neither doth corruption inherit incorruption. Behold, I shew you a mystery; We shall not all sleep, but we shall all be changed, In a moment, in the twinkling of an eye, at the last trump: for the trumpet shall sound, and the dead shall be raised incorruptible, and we shall be changed." 1 Corinthians 15:50-52*

In such a way as this, God was again able to brilliantly circumvent His own eternal decrees and laws that are unchangeable and without repentance and were most necessary at the time of issuance. Once again it must be said, *"to GOD the Lord belong escapes from death." Psalm 68:20.*

God gave the serpent the right to eat dust, but now through the substitutional sacrifice of Jesus, and His subsequent resurrection into a glorified body, God amazingly took man away from the dust that satan was eating. WOW! God had cursed the ground for Adam's sake, but now through the last Adam He arranged a way to remove man from the ground, the dust matter found in the Rakia heaven, the *ONLY* place the curse was allowed by God to be. WOW! WOW! WOW!

This receiving of a glorified body is the fulfillment of the promise given in scripture which declares those who are in Messiah Jesus become a new creation. It is at this point that faith becomes seeing for the old things are eternally passed away.

All those who are of the last Adam will walk in the full promise of God available in Messiah Jesus always. Never again to be affected by the weakness of the old body in any form; free from the serpent's attempts of domination; and free from the constraints and restrictions found in this temporary division of the heavens which separated man from the fullness of God.

> "Therefore, if anyone [is] in Christ, [he is] a new creation: old things have passed away; behold, all things have become new." 2 Corinthians 5:17

Second, in illegally bringing the curse and death upon the last Adam, and unwittingly sinning against Him, satan and the conspirators caused a judgment of reciprocity to be issued upon them by God. This meant that as satan was issued "limited" authorities over the only remaining living part of man, which at the time was his physical body, due to Adam's "limited" sin of disobedience; the last Adam was now given total dominion over the authorities of all the satanic conspirators due to their total sin against Him. This total dominion was to be, indeed, total, inclusive of whatever heaven the wicked ones held their authorities in.

THE "OLD" SHELL GAME

Remember, satan and the wicked angels are spirit beings, they do not have a division of life as man has. Actually, the triune nature of man's being has proven itself to be one of the most effective tools God used in the ensnaring of satan, for it allowed man to be apparently swallowable by darkness while actually helping protect man from the satanic effects of the transgression.

The angels don't have this apparently unique triune nature inherent to God and man, which is: spirit, soul, and body. Angels are just spirit, and their authorities lay only in their spirits. So in this case, the loss of power by the wicked angels is inclusive of all in their beings. They couldn't play the same "shell game" with God that He had used on them when He hid man's rights from them at man's spiritual death in the events leading up to the Adamic judgment.

Also, with the restrictions that tied His natural body to this physical earth no longer in effect, the last Adam in His glorified resurrection body had the ability and right to freely and legally enter into all the heavens to establish His newly acquired legal authority over all things before God.

This was the first time that a man was ever able to properly enter the upper heavens. And not just to exist there, but due to satan's illegal actions, and Messiah's glorified resurrection body, God was able to expand the realm of Messianic kingship and the dictatorial rule of Adam to include all heavens, and all things in the heavens as well as in the earth, and under the earth, in sheol. *(Matthew 28:18, Ephesians 1:20-23, Colossians 2:20, Philippians 2:9-11)*

The authority of the dominion of the Kingdom of Adam was now to be over and inclusive of everything within God's own Kingdom. All powers, authorities, and offices (with the exception of those of God Himself) were to be subject to the Son of man, Messiah Jesus, who was still functioning under the same mandate that Adam had originally received from God, and that was to fill the earth with God's blessings, (now the heavens also) and to bring all things into bondage to God's will.

The satanic conspirators were now to be subject to the will of God through the glorified Messiah in every heaven; leaving them no place of legalistic maneuvering or refuge for their wicked perverse ways.

The absolute tyranny of love was now established everywhere; and this great Ruler of the earth and heavens, the last Adam, the Son of man, Messiah, is able to be seated on the right hand of Power through the acquiring of His glorified body. He is seated in the highest heaven as a sign of His legally acquired authority not only upon the earth, but over all things in the heavenly places as well. Waiting for the day appointed by God in which His enemies are made His foot stool. *(Psalm 110:1, Luke 22:69, 1 Corinthians 15:25-27)*

The wicked conspirators could never have comprehended that their own actions upon the earth were to be the cause of their downfall throughout all the heavens. They couldn't have understood that it was their own deeds which allowed the Kingdom of Adam to be reestablished and released through Messiah; and that the Kingdom of Adam would grow beyond its original borders to encompass authority over everything in all the heavens and cause it to spread God's absolute will upon creation everywhere they were.

This pair of Kings is always a winning hand

The Kingdom of Adam and the Kingdom of God were becoming one in both place and leadership. The Most High was at this time in both authorities and upon both thrones now located in the highest heaven, and God's will was coming to pass in a mighty way. The hooks were in. The line was tight. All that remained undone was to pull the old serpent in for his final judgment.

The anointings and rights of the wicked conspirators were being continually whittled away by their own actions and reactions to God's plans. These wicked ones were being brought ever closer to the day when their own deeds would lead to their ultimate removal. This was the setting of the second set of hooks into the jaws of leviathan which only God was able to do through the blessed life of the King Messiah, the Word of God made flesh.

CLARITY

One thing needs to be added to our look at the narrative in order to keep things in clarity; and that is an explanation on the power/authority over the evil ones inherited by Messiah after the resurrection.

Although the evil ones were, indeed, subjugated to the will of the Messiah in all things as all power was unquestionably given unto Him, however, the illegal actions that led to Messiah's death at the hands of the conspiratorial angels was not considered by God to be a rebellious act, which as a consequence would carry a removal from office and a sentence of hell. For the wicked in that instance did not purposely set out to rebelliously break against the laws and statutes of God which upheld Messiah; rather, they "accidentally" overstepped their bounds in their greedy actions erroneously thinking themselves permitted to do so as Messiah was "made sin" on our behalf, and as such He appeared to be legally "killable".

This meant that just as the wicked were present in the area of authority of the first Adam, albeit subjugated to him there; so too are they still present and now under the authority of this last Adam, also equally subjugated to Him in all ways. The key here is to understand that the wicked angels are under Messiah's authority during this time of the duration of the age of grace, under His authority and not yet removed from their places of office.

ALL THINGS ARE ACCOMPLISHED THROUGH A BODY

Therefore, just as under the rule of the first Adam the wicked were present, attempting to bring about perversion, wickedness, and death where they could, so too are they still here during the rule of this last Adam trying to bring about the very same profane things. That being said, it has become the responsibility of the last Adam to control, limit, and restrict the wickedness that is present; the same which is placed under His authority by God the Father.

How is this to be accomplished with the Son of man now present in heaven at the right side of Power and not personally here on earth to do the task? In the very same manner as everything else in God's creation is accomplished: through the use of "the body".

The body is the mechanism for affecting the world around a being, and as scripture states, the corporate group of believers on this earth who have accepted the Lordship of Jesus is the "body of Messiah" during this age. As such, it is the portion of the Lord which is responsible to bring forth, represent, and enact His will.

This structure of Adamic rule over the wicked in creation will be in place until the time of the removal of the "church" through the catching away of the believers and the subsequent beginning of the removal of the wicked conspirators due to their illegal actions occurring in the seven year tribulation period which leads to the physical return of Messiah Himself to remove the wicked from their offices and judge them of their soon to be rebellious deeds.

RECAP REDUX

Let's recap a few things:

One: The nature of God's Kingdom was the foundation for free will found among all beings; and this "free will" was the legal basis for the wicked to launch their conspiracy.

Two: Adam's Kingdom had no free will provision in it; contrarily, Adam was under Godly mandate to bring into bondage all things in his domain. This made Adam's authority absolute within His dominion.

This pair of Kings is always a winning hand

Three: Messiah Jesus inherited the Adamic kingship.

Four: Messiah's Kingdom of Israel inherited the role of Adam's Kingdom.

Five: The sacrificial death of the sinless last Adam was illegally carried out by the wicked conspirators; therefore they became guilty of breaking against the Word of God, as well as against the anointings upon Messiah. This led to the subjugation of the wicked conspirators' authorities unto the One they had wronged.

Six: Upon the resurrection of Messiah, He took upon Himself a glorified resurrection body.

Seven: All who choose to accept the kingship of Messiah will receive a glorified body like His upon His coming to take the righteous home in the resurrection of the holy at the catching away of the righteous.

Eight: This glorified body which is no longer of the physical creation is not constrained by the laws of the natural physical creation, or by sin and satan, any longer.

Nine: This glorified body was no longer bound to the Rakia heaven like the original dust body was, and that gave Messiah the ability to be the first man ever to enter into all the heavens to establish His Adamic rule of absolute compliance, His holy dictatorship, over all things throughout all the heavens in the Kingdom of God.

Ten: The subjugation of all things, including the wicked angels, unto the authority of the last Adam which took place upon Jesus' resurrection was to restore unto this creation a format of rule last seen in the days of the first Adam; and this structure will remain in place until the ultimate removal of the wicked from the creation of God by Messiah.

Eleven: This was all a part of the process which the Lord God designed from the beginning for ridding His Kingdom of the evil conspirators.

JOB'S JOB

But wait, there's still more! The reason the analogy of "the hooks in satan's jaws" has been used so often throughout our look at the creation/redemption sagas, is that the events which take place in the redemption narrative are very similar to what had happened in the events surrounding God's servant, the man Job.

In fact, it is in both the life of Job and in the Book of Job that the explanation lies. Job was, in fact, a prophetic picture of a mankind which doesn't quite understand what is happening to itself in the creation unfolding around it, and the reasons behind it all.

After Job's frustrated speech, the Lord God explained to Job in the forty first chapter of the Book of Job that He alone was the only one able to put hooks into the jaws of leviathan (satan), and that Job had unknowingly served Him in the effort of ensnaring the great beast by being the object of unwanted satanic attention and activities. Just as mankind has been the subject of uninvited satanic interest since the days of Adam.

The Book of Job also makes it clear that God Himself was the one who turned satan's attention toward Job; perhaps, in much the same way that a fisherman tries to get the attention of a fish (in this case a leviathan) by using a lure. Job was a prophetic picture of mankind in general, and that included the persons of the first and last Adams in particular.

The name Job actually means "hated" or "persecuted", and reflects the trials and tribulations which mankind has gone through since Adam first sinned against God in the garden. Also, quite similarly to Job, Adam wasn't exactly near or dear to the hateful satan who wished to persecute him and anyone else as much as he could. As we have read earlier, the very purpose of this universe, the garden, and the Adamic Kingdom, was to bring about a format that would lead to the downfall of satan, the serpent, leviathan, and bring about his permanent removal from God's Kingdom. Job brings this story to light.

The satanic plot against Adam in the garden was actually the event pictured in the first satanic attack against Job. (*Job 1:6-22*)

In that attack everything was taken from Adam except for His physical life and he was destitute; just as Job was after satan's first assault against him.

Now, in the second satanic attack against Job, satan was allowed to increase his persecution of the man, by harming Job's body, but satan was not to kill him. In fact, satan was expressly forbidden from taking Job's life. (*Job 2:1-10*)

This second prophetic picture is fulfilled and carried out in satan's attack upon the second, or last Adam, but with one large difference: satan did, indeed, illegally bring physical death upon the last Adam, the Messiah; contrary to God's commands unto satan upon their second discussion of Job not to take the life of the "persecuted one"; a reference to the suffering Messiah.

Through satan's "accidental" disobedience in the matter, leviathan was totally hooked by surprise with his swallowing of this Adamic bait, and the serpent was ensnared by the only One in existence who could trap him. That one, of course, is Almighty God, and using the persecuted one His unique servant, man, was the way He chose to do it.

ANOTHER ARBOREAL ADVENTURE

Indeed, so similar to Adam's fall was God's plan for satan's demise, that just as Adam's partaking of that which hung upon a tree brought about the end of Adam's rule; so too, that which hung upon a tree, Jesus, was to bring about the fall of satan!

Adam the King lost his rights, and what's more, he lost his life by the way he handled his situation with a certain tree, the tree of the knowledge of good and evil and that which hung upon it.

satan was also to lose his rights and his life through his interaction with a particular tree; the cross at Calvary upon which our Lord was hung. It's the law of reciprocity at work once again.

Our Lord, Messiah Jesus, was made sin on our behalf. Sin is evil, that which separates from God, and Messiah as sin was placed upon the tree by the hand of man, to be an atonement for our sins. This is God's perfect plan; Jesus, who was and always shall be holy and good, simultaneously became sin, which is evil, for our sakes. And through His being placed upon the cross; God, unbeknownst to man or angels, reinstated the tree of the knowledge of good and evil into the world for satan to be tempted with. Isn't that TOO amazing!?!

The very hand of man which had removed the fruit from the tree so long ago in the garden was now allowed by God to return the fruit back to the tree! WOW!

God arranged for the fruit of the tree of the knowledge of good and evil which man in the garden removed, to now be returned by man through man's placing of Messiah on to the cross; and this time it was satan, the god of this world, as the defender of his Adamic rights who was to overextend his reach by removing the "fruit", the life of the righteous Messiah, from upon the tree.

satan was partaking of the fruit of the tree in direct violation of God's decree in the garden that death awaits those who eat of it. God had also clearly warned satan directly in the Book of Job, upon their second recorded discussion of Job's situation, not to take the life of Job, the persecuted one, the man who was a picture of the suffering Messiah. (*Job 2:6*)

Looking back at the Genesis narrative we can see that it was God Himself who created all trees, and He was also the One who planted the trees into the garden of Eden. The tree of knowledge of good and evil was according to scriptural record also one of those trees planted into the garden by God, and it was again "replanted" by Him onto the earth at Calvary to serve in this most crucial and amazing event. This also explains why there is no further mention of this tree in the biblical narrative. The tree of life is found to exist in the future; but the tree of knowledge of good and evil is nowhere to be seen, for God had uprooted it from the garden and replanted it onto the earth for use in this one crucial event.

Furthermore, speaking of the cross, the scriptures state in Galatians 3:13: *"...Cursed is every one that hangeth on a tree"*. satan not only illegally took the life of the persecuted one (Messiah), but in taking that fruit, satan partook of the curse and of the sin which was placed upon the tree; and he became the recipient of the evil which was upon it.

satan subjected himself to the curse that was manifested upon the fruit of the tree which was Messiah, and he opened himself up to God's judgment in doing so, just as Adam had taken unto himself the curse through the knowledge of evil during his own brush with the fruit.

satan was to lose control of his rights just as Adam had, through the tree; or more accurately, through partaking of what hung upon it; that which was representing both good and evil. And the curse, which was upon Him who hung on the tree, as we well know, brings about death.

satan therefore brought death, separation, loss of anointings, and a judgment upon himself very much like Adam had in the garden those many years before, by partaking of the very fruit of the tree of knowledge of good and evil. WOW!

It's difficult to stop saying "WOW" about this subject! God is so incredibly amazing! WOW! WOW! WOW! (*2 Corinthians 5:21, Galatians 3:13, Isaiah 53:12, Deuteronomy 21:22-23*)

GLORIFIED BODIES

Okay, onward! It is precisely the glorified body of the last Adam, the Messiah, which enables Him to legally and freely move throughout all the heavens, as well as to reenter the earth at any time of His own choosing.

Keep in mind, however, that the dead in Messiah who are now presently with the Lord do not have their expired physical bodies with them which kept them tied into Rakia; nor do they yet have their glorified resurrection bodies since the resurrection of the righteous hasn't occurred as of yet. So, the righteous still have a need to be in paradise, which is now located in the highest heaven, in the presence of God. For paradise was and is a part of the triune heavens of man's abode.

However, upon the receiving of their glorified bodies, which the last Adam, Messiah Jesus, already has, the righteous dead, and those of God who are alive when the Lord comes for His own, will then be able to traverse the heavens in the service of the Most High God without the constraining laws of Vilon or the restrictions of the physical world upon them.

It is precisely the glorified bodies that all the righteous receive upon the resurrection of the holy at the catching away of the saints which occurs at the beginning of the tribulation period that enable them to return to earth with the Lord upon His triumphant second coming at the end of the seven year tribulation period. (*Jude 1:14, 1 Thessalonians 3:13*)

Well, what kind of material is the glorified body made of? This is strictly theory, a presumptive guess; with no direct scriptural references to validate it, but most likely, the glorified body is made of the initial substance of all creation, the substance of the original heavens, the "waters" that were present in the first chapter of Genesis.

This is similar to the way the physical body of man is made of the same substance as the Rakia heaven is composed of, in which man today exists. These waters or heavens were the basis of all the heavens that were separated from, or created from them, and which will again one day be united together in them. Therefore, it stands to reason that the glorified body is of the original matter which existed in God's perfect will in the beginning.

If such were the case, it would also explain how the glorified body is so freely able to enter into all of the separate heavens with ease, seeing as it is fashioned of the original material from which they were all taken. Once again, it needs to be stressed that this explanation is strictly conjecture and opinion.

Now, it is interesting to note, however, that the Lord Jesus was already in possession of such a glorified body before His death as the disciples were witness to Him being in His glorified body on the Mount of transfiguration speaking with Moses and Elijah, both of whom were not part of the physical world in the same manner that Messiah was at the time the event took place. Therefore Messiah needed to be in His glorified body while that conversation took place as it was the one way in which He could remain upon the earth and still take part in this visitation with those from the heavenly realms. (*Matthew 17:1-5, Mark 9:2-10, Luke 9:28-36*)

Chapter twenty

Covert coverings

BY LAND, SEA, OR AIR

A further brief look at the angel called satan and why scripture refers to him by the three different names of serpent, dragon, and leviathan reveals some interesting details which are important to understand if we are to get a better idea of why it was this particular being called satan that first started the great wicked conspiracy. The Bible refers to satan by these three names precisely due to the fact that all of these creatures are reptiles, and are unusual in that all three are able to exist in multiple environments with ease, as many reptiles do, whereas most other animals cannot.

This most unique spiritual reptile (satan) is called these different names depending on which spiritual "environment" it is found to be in when it is spoken of. Unlike most other "beasts", this reptilian is one that is equally at home in all surroundings in which it finds itself, whether on the land, in the sea, or in the air. It is the unusual capability of this cherub once called Lucifer to fit in and dwell in any spiritual atmosphere, to be native in it, as it were, which gives it these unique reptilian qualities, and apparently only satan held the authorities necessary in all of these unique places to be considered a denizen of them all.

Although, in order to more properly fit in everywhere, satan apparently felt it necessary to appropriate as much additional authority from others as possible. Nevertheless, that appears to not have affected his conscience too much!

The Genesis Mousetrap

Each reptilian title held by satan is that of a creature which can live in multiple different environments and move effortlessly back and forth between them. The following is a brief look at the attributes unique to each particular species:

<u>The serpent</u>: Found on land and in water. satan was in the garden upon the earth in the Shechakim heaven embodied as the serpentine reptile he had become. When on the "land", in the garden, a serpent was the most appropriate animal to describe him. He was a native species, a beast of the field, with offices and authority in the triune heavens that he longed to pervert, and attempt to pervert.

Remember also, many snakes love to move in the water(s), which as we have seen is a metaphor for the heavens. This angel with a penchant for the heavens (waters) was no different in that respect than its natural water loving serpentine relations. This serpent is cunning, sly, and needless to say, very cold-blooded.

<u>The dragon</u>: Found in the air and on land. In his movements through the heavens, satan was referred to as a dragon, a winged snakelike reptile which was at home soaring among the fowl of the air. Yes, as Isaiah 14, Revelation 12, and many other scriptures indicate, satan seems to be quite comfortable in this area where he moves in the upper heavens in close proximity to the things of God.

This huge winged creature is callously manipulating his authorities in his attempt to usurp the rights of God in creation, and yes, according to popular thought and tradition, dragons do live and move comfortably on the ground as well. Most notably, it is said that when on the ground dragons take every opportunity to terrorize the indigenous human population around them.

<u>The leviathan</u>: Found in water and on land. The great snake of the waters, the sea serpent (Well, that says it all right there.), so at home among the teeming masses of life that constitute the rightful inhabitants of the vast seas. It's quite telling that this most wicked of angelic beings has as one of its native haunts, the seas; the great nations of the family of man, which were established as God's great fishing pond in which to catch the reptilian beast that slithers, flies, and swims toward its

infamous end. And when this reptile is caught and punished under the name of leviathan in the seas of man that will also entail its removal from its heavenly haunts as the dragon, and its terrestrial days of snaking about will also be at a long awaited end.

This aquatic creature being the amphibian that it is, is also biblically known to find its way up on to the dry and dusty ground on occasion. Perhaps its twisted serpentine behavior has something to do with the reasons it has for doing so. (*Psalm 74:14*)

On a side note: it is interesting to see just how this swimming reptile is so at home among the "fish"; which on a prophetic level picture the obedient and righteous of God. Leviathan is not one bit bothered by keeping company with those it holds such animosity towards. One look at the world in which we live, whether past, or present, will confirm for us that the evil ones always attempt to come in next to, usurp, or infiltrate the righteous wherever they are found. The evil called leviathan is not at all bothered by getting close to "fish", as it hopes to be able to catch more than a few for dinner!

THE COVERING ANGEL

Quite often it's assumed that a wicked being such as satan wouldn't be of any use to the Holy God, and such beings certainly don't intend to be; but our Majestic God of Creation often uses the transgressionary works of the evil ones to bring about results they themselves did not intend in their actions. God does so simply to bring to naught the works of the evil ones by their own hands. In other words, He has them negate their own attempts of perversion through the unintended consequences of their actions.

Also, since the wicked angels are in His Kingdom, they remain at His service and must submit to His use when called to, no matter how they would wish to avoid doing so.

A clear illustration of this was found in the angel of death; who through enacting his authority upon the dust body of man actually freed man from satan's grasp, negating the curse that was upon man through his dust body.

In the office of the covering cherub, held by the former Lucifer, we can see another great example of the Lord's ability to use the perverted attempts of the wicked to bring about a beneficial result in His creation.

> "Thou art the anointed cherub that covereth; and I have set thee so: ..." Ezekiel 28: 14

As we have seen, satan has perversely tried to cloak the light of God from creation through the use of his office, and we have also seen how God used satan's shadow to hide sinful Adam and Eve from His glory so they wouldn't be destroyed by His holiness. This is exactly how satan must function in this particular office to benefit the creation which he attempts to curse until the day he is removed. With his office intact, satan in his twisted way attempts to hide the knowledge of God, the truth of His power, and the genuine reality of all things from creation and the children of Adam who came under his dark shadow. But, consequently, as a result of his remaining in office and doing so, he must also cover and shield sinful man and all creation from the holy glory of God before which nothing tainted by sin could survive.

Remember, the Bible clearly states that there is no darkness in God, so He uses the wicked angel to protect His beloved albeit sin stained creation from Himself until the final removal of sin from creation can be accomplished and creation can once again dwell in the presence of His glory. (1 John 1:5)

There are many examples of this protective covering of darkness given throughout the scriptures; we've already read about its application in connection with Adam and Eve, but let's look at a few more:

> "And when the sun was going down, a deep sleep fell upon Abram; and, lo, an horror of great darkness fell upon him." Genesis 15:12

This horror of great darkness that fell upon Abram wasn't God or His awesome presence, but was clearly evil in nature. Think about it, a dark horror isn't the Holy God! Our God is altogether beautiful. However, due to the nature of His visitation with Abram, and the particular office in which He saw fit to manifest Himself, the Lord needed to veil Himself in this cloak of darkness to protect Abram and creation from His direct presence.

Next we'll look at the events surrounding Moses:

> "And the LORD said unto Moses, Lo, I come unto thee in a thick cloud, that the people may hear when I speak with thee, and believe thee for ever." Exodus 19:9

Please notice the reason God gave for coming in a *"thick cloud"*. It was so that the people could hear when He speaks with Moses and believe forever. Since a demonstration of His reality and of His favoring of Moses were the reasons given, a more dramatic presentation of God's might would have been better achieved without the presence of the *"thick cloud"*, but God needed its cover to separate man from His holy glory.

Interestingly, the word for cloud used in this verse is the Hebrew word "anan". "Anan" is a noun which does mean cloud, but the same word "anan" used as a verb clearly means: "to make appear"; "to conjure"; or "to practice witchcraft".

The reason these two seemingly unrelated meanings are associated with this word "anan" (cloud) is that clouds many times function to darken, obscure, and cloak other things with their own perceptible, but nevertheless somewhat translucent covering. Therefore, they are also a great example of the shadow covering of satan in that although it hides God's glory and truth, it has no real power to separate us from the Lord. While satan does need to cloak God from fallen mankind through the use of his unnatural cover he cannot actually separate us from the Father in any real way. Though given the opportunity, he would more than willingly, wickedly try to do so.

Notice that in this verse the Lord wasn't a part of the cloud itself, but He was covered by it lest His glory consume man. With that in mind, we can also see that once the Lord is able to move close enough to us due to our repentance and humbling through Messiah, the "veil" which attempts to cover Him, although present as long as we are in the flesh, isn't hindering our access to Him or knowledge of Him as it had before.

Clouds always appear darker, thicker, and seem to obscure more the farther we are from them and that which they cover. A dark cloud on the horizon always seems more ominous in appearance than it actually is when it is near. Our accepting of God's grace allows us to approach Him, and for Him to approach us. In doing so, the effects of the thick cloud substantially lessen, and we then come to realize the cloud's once forboding and ominous qualities are actually more illusional than real.

However, this look at the dark coverings is in no way meant to imply that every cloud which covers the Lord is satan's shadow. Far from it, there is His own cloud of glory that is the tangible manifestation of His holiness. One form of this is represented by what the Hebrew language calls "Shekhinah", the manifested thick cloud presence of His Spirit. This "Shekhinah" glory cloud is found in 1 Kings 8:10-11 among other places.

Moreover, on the eighth day, in the creation to come spoken of in the prophets and in Revelation, there will be no form of separating and obscuring covering cloud, as there is no more reason to separate man from the Lord. (*Revelation 21:23; 22:5*)

> "And mount Sinai was altogether on a smoke, because the LORD descended upon it in fire: and the smoke thereof ascended as the smoke of a furnace, and the whole mount quaked greatly." Exodus 19:18

Our God is a consuming fire; and just as a fire has smoke due to the impurities present in the substances it burns, God was also cloaked in this smoke because of the sin in His creation which burns when His Holiness comes in contact with it. All impurities burn away in His presence, which is another reason all creation with even the slightest stain of sin still needs to be separated from Him, lest they be utterly consumed, and that includes natural man. (Deuteronomy 4:24; 9:3, Hebrews 12:29)

> "And the people stood afar off, and Moses drew near unto the thick darkness where God [was]." Exodus 20:21

> "These words the LORD spake unto all your assembly in the mount out of the midst of the fire, of the cloud, and of the thick darkness, with a great voice: and he added no more. And he wrote them in two tables of stone, and delivered them unto me." Deuteronomy 5:22

In the two preceding verses we can again see that the thick darkness was where God was. He was using the darkness as a protective shield for the people so they wouldn't be consumed by His glory.

CARRIED BY ONE CHERUB

> "He bowed the heavens also, and came down; and darkness [was] under his feet. And he rode upon a cherub, and did fly: and he was seen upon the wings of the wind. And he made darkness pavilions round about him, dark waters, [and] thick clouds of the skies." 2 Samuel 22:10-12

> "He bowed the heavens also, and came down: and darkness [was] under his feet. And he rode upon a cherub, and did fly: yea, he did fly upon the wings of the wind. He made darkness his secret place; his pavilion round about him [were] dark waters [and] thick clouds of the skies." Psalm 18:9-11

All right, the following statement is merely a possibility, and it is not meant to express fact; but it is interesting to note that in the preceding two verses there was only one cherub, and specifically only one cherub, present.

This cherub carried the Lord from beneath in these specific instances where darkness was also noted to be covering the Lord from beneath, enshrouding Him in its cover. Whereas in other scripture verses which speak of multiple cherubim carrying the Lord darkness is not mentioned as being present, shielding Him in His glory. Therefore it brings up the possibility that this one specific cherub which is referred to in these verses carrying the Lord when darkness needed to be present, could be, just perhaps, could be, the wicked covering cherub having to fulfill the duties of his office. For, as we have seen, darkness is not of the Lord's own person.

> "This then is the message which we have heard of him, and declare unto you, that God is light, and in him is no darkness at all." 1 John 1:5

Let's take a look at what happened when King Solomon built and inaugurated the temple unto the Lord in 1 Kings 8: 12-13 and in 2 Chronicles 6:1-2:

> "Then spake Solomon, The Lord said that he would dwell in the thick darkness. I have surely built thee an house to abide in, a place to be settled for ever." 1 Kings 8: 12-13

> "Then said Solomon, The Lord hath said that he would dwell in thick darkness, But I have built an house of habitation for thee, and a place for thy dwelling for ever." 2 Chronicles 6:1-2

This thick darkness wherein the Lord said He would dwell wasn't the perfect and permanent will of God, but He had to use it as a way to approach man and to move in His sin tainted creation. However, due to Solomon's obedience in building the Holy temple according to the strict instructions of the Lord (this was important seeing that the earthly temple was a replica of the heavenly temple) God was able to enter the proximity of man in a way that ensured the safety of His created without the total cloaking of His presence by a dark cloud.

This is why Solomon used the terms: "...*The Lord hath said...*, *...But I have built...*". This was a monumental change in God-man relations; the temple started to negate the need for the presence of the one who casts dark shadows.

To walk the way of life a bit further, after the resurrection of Messiah had occurred and the day of Pentecost had come, the following was written by Paul:

> "What? know ye not that your body is the temple of the Holy Ghost [which is] in you, which ye have of God...". 1 Corinthians 6:19

Covert coverings

The physical bodies of individual repentant believers, from the time of Pentecost onwards, have become the abode of the Holy Spirit, further lessening the need of the covering agent to exist as a separator in any capacity, as God Himself was increasingly sanctifying His own through His Spirit, and returning creation unto Himself. Light was increasingly shining out of darkness....

Now, let's briefly go back to a subject which has been touched on before, and that is the passing away of Moses, the prophet of God. As previously stated, Moses passed on due to his entering the unshielded presence of God. Moses was allowed into the presence and allowed to see God's glory uncovered. This was possible as satan was not present in that special meeting to cloak God's glory. The result of this event was Moses' body expired from the lack of a cover between him and the Lord.

The lack of satan's presence at that event is corroborated by satan's insistence to the archangel Michael that he as the angel of death must be legally given Moses' body to be killed. This clearly meant satan wasn't there to bring about Moses' death as Moses passed from witnessing the glory without the concealing cloud. (*Deuteronomy 34:1-8, Jude 1:9*)

The Genesis Mousetrap

Chapter twenty-one

It's getting dark out there

THE BRIGHT EVENING LIGHT OF MORNING

As the world moves ever closer to the end of the age of grace and to the second coming of the King Messiah, the Bible makes one thing abundantly clear; darkness of all manner will increase upon the earth. (*Matthew 24:3-44, Mark 13:8, Luke 17:26+28, 2 Timothy 3:1-5*)

All sort of evil associated with godlessness such as anti-Semitism, natural disasters, apathy, false religions, immorality, pride, selfishness, addictions, hatred, disease, wars, death, demonic activity, etc. etc., increase as the end of grace fast approaches. For these things themselves are among the forms and byproducts of the dark shadow that descends upon the earth in an ever increasing cloaking of the glorious light filled coming of Messiah.

Sadly, many will be so blinded by the veils and cloaks of darkness: such as poverty, lack, and sickness (the daily unmet needs of their physical bodies) with which satan attempts to manipulate the lives of man where he can in order to conceal from them the truth of the imminent arrival of Messiah, that many will, indeed, be unaware of His coming.

Equally sad, and still more manipulative in nature, is the much thicker blindfold which is placed upon many; that is the blindfold of the love of the world upon their eyes and hearts. It is the seductive veil of the satanic darkness of materialism and the lusts of the flesh which surrounds many peoples' lives in their eternal quest for the illusive joy of more.

The Genesis Mousetrap

So enthralled are they with the lies of this world that they aren't even aware of the times they face, or the reasons for them, or of the great truth of the returning King Messiah. Instead, they will blindly root about under the increasingly thick and perverted shadow of satan, scavenging through the seemingly tasty garbage of the flesh that he has deceived them with like a herd of hungry hogs totally unaware of the pretentious and wicked butcher standing by the gate. These are they who refuse to raise their heads in order to see that they must repent of their self-destructive ways before it's too late; for the King of Glory fast approaches and time runs out for all.

The darkening of creation and the increase of evil in the events of our days culminate with the seven year tribulation period that is filled with all the things which God hates; things which come from the hearts' of those spirits who dwell in darkness and evil. How are such wicked things able to seemingly thrive as the Lord of Glory approaches earth to reinstitute holiness and absolute rule? Wouldn't things become consecutively better and more idyllic the closer the Holy One approaches?

Well, the closer the Lord comes, the more need He has to move in thicker and thicker darkness; covering Himself for the sake of His created and the sin stained creation that He so loves. If the Lord were to approach creation as the King of Glory without this dark veil covering Himself creation would be destroyed due to its own sin. It would burn in His presence. Therefore, as His holy presence approaches and the light of His countenance increases towards the creation He needs to allow darkness to increase.

The cloak must thicken so that the fallen family of man and this sinful creation wouldn't be destroyed by the brightness of His holiness before Messiah Jesus actually arrives to re-establish the throne of David and safely cover creation with His own righteousness. The greater the light and the closer it approaches, the greater the need for the dark covering to shield man and creation. These two events of ever escalating light and darkness are of a necessity simultaneously occurring.

Therefore the fruits of holiness; faith, hope, and love should strengthen among the humble remnant in the body of believers who jealously guard their faith as their Lord ever approaches. Their light should steadily increase, while the evil intents of the wicked children of darkness grow ever more blatant and perverse; emboldened and seduced by the spiritual night that befalls sinful man as the cover thickens. (*Revelation 22:11, Ezekiel 3:27, Daniel 12:10*)

BELIEVERS?

Seeing how this spiritual cover of darkness is increasing upon creation in every format available to it, so that it may fulfill its mandate to cover the ever nearer arrival of the Lord of Glory; it is not then surprising that many who have at one time considered themselves to be believers in Messiah no longer are. They have grown cold, and died away from the fire and light of Messiah, becoming ensnared by some of the many tentacles of the satanic deception.

It should also not be surprising that many who call themselves Christians in this day really aren't. They claim the titles of the righteous, but have no love of God, or of His creation; they exuberantly twist His will and His Word in an ever increasing escalation of their pretentious false religion consisting of public displays of self righteousness entwined with highly visible acts of good works. (*Matthew 24:12, 2 Timothy 3:1-5*)

These modern day Pharisees intend to muddy the Torah of the Holy God with their so called holy lifestyles; works of the flesh which are intended to deceive others into thinking that these spiritual scalawags are the pure and good, while they eagerly try to hide the holiness and power of the living God behind the evil cloak of their dead and twisted religion.

These breathing white sepulchers contain only death and damnation in their beautifully adorned public lives while their hearts grow as dark as the "god" they are secretly in bondage to. Under the gilded veneer of their "Christian" morality they themselves often lead the way toward all the evils found in satan's darkness, and they actually do so quite arrogantly and without remorse. These are not just average "hypocrites"; for having lived in spiritual conceit and deceit for so long they have become "jaded hypocrites", more interested in the lies of fleshly religious self-satisfaction than they are in humbling themselves unto the God of

The Genesis Mousetrap

all creation. This is why Jesus wisely asked in Luke 18:8, *"...Nevertheless when the Son of man cometh, shall he find faith on the earth?"*

The righteous remnant appears a remnant indeed. The darkness is ever increasing upon the entire earth and those "believers" who think they stand firm in their superficial lives covered with self righteous works of satan's design need to take heed, lest they themselves are the ones who fall in the night. (*Matthew 6:2-5; 15:7-9; 23:1-29, Mark 13:35-36, Luke 12:45-47, Revelation 2:5*)

THE TEN

Another example of the end time darkness and the way it affects the believers is found in Matthew 25:1-13. The night had waxed long and the ten virgins grew tired of waiting for the bridegroom; they grew very tired....very tired indeed.... so they did what everyone does when the time of darkness envelopes the earth, they all fell asleep.

When the call went forth in Matthew 25:6, *"...Behold, the bridegroom cometh; go ye out to meet him.";* it was still a time of darkness, midnight, as a matter of fact, and half of the virgins couldn't go forth to meet Him as they didn't take care to have their lamps filled with oil to light. Oil is biblically representative of the anointing presence of God's Holy Spirit, the blessing of life. The five were foolishly unprepared for the bridegroom's arrival during the time the greatest darkness was upon the earth, and as a result they failed to go forth to meet the bridegroom (the Lord) to usher Him back at His coming.

This is also an important example of the immense value of having God's anointing, the blessing of life upon oneself; the five foolish virgins squandered their opportunity to get filled with God's Holy Spirit while there was time for them to do so; and were like all those who find themselves without His presence, unable to properly function in the blessings that are inherently upon their lives. (*Exodus 27:20, Leviticus 8:12, 1 Samuel 16:13*)

IF YOU'RE NOT IN.... DON'T GET TOO CLOSE!

One of the many misleading concepts which is quite prevalent in the world is the thought that if something is close enough, it's good enough;

it's acceptable, and actually quite admirable. For example, the silver medal is considered to be a very prestigious award; the second place finisher makes it onto the podium to receive honors with the winner. Children in math class are taught to round out numbers to the nearest whole figure, etc.

However, when it comes to the things of God, close is the absolute worst place to be. The Lord made it quite clear that we must either be for Him, or against Him; with Him, or far from Him, but the deceptively comfortable noncommittal middle is a place He hates for us to be.

> *"So then because thou art lukewarm, and neither cold nor hot, I will spue thee out of my mouth." Revelation 3:16*

> *"No man can serve two masters: for either he will hate the one, and love the other; or else he will hold to the one, and despise the other. Ye cannot serve God and mammon." Matthew 6:24*

NEAR IS WORSE THAN FAR!

Why is it that living nearish to God and being sort of close to Him is worse than being far from Him? It's because in a spiritual sense, satan stands near to God. That's right! The office of covering cherub is right there; up close and cozy to the throne of God, and it is very easy to get lost in the thick cloud of satan's deceptions if we choose to stand close, but yet at a comfortable distance from the Lord.

We may think we've found a pleasant place of compromise with the Almighty when all we're actually holding on to is the serpent's tail! And if we get into the attitude of: it's close enough therefore it's good enough; and since it looks like, sounds like, it must be, since it seems like, we step into satan's area of expertise; the close proximity, his area of operation, and allow ourselves to be partakers of his deception.

The Bible clearly makes reference to satan as a deceiver and a serpent, and one of the reasons it does so is that satan twists himself up so close to the truth, wrapping himself like the serpent he is around all truth of God in such a twisted way, that it becomes terribly difficult for natural man to discern fact from fiction if man doesn't press in to seek the Lord and the truth of God. It becomes very easy to fall prey to the notion that the serpent's way of being "godly" and spiritual is enough, that the lukewarm place is as close to God as any need be.

Natural fallen man doesn't want the heat of the holy fire which comes as a result of being in God's presence and thinks that satan's deceptive smokescreen holds an ideal temperature. In satan's sulfurous cloud, man can find a place which is neither hot with holiness and power nor is it the conscience grieving cold of outright blatant sin. This demonically inspired tepid view of holiness gives fallen man the false cover of deception in which pretense would ostensibly trump love.

All the while one ends up standing in the thick choking pollution of satan's lies; cloaked in, and worst of all, partaking of and adding oneself to a thicker blanket of deception than those who stand far from the Lord are capable of doing.

As strange as it seems, those who live in clear sin and open defiance of the Lord vehemently opposed to Him are less lost and less deceived than those who walk in satan's lukewarm cloud of pretend located next to real holiness; for the far off have no intentions of claiming to present the Lord and His truth to others. Those who are openly lost are so without the facade of godliness; but those who have entered into the lukewarm cloud caused by the deceptive fog of words carried on the serpent's intoxicatingly mellow breath add their own selves to the deception. In so doing, they are further thickening the cloud of deceit themselves, making it harder for the lost and hungry to find their way home to the Lord; these "comfortable Christians" cause it to be more difficult for the unsaved to approach the throne of Grace.

So, the Lord would rather see us cold than lukewarm; far rather than near; He doesn't want us to stand where satan stands, becoming one with his evil and blinded from the truth ourselves while we, either purposely or unintentionally, help the twisting serpent blind others who would wish to see. (*Ezekiel 34:18-22, Micah 3:5*)

GOD DESIRES ONENESS

Most of all, however, God wants us to be one with Him. He wants us hot, burning with the fire of His holy presence, shining with the light of

His Spirit and casting out the darkness from the creation around us by being conduits of His love and blessings, so that those who are near and those who are far off can come to know the depth of His tremendous grace. He would that all stand in the presence of the power of His love made available through His rich mercy in Messiah Jesus; and by so doing, we would leave no room for the darkness of the evil ones to hide His truth. No matter how deceptively close they may try to stand. (*Hebrews 1:7, Isaiah 57:19*)

THE ONES THAT CAUGHT AWAY

The ten virgins of Matthew 25:1-13 mentioned previously make a great lead off to this next issue: The rapture or catching away of the church and the reasons for it.

These ten virgins depict events surrounding this issue well. First of all, as the Bible mentions, they were all virgins; that is to say, they were not sullied by the sins of this world for they were cleansed through faith in the atonement work of Messiah. In other words, they were sanctified believers.

As scripture shows, the cry went forth, *"...Behold, the bridegroom cometh; go ye out to meet him."* but darkness was upon the earth and they all slept. The call that went forth indicated the bridegroom, Jesus, was coming. This call referred specifically to the Lord's second coming as He never did actually arrive during the events spoken of in this parable.

However, the five wise virgins did go out to meet Him (indicating the rapture) in order to usher in the bridegroom to receive the bride, as was the custom to do in the days of Israel yore. When the bridegroom would come for his bride, a group of friends and well wishers would go forth to escort him forth in a joyous procession.

The virgins who went forth to meet the bridegroom and to accompany Him back were the raptured saints which went forth to escort the Lord back to His beloved. That which is portrayed here is the catching away of the living saints and the resurrection of the dead in Messiah; all those of the body of Messiah, all those with the personal presence of the Holy Spirit upon their lives, must leave the earth before the great seven year tribulation can begin upon it. For the wicked and evil one is restrained by the Spirit of truth that indwells those in the body of Messiah here on earth; the evil is held back by those who have oil in their lamps to dispel the darkness. Therefore, the wicked cannot arise to their judgment, doom, and eventual removal from the earth which takes place during the tribulation until the time the righteous are removed.

This "removal" event then allows the wicked ones the necessary freedom through the vacuum of authority that exists due to the lack of the presence of the raptured (removed) body of Messiah from upon the earth to act in a way that brings judgment upon both the unrepentant that dwell upon the earth and also upon themselves. (*1 Corinthians 15:51-53, 1 Thessalonians 4:13-18, 2 Thessalonians 2:7; 2:1-17, Isaiah 26:19-21*)

THE DAY OF THE LORD

The seven year tribulation period is the transitional stage between the age of grace and the millennial Kingdom of Messiah. In this time, which will be a day of reckoning for all creation, the effects of the covering cherub will be most evident.

Biblically speaking, for the nations of the world, this timespan will be known as the "tribulation"; a series of events and Godly judgments that will bring about the end of the time of the gentiles; and for God's covenant nation of Israel this will be the *"time of Jacob's trouble"* as stated in Jeremiah 30:7. This period of time is also called the "birth pangs of the Messiah" as Israel will come into its much prophesied role as the deliverer of the manchild, and will experience the travails of the birth, the coming of the one who is the rightful heir to the Davidic Kingdom, the last Adam.

These two groups of people which are: Israel, and the nations of the world, will encounter very different but equally serious and painful events that will cause the satanically controlled gentile powers to fall, never to rise again; and shall bring Israel to a place where her blinders will be removed and her exile shall end, and she will cry out in humble prayer and supplication for the will of God to be done, for the King Messiah to arrive. (*Ezekiel 11:19-20*). In this period of time the satanic conspiracy comes to a boil, fervently blanketing creation in its evil darkness as never before, as the long anticipated King of Glory arrives. (*Jeremiah chapter 30*)

> *"Woe unto you that desire the day of the Lord! To what end is it for you? The day of the Lord is darkness, and not light." Amos 5:18*
>
> *"Shall not the day of the Lord be darkness, and not light? even very dark, and no brightness in it?" Amos 5:20*
>
> *"The sun shall be turned into darkness, and the moon into blood, before that great and notable day of the Lord come:" Acts 2:20*
>
> *"And it shall come to pass in that day, that the Lord shall punish the host of the high ones that are on high, and the kings of the earth upon the earth." Isaiah 24:21*

There is coming a day, a time of great judgment, that will bring about the end of the activities of the evil conspirators, and of the curse which they had so eagerly unleashed in their wickedness. These wicked angels are *"the host of the high ones that are on high"*, which were spoken of in the preceding verses.

The Lord will also remove from upon the earth and punish their willful confederates among the children of man; removing evil from the midst of His creation. Thus ending the evil twisting of God's will which the wicked ones had implementeded through their legal manipulations both in the heavens and upon the earth. The Lord will accomplish this through the arrival of the Adamic heir, the King Messiah to reinstitute the now trans-heavenly totalitarian Adamic Kingdom upon the earth.

These are the principal events of the seven year tribulation during which time the cloaking satanic darkness will be thickest upon the earth to conceal the Lord of Glory who will have almost arrived to rid God's heavens of the wicked beings.

This seven year tribulation period is in itself a picture of the seven creative days and seven Adamic days, and in this seven year timespan the events which are at the crux of the creation and redemption sagas are seen taking place in microcosm.

> *"And there appeared another wonder in heaven; and behold a great red dragon, having seven heads and ten horns, and seven crowns upon his heads. And his tail drew the third part of the stars of heaven, and did cast them to the earth: and the dragon stood before the woman which was ready to be delivered, for to devour her child as soon as it was born."*
> Revelation 12:3-4

Did you notice the dragon drew a third part of the stars of heaven with his tail? These are the wicked angels who chose to follow him; and how was it that the dragon was the one which cast these errant beings to earth at this time?

Remember now, the evil ones are still in the heavens all the way into the tribulation period. Due to the satanic covenant, the wicked angels are bound to one another, and satan was in a hurry to do what he could in order to prevent the successful arrival of the last Adam into the physical creation to establish and implement the rule of His Kingdom. This last Adam is the child of the woman (Israel) who was ready to deliver, and He comes to reestablish the Kingdom, reintroduce absolute rule upon the earth, and implement the time of judgments.

Notice, these wicked angels weren't cast down by God, rather, satan as instigator and head of the conspiracy was the one to cast them to earth at this time. Therefore, since God wasn't the one casting them down during this occasion the wicked were not yet forbidden by God from reentering their duties in the upper heavens. Instead, it was their leader satan who cast them down as he felt it necessary to have the wicked solely concentrate on finding a way to stop Messiah from arriving at the place where He initiates His absolute rule.

At this point in time, satan feels the need to send all of the evil spirits in His conspiracy to focus their twisted efforts of transgression solely upon the earth "realm". This is done in an attempt to not only conceal the coming of the Lord of Glory, which is his angelic duty, but to also pervertedly try to stop Messiah from coming altogether, for His coming marks the end of the satanic transgression.

In saying that satan cast the others down at this juncture, the Bible is also referring to the fact that for the first time satan and the other wicked ones were embarking on a "self initiated" rebellious endeavor. They were going to illegally attempt to stop the lawful Adamic heir from returning to His rightful kingdom; and so, due to their mutual conspiratorial covenant, and very limited time, the wicked all set out on their final, but highly treasonous venture at the behest of satan.

> "And all the host of heaven shall be dissolved, and all their host shall fall down, as the leaf falleth off from the vine, and as a falling [fig] from the fig tree. For my sword shall be bathed in heaven: behold, it shall come down upon Idumea, and upon the people of my curse, to judgment." Isaiah 34:4-5

These verses in Isaiah speak of the actions taking place in the following verse of Revelation 12:7 which shall be read next. In these verses of Isaiah we can see that God is saying He will utterly destroy and demolish the ranks of the wicked conspirators, the evil angels. This takes place in their heavenly authorities before He brings His wrath of judgment upon the earth, the authorities located therein, and the peoples thereof. His sword shall decimate the ranks of the wicked during the events which transpire on the Lord's day.

Isaiah 34:4-5 must be read again; it is so amazing to see God saying that He will unleash His sword upon the wicked angels! His sword shall be first bathed in heaven!

IT BEGINS

> "And there was war in heaven: Michael and his angels fought against the dragon; and the dragon fought and his angels, And prevailed not; neither was their place found any more in heaven. And the great dragon was cast out, that old serpent, called the Devil, and Satan, which deceiveth the whole world: he was cast out into the earth, and his angels were cast out

> with him. And I heard a loud voice saying in heaven, Now is come salvation, and strength, and the kingdom of our God, and the power of his Christ: for the accuser of our brethren is cast down, which accused them before our God day and night. And they overcame him by the blood of the Lamb, and by the word of their testimony; and they loved not their lives unto the death. Therefore rejoice, [ye] heavens, and ye that dwell in them. Woe to the inhabiters of the earth and of the sea! for the devil is come down unto you, having great wrath, because he knoweth that he hath but a short time. And when the dragon saw that he was cast unto the earth, he persecuted the woman which brought forth the man [child]." Revelation 12:7-13

This, my friends, is the moment of the wicked rebellion. This is the point in time when clear blatant illegal angelic sin occurs. This is where the satanic conspirators finally break into open defiance against the Lord and are subsequently removed from the heavens due to their illegal actions (and likely, due to their neglect of their heavenly duties as well).

As satan defiantly moves against the woman (Israel), and tries to devour the manchild she bore, he willfully defies the Lord of creation and rebels against the Most High. This is the event which finally allows God to begin the complete eradication of the now rebellious and sinful angels from His creation. This is what Isaiah 14 and Ezekiel 28 were referring to; the implementation of judgment upon the now openly rebellious wicked angels is beginning at this point.

This is where the wicked transgressors move from manipulating and twisting God's laws, and merely planning their evil rebellion by saying in their hearts: "I will do" etc. etc., and 'merely' covenanting to act against the Lord, to actually launching into an open premeditated break against the Holy God and His anointings upon all the righteous beings which the wicked will try to stop and thus negate. The conspirators will do all they can to halt or derail the reestablished will of the Lord in Messiah any way they can; and they do it knowing that the law will shelter them no longer.

After having sown the original seeds of destruction into the heavens many ages prior, the wicked now begin to reap the full harvest of their own doom. In this matter we are given yet another chance to see the law of reciprocity at work.

WHY WERE THEY CAST DOWN TO EARTH?

Now, why were the wicked angels cast down to earth at this time for their tribulation era sojourn after their rebellion, instead of being sent directly to hell? What reason was there for God to do such a curious thing?

Alright, as we have read, all the angels are bearers of blessings, anointings, and authorities that are based in offices in God's Kingdom; and some of these myriad blessings and rights, indeed, do extend well into this triune universe.

However, it was the fall of Adam into sin, and Adam's consequent submission to the satanic conspiracy which gave satan and his wicked ilk rights from and over the negligent Adam. These particular rights had their basis in the absolute Kingdom of Adam, and not in the free will Kingdom of God, and these Adamic rights were not illegally used by the wicked angels in their rebellious and failed activities to come which bring about their tribulation time fall from their offices of authority in God's Kingdom at the hands of Michael and the angels.

Remember, the authorities based in Adam's Kingdom are independent of the authorities based in God's Kingdom. Therefore, these wicked angels were still secure in their legally held and used Adamic rights even though they forfeited their angelic offices in the heavens of God's Kingdom. Had it not been for the control which the wicked angels had over these Adamic rights inherent to our universe, specifically inherent to the Kingdom of Adam, God would have been able to send the wicked straight to hell the moment the outright rebellion begins.

However, these rights and authorities in the "world" are what gave the wicked angels legal protection so that they could not be thrown directly into hell but had to be cast down to earth, into this triune universe which is the location of their usurped Adamic authorities. As stated, this takes place during the tribulation period after their open breach of law at the onset of the heavenly rebellion. Here, they were to stay until their hatred and lust came through into their inherited Adamic authorities in such a way that the wicked conspirators were to once again openly rebel by overextending their remaining rights; using those authorities specific to the Adamic Kingdom (at that point their only remaining rights) to rebel against the last Adam and His Kingdom of Israel located upon this earth.

This they will do in a planned open defiance of God's legally binding decrees upon all created. Those rebellious actions, in turn, give Messiah, the Adamic heir, the reasons and rights to execute the removal of the wicked in an uncontested way.

A CONFLICT OF INTEREST?

It may be asked: "If Jesus was given all power and authority upon His resurrection and ascension, with what power and authority do the wicked angels operate in at this time? If they both operate in Adamic rights, isn't there an inconsistency?"

No, there's no inconsistency at all. What needs to be remembered is that all of the Adamic authority which satan received and operates in is located in the realm of rights inherent to the physical body of man. This portion of the triune man is scripturally speaking unrepentantly wicked, and like the evil angels, would not humble itself to the mercy of God's salvation if it could.

The flesh of man is actually shown throughout scripture to be in league with satan, and as such, is irredeemable in its current state, as it is the source of evil influence in man and the location for the operation and effects of the curse.

That is one reason the glorified body is given to the believers at the resurrection of the righteous; to separate the believer from the source of the curse.

It is through this "piggybacking" on the rights of the flesh of willingly sinful collaborators in the family of man who refuse to submit themselves to the power of the grace of God found in the last Adam, Messiah, that the satanic transgressors can operate in this earth in such bodily based Adamic authority as unrepentant individuals yield to them; even though the wicked angels were defeated at the cross of Calvary. God will respect the free will and kingship inherent to man, and not enforce the grace that He has made available to all men, that is, until the time spoken of by the wicked spirits themselves, the time of the great judgment which they themselves said is coming, a time when the wicked (to use their own words as a basis of statement) shall be "tormented". (*Matthew 8:29*)

It is then that all of the King Messiah's enemies will be made His footstools, and Messianic rule becomes effectively dominant at the end of the tribulation and at the beginning of the millennial reign.

Conversely, the Adamic authority which Messiah operates in during this pre-millennial period, while total and absolute, has its basis in the once dead spiritual authorities of Adam which again came alive through Messiah in His sacrificial atonement for all men who accept His rule.

In this pre-millennial age these authorities become absolute in a person's spirit only once a person chooses to accept Messiah's Lordship in all areas of life and begins to voluntarily yield to the will and Spirit of God who comes to glorify the Messiah. Such a person is then transformed by God's indwelling Holy Spirit into the image of God, as Adam originally was. How quickly the transformation happens in the different facets of a person's life, and how much transformation ultimately takes place in the physical portion of the person as it is brought into submission to the spirit, still remains up to the individual believer in Messiah. (*John 16:13-15*)

Furthermore, these absolute rights of Messiah will only become universally unresisted in the creation at the onset of the eighth day when all flesh (meaning all of mankind), including those which cannot and will not yield to Messiah, comes to an absolute, complete end.

Until that time, mankind lives in a constant strife in creation between the flesh of man, which sanctions evil as long as it lives, and those in mankind who favor not the flesh of man, but the spirit: Which through faith in Messiah is reborn at the substitutional death of the flesh upon the voluntary acceptance of His atoning sacrifice and accepted Lordship.

However, as the Messiah returns to rule at the end of the tribulation period, this rightful heir to all Adamic authority has the legal right, and actually, the obligation, to reign over all who voluntarily subjugate themselves to Him; and He is also obliged to remove those who won't.

CAST OUT

Just for additional clarity, in the biblical use of the term *"cast out into the earth"*, it is not meant that the wicked angels were thrown into the Rakia heaven, the physical portion of this creation; rather, this refers to them being cast into the heaven where their authority has always been located in this universe, and where Adamic authority was and is located, and that is into the spiritual Shechakim side of the universe.

From there they will not be able to ascend into the upper heavens any longer; the Kingdom of our God will have been cleansed by the power of His Messiah. Instead, the wicked are confined to Shechakim from where they attempt to manipulate Rakia, the heaven containing the dust matter of Adam's body which the serpent received rights over.

Using the power of their authorities over their willing cohorts in the family of man, the wicked will try to destroy the seat of the Kingdom of the last Adam upon the earth, the Kingdom of Israel. This leads to their final rebellion through the use of their appropriated Adamic authorities, and their final removal during the end of the second three and one half year portion of the seven year tribulation.

A second and equally compelling reason exists for why God expelled the wicked from the heavens and set them into the earth realm for a short period of time. The Lord made this very clear in scripture; He wants all creation to see the defeat and destruction of the wicked. He wants all people upon the earth to understand the magnitude of evil that is present in the wicked angels; and the Lord wants all people to see that without Him and the powers that are in the offices He has given to the angelic, or to anyone else, satan and the evil ones are inconsequential in themselves.

These evil beings wrought great havoc and destruction in the heavens, and upon the earth in particular due to Adam's perceived carelessness in the garden. They existed only to steal, kill, and destroy in their insatiable quest for the unattainable rights to be God. They had polluted the heavens with a most foul evil and the Lord wants to make an open show of them before every being in creation. He will humiliate the wicked ones before man, before those of His beloved creation that the wicked were trying to destroy, by showing how weak these depraved and perverted individuals really are without His authorities and offices of power. In those days the children of Israel will make poems and proverbs, and sing taunting songs about the presumptive destroyer who himself was destroyed through God's great mercy. *(Isaiah 14:4)*

> *"Thou [art] the anointed cherub that covereth; and I have set thee [so]: thou wast upon the holy mountain of God; thou hast walked up and down in the midst of the stones of fire. Thou [wast] perfect in thy ways from the day that thou wast created, till iniquity was found in thee. By the multitude of thy merchandise they have filled the midst of thee with violence, and thou hast sinned: therefore I will cast thee as profane out of the mountain of God: and I will destroy thee, O covering cherub, from the midst of the stones of fire. Thine heart was lifted up because of thy beauty, thou hast corrupted thy wisdom by reason of thy brightness: I will cast thee to the ground, I will lay thee before kings, that they may behold thee. Thou hast defiled thy sanctuaries by the multitude of thine iniquities, by the iniquity of thy traffick; therefore will I bring forth a fire from the midst of thee, it shall devour thee, and I will bring thee to ashes upon the earth in the sight of all them that behold thee. All they that know thee among the people shall be astonished at thee: thou shalt be a terror, and never [shalt] thou [be] any more." (Ezekiel 28:14-19)*

May these verses be fulfilled soon… and in our time. AMEN!

The Genesis Mousetrap

Chapter twenty-two

THE MUST ATTEND EVENT OF THE MILLENNIA(L) REIGN

YOM KIPPUR

One of the many issues that has greatly baffled countless generations of mortal man for thousands of years, and which still keeps scores of people awake at night in anxious pondering, is the perplexing question of: "Will there be life after devil?" (It's a quip, folks).

Well, the answer is naturally, yes; but in order to get to the millennial Sabbath (Now approximately 99.993% devil free!) we need to look at and understand how we get there, and the seven feasts of God which were mentioned earlier hold a key to help us in this process. These feasts were, are, and will always be, filled with God's wisdom and eternal truth; but one of these feasts is also very telling on the issue of the covering cherub, and of the coming lack thereof. That feast, of course, is Yom Kippur. So, this is the feast which will be looked at as it is most relevant to the issues at hand.

By no means is this meant to be an exhaustive look at Yom Kippur, which like all the feasts is stunningly rich with God's voice of truth and prophesy. There simply isn't the room in this book to go into all the details, so we'll do a quick overview of some of the covering related issues necessary for entry into the Millennial reign.

The feast of Yom Kippur is kept by Jews all over the earth as the single most important day of the year. God gave the biblical command that all Israel must humble themselves before Him on the day of Yom Kippur;

and any who were not afflicted on that day would be cast out of the inheritance of Israel. That is a really, really, big deal, and it signifies the vital importance of this event. (*Leviticus 23: 26-32*)

COMPLIANCE IS SERIOUS BUSINESS

The Day of Atonement is a day of serious repercussions, a day of amazement, a day to humble oneself before the Almighty; for it is the day God covers those of His people who choose to present themselves before Him. The Hebrew term "Yom Kippur" directly translated into English means "day of covering", and is so named in recognition of the fact that it is God who covers His own in His great mercy. (*Leviticus 16*)

How does this apply to our look at the covering cherub? Well, as it has already been stated, this feast is the single most important day of the year, and as a prophetic event it retains that status. Like all the feasts, indeed, like everything in the Word, the Day of Atonement has four unique depictive issues or events which it refers to. For the Day of Atonement these events are:

- The individual covering and sanctification.

- The national covering and sanctification.

- The prophetic individual covering and sanctification; fulfilled during Messiah's first appearance.

- The prophetic national/kingdom wide covering and sanctification; to take place after Messiah's second coming.

The effects of the covering cherub and the coming lack thereof are most evident in the fourth level mentioned; that being the prophetic national kingdom wide covering which will be discussed shortly; but at this point, we'll delve into the first two levels mentioned in order to build the necessary framework to better understand the other levels.

In the temple period on this great day two goats were brought up for a once yearly sacrifice; this was so that Israel would be in compliance to the scriptural mandate. The High Priest would lay his hands upon one and declare it for God as a blood sacrifice given on behalf of His people. The High Priest would also place his hands upon the other and declare it for "Azazel"; and in so doing, transfer the sin of the nation upon that particular goat. This became the infamous "scapegoat" of lore.

Now, according to Jewish tradition, Azazel was one of the highest ranking of the transgressionary angels, and apparently one who was responsible for enforcing the wages of sin upon the people. The wages of sin being death according to Romans 6:23.

The goat that was declared for God was slaughtered on the Temple grounds and bled. The blood of this goat was then offered to God as a sacrifice; a covering for the people; a way for them to stand before God another year without being cast out of the promise of Israel due to their unending frailty of sin.

The other goat, the one that had the sins of the nation placed upon it, "the scapegoat", was brought out of the temple and chased into the wilderness to die. It was given to Azazel as a substitutionary death; for it carried the sins of the nation upon it, and the wages of sin are death. So, that particular goat, the scapegoat, had to die in order to satisfy the decrees and ordinances of God made to clarify the rules of the order of the lower heavens which Adam and the serpent made for themselves during the events that led to, and included, Adam's fall into sin. The serpent was due his sin laden dust, and it was given to him in the substitutional form of the goat.

Now, before the goats were sacrificed, a scarlet cloth was nailed to the temple door. This cloth signified the sin of the nation hanging upon a tree, in this case a wooden door (Jesus Himself said: *"I am the Door"*, another picture of Messiah's death on the wooden cross, He became sin and scarlet with blood, and was hung upon the "tree" to be given on behalf of our sins).

After the deaths of the sacrificial goat and the scapegoat, the scarlet cloth would turn white to signify the acceptance of the sacrificial offerings by God. This change of color was to indicate God's acceptance of the sacrificed goat as a sin covering, and that the substitutionary sinful dust of the earth, the scapegoat, was "eaten" by the serpent of death in accordance to the rights God decreed unto it in Genesis 3:14.

Through this sacrificial format, the laws of God upon the nation were judged to be satisfied both individually and nationally, and the laws and

The Genesis Mousetrap

order of the fallen earth as established by the actions of Adam and the serpent were deemed to have been kept.

TYING LOOSE THREADS TOGETHER

This thread of information winds its way into the fourth chapter of the Book of Luke where it ties in with some of the other strands of knowledge that we have been previously knitting together.

> *"And all they in the synagogue, when they heard these things, were filled with wrath, And rose up, and thrust him out of the city, and led him unto the brow of the hill whereon their city was built, that they might cast him down headlong. But he passing through the midst of them went his way,"* Luke 4:28-30

Just what is going on in these verses, and how does it apply to our look at things? The one original sin of Adam was disobedience. A look back in this book will remind us that Adam knew he needed to sacrifice in order to bring about atonement, but he chose to do it incorrectly, in disobedience against his better knowledge of God's laws as Adam's way appeared to be a seemingly easier form of compliance.

As we move the hands of time forward some 3400-3700 years, we can see that the children of Israel had over the centuries developed some extra biblical traditions of their own which they had added to God's laws and instructions (much like Adam had). This ingrained altering of Godly decree came to also affect the observance and delivery of the Yom Kippur sacrifice.

The apparently harmless modifications of the scriptural instructions concerning the Yom Kippur decrees was most evident in the casting of the scapegoat down a cliff to its death, rather than the exiling of the goat into the desert to die as Torah instructs in Leviticus 16:10. Over the centuries the nation of Israel had found it to be both a more convenient and a faster way to carry out God's decrees by simply casting the scapegoat down a nearby cliff to die quickly rather than exiling the goat to die in the desert over an unknown period of time.

The must attend event of the millennia(l) reign

This slight change in procedures didn't alter the outcome of events. The scapegoat died in the desert, either way; and all seemed well. But, as our father Adam so painfully taught us, incorrect compliance with God's Word is disobedience, and disobedience is sin.

The consequences and severity of the breach against God's will may not manifest themselves immediately; especially due to what may seem to be trivial changes in otherwise correctly implemented procedures; "after all", says the mind of man, "it would seem the intent is what matters most; and in this case, a dead goat is still a dead goat". However, these goats were the Yom Kippur offering brought before the Holy Lord; and they were prophetically picturing Messiah's sacrifice. As such, they were crucially important and were serving a vital purpose. The sacrifices were not to be altered or perverted in any way as they were God given pictures of important events to come.

The scapegoat which was cast off of a cliff to die, died much sooner than the one correctly released into the desert would have; and herein lays the problem. The living prophecy of Yom Kippur was lived out incorrectly.

The people of the synagogue mentioned in Luke 4:28-30, being the descendants of the disobedient Adam that all naturally minded unrepentant men are, and being firmly ensconced in this incorrect sacrificial tradition, attempted to cast Jesus off of a cliff to die as an innocent scapegoat in the very early moments of His Messianic ministry.

Were they aware that there was a deeper spiritual issue at work in their actions? No, they were just an angry mob of people who would have unintentionally fulfilled an incorrectly instituted version of scripture and prophecy due to the fact that the sin of national disobedience through incorrect compliance of scripture opened the door for the wicked spirits to manipulate them in this way.

The wicked conspirators, anxious in their quest to rid the earth of its rightful King, attempted to have Messiah killed and removed as soon as possible, much in the same manner as the scapegoat traditionally had been, by having Him expeditiously thrown off of a cliff and prematurely slain by a people which had a long standing tradition of disobediently complying with Godly sacrificial law.

The Genesis Mousetrap

This brings us back to the vitally important lesson we first learned through Eve's conversation with the serpent: Be vigilant not to alter or change the Word of God in any way; for everything about it has a deeper significance than we could envision, and the consequences of doing so can be most severe.

THE THIRD LEVEL

In the third or prophetic individual sanctification level of personal atonement or salvation, Jesus did, indeed, fulfill both of these pictoral sacrifices upon His death.

First, as a sin offering: by being made sin and dying in the place of everyone who would proverbially place their hands upon Him (as the High Priest did to the goats) and declare Him to be their substitutional sin offering, He eternally satisfied the decrees of God and the requirement of dust for the serpent.

Secondly, as a blood offering, by being offered to God, the shed blood of Jesus will cover, and not only cover, but it will cleanse the sinner and make righteous the individual person here and now, so that the individual born again people who choose life in Messiah can live before the Holy God and not be consumed with the fire of holiness brought into their lives by His Spirit. (*Hebrews 9:12; 10:4*)

THE FOURTH LEVEL

In the fourth or national prophetic atonement level; that is, in the sanctification of Israel which leads to the redemption of all creation, the Day of Atonement allows for the removal of the wicked ones from God's Kingdom at the end of the tribulation. It is there that the feast of Yom Kippur takes on yet another extremely important role. What we needed to learn from the days of the temple sacrifice was that the goat declared for God was sacrificed to cover the nation, in order to allow an imperfect nation the ability to stand before the perfect God and not be destroyed. This has great significance in the great day of the Messianic Yom Kippur to come.

After the arrival of Messiah, at the end of the seven year tribulation when the wicked angels have been cast out of heaven and banished into hell for punishment in outer darkness, the commencement of Yom Kippur will begin and the Lord will judge the nations according to their behavior toward His people, and consequently of their sin.

In this subsequent judgment of the sheep and goat nations spoken of in Matthew 25:31-46 (the sheep nations are those who are judged to have been kind to God's people, whereas the goats are those which were disobedient to His will), Messiah Jesus Himself will become the covering for Israel; sanctifying the nation with His blood, and He will be covering the sheep nations with His righteousness and holiness so that they may enter into the presence of God in His millennial Davidic Kingdom. More precisely, He will be covering the sheep nations with His power and righteousness, with His blood, but not sanctifying them.

This is a very unique and unusual event which will occur only one time in the history of the redemptive process. This event of covering is not to signify or accept the national salvation of Israel which will have previously occurred upon Messiah's physical appearance in the second coming as a result of Israel's repentance and prayers. Nor will it be to signify the salvation of the sheep nations that survive His post tribulation judgment, for those sheep nations have not yet experienced and may well never experience a national salvation. Rather, they have been given the grace to enter the millennial era due to the kindness they have shown toward God's own in the Godly hope that they too would repent and choose grace during their time in the millennial Sabbath.

The wicked goat nations conversely will be sent away to die (sent to hell) for their part in the sinful rebellion, much as the scapegoat was. For this day is the culmination of the removal of the sinful beings' grip from upon the earth in preparation of the millennial age.

So then, the great Messianic Yom Kippur, the day of covering, is to arrange for the physical people of the entirely saved nation of Israel; and for the people of the unsaved but obedient sheep nations; as well as all of the natural creation, to survive the manifest glory of the Holy God which would no longer be covered or veiled behind the dark curtain of the covering cherub due to satan's removal from office and his one thousand year binding in the bottomless pit.

Messiah Jesus, the Son of man, will stand as a perfect covering for the creation He judged to be worthy of His rule and over those individuals which He accepted into His millennial Kingdom. Messiah will shield this still imperfect creation from the manifest glory of the Holy God so that the Kingdom of Messiah's authority wouldn't be destroyed due to the fact that satan (the former Lucifer), the covering angel of the Most High is removed from office, and is no longer hiding the majestic radiance and power of the Almighty.

It is imperative that Messiah step into the office which was left empty by the removal of satan upon his rebellion and judgment. For without Messiah's shielding cover, all of creation would die under the power of God's manifest holiness. If it weren't for Messiah's covering, God's great glory would shine unfiltered upon the physical earth that is not yet made holy through the voluntary personal salvation of every individual child of Adam present in the physical creation, and by the expulsion of the remaining unrepentant sinners therein to an eternity in the lake of fire, or through the passage of the required time, which is a week of days, that is needed to separate certain uncleanliness from God.

Remember, there is still sin present in men and in creation during Messiah's millennial reign; although it won't dominate creation through the manipulation of the dust of the earth, the body, as it does now since the rebellious angels will be removed and the curse will be broken as the King, the last Adam, rules creation with His righteous iron rod.

Unlike the wicked cherub who Messiah will have replaced in this office through His works and God's faithfulness, Jesus as the atoning cover will be shielding the holiness of God in the way it was meant to be covered, in a respectful and complimentary canopy of shelter, as a sign of respect to the Highest.

He won't be hiding God or truth behind intricate deceptions and falsehoods, weaving lies into a net so tight that nothing could survive the strangling darkness of the perverted oppression it causes as satan had done in his use of the office. No, no. Jesus, the Word of God, God Himself, the wearer of many crowns, will do what He has always done when things weren't going well for the creation He so loves. He will take upon Himself the added role vacated by the covering cherub on the Day

The must attend event of the millennia(l) reign of Atonement upon His second advent, and in so doing, respectfully cover His creation with the righteousness that comes as a result of His own shed blood; allowing natural man to walk without the dark blindness and heavy yoke of satan's oppression for the first time since Adam's fall in fulfillment of His Words spoken so long ago. (*Matthew 23:37, Luke 13:34*)

The Genesis Mousetrap

Chapter twenty-three

The end of the days

THE THOUSAND YEARS

The entry of the creation into the millennial era is the event that begins God's declared Sabbath rest from the creative and redemption narratives. This takes place upon the beginning of the seventh day of creation; the six days of "work" having been completed at that point. The last Adam, Messiah, having arrived late on the sixth day, and having been blessed by God to rule over everything created. (*Genesis 1:26-31, Matthew 24:29-30*)

The millennial Kingdom is the first time the Adamic mandate will actually be fulfilled upon the earth as the King Messiah initiates His absolute rule; His tyranny of love over the entire earth.

It is worth noting that the wicked beings were unable to submit themselves to the absolute rule of God's will over their lives. The wicked conspirators couldn't bear to be in bondage to Adamic power and instead chose to remove themselves through rebellion and defiance rather than to languish in a state of perfect submittal to the Lord in His rule as the Son of man.

This thousand year reign, though free from satanic affliction, is still not a holy place, however, as natural unrepentant man, those born from the first Adam and dominated by the physical dust body, but not born again from faith in the second Adam, still constitute the majority of the people alive on the earth during this era. The Book of Revelation describes this time well in its description of the seventh church of Asia, the church of Laodicea:

> *"Because thou sayest, I am rich, and increased with goods, and have need of nothing; and knowest not that thou art wretched, and miserable, and poor, and blind, and naked: I counsel thee to buy of me gold tried in the fire, that thou mayest be rich; and white raiment, that thou mayest be clothed, and [that] the shame of thy nakedness do not appear; and anoint thine eyes with eyesalve, that thou mayest see."*
> *Revelation 3:17-18*

The people of this Messianic age, although they are not being constantly harassed or influenced by satan, are still as self centered as any who walk according to the flesh, and they erroneously begin to believe that it is their holiness, their righteousness, and their efforts, which have caused this era of great peace and contentment. Not realizing that it is the rule from Zion by the King Messiah which keeps righteous order, that it is His iron rod which enforces the blessings of prosperity upon the earth through His will and might, not their effots or wisdom.

It is this lack of personal repentance and absence of the realization of true salvation among the peoples of the earth that requires the one thousand year sabbatical covering of Messiah to keep the people from being destroyed by God's manifest presence. This is also the reason satan will be released for yet a season at the end of the seventh day; to give an opportunity for those who have not yet yielded themselves unto God to enter into rebellion against Him under the seducing darkness of evil.

Every being created with free will needs to make a choice, a voluntary decision about whether to partake of evil or accept grace; even those people in the millennial Sabbath.

Once satan has been unchained and released from the bottomless pit back into Shechakim, and has gone throughout the earth to raise those who would follow him into rebellion (unfortunately there will be no shortage of volunteers), he will then rally them to war against Messiah and His Kingdom of Israel.

This surprising event at the closing of the millennial Kingdom will be the final end to satan and the children of the flesh, the ones who choose

The end of the days

to walk under the influence of their own unrepentant natural minds. The only physical inhabitants of the millennial age who will be left to live upon the earth at the end of this final war of rebellion against the Anointed and His nation of Israel are those who have chosen to voluntarily align themselves with Messiah and humble themselves to His grace. This event is what the apostle John wrote of in Revelation, calling the peoples and events that are included in this great final insurrectionary battle *"Gog and Magog". (Revelation 20:8)*

This is more than likely the same battle spoken of in the Book of Ezekiel, chapters 38 and 39. Gog, the chief prince of Meshech and Tuval, and the head of this final worldwide conspiracy to destroy Israel and topple God's Messiah, is none other than satan, the serpent, leviathan, who had been released from the pit to give man a last necessary opportunity to rebel and to forsake the things of God.

> *"And you shall say; So said the Lord God: Behold, I am against you, Gog, the prince, the head of Meshech and Tubal. And I shall unbridle you, and I shall put hooks into your jaws and bring you forth and all your army, horses and riders, all of them clothed in finery, a great assembly, with encompassing shield and buckler, all of them grasping swords."* Judaica Press Complete Tanach translation, *Yechezkel (Ezekiel) 38:3-4*

The Lord, through his prophet Ezekiel, spoke of unbridling Gog, loosing him from the constraints previously placed upon him by God. This is an allusion to satan and all wickedness being confined and limited by the decrees of God, and subsequently loosed by command at a set time. Yet more specifically, it is a reference to satan being unbound after the thousand year incarceration, and then of the Lord subsequently putting hooks into the jaws of this Gog, precisely because it is Gog who is leviathan, and leviathan, as we have seen, seems quite adept at receiving God's hooks into his jaws.

Indeed, the original hooks were not removed from his jaws upon satan's temporary one thousand year incarceration, and Gog is tied into doing exactly what God wants, which is to offer the people of the millennial rule a free will choice of life or death; and to then have this

The Genesis Mousetrap

Gog lead those who love death unto their final end upon the hills of Israel. The Lord will not only unbridle and loose Gog, but He will also pull him into action by tightening the lines that are hooked into Gog's jaws and haul him into the land of Israel with his massive band of errant humanity in tow.

These hooks will include strong enticements for Gog to break against the covenant nation of God, which is Israel, and to raise the nations to war against the King Messiah, and after he does so, the long promised words of Isaiah will come to pass:

> "In that day the LORD with his sore and great and strong sword shall punish leviathan the piercing serpent, even leviathan that crooked serpent; and he shall slay the dragon that [is] in the sea." Isaiah 27:1

And so ends the saga of the self-proclaimed adversary of God. The trap was made; the bait was set; the beast had swallowed the hooks; the line was tightened; and the old dragon was pulled in to its ultimate destruction at the end of the seventh day.

Notice, that biblically speaking, the leviathan is predominantly pictured as being a sea creature; and the reason for this is that the seas are a metaphor for peoples and nations. It is through individuals found in nations, and in the nations of man themselves, that leviathan was enticed to move and attempt to bring about his will. So naturally, he will be most logically found, caught, and judged in the place he feels he can be most comfortable and active, and that place is in the seas of the family of man.

Remember, it was through the Lord's amazing plan of creation, and through the establishment of the house of Adam with its procreative rights and multitudes of offspring upon the earth, that God was able to create the perfect complex climate, the perfect seas with the perfect conditions, to fish out the evil leviathan from His creation using the perfect bait of man's authority.

Thusly, God will remove the serpent from the heavens once and for all, to be finally slain with the Lord's own sword; His sore, and great, and strong sword.

What is the *"sore and great and strong sword"* that the Lord will use to slay leviathan with?

> *"...and the sword of the Spirit, which is the word of God:"* Ephesians 6:17

> *"And out of his mouth goeth a sharp sword..."* Revelation 19:15

> *"And then shall that Wicked be revealed, whom the Lord shall consume with the spirit of his mouth..."* 2 Thessalonians 2:8

THE HOLY SPIRIT IS THE SWORD!

His Spirit is that sword with which He shall destroy the evil one! Remember, it was the Spirit of God which was most wronged in the darkening of the deep initiated by satan, and it was specifically the Spirit of God which set forth to negate the abysmal effects of satan's actions taking place upon the face of creation as stated in Genesis 1:2. For the law of reciprocity to be fulfilled, it is, and will be, the Holy Spirit which will ultimately end the wickedness of satan.

QUESTION: WHOSE WILL SHALL BE DONE? ANSWER: GOD'S.

It is at the end of the thousand year reign that the final judgment of the wicked beings takes place; this is also commonly referred to as the "Great White Throne" judgment. This judgment will be preceded by the second great resurrection of the dead which occurs at the end of the millennial reign and is in preparation for the final judgment of the wicked.

In this final resurrection for judgment, those saved among the family of man, along with the Lord God Himself, will judge the wicked angels and sentence them according to their deeds. All the remaining dead, those who are the wicked of man, will have been brought back to life, and subsequently judged according to their deeds and justly sentenced into their proper place in the lake of fire. (*Revelation 20:11-15, 1 Corinthians 15:26, Isaiah 24:21-22*)

Now, why is it that all the dead must be brought back to life in their natural bodies? Why couldn't they be left dead, and allowed to remain in either heaven in the case of the resurrection of the righteous, or in the case of the resurrection of the wicked, left in hell, and later transferred to the lake of fire? ....More questions? Who keeps coming up with them anyway? Okay, alright, I do, but still; OI VEI!

Seriously though, the reasons for the resurrections beyond the need for all beings to bow before the King Messiah; submit to His rule, confess the Lordship of Jesus to the glory of God the Father, and to receive their proper judgments; rewards in the case of the first resurrection (that of the righteous which occurs prior to the millennial reign), and punishments in the case of the second resurrection (that of the wicked during the great white throne judgment occurring at the end of the millennial reign), are actually quite interesting, and they are tied into the previously mentioned facts.

ALL WORKS OF "SELF" SHALL BURN

As concerning the righteous, in 1 Corinthians 3:13-15 the Bible states that the works of some shall burn in the fire and only their souls shall remain to be saved. This means every work and every effort done outside of the will of God, everything done without the anointing of life involved in it, no matter how good or how apparently holy, if it is done without the personal permission, will, and involvement of the Holy Spirit instigating and completing it will be brought to naught and be done away with. Such deeds which originate from "self" will not be found to exist upon the completion of God's judgments of the works of the righteous.

This specific word was referring to the judgment upon the works of the righteous individuals and the root reasons behind the source of their works! How much more applicable is it to the destruction of the works of the wicked?!

Now, an explanation for the reasons behind this fact: just as we clearly understand that Jesus has always existed and that He was crucified from before the beginning of time, and that He was always the King of Kings, so too must we also realize that God is the only "I AM", and that nothing has ever existed outside of Him; or can ever exist outside of Him.

The end of the days

This amazing omnipresent creator God never quit being the all encompassing ever present God, even though the wicked transgressors attempted to hide His will and presence and initiate their own works and deeds to supersede and negate those of the will of God. As we come to realize that fact, we can then better understand that nothing which the wicked among man or angels did of their own dark hearts was done according to the will or Spirit of God; but they were actually operating in their own twisted free will, moving perversely in their granted authorities to do their own vile works contrary to the will of the only One who is the all encompassing I AM.

For that reason, when the resurrections occur and judgments are passed, all the works ever accomplished in disobedience, wickedness, or rebellion (that is, performed outside of the will of God), shall be brought to naught and burn along with the wicked themselves. The very works themselves shall be negated and emptied from God's creation, and shall burn and be destroyed. There is a beautiful verse in first John which states this fact well:

> "....For this purpose the Son of God was manifested, that he might destroy the works of the devil." 1 John 3:8

Please follow this next statement carefully: This does not mean that God will negate merely the future works of the wicked angels or even the present works of the evil angels; but all the works of the evil ones ever commited, both of man and of angel, will be made to be of no effect!

Whether the wicked works occurred in the past, present, or future will be inconsequential to God's judgments. All the works of evil will be brought to nonexistence by the Lord God Most High. All works, acts, and deeds not born of and completed out of the Holy Spirit of God will be wiped out of all creational existence and memory in the eternal fires of the blazing lake!

The God who dwells outside of time, and yet in every time, cannot and will not stand for one vile deed to remain in the presence of His eternal holiness, past, present, or future. Come the last judgment, everything must either be eternally sanctified and rectified, or eternally removed and destroyed.

So, to finally answer the original questions; since satan and his ilk had charge of the first death, the physical death of man's dust body, and since all of the bodily deaths which occurred in man's history were carried out under the authority and mandate of the wicked satan, enacted through the curse of sin, they were done outside of God's will.

Therefore, just as God shall destroy the angel of death, satan; the works of satan starting with the first injustice and the first taste of death with its ill effects must, and will, be nullified to allow the will and peace of God to be restored into His creation; past, present, and future. Every death starting from Abel on up to the last person killed in the rise and demise of Gog and Magog at the end of the seventh day will be reversed and destroyed by the great and righteous Judge of creation so that He may rid the effects of unwanted evil from His midst.

Allow this previous statement to be said yet another way:

The reason for the resurrections of the dead is that the first death, the physical death of the body, was not, is not, and never shall be the intent or will of God. Rather, it was perpetrated and carried out pervertedly, but legally, by satan, the angel of death; under the format of the order established by Adam and the serpent as a consequence to Adam's sin, and not as a result of God's will. Therefore God will negate all the works of death which have taken place in the ages of creation prior to the final judgment, and He will remove all the myriad effects of the unsanctioned activities of the wicked beings, both of man and angel, that were brought about as a result of their free will attempts (whether intentional or unintentional) to curse His creation. For He, the great and only God, will not allow evil; past, present, or future to remain before Him, mocking Him, and forever defiling and polluting His beloved heavens.

Truthfully, when the final judgment arrives, God will not let stand any works that were not willed, inclusive of, or initiated by His Spirit. He will remove and destroy in the fire all works originating out of any source other than His love whether those works were seemingly good, bad, or ugly. For nothing truly exists outside of the Most High God; and with this time of the satanic darkening of the deep having finally ended, all creation can at long last experience God's unhindered power of love, and know what it means to say: "There is no power, there is no life, there is nothing, outside of Almighty God." This is also why Jesus said the following in the Book of Matthew:

> *"And fear not them which kill the body, but are not able to kill the soul: but rather fear him which is able to destroy both soul and body in hell." Matthew 10:28*

People, we had better get our priorities straight while we still have time in our lives to do so, and act while the grace of God is still available to us. It's not the rumblings of the serpent's eternally empty stomach that we should be concerned with, no matter how terribly noisy it may sound; or how large and bloated it may appear to be; or how grand of an illusionary shadow he's able to cast at this time. It's the awesome, holy, endless power and wisdom of the Almighty God of Israel that is due all of our fear and respect; now, and in the days to come. For the Lord will show Himself to be the great I AM, and He will prove before all beings that nothing exists outside of Him.

> *"It is a terrible thing to fall into the hands of the living God."* NLT Hebrews 10:31

satan's attempts to move in his anointings, authorities, and offices are actually a complete waste of his time and efforts since they are not sanctioned by the Holy Spirit, and because they are not, they have no lasting value or effect. Everything which the wicked conspirators and their cooperative cohorts in the family of man have ever done, no matter how successfully they may have seemingly accomplished their schemes, is going to be reversed, negated, and destroyed on a truly amazing day, at the final judgment.

Can anyone actually envision the depth of the defeat which the evil ones are going to suffer at the hands of the Lord God Most High? Is it even faintly clear? Perhaps the scale of the satanic conspirator's destruction and removal is just beyond the scope of human understanding.

Everything the wicked have ever done is going to be cancelled out in God's final judgment of the wicked beings of this era, and their works

The Genesis Mousetrap

won't be anywhere to be seen.... nowhere. These wicked ones who at one time battled angels, shook nations, humbled kings, brought great pain, ended countless lives, and dared to blaspheme the living and Holy God, will not even have the smallest fleabite work of theirs' survive, no matter how long ago it may have taken place. It's all headed to the lake of fire, the fiery trash dump of creation, where the unburnable burns forever, along with what remains to be found of the wicked ones themselves.

> "O death, where [is] thy sting? O grave, where [is] thy victory?" 1 Corinthians 15:55

> "He which testifieth these things saith, Surely I come quickly. Amen. Even so, come, Lord Jesus." Revelation 22:20

HELL SHALL BURN IN THE LAKE

It is at the end of these events, when hell is finally emptied of its contents, and all wicked beings have been judged and sentenced, sent to the lake of fire, that hell itself will also be cast into the fiery lake, never to be seen again. (*Revelation 20:14*)

All those who stand with God and His Messiah will bear witness to the unfathomable might of the God of Israel as He literally annihilates the very deeds and effects that brought such hardship unto mankind and unto the entire creation of God. From the first covering shadow to the last lie of satan, the Lord has promised to wipe our tears away, and He has said that the old things will not be remembered in the time to come. That is not because He will give the righteous a very large case of group amnesia! No, no, no. It is due to the fact that He will remove and destroy the very source of the tears from His creation, the actual events which caused them will be gone. As a result of this astonishing action, there will be nothing left for anyone to cry about. Nothing! The battles will have all been over; the loser and his works abolished from creation forever; and Jesus the King Messiah will stand alone as Lord. (*Isaiah 25:8; 65:17, Revelation 7:17; 21:4*)

Chapter twenty-four

Days, dreams, and visions

IT WAS A BEASTLY TIME!

During the reign of King Nebuchadnezzar of Babylon, a remarkable thing happened. This man who was one of the greatest monarchs in the history of the world saw a dream one night. In that dream he was visited by an angelic watcher who brought with him a warning from God, a notice to Nebuchadnezzar to turn from his prideful and disobedient ways which were to result in a strange and terrible fate coming upon him if he did not humble himself. It was a call to repentance which the king did not heed; an offer of mercy that he did not accept.

The fate which was declared unto him in the dream was such that he would lose his mind and reason; his office of kingship, and actually, his very humanity. This king was to become little more than an unusual animal for a period of seven years as a result of his pride, arrogance, and disobedience towards the warnings of the living God given to him in the dream.

The warnings of God were yet further clarified to the king through the words of the prophet Daniel. Daniel had clearly told the king of his need to humble himself and repent lest such a judgment were to come about, as it inevitably did. What is yet more remarkable is that when the God of Israel restored Nebuchadnezzar's mind back to him after the decreed seven years were completed, this man who had existed as an animal for those long years became full of adoration and praise for the very God whose Words he had so rashly scorned earlier.

The Genesis Mousetrap

This same God simultaneously restored unto Nebuchadnezzar his kingship as well as his reason, and restored it with increased *"excellent majesty"*, no less.

Now, it's fairly safe to assume that almost everyone would be exceedingly amazed if this sequence of events had happened to them. That they too would find it equally remarkable and humbling if the majesty of their reign was greater after their extreme debasement than it was before, as was the case with Nebuchadnezzar; but let's take a look at what the king had to say about his return to reason in the king's own words as found in the Book of Daniel.

> *"And at the end of the days I Nebuchadnezzar lifted up mine eyes unto heaven, and mine understanding returned unto me, and I blessed the most High, and I praised and honoured him that liveth for ever, whose dominion [is] an everlasting dominion, and his kingdom [is] from generation to generation: And all the inhabitants of the earth [are] reputed as nothing: and he doeth according to his will in the army of heaven, and [among] the inhabitants of the earth: and none can stay his hand, or say unto him, What doest thou? At the same time my reason returned unto me; and for the glory of my kingdom, mine honour and brightness returned unto me; and my counsellors and my lords sought unto me; and I was established in my kingdom, and excellent majesty was added unto me." Daniel 4:34-36*

The entire account of this event can be found in the fourth chapter of the Book of Daniel. In reading this account, we can see that Daniel gave Nebuchadnezzar a God given and accurate interpretation of his dream and its consequences: But, could it be possible that this story out of the pages of the holy Word of God could also be telling us something else? Well, the astute reader will by now be able to answer with a resounding: "Yes! Absolutely!" Now we have only one more hurdle to overcome; learning what the "something else" is.

Well, to do that, let's return to our friend who had the royal problem to begin with: Nebuchadnezzar; his beastly time, and the explanation of it.

A further explanation

Nebuchadnezzar in this instance was also a prophetic picture of Adam, of mankind. Similarly to Adam, Nebuchadnezzar was the supreme king on the earth during his reign, everything was subjugated before him; his very rule was sanctioned and decreed by God.

This person who scripture called, "the basest of men" (Daniel 4:17) was in this manner also much the same as the "dust being" called Adam. In that Adam was perhaps the basest or lowest of God's sons due to his uniquely physical and limiting origin; but he was nonetheless given dominion and elevated to a stature far above his peers among God's sons in this triune universe. Tellingly, both Adam and Nebuchadnezzar fell into sin, ignoring God's will and the fact that His majesty and might was the source which prepared both of their great realms for them to rule in humility and honor; not in arrogance and pride.

A PERFECT PICTURE

Oh, about the seven years Nebuchadnezzar spent as an animal? These are pictures of the seven days; that is to say, the seven thousand years of Adam; in which mankind was debased, removed from the fullness of God's will and the glory and honor of walking as flames of holy fire, as "aish" in these heavens of God.

The Bible actually says in Daniel 4:25 that Nebuchadnezzar was made to dwell, *"with the beasts of the field"*. Those who have been following along closely will immediately notice that the term used in this verse of Daniel which says, *"thy dwelling shall be with the beasts of the field"* has an underlying reference to the events of Adam; that is, of mankind, existing with and among the beasts of the field (the subtle beings) which were spoken of in the early chapters of Genesis.

This corrupt co-habitation was to last for the predetermined length of time that is pictured here as the seven years of Nebuchadnezzar which are the seven days, or seven thousand years of man. Fallen mankind exists in a state of physical subjugation to the perverted natural elements which are influenced by the wicked portion of the angelic host, with Adam (man) unwillingly included in the conspiracy of darkness among the less than obedient angels who function in God's heavens, the conspiratorial ones.

Hence the use of the term *"with the beasts of the field"*, applies to fallen man whether specifically to Nebuchadnezzar or to all men; as man became like one of the less than obedient beings for the duration of his remaining exilic physical tender here on earth.

Adam was placed under satan's shadow and under the first death, cut off from all he had been; debased and living as an odd and unwilling member of the satanic conspiracy as a result of the sin and pride that resulted in God's judgments which came upon him. This was further explained in the events which occurred to Nebuchadnezzar during his seven year exile as decreed by the watchers.

As Nebuchadnezzar was lowered to the level of a grunting mindless beast, so too was his father Adam before him lowered from his elevated position as a king made in the image of the Almighty in which he ruled with such glory that the natural mind cannot in this day comprehend; to exist as a being which is given over to ostensibly be only and totally physical in all things.

This beastlike life, which is the present existence of fallen natural man who exists under and is oppressed by the perverted laws of this natural world, has man driven by wickedness and brute tendencies. Mankind is lowered to living as a natural beast, knowing only of bodily need; debased, weakened, and killed by things which could previously not hurt Adam. Man has descended so low as to even teach and be taught by others of his kind that he is both descended from, and is one of the animals, "the beasts", with which he now dwells.

Both the way the natural lives of people are spent on this sin tainted earth as they are now affected by the actions of the wicked legalists in the same diabolical manner as the lives of the natural beasts are and were before them, through the evil angelic twisting of Godly laws, as the wicked seek to govern all flesh in this physical world; as well as the way that the governance of the Adamic spirit over all others in this universe was lost, were shown in this example of Nebuchadnezzar which speaks of the manner and timetable of the fall and redemption of man.

Yes, Adam fell, and how he fell! As Nebuchadnezzar aptly illustrates to us; without the grace of God, and without His redemption, we are but mindless grunting beastlike beings, poor shadows of what we were;

incapable of even comprehending the amazing things the Lord had prepared for us; or of living in the paradisiacal place we as the children of Adam were created to be in. Mankind now dwells, without better knowledge, among the *"beasts of the field",* which are not fit company for man, as Adam himself came to realize in Genesis 2:20.

However, upon the end of the decreed time of judgments, mankind will lift its eyes toward heaven as Nebuchadnezzar did so many years ago and give genuine thanks and praise unto the Lord God of hosts. Upon doing so, the collective reason of man will return upon the end of the seventh day; and those humble ones of Adam in Messiah will be returned to the place of kingship in Messiah Jesus, the last Adam.

The very same who will reestablish these heavens and all contained within them as a place befitting the fire which He originally came to launch during His first appearance. With the judgments of God having run their course, Adam, that is, mankind, will finally be restored to the true place and nature which Adam was created to be of. With added excellent majesty, no less! For, thanks to the grace of the King Messiah, God Himself shall dwell among His people!

This is what King Nebuchadnezzar shows us of our days in the Adamic exile: Debased, outcast, shunned and low, unable to move in our God given authority due to our own sin and pride, both individually and collectively sent out to pasture, but praise God! The Almighty sent a redeemer, and the Lord will yet restore His creation and fulfill His Words of blessing spoken to Adam and Eve those seven days ago, and that He will do through His Messiah!

JUST A TEMPORARY HOME

This temporary fallen state of things brings us to a short look at another of the great feasts of the Lord which He Himself gave unto Israel to celebrate as an eternal and holy convocation; one that has already been previously mentioned among the seven and that feast is "Sukkot", also known as "the feast of Tabernacles".

This beautiful feast, held as a witness to God's goodness, carries with it an underlying theme that speaks of these seven days of creation and man's part in them; as well as of man's separation from His rightful or permanent state of being during this time of the seven Adamic days.

All of Israel had to make temporary little dwellings in which to reside for the duration of the feast which was to last for a total of seven consecutive days. Sukkot really is the feast of seven. Seven days in duration; this seventh feast which takes place in the seventh month is a picture of mankind's, and indeed, creation's temporary removal from the surroundings it was to permanently have in God's heavens; as man was to temporarily dwell in a short term little structure called the heaven of Rakia in an Adamic exile that was to last for a period of seven thousand years, seen in the seven creative days of Genesis, which ultimately lead to the "olam haba", the "world to come".

Sukkot is the joyful feast. The time of merriment and happiness; this would seem a bit odd upon a superficial inspection of the location it is to be held in, namely, in a "sukkah", a booth. A flimsy structure that leaves one seemingly exposed to the elements, uncomfortable in contrast to the permanent dwelling from which one came; and God willing, will once again return to. Yet happiness was, and is, the operational word for in this feast Israel celebrates the goodness of God.

In this time of dwelling in the sukkah, joy is extremely important; just as it is for the life of the believer who comes to understand the temporary nature of this existence. As Israel dwelling in its small temporary booths is to be joyful, due to all that the Lord has done to redeem and bless them, so too the believer dwelling in this temporary heaven, and in this temporary physical form and world, needs to be constantly joyful for all the amazing things God has done and continues to do for the redemption of His beloved.

Yes, we can be, and truly must be joyful knowing that this little sukkah, or booth, called our heavens is a place where the glory of the Lord was, is, and shall again be revealed. We are to rejoice regardless of how vulnerable or exposed we may seemingly be to the elements in creation just as Israel is during this seven day feast of our God.

Another point about the purpose of the use of a fragile structure during this time: It is to show us that the separation between man and the God of all glory really isn't as thick or as solid as we often think it is. In fact, God wants us to understand through the use of the sukkah, the fragile temporary structure used in this celebration, that very little; and actually nothing substantial separates us from Him during our sojourn on this earth. Nothing but a frail little structure called the curtain heaven of Vilon stands between man and the glory of the God of all the heavens. (*Leviticus 23:34-43*)

> "Rejoice in the Lord alway: [and] again I say, Rejoice."
> Philippians 4:4

Of course, we can't go further without noting the allusion this feast also makes to the millennial reign which is itself a seventh day time of rejoicing and freedom from bondage and tyranny for the entire creation. In that time, the wicked angels shall have been removed as this temporary triune structure of heavens is prepared for the seventh or Sabbath day to house creation in the peace of Messiah.

SEVEN TO ONE

> "And in that day seven women shall take hold of one man, saying, We will eat our own bread, and wear our own apparel: only let us be called by thy name, to take away our reproach. In that day shall the branch of the LORD be beautiful and glorious, and the fruit of the earth [shall be] excellent and comely for them that are escaped of Israel."
> Isaiah 4:1-2

"In that day shall the branch of the LORD be beautiful and glorious...". The Hebrew word for branch in the previous verse is "tzemach". This word is used on occasion in different passages of scripture as a descriptive reference to the anointed Messiah of Israel.

In the day this "branch" of God shoots forth; that is to say, when the Messiah is visible to all and comes in power (during the start of the Millennial age), a very amazing and holy thing happens. Seven women will take hold of one man saying, "Take us to be your own; let us be called by your name, we will ask nothing else of you, just take away our shame."

This "one man" spoken of is none other than the Messiah, the last Adam Himself; and the seven women are the seven days of creation, the seven heavens of division.

The very creation itself will cry unto the rightful Heir of all things and seek to be made whole when He arrives in power and glory and finally re-establishes the throne of David. That wholeness which creation yearns for is something only the righteous King Messiah can give; to have the reproach of separation, division, and partition from time and space removed is that which the creation is longing for; to be once again accepted and one before the Lord is the plea of the "olam".

The seven women these verses speak of; the seven divisions of time and space (the days and the heavens), will desperately plead for Messiah to sanctify them and accept them unto Himself. They cry for Him to return them unto righteousness even though they were long and far removed from the holiness and unity of God, as they endured an existence in the spiritual famine and poverty of separation first brought about during satan's darkening of the deep.

At the end of the seventh day, the very fabric of creation itself will stretch forth and weep for acceptance and atonement in a desperate longing the magnitude of which has yet to be seen or felt in any age. As this creation, once tinged by the satanic cover of darkness and then decreed by God to serve in a divided and fragmented state of time and space, sees the manifestation of the promise of God fulfilled in Messiah, it then cries for the end of reproach which only He can give by making the seven His own; giving them honor instead of shame.

Messiah will take the reproach of the creation away by allowing the divided and removed to be called by His name just as a husband takes a wife to be his own and gives her his name. The *"fruit of the earth"* shall, indeed, be comely for those of Israel in that time, for Israel shall have a King, and creation will be allowed to come home.

Chapter twenty-five

A further explanation

THE END OF THE BEGINNING

As the millennial kingdom comes to an end the creation narrative is far from over. On the contrary, there are huge things in store for creation as the eighth day sets in. Now, to understand why these events had to wait until the creative/redemptive week of days was over, we need to understand a little bit about the laws of God. In order to do that, we need to go to the laws and statutes of God found in scripture.

The first issue centers on the question of why the direct presence of God could not approach man throughout the redemptive week of days. As we've seen, the answer centers on the issue of sin; but we also need to realize that it had more to do with how man has chosen to handle himself in his approach to the problem.

Ever since Eve first ate of the fruit of the tree of knowledge of good and evil (in a disastrous attempt at self improvement due to her unattainable desire to make herself more perfect than she already was), followed by Adam's half-hearted and disobedient attempt at dealing with the situation, mankind throughout history has always desired to achieve improvement and perfection through the implementation of self centered works which are an abomination before the Lord. That is why He cannot allow us near in that vile state.

WE CANNOT ATTAIN PURITY THROUGH EFFORT

We have always attempted to achieve a level of purity, cleanliness, and acceptance which we simply cannot attain on our own; and in our own efforts we have defiled ourselves and the creation around us as we have not wanted to humbly accept the Lord's freely offered cleansing works of grace. Therefore, the Lord needed to keep His distance from man during our prideful attempts at achieving righteousness on our own. This sin of attempting self righteousness took a certain time to work its way out of the body of mankind; it took a week of days. This was the biblically allotted time required before God could re-enter man's presence and allow man to re-enter His.

Now remember, everything that is written in the scriptures has four different streams of interpretation, and nothing in the Bible should be thought to be only speaking of its obvious meaning. For example: everything the Lord God commanded the children of Israel to do in their lives had a prophetic implication; a deeper meaning than what the directed acts actually entailed.

An event such as keeping the Sabbath holy was actually to prophetically live out the promise of the unique rest found in the millennial reign to come; and the prohibition of eating unclean animals was to signify the need to avoid partaking of various and sundry sinful issues and behaviors.

Consequently, in scripture we find many ordinances that prohibit our contact with others due to our voluntary and involuntary actions which have brought about, and caused, our defilement. As stated, this time of separation due to defilement was biblically decreed to last for a period of seven days. Some examples of this can be seen in the following verses: *Leviticus 12:2+5; Chapter 13; Chapter 14; Chapter 15; 15:24, Numbers 19:11; 19:14-16.*

However, the most telling example of the need for a seven day separation is found in Leviticus 15:19-29. It details the fact that our actions of cleansing ourselves is what keeps us separated from the Lord for a set time of seven days due to the impurity brought forth as a result of self effort.

From the time of Adam's and Eve's first attempt to better themselves and to achieve purity, seven days were set for the bride of Messiah to be separated from the presence of God due to her impurity. These seven days were the seven thousand years of man's authority and effort here

A further explanation

on earth. It was a time when there could not be direct unity in the creation; this may well be the reason that the 'bride of unity', new Jerusalem, is even now found in a separate heaven of its own according to traditions found in Judaism; the heaven of Zevul, waiting for the day it may arrive into the newly reunited world to come.

ISAIAH EXPLAINS IT WELL

"But we are all as an unclean [thing], and all our righteousnesses [are] as filthy rags; and we all do fade as a leaf; and our iniquities, like the wind, have taken us away." Isaiah 64:6

This verse in Isaiah captures the issue very well, although the translators hid and "sanitized" the original meaning of the verse so that the unadulterated Word of God wouldn't be too offensive or distasteful for sensitive people to endure. Sadly, it seems the "Good Book" wasn't good enough for the "good people" to read without cleaning it up a little first. Do read on.

In fact, this verse speaks of mankind's predicament exactly; and a look at the Hebrew shows us that this verse perfectly ties into what Leviticus 15:19-29 was speaking of.

Let's look at the term: *"But we are all as an unclean thing"*. The term "unclean" refers to being defiled or polluted in a physical or moral way; and the phrase *"and all our righteousnesses are as filthy rags"* refers precisely to our own efforts of cleansing impurities from ourselves in the normal feminine physiological manner. The resulting condition and the *"filthy rags"* it causes are an affront and abhorrence to God.

Anything that we do ourselves to attain self purity is horrendous to the Lord God for it does not produce life in any form. The cleansing process inherent to the natural actions of mankind, the bringing forth of our own unclean tainted blood and effort in an attempt to attain purity and spiritual righteousness in self; along with the attempt of a self transformative preparation in the hope of a better more productive time to come has caused God to hide Himself and move away from us due to the fact that His blood, His Spirit, and His love were not accepted by mankind.

SPIRITUAL REASONS BEHIND THE PHYSICAL

Remember, we are speaking of the spiritual and prophetic meanings behind these verses. The Lord often uses those things common to mankind as living examples; as ways to make points we can relate to, such is the case here.

It should be quite evident to us that one cannot become spiritually holy through the efforts of one's own sinful and defiled nature, or by using fleshly endeavors or works to attain cleanliness. Yet, this simple but Godly logic seems beyond the grasp of the natural mind.

This incapability of man to properly purify self is why it took the pure lifeblood of the last Adam, Messiah Jesus, to wash us clean. Our own soiled blood and the natural effort of the flesh just cannot do it. It needs to be God's perfect work of love.

Therefore God's direct presence will be withdrawn from creation these seven days until the time it takes to process the efforts of cleansing uncleanliness out of mankind's system has past; and this uncleanliness, as illustrated, is caused by the self-induced natural effort of man to attain cleanliness. Only then can the full effects of the Lord's sanctification and presence be felt throughout creation. This is just as God explained it in His holy Word.

Those of you who understand will also note that the particular type of *"filthy rags"* mentioned in this verse come about as a result of our not being fruitful. They are a result and a sign of our unproductiveness, infertility, and of our separation from God who is referred to biblically as the husbandman, as He is the source of all life and blessing. (*John 15:1*)

However, upon the start of the eighth day our *"filthy rags"* will be seen no more as all mankind and the entire creation will finally become fruitful again due to the fact that the direct presence of the Lord, the Creator of the heavens and the earth will be united with us in His new Jerusalem; and His creation shall bear Him much fruit.

A further explanation

THE ROLLING AWAY OF THE "OLD CLOTH"

Now, at the end of these seven days when all impurity has been dealt with and the time of separation is over, the unity of creation can be reestablished. So, there won't be the need for this temporary structure of division in the heavens anymore. (*Hebrews 12:26-27*)

It will be during this time, in the close of the thousand year reign of the King Messiah, after all his enemies have been made His footstool, His rule having become absolute in all the heavens and all those who have attempted to transgress against the Lord God having been sent to the lake of fire, that the Adamic mandate will have become fulfilled. The last Adam will have done exactly what Adam was created to do. He will have protected the garden; filled the whole earth with it; and brought all things that went against God's will into bondage and submission to the Word of God.

Messiah will then usher in the unification of the heavens. It is written that Messiah will be the last one standing upon this old physical creation, this earth of Rakia, as he is the first and the last; the Alpha and the Omega; the beginning and the end. (*Revelation 22:13*)

> "For I know [that] my redeemer liveth, and [that] he shall stand at the latter [day] upon the earth:" *Job 19:25*

This then brings about what the scriptures spoke of when we read about the heavens being rolled away like an old cloth. As the Lord stretched out the heavens like a curtain, in the same manner He is well able to roll them up again. Notice, and keep in mind that the following descriptions best portray heavens which are a thin veneer or a covering veil over things. (*Isaiah 42:5*)

> "And, Thou, Lord, in the beginning hast laid the foundation of the earth; and the heavens are the works of thine hands: They shall perish; but thou remainest; and they all shall wax old as doth a garment; And as a vesture shalt thou fold them up, and they shall be changed: but thou art the same, and thy years shall not fail." *Hebrews 1:10-12*

> *"[It is] he that sitteth upon the circle of the earth, and the inhabitants thereof [are] as grasshoppers; that stretcheth out the heavens as a curtain, and spreadeth them out as a tent to dwell in:" Isaiah 40:22*
>
> *"Who coverest [thyself] with light as [with] a garment: who stretchest out the heavens like a curtain:" Psalm 104:2*
>
> *"Oh that thou wouldest rend the heavens, that thou wouldest come down, that the mountains might flow down at thy presence," Isaiah 64:1*

The word "rend" used in the preceding verse is the Hebrew word "qara"; it speaks of the way something would be torn, split, or cut like a fabric or a curtain. The prophet Isaiah is calling for God to rend the heavens and to administer justice. It would seem very plausible to assume that the curtain heaven of Vilon (the separative barrier) is the heaven specifically or at least inclusively alluded to in these preceeding verses. (*Isaiah 34:4, Isaiah 51:6*)

GOD IS NOT A MALICIOUS DESTROYER

Many have assumed that these two previous verses of Isaiah, and others like them, indicate that God will take the entire physical creation and do away with it; or perhaps destroy it and then craft an altogether new realm, but as we have seen and read, this will not be the case.

First of all, God is not a malicious destroyer, particularly of His own works and of His own beloved waters (the heavens), which He set apart and designed specifically to serve Him in ridding creation of evil.

Secondly, as the apostle Paul wrote in Romans 8:19-22, all of nature is waiting for the end of the curse; for the time of freedom to arrive.

Now, consider this: Why would the Holy One have all of nature longingly await Messiah's arrival and His restorative works, if after He arrives and is done restoring all things to the Adamic state in the millennial kingdom (as He has promised to do), He would then turn around and dispose of everything that has waited on Him for liberty and restoration?

A further explanation

That is simply not the way God operates. He doesn't condemn or curse those which He Himself sets to wait upon Him to free them and bless them. He will not doom any that He has set to humbly await His arrival, not even if the ones in question are animals, or plants, or the heavens in general. For as we have seen, everything the Lord does or speaks is as eternal as He is Himself, and since He is the One who has set creation to earnestly wait upon Him, the Eternal One; He will eternally liberate this creation from the curse and not destroy it for the sake of His own eternal Word.

This brings us to one unmovable point. God cannot undo that which He has spoken into existence. His Word is an unbreakable fact and cannot be undone; He will not arbitrarily destroy the heavens which He willingly spoke into existence to serve Him in the process of ridding creation of the satanic conspirators. (*Psalm 93:1)*

FOR EVER IS FOREVER

"[One] generation passeth away, and [another] generation cometh: but the earth abideth for ever." Ecclesiastes 1:4

"And he built his sanctuary like high [palaces], like the earth which he hath established for ever." Psalm 78:69

In fact, the term "for ever" used in these previous verses is translated from the Hebrew word "olam"; but "olam" just as commonly carries the meanings of the words "world" and "universe" in its use. For example: in many Hebrew prayers God Himself is often referred to as the "Melech ha Olam"; the "King of the Universe".

"Olam" is another example of those great Hebrew words which try to teach us deeper truths than we first realize. This multiple meaning is yet another way which we are given to see that the creation made and upheld by God's Holy Word will not be destroyed; but rather, it will, indeed, last forever just as His Word and intent always does.

ANOTHER EXAMPLE

What is actually meant by the verses which speak of the heavens being rolled up like a curtain, carpet, garment, or cloth, is the removal of the old superficial ways which can finally occur on the eighth day of creation. The removal of the reasons for the restrictive and separative laws of Vilon, and of all the excess surface clutter which satan was able to tinge by casting his dark shadow upon it. It is the removal of the superficial veneer; the removal of the curtains of separation.

The clarification of this is once again found in the Torah of the Lord Most High. Yet again, it must be said that the Word of God is living, and always refers to a number of things simultaneously, never just to the obvious. Everything God commanded the children of Israel to do has a prophetic implication which speaks of things to come; they are not just quaint cultural customs initiated to keep the nation of Israel busily occupied with meaningless religious practices.

The explanation to this issue is found in the commandment God gave unto Israel to circumcise all the newborn males on their eighth day of life as a sign of the covenant which exists between God and the house of Israel. This was the removal of the old preexisting natural way which was considered to be the norm up to that point. What came about as a result of this action was something which was always there, but was still altogether new.

Notice, in this eighth day event no destruction or alteration was involved; merely the removal of the old surface so that the new could come forth. This precisely pictures the removal of the restrictions of separation found in the heavens as a cloth, a curtain, or can we say, a surface, or perhaps of a skin which covers the heart of the issue and keeps the heavens separate from each other in an unnecessary way.

Upon the removal of this old surface at the beginning of the eighth day, the Lord can reunite the heavens and bring forth a new thing; a new heaven and a new earth, the "olam haba"; and this act of the removal of the old will be as a sign of the covenant which the creation God so loves has with Him. The new format of the eighth day was always there and always existed; it was just hidden beneath the surface of our present state of being. (*Isaiah 65:17; 66:22*)

> "*Of old hast thou laid the foundation of the earth: and the heavens [are] the work of thy hands. They shall perish, but*

> *thou shalt endure: yea, all of them shall wax old like a garment; as a vesture shalt thou change them, and they shall be changed:" Psalm 102:25-26*

What other causes are there for these events to take place upon the eighth day? Alright, we have found yet another question worthy of response. Medical science has explained that the blood of a person doesn't reach its maximum coagulatory effectiveness until the eighth day of life. If a person would bleed any sooner, the blood flow wouldn't halt itself nearly as quickly or as easily as it does when blood can solidify properly on its own. So, the eighth day of life is the earliest time in which the event of removal could safely and easily take place.

The same holds true for the removal of the heaven of Vilon, the spiritual laws, this physical matter, and the upholders of the different spiritual substances of the heavens. If these separators are removed too soon God's covenant partners would be subject to needless harm due to His direct unveiled holy presence which would be too great for the unprepared creation to bear. The result of such a premature removal of the dividing structures and curtains of the heavens may cause a great blood flow that would not cease until man and creation itself would be destroyed. The Lord absolutely doesn't want that.

The Bible states, should God even look upon the earth it trembles. How much more would happen in the face of His full presence if creation wouldn't be ready? However, He does have a great desire to remove all barriers within creation that cause disunity as quickly as possible; and by the eighth day creation will finally be mature enough. It is the earliest possible time. (*Psalm 104:32*)

Was there another reason that the heavens couldn't have been unified sooner? Remember, another answer for that question was found in our previous look at feminine physiological purification which required a full seven day cessation of contact after its beginning, as stated in Leviticus 15:19-29.

The Lord God Most High has used both masculine and feminine physiology to explain unto us the reasons behind the timelines necessary in His restoration process, and in the reunification of creation. He needed to allow a set time for things to work themselves out to a point where His efforts wouldn't be polluted, fruitless, cause any harm to His covenant partners, or bring about unwanted complications into the restorative effort which may cause yet further delay.

> *"For God speaketh once, yea twice, [yet man] perceiveth it not." Job 33:14*

> *"For God may speak in one way, or in another, Yet man does not perceive it." NKJV™ Job 33:14*

THE TIME FOR FIRE

> *"But by the same word the present heavens and earth have been stored up (reserved) for fire, being kept until the day of judgment and destruction of the ungodly people."* Amplified Bible, *2 Peter 3:7*

The Book of Second Peter speaks of a time when the earth will be burned with fire at the end of days. This is not a hurtful, destructive, or a punitive event as many have supposed, although it will have that effect on any lingering ungodliness. Rather, this is the culmination of the will of Messiah and the very purpose He came to the earth as He Himself said in the following verse:

> *"I have come to cast fire upon the earth, and how I wish that it were already kindled!" Amplified Bible, Luke 12:49*

This fire spoken of by both Messiah and the apostle Peter, the fire which the Lord so longed to see blazing, is the indwelling presence of the Holy Spirit which transforms and makes holy all which have His sanctifying presence transform their being. This spreading of fire or holiness to transform the earth and all in it was an essential part of Adam's original mandate which Messiah came to fulfill.

This was even attested to in the very names found for man and woman used in the Hebrew language, and they are: "aish" meaning man; and "aisha" meaning woman. These are simply masculine and feminine forms of the same word which has as its root and relative the word: "eish"; which is the word for fire.

Furthermore, a look back a few pages will remind us that the Hebrew words for "skin" and "light" are homonyms, as both are pronounced "or". This light of God which was upon man can be well understood to represent man's rightful skin or covering when we realize that man was intended to be a being of living fire. A walking, talking, flame of the fire of the Holy Spirit burning bright unto the Lord, bringing light into His creation.

Hopefully these facts have helped kindle or rekindle the flames of God's Spirit and knowledge to burn brightly in the hearts of His people today as well.

The apostle Paul spoke of this same fiery fact in the Book of Hebrews:

> "And of the angels he saith, Who maketh his angels spirits, and his ministers a flame of fire." Hebrews 1:7

The ministers of God were created to be flames of fire. Man and woman were created to be as living flames of holy fire spreading the very nature of God's Spirit throughout creation; and Messiah came to fulfill that assignment, to restore man and woman to their original state of being.

They were created to be flames of God's fire burning in holiness for the Lord, transforming all that was around them into a creation acceptable and pleasing to His will; and God's original intent shall always, always, come to pass.

The Apostle Peter speaks of the day when God's will is fulfilled in this particular issue. This incendiary event which Peter speaks of is actually the second "baptismal event" of the earth; the baptism of fire. The first baptism was the flood, the water baptism of Noah's day spoken of in Genesis chapters 5-10.

> "And the waters prevailed exceedingly upon the earth; and all the high hills, that [were] under the whole heaven, were covered." Genesis 7:19

This was the flood that cleansed the earth from its evil and changed it from its nearly total ungodly former state allowing it to continue to exist before the Lord. Yes, the flood was an event of judgment, but a judgment of God upon the wicked will always bring about blessings for the righteous, allowing for the birth of a new thing. This flood of Noah's day was a saving event where the earth and mankind were allowed to be born again into the purer ways of God as the old wicked things were to be forever passed away and buried.

In the fact that the earth was immersed in the cleansing waters of God and in His blessing of rain all things became new; just as an individual has the salvation experience when they are born again and their old sinful selves are allowed to die in Messiah. Both the Noachic flood and the personal individual salvation experience are immersions into the cleansing waters of God to put away the old, and are necessary in order to be able to partake of God's grace in the new life He mercifully provides in Messiah.

Notice that even in the occurrence of an individual's new birth experience, the individual isn't visibly perfected. Although, the individual is saved and made righteous through faith in Messiah; given a new spirit and a new life, and is therefore able to begin growing into the things of God since sin has been dealt with. It's the same with the earth and its immersion flood. It may not have been visibly perfected at the time of its cleansing, but it found grace through God's intent and Noah's faith; and evil was dealt with so that the earth was saved to grow into the day of Messiah, the day of perfection.

The flood of Noah was the first baptismal event which is experienced: the baptism of water; and the event which Peter spoke of is the second baptism which the Bible refers to: the baptism that comes when we are truly ready and hungry to serve the Lord our God, and thusly able to receive His permanent infilling presence; that is the baptism of fire.

In the end of days this baptism of fire will come to pass as an earth-wide event just as the water baptism of Noah was. The baptism of fire, or sanctification by the infilling presence of the Holy Spirit, is a monumental change; a permanently existence-altering event and is exactly what the earth has been preserved for. First the creation was saved through water, and then it will be empowered through fire. Brought, launched, and kindled by the Messiah, the Lord Jesus Himself.

What is the earth to be empowered for? This holy fire is the personal presence of the Holy Spirit of God Himself which comes to sanctify creation, and is necessary as a preparatory work of God to make ready the creation and enable it, to completely change it into a place which can be reunited with the upper heavens in accordance with God's original intent. This is done so that it may be fit for the arrival of the new Jerusalem, and even more importantly, for the arrival of the Most High God who will come to dwell upon the "new" earth. (*2 Peter 3:7-13*)

WHAT DO ADAM AND DAVID HAVE IN COMMON? JESUS.

Upon the completion of these events the need for a separate Adamic kingship will have come to an end, along with the need for separate heavens; for it will be the time of the reunification of creation.

A veiled reference and explanation of this day is found in scripture in the lives of Adam and King David. As we have seen, the kingships of Adam and David were covenantal building blocks of Messiah as He is the inheritor of the authorities unique to both.

Adam was the portrait and foreshadow of Jesus, the last Adam; the one in whose offices and authorities Jesus walked as the perfect Son of man. Adam was told by God that He would die on the day he eats of the fruit of the tree of the knowledge of good and evil; and Adam did, indeed, die spiritually on that day. Now, let's also remember the scriptures make clear that one thousand years to God is as a day. (*Psalm 90:4, 2 Peter 3:8*)

Scripture also shows that Adam physically lived nine hundred and thirty years before he physically died, so he died well within the timeframe of the biblical day in which his disobedience caused him to eat of the fruit.

Moreover, rabbinical tradition says Adam died precisely on his birthday. Whether Adam died on his birthday or not isn't a necessary fact of information, but it is interesting when we realize what is transpiring in a prophetic sense. As we are all well aware, Adam fell short of completing his task of bringing this creation into bondage to the mandate of God. This is also indicated by his dying short of reaching his full biblical day: a full one thousand years of life, which was theortically possible to attain within the stated margins of God's judgment decrees.

This brings us to King David of Israel; the inheritor of the Adamic promises through Abraham, as well as the recipient of the Messianic covenant which God made with him personally. The Bible makes clear that the lives of the biblical individuals are as stories and prophesies of the things of God, showing hidden details of other important events, and the life of King David is no exception. In certain respects, David's life reveals details of his greater Son's life and Kingdom.

> *"Remember the days of old, consider the years of many generations..."* Deuteronomy 32:7

David was the greatest King the nation of Israel ever had; and the one from whose throne Messiah Himself will rule, for He is called David's greater son. Briefly put, here are some similarities between David and Messiah: King David was the great King of Israel; so is Messiah. David inherited his throne from a disobedient predecessor; so did Messiah. David was a very humble king; so is Messiah; David was a great warrior; so is Messiah, etc. etc.

Thusly, we come to the point being made. King David lived exactly seventy years according to the Bible in 2 Samuel 5:4; and in an equally interesting tidbit, rabbinical tradition says that David died precisely on his birthday as well. This unusual occurrence is also said to have happened to Adam. What is the significance of this? The seventy years of David's life are a numeric picture of the seven complete days of creation, and his death in his seventieth year prophetically represents the end of the independent Adamic/Davidic throne at precisely the end of the seventh day, at the close of the millennial reign.

Also, when David's seventy years are added to Adam's nine hundred thirty years, we get precisely one thousand years. The ages of both men together represent a full day of life for the dominion of man! These kings had their kingdoms finally united in the crowns of Messiah whose rule saw the full Adamic day completed and fulfilled during His millennial one thousand year reign.

The full day of Adam was found in combining the lives and authorities of the two kings; Adam and David; who were both covenantal forerunners of Messiah; and their rule was finally realized in Messiah, who is biblically referred to as both: the "last Adam" and the "son of David"; the only heir to both kingdoms. Rabbinic scholars have long made a numeric connection between the lives of these two individuals: Adam and David.

Messiah, as the inheritor of this Adamic Kingdom will bring it to its full day in His complete unified rule of creation through His Davidically inherited nation of Israel. At the end of the full day, when the two thrones and Kingdoms held by God in Messiah (the Kingdom of Adam and the Kingdom of God) finally become reunited, the need for the separate Adamic/Davidic kingship is no longer necessary. Therefore the Adamic/Davidic kingship is merged into one with the Kingdom of God.

Again, this is not to say that the Adamic/Davidic Kingdom(s) are done away with, but they are seamlessly reunified with the eternal Kingdom of God. The King that sits upon David's throne (Messiah) shall cede all power and authority back to God the Father, the source of all things. At that time of unity His unique totalitarian Kingdom is no longer required to be a separate entity from that of the Kingdom of God.

> "Then [cometh] the end, when he shall have delivered up the kingdom to God, even the Father; when he shall have put down all rule and all authority and power." 1 Corinthians 15:24
>
> "For he must reign, till he hath put all enemies under his feet." 1 Corinthians 15:25
>
> "And when all things shall be subdued unto him, then shall the Son also himself be subject unto him that put all things under him, that God may be all in all." 1 Corinthians 15:28

As it has been said many times before, God's Word cannot return unto Him void. His original intent will always be done. Therefore, having been given all power in the heavens and upon the earth, the Word of God, the last Adam, the Son of man, will stand before the Father and submit all authority back to the source from which it came; to the Father and God of our Lord, Messiah Jesus.

My dear brothers and sisters, that one event alone is worth everything to see. After all the amazing works of God to save His creation and purify His Kingdom from the transgressing evil are completed; after all the great and wondrous gifts that He created and which He bestowed upon His son Adam, whom He made a king, and who through disobedience had apparently lost everything that was given unto him, including mankind and all of creation, the last Adam will have successfully redeemed mankind and God's creation.

He will then present the redeemed creation, all of the heavens, back unto God as He will have put an end to the transgressing evil which wrought harm to His Father's Kingdom. Having received all power and all authority throughout creation through His obedience and sacrifice Messiah will be able to stand before the Father and present creation whole, redeemed, and renewed back unto the personal authority of God the Father.

In so doing He may perhaps say something like this: "Father, in your wisdom and mercy you gave your son Adam a kingdom and a mission; to bring everything created into bondage to your will and to fill the earth with your blessings. I, the Son of man, the last Adam, have done so and fulfilled your mandate and your will. All that you have desired is done and all that you have required of man is complete, the assignment is fulfilled. Since there is no more that you require of the Adamic kingship, I now yield all authority back to the source from which it came; back to the One God to be protected forever in the power of your might. That your will may always be done; that creation may truly be one."

HIS NAME SHALL BE ONE

On that day, the two Kingdoms will have become one; and the One God, Soul, Body, and Spirit; that is Father, Son, and Spirit will be upon the throne of the heavens in new Jerusalem in the reunited heavens with all power, ruling and reigning forever. (*Revelation 22:1-5*)

A further explanation

Then, with all work done; all evil destroyed; and all things sanctified by His power, the Lord will be one and His name will be one; the heavens shall be one and we who accept His grace shall ever be with the Lord who is always victorious in all things. Amen and Amen.

> "And the LORD shall be king over all the earth: in that day shall there be one LORD, and his name one." Zechariah 14:9

> "...and so shall we ever be with the Lord." 1 Thessalonians 4:17

THE EIGHTH DAY

We might as well start this off with another question: so.... here goes.... If creation is without end and time is infinite, why are we only speaking about the subsequent eighth day which follows the seven days of creation and not of nine, ten or limitless more days to come? Okay, if we look back at the creation/redemption saga, we will see that the seven days of creation had something which separated them one from another; and of course, that something is night. Night is a time of darkness; a testament to evil in our midst; something which came to pass that was other than the perfect will of God.

Night, in a different sense, is also a time to recover from the day's work, and a time to gain strength for the new day ahead. The eighth day, however, is not a day of work or repair as all things have been completed and changed and all evil has been removed, creation having been perfected and sanctified by the Lord.

Yet one more reason that night no longer exists in the "olam haba" is found in the Book of Revelation where it states that God Himself will be a light unto them in that era; and God's light never diminishes. (Revelation 21:3; 22:5)

It must be remembered that these seven days of creation were themselves a temporary structure designed to do away with darkness; and without darkness there can be no night to cause a division of days. Therefore, the days do not change as there is no more perfecting or lessening of darkness to be achieved.

So, in essence, the eighth day, or the first day of the world to come, lasts forever and is inclusive of all existence beyond itself, as the temporary structure of division which made possible the physical time sensitive creation of Rakia where times of day and night existed has been unified with the other heavens and they have all been perfected through Messiah's sanctification.

THE OLAM HABA

Now to briefly look at some of the things found in and about the "olam haba" (the world to come) which will exist in the time of the coming rule of God from the eternal new Jerusalem.

> *"He that overcometh shall inherit all things; and I will be his God, and he shall be my son." Revelation 21:7*

The righteous believers of the ages will all be there; they shall be called God's sons. This is in order to fulfill the original intent of God for man. God had declared in the Adamic blessing that Adam was the son of God and enabled him to become fruitful; all those of the last Adam are now the product of that fruitfulness and called God's sons, again and forever.

> *"And he shewed me a pure river of water of life, clear as crystal, proceeding out of the throne of God and of the Lamb." Revelation 22:1*

The first thing to be noticed in this verse is that the throne of God and of the Lamb is mentioned in the singular, referring clearly to one throne. All major English translations have the throne referred to, and written of, in the singular; the original Greek has it written in the singular. It is not a translatorial error to write of one throne. It is one throne at this time due to the fact that the two kingdoms ruled by God through His different manifestations of Father God, and Jesus, Son of man, have become one; and all creation has been unified under that one throne in this blessed era.

The precious river of life is found there, flowing from God's throne as it always has. This river is the flow of the Holy Spirit of God which carries

A further explanation

forth the Word and will of God from the presence of the Father. It is the same river that Genesis 2:10, among other scriptures, spoke of; it has never stopped, and never will stop flowing. This river enters into creation with the life and intent of God coursing in its crystal currents.

Revelation 22:2 states that the tree of life will be there; blessing the creation as God has always intended for it to do.

Revelation 22:3 tells us that there will be no more curse; and again mentions the one united throne of God and of the Lamb.

Revelation 21:8, and Revelation 22:15 both clearly state that the wicked and sinful are not a part of the world to come, but are outside of it.

What does all of this remind us of? Hmm.... A place where we can find the river of life; the tree of life; the lack of the curse; the lack of the wicked and sinful; a place where the righteous people, the sons of God, live...... Why, it's the garden! We find the Holy garden again! The seed of the garden; the prototypical example of God's will which He Himself planted, and which Adam was given to protect and to grow, will have been protected and grown by the last Adam to include all things in all the then unified heavens. The last Adam will have, at this point, restored all things to God's most Holy design which He Himself planted so long ago to the east of Eden and having done so, God Himself will enter into it in His full being to dwell with His children forever! No more *"cool of the day"* visits necessary now... WOW!

The garden format in that time will have filled the structure of the unified heavens with God's perfect will. It was grown and protected by Himself and is inclusive of all His many sons with its heart being the new Jerusalem, the glory of God; the Redeemer of His creation.

THE ANGELS WILL NOT HAVE COTROL OF THE WORLD TO COME

> *"Behold, he put no trust in his servants; and his angels he charged with folly:" Job 4:18*

One highly interesting fact to be mentioned about this coming time of the "olam haba", is that the angelic host which in this present time operates and controls everything which they oversee through the unrepentantly given blessings, offices, and authorities which they have received from God, will no longer be functioning in the same manner of operational authority as they have up to that time. For as we have seen, one of the paramount reasons the temporary seven day division of the heavens was established was to return all of the authorities which God had given to others back unto Himself; unto His protection through the last Adam, Jesus, so that those blessings could not be used by any to harm others or to defile creation any longer.

The misuse of power was a folly which angels, specifically the angelic conspirators, had grievously partaken of in the past and one to which all beings other than God seem susceptible. This is not to say the angels will be done away with, or that they will be made powerless; rather, it brings into creation an operational structure which in essence lacks the right of perversional free will.

Yes, all beings created will always have the inherent ability of free will; but since ALL power and ALL authority will have come back to God through Jesus inheriting many crowns; and since all beings (both holy angels and repentant man) which will be present in God's creation from the eighth day onward will be there voluntarily, as a consequence of their free choice, all beings in creation, whether man or angels, will have authority to function only as they move in their free will in obedience to the perfect will of God. Thus, the rights to the abilities of distorted autonomous behavior are ended for all in this coming time as God shall have decreed and brought about perfection in His realm.

Simply put: the operational structure of the world to come will not be under the subjection of angelic authority, it will be totally under God's personal authority as Jesus had bought and received all things unto Himself and returned all things and Himself unto the Father.

The prophet Isaiah prophesying on behalf of God spoke the following about the Word of God; and it well explains this issue. Remember, the Word is Jesus who has and will have returned unto God with all of sanctified creation in tow.

A further explanation

> "So shall my word be that goeth forth out of my mouth: it shall not return unto me void, but it shall accomplish that which I please, and it shall prosper [in the thing] whereto I sent it." Isaiah 55:11

Scripture also makes the previously mentioned issue of the coming lack of angelic authority over the things of the world to come quite clear; a few supporting verses follow:

> "For unto the angels hath he not put in subjection the world to come, whereof we speak." Hebrews 2:5

> "And all the host of heaven shall be dissolved, and the heavens shall be rolled together as a scroll: and all their host shall fall down, as the leaf falleth off from the vine, and as a falling [fig] from the fig tree." Isaiah 34:4

HEBREWS

The first two chapters of the Book of Hebrews are filled with relevant and complimentary information to what has been presented heretofar, and serve as a wonderful condensed version of support information to what has been previously touched upon. Take the time to read the chapters slowly and contemplatively; they are quite revealing.

Hebrews 1:1-2:18 presented the way it was originally written, in letter form:

> "God, who at sundry times and in divers manners spake in time past unto the fathers by the prophets, Hath in these last days spoken unto us by [his] Son, whom he hath appointed heir of all things, by whom also he made the worlds; Who being the brightness of [his] glory, and the express image of his person, and upholding all things by the word of his power, when he had by himself purged our sins, sat down on the right hand of the Majesty on high; Being made so much better than the angels, as he hath by inheritance obtained a more excellent

name than they. For unto which of the angels said he at any time, Thou art my Son, this day have I begotten thee? And again, I will be to him a Father, and he shall be to me a Son? And again, when he bringeth in the firstbegotten into the world, he saith, And let all the angels of God worship him. And of the angels he saith, Who maketh his angels spirits, and his ministers a flame of fire. But unto the Son [he saith], Thy throne, O God, [is] for ever and ever: a sceptre of righteousness [is] the sceptre of thy kingdom. Thou hast loved righteousness, and hated iniquity; therefore God, [even] thy God, hath anointed thee with the oil of gladness above thy fellows. Thou, Lord, in the beginning hast laid the foundation of the earth; and the heavens are the works of thine hands: They shall perish; but thou remainest; and they all shall wax old as doth a garment; And as a vesture shalt thou fold them up, and they shall be changed: but thou art the same, and thy years shall not fail. But to which of the angels said he at any time, Sit on my right hand, until I make thine enemies thy footstool? Are they not all ministering spirits, sent forth to minister for them who shall be heirs of salvation? Therefore we ought to give the more earnest heed to the things which we have heard, lest at any time we should let [them] slip. For if the word spoken by angels was stedfast, and every transgression and disobedience received a just recompence of reward; How shall we escape, if we neglect so great salvation; which at the first began to be spoken by the Lord, and was confirmed unto us by them that heard [him]; God also bearing [them] witness, both with signs and wonders, and with divers miracles, and gifts of the Holy Ghost, according to his own will? For unto the angels hath he not put in subjection the world to come, whereof we speak. But one in a certain place testified, saying, What is man, that thou art mindful of him? or the son of man, that thou visitest him? Thou madest him a little lower than the angels; thou crownedst him with glory and honour, and didst set him over the works of thy hands: Thou hast put all things in subjection under his feet. For in

A further explanation

that he put all in subjection under him, he left nothing [that is] not put under him. But now we see not yet all things put under him. But we see Jesus, who was made a little lower than the angels for the suffering of death, crowned with glory and honour; that he by the grace of God should taste death for every man. For it became him, for whom [are] all things, and by whom [are] all things, in bringing many sons unto glory, to make the captain of their salvation perfect through sufferings. For both he that sanctifieth and they who are sanctified [are] all of one: for which cause he is not ashamed to call them brethren, Saying, I will declare thy name unto my brethren, in the midst of the church will I sing praise unto thee. And again, I will put my trust in him. And again, Behold I and the children which God hath given me. Forasmuch then as the children are partakers of flesh and blood, he also himself likewise took part of the same; that through death he might destroy him that had the power of death, that is, the devil; And deliver them who through fear of death were all their lifetime subject to bondage. For verily he took not on [him the nature of] angels; but he took on [him] the seed of Abraham. Wherefore in all things it behoved him to be made like unto [his] brethren, that he might be a merciful and faithful high priest in things [pertaining] to God, to make reconciliation for the sins of the people. For in that he himself hath suffered being tempted, he is able to succour them that are tempted."

It is also recommended that Psalm 8 be read; as it speaks of the Lord's ordered path of delivering creation from His enemies by raising the promised Son of man unto the place of dominion.

ALL WRAPPED UP

Can you not see it?.... Do you not yet understand?.... Is the Word of God not evident enough?.... Was satan not a clear enough example?.... My brothers and sisters, please try to realize what God wants us all to know: Those who attempt to function without the anointing of life; the blessing of God's own Holy Spirit present in their lives cannot succeed.

satan and all of the evil angels are doomed to failure. They cannot succeed in anything they attempt to do; and the more they try, the more they heap defeat upon themselves until they find themselves utterly destroyed.

They cannot function; no one can successfully function; no matter how powerful they are; no matter how anointed they are; no matter how hard they try; or how many times they try to do anything; without the anointing of life, the precious personal anointing of the Holy Spirit of God Himself upon them, they are destined to failure. For without Him, all other blessings, anointings, and efforts are doomed to failure. Whether angel or man; whether great or small; the anointing of life, the presence of God in one's life through His Spirit is essential to the proper implementation of all God's other blessings.

The evil angels are lost; their efforts are lost; their works are lost; their lives are lost; but by the grace of God found in Messiah Jesus we as the children of man do not need to suffer the same terrible fate which they encounter. We don't need to be lost. We can accept His mercy and receive the anointing of life which empowers all of God's blessings to properly function in our lives. The Most High God has made a way for us to once again receive the personal presence of His Spirit and for us to stand clean before Him and reenter the blessings of the Kingdom man was originally made for; and that way is salvation.

Messiah Jesus is that salvation. The Hebrew name for our beloved Jesus is actually "Yeshua", and this name literally means "God's Salvation". This Salvation is the way of the tree of life; He is the only path to God. No one can be saved by God without accepting the authority of Yeshua, God's Salvation, over themselves; and without partaking of His death through faith in this wonderful grace.

In this person of God's Salvation, we can receive a new life and a separate destiny from that of the wicked ones who have chosen the path of death and destruction. It would be wise to accept Yeshua, His Lordship and His Spirit, and walk away from all the evil of the world which tries to drag down and bind the children of Adam, to experience the grace of God and true freedom in Yeshua, wouldn't it?

A further explanation

Since we are given that rare privilege of a new life; of being born again into God's life through His Spirit, we should all jump at the opportunity while it's still available! Right? If you haven't accepted Yeshua Jesus as your Lord and Savior, and you would like to, you can say a simple prayer of your own; or you can say the following:

Father God, I have sinned against you. I come from a people that has sinned against you; and from a world that has sinned against you, but I repent. I ask you to wash me clean from my sins and allow me to partake of your grace which is complete in Jesus. Please come into my life and lead me as my God from this day forward as I now make Messiah Jesus Lord of my life. In Jesus' name I pray. Amen.

If you have prayed that prayer, welcome home! This is a birthday for you! You and your "Abba" (That's Hebrew for "Daddy") have a lot to catch up on! Stay in prayer, speak with Him, and study His Word, the Bible. Through His Spirit, He will teach you what it means to live in Yeshua Jesus. Remember that God is good; and His mercy endures forever. You will get to see forever come to pass! Praise God.

> *"The LORD [is] nigh unto them that are of a broken heart; and saveth such as be of a contrite spirit." Psalm 34:18*

Now, for those believers who have not yet received the infilling and permanent presence of the Holy Spirit; or for those who do not yet have tangible signs of such like the ability to speak in tongues during prayer or worship, and do wish to become fiery flames for our God: the path is so simple. Love the Lord your God more than anything else; make it a point to cherish Him, and to seek His will and kindness carried out toward others. Once the welfare of God and of other people become the very cry of our souls, the Holy Spirit can enter our lives and our beings in a whole new way to help us realize and implement God's will, love, and justice in this earth, and nothing will be the same. Your prayers, praise, worship, and love will then come from the depths of a heart that beats the life of God.

> *"Thou shalt love the Lord thy God with all thy heart, and with all thy soul, and with all thy strength, and with all thy mind; and thy neighbour as thyself." Luke 10:27*

THE END

Well, that brings us though our short little look at some of the amazing events of the past, present, and future spoken of in the Word of God. I pray that you, dear reader, will be well; be blessed; be saved; and be prepared for the amazing events ahead for those who have not only peace with God; but also the peace of God which is only available in Yeshua Jesus, the Torah Word made flesh. Shalom.

Look for more books, products, and information from: T. M. Kymalainen and Time to Return Ministries LLC.

Visit our website at: www.timetoreturnministries.com

Or e-mail us at: timetoreturn@gmail.com

www.ingramcontent.com/pod-product-compliance
Lightning Source LLC
Chambersburg PA
CBHW060449170426
43199CB00011B/1145